ZONDERVAN

HANDBOOK

OF CHRISTIAN BELIEFS

Zondervan Handbook of Christian Beliefs
Copyright © 2005 by The Zondervan Corporation

The authors assert their moral right to be identified as the authors of this work.

Published by Lion Publishing plc, Mayfield House, 256 Banbury Road, Oxford OX2 7DH, England   www.lionhudson.com

This edition published by special arrangement with Lion Publishing in 2005 by Zondervan, *Grand Rapids, Michigan 49530*

Library of Congress Cataloging-in-Publication Data

The Zondervan handbook of Christian beliefs / Alister E. McGrath, general editor ; James I. Packer, consulting editor.—New ed.
    p. cm.
    Rev. ed. of: Guide to Christian belief for the non-specialist reader.
    ISBN-10: 0-310-26273-9
    ISBN-13: 978-0-310-26273-2
    1. Theology, Doctrinal—Popular works. 2. Theology, Doctrinal—Handbooks, manuals, etc. I. McGrath, Alister E., 1953–
II. Packer, J. I. (James Innell) III. Guide to Christian belief for the non-specialist reader.
BT77.Z66 2006   2005012578
230—dc22   CIP

This edition printed on acid-free paper.

Scripture quotations are taken from:
Holy Bible: New International Version®. NIV®. Copyright © 1973, 1978, 1984 by International Bible Society. Used by permission of Zondervan. All rights reserved. The "NIV" and "New International Version" trademarks are registered in the United States Patent and Trademark Office by International Bible Society. Use of either trademark requires the permission of International Bible Society.

New Revised Standard Version of the Bible, copyright © 1989 by the Division of Christian Education of the National Council of Churches of Christ in the United States of America, and used by permission. All rights reserved.

Authorized Version of the Bible (The King James Version), first published in 1611.

All rights reserved. No part of this publication may be reproduced, stored in a retrieval system, or transmitted in any form or by any means—electronic, mechanical, photocopy, recording, or any other—except for brief quotations in printed reviews, without the prior permission of the publisher.

Printed and bound in Singapore

---

06 07 08 09 10 11 12 • 10 9 8 7 6 5 4 3 2 1

ZONDERVAN
HANDBOOK
OF CHRISTIAN BELIEFS

ALISTER E. MCGRATH
General Editor

JAMES I. PACKER
Associate Editor

ZONDERVAN™

GRAND RAPIDS, MICHIGAN 49530 USA

ZONDERVAN.COM/
AUTHORTRACKER

Contents

GENERAL EDITOR
Alister McGrath
Oxford University, UK

ASSOCIATE EDITOR
J. I. Packer
Regent College, Vancouver, Canada

CONSULTANT EDITORS
Atsuyoshi Fujiwara
Tokyo Christian University, Japan

Dr Rolf Hille
Albrecht-Bengel-Haus, Tübingen, Germany

Stephen Noll
Uganda Christian University, Uganda

Jo Bailey Wells
Ridley Hall, Cambridge, UK

Carver T. Yu
China Graduate School of Theology, Hong Kong

CORE WRITING TEAM
Gerald Bray
Beeson Divinity School, Birmingham, Alabama, USA

John Stackhouse
Regent College, Vancouver, Canada

Graham Tomlin
St Paul's Theological Centre, London, UK

Peter Walker
Wycliffe Hall, Oxford, UK

Christopher Wright
Langham Partnership,
London, UK

1 Faith

2 God

3 Jesus

4 Salvation

5 The Church

6 The Christian Hope

Concise Anthology of Christian Thought   302

Glossary   322

Index   345

Editor's Introduction

This handbook sets out to introduce basic Christian beliefs simply and clearly. It explores what Christians – the world's largest religious community – believe, where these beliefs come from, how they have developed over the centuries, and their place in the contemporary church and world. It is designed to help Christians to deepen their knowledge of their faith, and non-Christians to gain a basic understanding of Christian belief, including some of the important debates over matters of doctrine. Above all, it aims to demonstrate how Christian beliefs are grounded in the Bible.

So why study what Christians believe? Why devote an entire book to explaining and exploring these beliefs? Many answers might be given. One of the most important is the deepened appreciation it brings to the life of faith of the believer, and the journey of reflection and personal growth it stimulates. For the great Christian theologian Augustine of Hippo (AD 354–430), there was a genuine intellectual excitement to wrestling with God. Augustine wrote of an 'eros of the mind' – a sense of longing to understand more about God's nature and ways – and the transformative impact that this could have on people's lives. Other Christian writers have stressed the practical importance of theology, noting how it is essential for the ministry of the church. Christian preaching, spirituality and pastoral care, many argue, are grounded in basic Christian beliefs. Those not sharing Christianity's beliefs can still gain something of an understanding of this relationship of theory and practice.

Beliefs, then, are of major significance. They shape our mental world, and provide us with a map of the complex and often baffling world we inhabit. Christians' beliefs provide them with a fundamental framework for living out their faith. For example, their belief about the future hope of heaven has a huge impact on their attitude to living and dying. It makes a world of difference to the way they behave and the way they think.

Again, Christians don't just believe in God; they believe certain things about God, which shape their entire outlook on life. Christian faith is not an unstructured assortment of emotions or feelings. Christians believe that God has certain fundamental characteristics – such as holiness, trustworthiness, and graciousness. They believe that he loved the world so much that he sent Christ into the world to redeem humankind. The Christian doctrine of the Trinity tries to summarize an immensely rich and powerful vision of God, as portrayed in Scripture. It is not the easiest of doctrines to understand – but it reminds people of the overwhelming majesty, glory and radiance of God. These fundamental beliefs about God affect the way in which Christians pray, worship, and tell others about this distinctive God.

Christian beliefs about Jesus Christ are also clearly of immense importance. Jesus Christ is the beginning, the centre and the end of the Christian message of hope. It is certainly true that at the heart of the Christian faith there stands a person, not a belief. Yet it is important to appreciate that Jesus is a person who gives rise to beliefs the moment someone begins to wrestle with the question, 'Who is Jesus Christ?' or 'What is the best way of representing his significance?' One cannot proclaim, worship, adore or imitate Jesus Christ without holding certain beliefs about him. It makes all the difference in the world whether Jesus is a particularly splendid human being whom we are asked to imitate, or the Son of God who entered into this world to redeem humankind. For believers, getting their ideas about Jesus right is fundamental to Christian living and witness. Beliefs matter – and they make a difference to what Christians think, hope, and do! That's why this book is so important.

This introductory guide to Christian belief begins with a brief survey of Christian history. After this comes a discussion about the nature of faith, designed to help the reader understand the distinctive characteristics of the Christian understanding of faith, and its relationship to reason and culture. This is followed by five major sections that deal with the central themes of the Christian faith – beliefs about God and the creation, Jesus Christ, salvation, the church, and the Christian hope. Each of these chapters explores what Christians believe, and how these beliefs are rooted in the Bible.

The first chapter is a highly engaging exploration of the nature of faith by John G. Stackhouse. Based on his extensive experience of teaching philosophical theology and apologetics at Regent College, Vancouver, Stackhouse guides his readers through the many themes associated with the idea of faith, including those issues relating to Christianity's encounter with a postmodern world-view and other world faiths.

This is followed by an extensive, carefully argued account of the Christian doctrine of God by Gerald Bray, professor of theology at Beeson Divinity School. This explores the classic themes of the Christian vision of God, including a careful account of what it means to say that God is a 'person', or to speak of a 'personal God'. Bray's special interest in the doctrine of the Trinity shines through this article. His thorough exposition of the basis of this doctrine is of especial

importance in the light of growing Islamic criticism of Christianity about this specific point.

The person of Jesus Christ is clearly of critical importance to just about every aspect of the Christian faith. To give one example of especial importance to believers: evangelism concerns telling people about Jesus. So what needs to be told? How best can believers communicate his identity and significance? If Christian evangelism is

This detail of a mosaic by Edward Burne-Jones depicts Augustine of Hippo, a fourth-century bishop who was one of early Christianity's most influential thinkers.

to be effective, it must be faithful to who Christians believe Jesus really is. And that means reflecting long and hard on the biblical witness to him. Drawing on his experience of explaining the basis of Christian beliefs about Jesus to Oxford students, Peter Walker gives a vivid and highly readable account of the biblical portrayal of Jesus and its implications for Christian thought and life. This clear, authoritative account of the Christian understanding of the person and place of Jesus Christ lays the foundation for an informed response

An icon showing Christ the King reigning in majesty.

both to rationalist critiques of traditional Christian approaches to the incarnation and resurrection, and especially to Islamic critiques of the central Christian affirmation of the divinity of Christ. In many ways, this article is the centrepiece of this book, its themes radiating outwards and interconnecting with other articles and themes.

The identity of Jesus Christ is closely linked with the work of Christ. To put it simply: who Jesus is determines what Jesus does. Graham Tomlin provides a succinct account of the fundamental themes of the Christian doctrine of salvation. Salvation is shown to be a complex and rich idea, with past, present and future implications. Tomlin demonstrates the importance of the concept of salvation to the Christian faith, explores the various ways in which this idea is expressed in the Bible, and the long Christian tradition of interpreting and applying the biblical material.

Although some western Christians tend to think of their faith in a somewhat individualist way, the dominant tendency in Scripture and Christian theology is to think of faith in much more corporate terms. Believers are members of the body of Christ – the church. But what is the church? What is it there for? What role does it play in maintaining and spreading faith? How does it maintain its distinctive identity and mission? Chris Wright, an experienced theological educationalist with a deep love for mission, explores the various aspects of the Christian understanding of the church and the vision of a restored humanity that it proclaims and embodies.

Finally, we turn to consider the Christian hope. As the apostle Paul points out in his discussion of the resurrection (1 Corinthians 15), if we are without hope, we are indeed utterly lost. What does the Christian faith have to say about the future, and how this affects life in the present? In this concluding chapter, I set out some of the basic themes of the Christian vision of the future, and its transformative impact on life and thought.

Inevitably, this handbook can only serve as an introduction to Christian belief. It is, however, hoped that this introduction to the basics of Christian thought will allow its users to deepen their understanding of the core themes of the Christian faith, their historical development, and their contemporary application.

It remains for me to thank all those who have worked so hard to make sure that this book will meet the needs both of Christians wanting to explore key issues of faith and of others wishing to discover more about the basics of Christian belief. It is our belief and hope that this volume will be a valuable and user-friendly introduction to the basics of Christian belief, enabling its readers to discover more of the riches and treasures of the gospel message.

ALISTER MCGRATH
Oxford

A Very Brief History of Christian Belief

ALISTER MCGRATH

It is impossible to study Christian belief without a basic understanding of the history of the church. Every generation of Christians has tried to make sense of the Bible, develop its ideas into a coherent system of thought, and apply those ideas to the world around them. Today's rich legacy of Christian thought reflects this long, sustained process of engagement with the biblical texts, and wrestling with their true meaning. It is impossible to study Christian belief without overhearing debates from the past, or encountering the ideas of significant historical Christian writers. This chapter therefore aims to provide the reader with an overview of this long history of Christian reflection on how best to make sense of the Bible and represent its contents. At least some knowledge of this history is important to a proper understanding of what Christians believe. This very brief introduction to the history of Christian belief identifies some landmarks that readers may find helpful.

The New Testament

The starting point for Christian theology – to use the technical term for the study of Christian belief – is the New Testament, a collection of twenty-seven documents dating from the first century (often referred to as the 'apostolic period'). The 'books' of the New Testament can be broken down into a number of different categories – such as the gospels and the letters. Their common theme is the

identity and significance of Jesus. The first four books of the New Testament are collectively known as 'gospels'. These can be thought of as four portraits of Jesus, seen from different angles and drawing on various sources. The first three of these – Matthew, Mark and Luke, sometimes collectively known as the 'synoptic' gospels, have many features in common, and are widely regarded as drawing on common sources in circulation within early Christian circles. Each of the gospels has its own distinctive character. John's Gospel is noted for its emphasis on the signs pointing to the identity of Jesus, and especially its distinctive 'I am' sayings.

The gospels are followed by a history of the expansion of Christianity in the Mediterranean world – the Acts of the Apostles – which is widely regarded as having been written by Luke, the author of the third gospel. Taken together, Luke's Gospel and history of the early church form the largest single document in the New Testament. In his Gospel, Luke informed one 'Theophilus' (probably a well-placed Roman official who had become interested in Christianity) of the basic details of the life, death and resurrection of Jesus.

There then follows a significant collection of letters, sometimes referred to using the older word 'epistles'. Most of these are from Paul, an early convert to Christianity from Judaism, who was especially involved in bringing the Christian gospel to the Gentile (that is, non-Jewish) world. One of Paul's particular concerns is the relationship of Christianity and Judaism. Although Paul's letters are generally written to churches (for example, at Rome and Corinth), some are addressed to individuals, such as Timothy and Titus. The New Testament also includes letters from James, Peter, John and Jude, as well as the letter to the Hebrews, whose authorship remains unknown. These letters provide encouragement and guidance to believers, as well as expanding on some central themes of Christian doctrine. The New Testament concludes with The Revelation of John, a dramatic book of visions concerning the end of the world, intended to encourage believers as they faced persecution at the hands of the Roman authorities.

The Early Church

The period immediately following that of the New Testament writers is often known as the 'patristic' period – from the Greek word *pater*, meaning 'father' – in other words, a respected Christian teacher such as Athanasius (c. 300–373) or Augustine of Hippo (354–430). This period is usually held to begin in about AD 100, and end with the Council of Chalcedon in AD 451. During the early part of this period, Christianity had yet to secure the status of a legally tolerated religion, and was periodically persecuted. Yet the conversion of Constantine, who went on to become the first Christian Roman emperor, led to Christianity initially being tolerated, and then favoured, throughout the empire.

It was a critically important period for the shaping of Christian belief. Like a series of threads, the ideas of the New Testament needed to be woven together. The patristic period was a time of reflection and synthesis, when the contents of the New

Testament were unpacked, examined and explored. A series of important controversies forced the church to give careful thought to how best to represent the biblical witness. The Gnostic controversy of the second century led to intense debate over the relationship of Scripture and tradition. Gnostic distortions of the biblical message led the church to lay down

An icon of Paul the apostle.

basic principles for how the Bible was to be interpreted. It is no accident that this period witnessed the emergence of creeds as public, authoritative declarations of faith. Unlike the maverick interpretations of Gnostic writers, the creeds provided succinct, reliable summaries of the central themes of Christian belief.

The most important debates of this period focused on the identity of Jesus Christ. What is the best way of expressing the New Testament's vision of the significance of Jesus? Although the discussion began in earnest in the second century, it became of especial importance in the fourth century, when the Arian controversy broke out. The chief figure in this debate was Arius (c. 256–336), who argued that Jesus was to be regarded as an especially gifted human being, who outranked everyone else – but was not to be considered divine. He was countered by Athanasius, who argued that this approach to Jesus made it impossible for him to save humanity. Only God could save, he insisted. So if Jesus was not God, he could not bring salvation. Athanasius also pointed out that Christians had worshipped Jesus since the time of the New Testament itself. If Jesus were not God, this would amount to idolatry – worshipping a human being, not God himself.

In the end, after much debate and careful study of the New Testament texts, a definitive statement of Christian belief was set out by the Council of Chalcedon. The Council declared that Jesus Christ was to be regarded as truly human and truly divine. Arius's idea that Jesus was an outstanding human being was decisively rejected as inadequate. This framework has been accepted by most Christians ever since.

Another area of Christian thought to be explored thoroughly at this time was the doctrine of God. Although the doctrine of the Trinity is often regarded as one of the most difficult aspects of Christian thought, patristic writers increasingly saw it as essential to make sense of the New Testament witness to who God was, and what God had done. Although the idea of God being 'three in one' was difficult

Magdalen College, Oxford. The establishment of universities in the Middle Ages took the study of theology and issues of faith beyond the monastery walls.

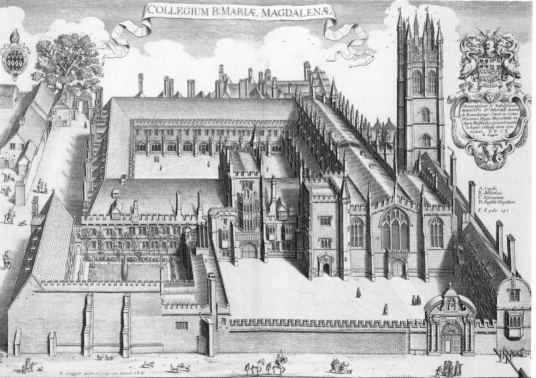

COLLEGIUM B: MARIÆ, MAGDALENÆ.

to grasp, there was a growing consensus within the church that this was the only way in which the biblical witness to God could be faithfully maintained. Simpler ways of representing God were not good enough to do justice to the biblical revelation of God.

The Middle Ages

The collapse of the Roman empire in the fifth century brought about a new period of uncertainty for Christianity in the West. The protection it had enjoyed from the state was now at an end. Many Roman pagans blamed the fall of the empire on the rise of Christianity. If Rome had remained faithful to her traditional religion, they argued, this would never have happened. In the East, however, Christianity remained relatively undisturbed, although the rapid rise and spread of Islam in the eighth century led to severe difficulties in North Africa. The great city of Constantinople (modern-day Istanbul) became of increasing political and religious importance throughout the region, and served as a mission base for the evangelization of many parts of eastern Europe.

In the West, the church was harried by constant waves of barbarian invasions. Monasteries became increasingly important in keeping the Christian faith alive during the periods of instability. An important turning point was the inauguration of the Holy Roman empire under the reign of Charlemagne (742–814). However, this did not produce the long-term stability that many had hoped for and the 'Carolingian renaissance' proved short-lived.

Two centuries later, however, the much hoped for stability began to emerge in western Europe, with the church playing an increasingly important diplomatic role. The role of the monasteries in exploring issues of

A fifteenth-century painting of Thomas Aquinas, the philosopher and scholar who is widely regarded as the greatest Christian theologian of his time.

faith was challenged through the establishment of the universities – such as Bologna, Paris and Oxford during the Middle Ages. This did much to encourage the study of Christian theology and the exploration of its relationship to philosophy. The rediscovery of the writings of the classic Greek philosopher Aristotle led to a new interest in how Christian beliefs could be presented and systematically developed. This is especially clear in the writings of Thomas Aquinas (1225–1274), widely regarded as the greatest Christian theologian of the period. Aquinas's massive work usually known by its Latin title *Summa Theologiae* ('the totality of theology') set out to explore the relevance of theology to every aspect of human thought. It has often been described as a 'cathedral of the mind' on account of its complexity and grand scale.

This type of 'scholastic theology' became highly influential during the

A contemporary German print showing Martin Luther at the Castle Church door in Wittenberg, 1517.

Middle Ages. Yet there were problems with these approaches to Christian belief. Most medieval theology, for example, made use of the Vulgate – a Latin translation of the Bible which was increasingly recognized to be unreliable as time progressed. There was growing pressure to revise the translation in the light of the original Hebrew and Greek texts of the Bible. There were also concerns that scholastic theology was not closely related to the biblical text and was isolated from the life of ordinary Christians.

The Renaissance

Meanwhile, an alternative approach to Christian theology was developing. The Renaissance was a major movement concerned to bring about the renewal of culture in western Europe. It aimed to do so by appealing to the classical period. Why not bring the glories of ancient Rome and Athens back to life? The most satisfying way of renewing European culture was by returning to its roots in the classical period – an approach summed up in the Latin slogan *ad fonts* ('back to the sources').

Many Christian writers were inspired by this approach. If western culture could be renewed by going back to its original sources, why not do the same for the church and for Christian belief. For Erasmus of Rotterdam (1466–1536), perhaps the greatest Renaissance writer, Christianity could be renewed by going back directly to the New Testament, and studying it in the original Greek language. This, he believed, would lead to a simpler, more authentic approach to Christian beliefs, which lay Christians could understand and appreciate.

The Reformation

This approach to Christian belief ended up sparking off a revolution in western Europe. Erasmus had argued for a return to the New Testament, in its original language, as the basis for Christian belief. Yet many ideas developed during the Middle Ages had been based on the Vulgate, and the surge of interest in studying the Bible in its original language led to translation mistakes being identified. But it was not simply translation errors that were noticed: sometimes, beliefs had been based on these faulty translations. A re-examination of belief was necessary, to check out which beliefs were firmly grounded in the Bible, and which were not.

The first phase of this process of re-examination was sparked off by the German reformer Martin Luther (1483–1546). He sought to re-establish the centrality of the Bible to the teaching and structures of the church. Luther was especially concerned by the sale of indulgences – pieces of paper which promised the bearer forgiveness of sins, as a result of payments to the church. For Luther, this was completely unacceptable. He believed that the church of his day had lost sight of Paul's doctrine of justification by faith. Only by recovering this doctrine could the church legitimately claim to call itself 'Christian'. Luther's programme of reform was thus a call for the church to re-examine itself, and bring itself into line with the Bible.

Luther's programme was developed further by John Calvin (1509–64). Calvin set out to re-establish the centrality of the Bible to the life and thought of the church by placing it at the centre of its preaching and thinking. He did this by writing biblical commentaries, developing an expository style of preaching, and by formulating an approach to theology which stressed the role of the Bible. This third aspect of his mission was set out in his *Institutes of the Christian Religion*, which is often thought of as the Protestant equivalent of Aquinas's *Summa Theologiae*.

The Roman Catholic Church rose to the challenge of the Reformation in various ways, not least by responding to many of the criticisms directed against it by reformers such as Luther and Calvin. The movement that is known as the 'Catholic Reformation' set out to eliminate many of the abuses identified by the reformers. Nevertheless, significant differences of belief remained between Protestants and Roman Catholics, especially relating to the authority and institutions of the church.

The religious controversies of the period led to a new emphasis on the importance of Christian education and of developing new ways to deepen people's knowledge of their beliefs. One important development associated with this period is the emergence of 'catechisms' (from the Greek word for 'instruction'). These are primers of Christian belief, usually taking the form of questions and answers. A good example is the Westminster Shorter Catechism, which opens with the following question:

Question: What is the chief end of man?

Answer: Man's chief end is to glorify God, and to enjoy him forever.

These catechisms were widely used for teaching basic Christian beliefs and are still used today. The most widely used modern catechism is currently the *Catechism of the Catholic Church* (1990).

Revival

After the reforms of the sixteenth century, Protestantism entered what many regard as a period of stagnation. The movement widely known as 'Protestant Orthodoxy' stressed the importance of correct religious beliefs, but seemed to its critics to lack religious fervour. The movement known as 'Pietism' emerged in the seventeenth century, largely as a reaction against this emphasis on correct belief. While not denying the importance of theology, Pietism placed an emphasis on 'a living faith'. It was important to live a life that was transformed by the gospel, rather than merely to accept its ideas. It was the heart, not only the head, that needed to be renewed through faith. Religious feelings were just as important as religious ideas.

In the English-speaking world, Pietism is best known in the forms associated with John Wesley (1703–91) and his brother Charles (1707–88), who founded Methodism. To begin with, Wesley was convinced that he 'lacked the faith whereby alone we are saved'. He discovered the need for a 'living faith' and personal experience of Christ in the Christian life as a result of his famous

A portrait of John Wesley, founder of Methodism.

conversion experience at a meeting in Aldersgate Street in May 1738, in which he felt his heart to be 'strangely warmed'. Wesley's emphasis upon the experiential side of Christian faith, which contrasted sharply with the dullness of contemporary English religious life, led to a major religious revival in England. Yet this revival was part of a much broader movement – an evangelical upsurge which affected Protestantism in many parts of the western world, including North America, in the early eighteenth century. The 'Great Awakening', which had its origins primarily in New Jersey and Pennsylvania, swept across much of New England in the mid-eighteenth century. Preachers such as George Whitefield (1714–70), a colleague of the Wesleys, and Jonathan Edwards (1703–58) had a major influence on creating a new enthusiasm for faith.

The Modern World

The history of Christianity in the West in recent centuries has been dominated by the movement known as 'the Enlightenment' (see also page 50). This movement in western culture stressed the importance of human reason and was critical of many traditional Christian beliefs. For example, it held that the traditional Christian understanding of Jesus Christ as 'truly God and truly human' was illogical nonsense. Instead of basing beliefs on the Bible, rationalist writers argued that the only reliable source of human knowledge was reason.

Christian writers rose to this challenge in a number of ways. One of the most significant approaches is found in the writings of C.S. Lewis (1898–1963), who stressed that Christian beliefs are not contrary to reason; rather, they go beyond what reason can establish. Lewis also pointed out that an excessive emphasis on reason failed to do justice to the relationship between beliefs and the imagination on the one hand, and emotions on the other. It was, he argued, necessary to recover a more rounded understanding of the impact of belief on every aspect of human existence. Christian belief provided a framework through which every aspect of human existence could be understood. As Lewis once remarked, 'I believe in Christianity as I believe that the sun has risen: not only because I see it, but because by it I see everything else.'

In recent years, however, the validity of the rationalist critique of traditional Christian belief has itself been challenged. The rise of 'postmodernism' can be seen as a reaction against the western idea that there is some universal rationality, which determines what is 'rational' and what is 'irrational'. Instead, postmodernity argues for the recognition of many different ways of reasoning and thinking. Although this development has caused some difficulties for Christian belief – for example, it is widely believed to encourage pluralism and relativism – it has nevertheless liberated Christian belief from the straitjacket of pure reason. The limits of reason have finally been recognized within western culture.

However, one of the most important developments in recent Christian history has been the expansion of Christianity into non-western regions. Today, Christianity is a global religion, whose centre of gravity has shifted away from the West to the South and East. Latin America, Africa and South-East Asia are the new heartlands of the Christian faith.

This process of expansion has raised important questions for Christian belief. For example, the main global dialogue partner for Christianity is no longer western

secularism, but Islam. And there is increasing interest in the relationship of Christianity to various forms of Hinduism and Buddhism, as Christians in Asia explore how their faith can be thought of as the fulfilment of these ancient wisdoms. For many writers, the future strength of Christianity lies in these regions.

This observation concludes my very brief account of the history of Christian belief, intended to help readers gain a sense of direction as they prepare to explore the rich tapestry of Christian belief. And where better to start than by exploring what that word 'belief' means? What do Christians understand when they say that they 'believe in God'? Or talk about 'faith'?

C.S. Lewis, twentieth-century Christian scholar, apologist and writer.

1

Faith

JOHN STACKHOUSE

Facing page: A miniature from *The Bedford Hours* depicting Noah overseeing the construction of the ark.

What is faith? To answer this question, we may begin by looking at some of the great role models of faith. What difference does faith make to someone? And what does it mean to say that they have faith in God? The first spiritual hero in the Bible about whom there is any extended narrative is Noah. And he turns out to be a shining example of faith. God tells Noah something hard to believe: The world as he knows it will be coming to an end by a flood such as the world has never seen. But God promises to save Noah and his family (Genesis 6:9–22). Noah is then given something to do in the light of this revelation. He is to build an ark and store inside it his family and enough animals to replenish the earth.

Noah believes God. Noah obeys God. Noah has faith.

In the pages of both the Old Testament and the New, we find Abraham as the favourite example of faith. Indeed, the explicit terminology of faith and faithfulness appears first in the story of Abraham. God tells Abraham to leave his home in ancient Sumeria, near the Tigris and Euphrates Rivers present-day Iraq or Kuwait), and move to a land that God would show him (Genesis 12:1–4). God also tells Abraham that, as old as he and his wife are, they nonetheless will have offspring that will multiply eventually into a nation whose influence will bless the entire world (Genesis 15:1–6).

Abraham believes God. Abraham obeys God. Abraham has faith.

No word is more central to the Christian religion than faith – so central, in fact, that we often speak of Christianity itself as the Christian *faith*. And yet it is a word that has been widely misunderstood in our day – so misunderstood, in fact, that many people hesitate to embrace Christianity for fear that they must give up their commitment to intelligent thinking ('faith versus reason') and take a mindless, groundless chance on they-know-not-what (the 'leap of faith'). So what is faith? And why would so many apparently thoughtful and sober people – from Jesus himself to many of our contemporaries today – commend it to us?

What is Faith?

Faith is a rich word in the Bible. In fact, faith is translated by several words in ancient Hebrew, the language of most of the Old Testament, and several words in koine (or 'common') Greek, the language of the New Testament. And in this network of words is a fascinating linkage: belief and action.

The related Hebrew words include the following meanings: 'to fear God' (usually an expression of moral obedience, as well as religious awe; Deuteronomy 10:12; Job 28:28; Psalm 111:10); 'to believe'; 'to be confident'; 'to trust or to be trustworthy'; 'to be loyal or reliable'; 'to be true or truthful'; 'to be firm or established'; 'to heed or pay attention'; 'to obey or follow'; and 'to be righteous or holy'. The related Greek words in the New Testament include the meaning 'to be persuaded'

(Hebrew has no word for persuade or convince), as well as the same range of words as in the Old Testament.

The duplication of these various definitions is illustrated by the familiar word *amen*. Originally an adverb in Hebrew, it is used as a word of response to what is said by someone else: '[That is] truly [said]' or '[That was] reliably [spoken].' We should note in passing Jesus' prefacing of his own teachings with 'Amen, amen' – rendered 'Verily, verily' in the King James Version of the Bible and 'Truly,

Trusting in God as Saviour is more than intellectual assent: it also requires personal commitment.

truly' in more recent renditions. Such usage was unprecedented and signalled his unique claim to authority. Consider in this context Jesus' characterization of his words as a sure foundation for living, as dependable as a stone foundation (Matthew 7:24).

'Amen' becomes a word of self-involvement, particularly in response to the commands of God. The people of Israel respond to the Levites' solemn pronouncements of curses with 'amen', thus committing themselves to the avoidance of those actions upon which the curses have been uttered (Deuteronomy 27:14–26). A later generation responds the same way when Nehemiah denounces those who do not free their fellow Jews from debts, thus promising both to obey Nehemiah's directive and to repudiate their disobedient fellows (Nehemiah 5:13). We see, then, that to say 'amen' is not merely to recognize the accuracy or aptness of what is spoken, but is also to declare one's intention to act in accordance with what is spoken: *Since* what has been said is true and reliable, *then* I will faithfully respond to it. Thus we must recognize that the common modern Christian use of 'amen' simply as a sort of coda to a prayer or hymn is a sad attenuation. When we say or sing 'amen', it must be as a sacred vow that we intend to fulfil.

The English language does not have a verb that precisely corresponds to the noun 'faith'. We don't 'faith', nor do we 'faith' anything. We 'believe' something or someone. But in the languages of the Bible, faith is not restricted to intellectual assent. It is not merely an acknowledgment that such-and-such is the case. Faith generally takes place in a personal relationship, so that one believes something because one believes the someone who said it. And with that belief, in the context of a relationship of mutual promise and help – what the Bible calls a covenant – comes implications of action. The common formula is as follows: Since I believe X is true because you have told me so, and I believe you to be true, then I will perform my part in our agreement, and I believe you will do your part as well. Thus we have the expression to 'keep faith' with someone.

Indeed, a common motif in both Testaments is the imitation of God: Since God is faithful, so the people of God are to be faithful; since God is truthful, so his people are to be truthful. In fact, one of Jesus' great titles in the book of Revelation's depiction of his second coming is 'Faithful and True' (Revelation 3:14; 19:11).

Thus in biblical faith the key element is *trust* – a combination of belief and action. 'I trust you' is a meaningless phrase if not connected with some sort of action. The lifeguard swims out to me as I flounder in a choppy sea, and he yells at me to calm down and take hold of him properly. 'I trust you' is a meaningless declaration at that point if I do not obey him out of confidence that he will save me.

Such a combination applies not only to crises but also to daily life. When a couple recite their marriage vows, they are not merely declaring their ideas about the other person: 'Yes, come to think of it, I do believe you're rather a fine person and it would be splendid to spend the rest of my life with you. What a terrific concept. And now, goodbye.' No, the two of them make vows that oblige them to act in particular ways that are indeed consonant with their ideas: '*Since* I believe that you are a fine person, that I love you, that you love me, and that we desire to build a life together – and thus I believe not only these things about you, but I believe *in you* – *then* I promise my love to you forever and will act in all of the ways that are implied in such a promise.'

The motif of marriage is in fact used powerfully in the Bible to represent

God's relationship with his people – from the broken-hearted prophet Hosea taking back his adulterous wife once again as God once again forgives unfaithful Israel, to the glorious Christian hope of the church joining Jesus at his second coming in the marriage supper of the Lamb (Revelation 19:9).

In Christian usage, faith sometimes does refer to beliefs. It occasionally seems to do so in the New Testament, as in the apostle Paul's counsel to Timothy: 'If you put these instructions

Faith, like marriage, is an agreement based on belief, trust and commitment.

before the brothers and sisters, you will be a good servant of Christ Jesus, nourished on the words of the faith and of the sound teaching that you have followed' (1 Timothy 4:6). Even here, though, we might understand a fuller interpretation of 'faith': the 'teaching' can be seen as merely the intellectual component of the whole way of Christian life denoted as 'the faith', and thus 'the teaching' is literally 'the *words of* the faith'. It is actually quite rare to find in the New Testament 'the faith' unequivocally reduced to simply a body of truths, although some rationalistic theologians indicate otherwise (consider examples

'Faith is taking the first step even when you don't see the whole staircase.'

Martin Luther King, Jr

The Origin of the Creeds

The word 'creed' comes from the Latin word *credo* ('I believe'), and refers to a publicly authorized statement of faith. The earliest and simplest Christian confession of faith seems to have been 'Jesus is Lord!', a formula which is found at several points in the New Testament. As time passed, the need for official, public declarations of faith became increasingly obvious. Converts to Christianity were asked to confirm their faith at their baptism using short statements of faith. These gradually became expanded into what we now know as 'creeds'. These often have a recognizably Trinitarian form, affirming belief in God as creator, Christ as saviour, and the Holy Spirit. The creeds have never been thought of as alternatives to the Bible. Rather, they are to be seen as reliable and trustworthy frameworks for making sense of the Bible, safeguarding the church against serious misinterpretations of the Bible – such as those which emerged during some of the controversies with Gnostic groups in the second century.

The two most important Christian creeds are the Apostles' Creed and the Nicene Creed. The Apostles' Creed evolved over many years, with its final versions dating from the eighth century. It consists of twelve individual statements of faith. These are traditionally ascribed to individual apostles, although there is no historical justification for this belief. In its western form, the creed reads as follows:

1. I believe in God, the Father almighty, creator of the heavens and earth;

2. and in Jesus Christ, his only Son, our Lord;

3. who was conceived by the Holy Spirit and born of the Virgin Mary;

4. he suffered under Pontius Pilate, was crucified, dead and buried; he descended to hell;

5. on the third day he was raised from the dead;

6. he ascended into the heavens, and sits at the right hand of God the Father almighty;

7. from where he will come to judge the living and the dead.

8. I believe in the Holy Spirit;

9. in the holy catholic church; the communion of saints;

10. the forgiveness of sins;

11. the resurrection of the flesh;

12. and eternal life.

During the twentieth century, the Apostles' Creed has become widely accepted by most churches as the basis for ecumenical discussions aimed at deepening understanding, and encouraging cooperation.

The Nicene Creed is particularly concerned with safeguarding the identity of Jesus Christ against misunderstandings and inadequate representations of his significance. This creed dates from the fourth century, and takes its name from the Council of Nicea (AD 325), which set out the orthodox understanding of the identity of Christ. The creed includes explicit statements of the divinity of Christ, declaring that he is to be thought of as 'true God from true God, begotten not made, being of one substance with the Father'.

FAITH

commonly offered by those of this opinion such as Romans 1:5; Galatians 1:23; Jude 3).

In the early church, however, theologians talked about the 'rule of faith', by which they meant a brief statement of Christian doctrine that served as a guideline for assessing heresy. Such statements of faith, when authorized by widespread usage or official sanction, became known as 'creeds' – a term that comes from the Latin beginnings of the two most famous early instances, the so-called Apostles' Creed and the Nicene Creed: 'I believe…' or *credo*. In medieval Christianity and in Roman Catholic teaching since the controversies with Protestants in the sixteenth century, faith sometimes has meant 'assenting to the teaching of the Church'. This definition of faith was posed particularly in opposition to what was supposed to be the basic Protestant sense of faith as a merely affective trust in God's mercy regardless of doctrinal correctness. (Protestants, and particularly Martin Luther, could sound this way – but the Protestant Reformers' characteristic passion for correct doctrine shows that faith for them was never actually divorced from intellectual concerns.)

Yet no main branch of Christianity has ever narrowed faith purely to intellectual conviction, to the realm of ideas alone, to a bare 'I believe…' without any heartfelt concern or any practical implication. Indeed, one of the more intriguing verses in the Bible suggests that demons themselves believe certain truths about God and 'shudder' in response. They see the truth, but respond wrongly to it (James 2:19). Nor has any main branch of Christianity ever narrowed faith purely to a sort of affection or existential decision to trust God without doctrinal content or moral entailment. In fact, it is difficult to imagine just what 'contentless' faith would be like, or

why someone would be persuaded to engage in it.

Some readers of the New Testament – such as Martin Luther – have seen an opposition between Paul and James on this sort of point, as if Paul is defending faith-as-mere-trust while James champions faith-plus-works. Thus Luther was doubtful that the epistle (or letter) of James should be included in the Bible! But there is no opposition, especially when we recall that both Paul and James are Jewish Christians. Their whole heritage of faith is a holistic one, rooted in the covenant between God and his people. To be faithful means to believe what God says; to trust God's forgiveness for the past and his provision for the future; and to cooperate with God in the present in whatever his work demands.

Consider Habakkuk's conviction, echoed by Paul: 'Look at the proud! Their spirit is not right in them, but the righteous live by their faith' (Habakkuk 2:4; cf. Romans 1:17; Galatians 3:11). One might read this passage as suggesting bare belief, a sort of inward trust in God without any requirement of action. Yet consider Habakkuk's contemporary Ezekiel, perhaps a sort of 'James' to Habakkuk's 'Paul', who writes: 'If a man is righteous and does what is lawful and right… follows my statutes, and is careful to observe my ordinances, acting faithfully – such a one is righteous; he shall surely live, says the Lord God' (Ezekiel 18:5, 9). Paul and James share this heritage from the Old Testament.

In fact, Paul characteristically wants to make sure we understand that we cannot merit God's favour by our good works. In this, he is particularly concerned to refute certain later Jewish emphases on religious law-keeping as a means of earning God's approval. He cites Abraham often as his example: 'For what does the

'He who hears the word of God and does not obey is out of his mind.'

Euripides

'In faith there is enough light for those who want to believe and enough shadows to blind those who don't.'

Blaise Pascal

'The faithful see them (the things that are of faith), not as by demonstration, but by the light of faith that makes them see that they ought to believe them.'

Thomas Aquinas

Scripture say? "Abraham believed God, and it was reckoned to him as righteousness" (Romans 4:3; see Galatians 3:6). Abraham did not earn God's blessing. No one can do that, since 'all have sinned and come short of the glory of God' (Romans 3:23). God graciously *counted* Abraham as righteous as Abraham put his trust in God, and so God blessed him.

Paul makes clear that Jesus Christ has, so to speak, been the faithful one on both sides of the divine–human encounter. In Christ, God has played both the role as faithful judge and saviour and the role of faithful human respondent (Galatians 3:23–25). Jesus is both 'God with us' and the 'Son of Man'. Thus as we put our faith in him, we become literally 'in him', and are both reckoned righteous by God's justice (what Protestants typically call 'justification') and progressively purified into holiness by God's transforming power (what Protestants

call 'sanctification'). Roman Catholics tend to use the term 'justification' in both instances, while Orthodox Christians more commonly use the language of being 'partakers of the divine nature' (2 Peter 1:4). So Paul crucially steers readers away from any sense of their own righteousness and towards the forgiveness of sins and regeneration in new spiritual life as gifts of God that humankind so desperately needs.

The New Testament writer James, for his part, wants to make sure his readers understand that they cannot claim to have genuine faith without evidencing good works. And he, too, as a good Jewish believer writing to other Jewish believers, cites the example of Abraham who *believed God* – which for James, as for Jews in general, simply includes the idea of obedience:

Was not our ancestor Abraham justified by works when he offered his son Isaac on the altar? You see that faith was active along with his works, and faith was brought to completion by the works. Thus the Scripture was fulfilled that says, 'Abraham believed God, and it was reckoned to him as righteousness', and he was called the friend of God. (James 2:21–23; compare Genesis 22:16, 18; 26:3–5.)

Different audiences with different challenges prompt Paul and James to different, but complementary, emphases. And this is how most of the church has understood these emphases through the centuries.

Paul himself nicely summarizes this connection of faith and works in the following way:

For by grace you have been saved through faith, and this is not your own doing; it is the gift of God – not the result of works, so that no one may boast. For we are what he

When Abraham offered Isaac on the altar, his obedience proved the genuineness of his faith.

has made us, *created in Christ Jesus for good works, which God prepared beforehand to be our way of life (Ephesians 2:8–10)*.

It is also worth noting that Paul lists 'faithfulness' among the fruits of the Spirit (Galatians 5:22).

The voice of the apostle John should be added to this dialogue. Scholars have noted how in John's writings the concept of faith can sound as if it has been narrowed to mere intellectual assent to orthodox teaching. His Gospel, for instance, is written 'that you may come to believe that Jesus is the Messiah, the Son of God, and that through believing you may have life in his name' (John 20:31). Among the most-quoted verses in the Bible is his epitome of the gospel: 'For God so loved the world that he gave his only Son so that everyone who believes in him may not perish but may have eternal life' (John 3:16). And John's major epistle has a similar-sounding objective: 'I write these things to you who believe in the name of the Son of God, so that you may know that you have eternal life' (1 John 5:13).

Yet it is also in the Johannine writings that Christians encounter some of the Bible's strongest affirmation of the necessity of obeying and loving God, of serving one's neighbour, and particularly of caring for one's fellow believer. John quotes Jesus in the Upper Room on the night he is betrayed: 'I give you a new commandment, that you love one another. Just as I have loved you, you also should love one another' (John 13:34). Again, in his major epistle, John himself clearly links belief and action: 'This is his commandment, that we should believe in the name of his Son Jesus Christ and love one another, just as he has commanded us. All who obey his commandments abide in him, and he abides in them' (1 John 3:23–24).

There is no 'cheap grace' in John, as there is none in Paul or James. There is no easy salvation by mere belief, no faith without works. Christian faith – the fundamental commitment of the Christian to God in Christ – entails holiness:

If we say that we have fellowship with him while we are walking in darkness, we lie and do not do what is true... Whoever says, 'I have come to know him', but does not obey his commandments, is a liar, and in such a person the truth does not exist; but whoever obeys his word, truly in this person the love of God has reached perfection. By this we may be sure that we are in him: whoever says, 'I abide in him', ought to walk just as he walked (1 John 1:6; 2:4–6).

Christian teaching – Roman Catholic, Orthodox, and Protestant – thus has declared the faithful response to God to include the whole person, sometimes summarized as 'head, heart, and hands'.

And it is a *response*. Mainstream Christian teaching has always maintained that in each individual's salvation God makes the first move, the last move, and the most important moves in between. All anyone can do is respond to his gifts, literally his 'graces'. Without his initiative, his sustenance, and his perseverance, no one could hope to be saved. We certainly *would not* choose aright if God did not lift us out of our sinful disposition to a place of genuine choice.

Christians have disagreed with each other, sometimes vehemently, about just how God does affect our wills and thus about the nature of our 'genuine choice'. The history of theology is replete with these arguments – from Pelagius versus Augustine to Ockham versus Aquinas, to Erasmus versus

'Faith is reason grown courageous.'
Sherwood Eddy

'If you believe what you like in the gospels, and reject what you don't like, it is not the gospel you believe, but yourself.'
Augustine of Hippo

FAITH

'Faith is understanding's step, and understanding faith's attainment.'

Augustine of Hippo

Faith is the root from which hope grows and love blooms.

'Everything depends upon faith. The person who does not have faith is like someone who has to cross the sea, but is so frightened that he does not trust the ship. And so he stays where he is, and is never saved, because he will not get on board and cross over.'

Martin Luther

Luther, to Arminius versus Calvin. But all orthodox Christians agree that sin has corrupted all of humanity to the extent that no one would ever choose God if God had not chosen them first and empowered them to choose him (John 6:65; 1 John 4:19).

But God is strong, and good, and patient, so Christians trust him to come through for them and to help them persevere as well. Indeed, the epistle to the Hebrews calls Jesus 'the initiator and completer of our faith' (Hebrews 12:2). And that is the God who Christians worship. Faith means not only moral obedience, but liturgical response as well. So closely intertwined are these two modes of grateful response to God that we must think of them simultaneously when we consider related words such as 'piety' and 'devotion'.

Furthermore, it is precisely because faith is a matter of personal relationship – of believing and trusting and obeying and worshipping God – that the whole Christian way of life can be called 'the faith' (Acts 6:7; 13:8; 14:22; 16:5). We see this usage in the earliest Christian documents, for

example, Paul himself testifies in his last epistle that he 'has fought the good fight' and has 'kept the faith' (2 Timothy 4:7). Indeed, the first Christians called themselves simply 'the believers' (Acts 2:44; 4:32; 11:21).

Love has been called the highest of Christian virtues. It lies at the heart of Christ's famous summary of the Law of God: 'You shall love the Lord your God with all your heart, and with all your soul, and with all your strength, and with all your mind; and your neighbour as yourself' (Luke 10:27). And Paul makes clear that the greatest of the Christian graces is love, not faith. But if love is the flower of Christian virtue, and hope is the stalk on which that flower blooms as it reaches up towards the light, then faith is the root that nourishes and secures the rest of the Christian life. Faith is the fundamental posture of the child of God. If Christians adopt this attitude towards God – humble, grateful, and obedient – God can give them every other blessing and lift them upwards into glory forever. If they refuse it, he can give them nothing at all.

God's blessing is, after all, the true focus of faith – and not what believers do. In one striking poetic allusion, Paul refers to faith as a shield (Ephesians 6:16), but rabbi Paul, who knew his Hebrew Scriptures thoroughly, means that it is the faithful God in whom we trust who is our protection, as the psalmist says: 'his faithfulness is a shield and buckler' (Psalm 91:4). Christianity teaches that God's blessing is astoundingly disproportionate to an individual's faith. God does for his people 'far more than all we can ask or imagine' (Ephesians 3:20). Jesus refers to a believer's faith as miniscule. Yet if it is oriented properly – humbly, obediently, and gratefully towards the God who loves his people and longs to do them good – its effect is gigantic, as is the God in whom they trust and who

Faith and Philosophy

The Greek philosopher Plato (c. 427–347 BC) once defined 'philosophy' as the quest for wisdom. Over the years, however, the term has come to mean something like 'the use of human reason to uncover the meaning of life' or 'the discovery of truth through argument'. Theology, on the other hand, is often thought of as the attempt to set out what can be known about God from revelation. One of the classic debates within the Christian church concerns how philosophy and theology relate to each other. Are reason and revelation opposed to each other? Or are they complementary? This question demands a careful study of the limits of human reason, as it attempts to wrestle with something that is ultimately far beyond its grasp – the living God. To what extent is reason able to cope with God? If God is above and beyond our world, how can human reason ever hope to make sense of him?

Some Christian writers have argued that, since human reason is fallen and finite, it is incapable of arriving at any satisfactory or reliable conclusions about God. In any case, why bother using reason, when all that we need to know about God has been disclosed in Scripture? At best, we can use reason to show how various biblical statements can be woven together. We must know God as he has revealed himself, not as reason argues that he must be. We find this concern expressed by the French theologian Blaise Pascal (1623–62), who argued that Christians believed in 'the God of Abraham, God of Isaac, God of Jacob, not of the philosophers and scholars'.

Others have argued that, while reason is clearly incapable of giving us access to a full, saving knowledge of God, it nevertheless points us in the right direction. One of the most important recent discussions of the relation of faith and reason is found in Pope John Paul II's 1998 encyclical letter *Fides et Ratio* ('Faith and Reason'). This letter sets out a classic Christian approach to the relation of faith to reason, arguing that they 'are like two wings on which the human spirit rises to the contemplation of truth; and God has placed in the human heart a desire to know the truth – in a word, to know himself'. The basic idea is that human beings long to know the truth, and are constantly searching for it. 'In the far reaches of the human heart there is a seed of desire and nostalgia for God.'

So can reason alone lead humanity to this truth? The letter pays a handsome tribute to philosophy, as 'one of noblest of human tasks', which is 'driven by the desire to discover the ultimate truth of existence'. Yet unaided human reason cannot fully penetrate to the mystery of life. God graciously chose to make these things known through revelation which would otherwise remain unknown. 'The truth made known to us by revelation is neither the product nor the consummation of an argument devised by human reason.'

The debate over the relation of faith and philosophy continues. However, there is at least a degree of consensus that, whatever its limits, we can use reason responsibly and carefully in exploring and defending the Christian revelation.

> 'There is no philosopher in the world so great but he believes a million things on the faith of other people and accepts a great many more truths than he demonstrates.'
>
> Alexis de Tocqueville

acts on their behalf: 'For truly I tell you, if you have faith the size of a mustard seed, you will say to this mountain, "Move from here to there", and it will move; and nothing will be impossible for you' (Matthew 17:20).

Faith and Reason

Aristotle famously divided our ideas into three categories: opinion, belief, and knowledge – with religious conviction being located in the middle category. Long before him, of course, religious thinkers wrestled with the question of how faith relates to knowledge. Is faith just a religious kind of knowledge? Is it inferior or superior to knowledge? Are faith and knowledge utterly different from each other, and even opposed to each other?

Two mistakes are common in this inquiry. The first is to think that faith is a peculiarly religious word and that it has nothing to do with everyday life. The second is to presume that faith has no relationship to knowledge, that the two stand as utterly separate categories of perception and assent.

In fact, however, everyday life constantly presses us beyond what we know (or think we know) and requires us to exercise faith. We frequently find ourselves compelled to trust beyond what we are sure of, to make commitments that go outside our sense of safety. And yet these moments of trust and commitment – these acts of *faith* – are intrinsically and importantly related to knowledge. Faith relies on knowledge even as it moves out from knowledge into the uncertain, and even the unknown. The most famous biblical definition of faith affirms this concept: 'Now faith is the assurance of things

Faith in Words: Religious Language

How can we express the magnificence of God in words? The Austrian philosopher Ludwig Wittgenstein once pointed out that words were incapable of adequately describing the aroma of fresh coffee. So if words cannot do justice to something as simple as this, how can they ever do justice to God? How can we hope to speak reliably about God?

These questions are fundamental to the debate about religious language – the ways in which the Bible and Christian theology speak about God. Two answers to this question are of especial interest: the ideas of *analogy* and *accommodation*. Both these express the idea that God reveals himself in forms that our human minds are capable of grasping. Both have a long history of use in the Christian tradition, and have proved their value over many centuries of discussion and debate.

The appeal to *analogy* is especially associated with writers such as Thomas Aquinas, the great medieval theologian. Aquinas argued that, since God created the world, there was a fundamental analogy between the creation and the creator. Aspects of the created order could thus mirror something of the nature of God. For Aquinas, the creation is analogous to – but not identical with – its creator. It can thus help us grasp something of the nature and character of God. God reveals himself in images and ideas which tie in with our world of everyday existence – yet which do not *reduce* God to the level of the everyday world. Aquinas is clear that not every aspect of the created order can reflect the nature of God; it is those aspects of creation that are identified in the Bible as having this capacity. Thus human kings and shepherds could help us 'visualize' what God was like. Just as a human shepherd guides and cares for his flock, so God leads and protects his people. Again, there is an analogy between the human process of purchasing the hoped for, the conviction of things not seen' (Hebrews 11:1).

Trevor cannot know for certain that the canoe bobbing by the dock will still float once he gets in it. But he cannot settle for being 'mostly convinced' and thus place most of his weight in the canoe while reserving some of his weight for the dock. If he tries to do so, he will soon be experiencing neither the canoe nor the dock. To enjoy the canoe, he has to get all the way in. He has to make a commitment. And he is prudent to do so. He is exercising rationally-based faith.

No one exercises 'blind faith' in anything – or anyone. Everyone has a reason to believe what he or she believes – even if someone else thinks it to be an insufficient reason, and even if it turns out in fact to be a poorly grounded belief. The relationship of knowledge and faith holds in matters both large and small, impersonal and personal. It would be silly to refuse to sit in a chair until its structural adequacy had been conclusively demonstrated. Who can wait around for an engineer to test every piece of furniture one might wish to use? And who can be sure that the chair will not fail one minute after the testing is complete? Parents of small children can never have an evening out if they refuse to trust every babysitter who applies for the job. A woman would be a fool to refuse to marry her beloved until the marriage had been guaranteed. Life for us humans means risk, and the wise person is the one who does not seek certainty, but seeks instead adequate reason to believe the best alternative available. Then he or she ventures

> 'Life is a battle between faith and reason in which each feeds upon the other, drawing sustenance from it and destroying it.'
>
> Reinhold Niebuhr

freedom of a slave and the divine process of purchasing the freedom of a sinner through the death of Christ.

The idea of *accommodation* is especially associated with John Calvin, who argues that God adapts himself to our capacity in revelation. In other words, God chooses to reveal himself in forms that are appropriate to our ability to grasp him. The analogy which lies behind Calvin's thinking at this point is that of a human orator. A good speaker knows the limitations of his audience, and adjusts the way he speaks accordingly. The gulf between the speaker and the hearer must be bridged if communication is to take place. The limitations of his audience determine the language and imagery the orator employs. The parables of Jesus illustrate this point perfectly: they use language and illustrations (for example, analogies based on sheep and shepherds) perfectly suited to his audience in rural Palestine. Paul also uses ideas adapted to the situation of his hearers, drawn from the commercial and legal world of the cities in which the majority of his readers lived. Calvin argues that God speaks to us in this 'adapted' or 'accommodated' manner as an act of grace, so that none may miss out on the riches of the Christian gospel.

The image of a loving shepherd and his flock helps us visualize what God is like.

'You call for faith:
I show you doubt, to prove that faith exists. The more of doubt, the stronger faith, I say, If faith o'ercomes doubt.'

Robert Browning

Christians believe that the beauty and majesty of the natural world point towards the existence of God.

forward in faith, trusting something or someone because of what she thinks she knows about that thing or person.

Some readers may wonder if I am depersonalizing Christian faith here into mere cognitive decision, rather than personal trust: 'On the basis of my knowing X, I shall therefore risk in the following way…' Yet the latter depends upon the former. One never trusts someone without a store of important knowledge on which one bases one's faith. Knowing you to be a kind and responsible person, for example, I entrust my pet to your care while I'm away on a journey. There is no virtue to trusting someone without good reason to do so! The apostle Paul brings these themes nicely together: 'But I am not ashamed, for I know the one in whom I have put my trust, and I am sure that he is able to guard until that day what I have entrusted to him' (2 Timothy 1:12).

There are important respects also in which the relationship between faith and knowledge is reversed. Faith, that is, can be a condition for acquiring knowledge.

Let's consider a scientific laboratory. A young physicist, Dr Alpha, is attempting to convince a senior scientist, Dr Beta, that she has found something important in her research that contradicts some of Dr Beta's work. Dr Beta is sceptical – and that's perfectly all right, we should think, especially for a rigorous and experienced scientist. But it turns out that poor Dr Beta also happens to have developed paranoid tendencies. He now suspects that other scientists are constantly trying to trick him or humiliate him. He no longer trusts them.

Now, how successful will Dr Alpha be in convincing Dr Beta? Not very. She can show him her lab notebooks. 'Hah!' he responds. 'Fictions!' She shows him the computer printouts.

Can God's Existence Be Proved?

Faith is not blind trust, opposed to the evidence of the world. Rather, faith believes that the world – which Christians see as God's creation – is studded with hints of God's existence and nature. It appeals to the apostle Paul's sermon preached at the Areopagus in Athens (Acts 17) in arguing that it is entirely reasonable to infer the existence of God from the wonders of nature and a human sense of divinity within us. These do not count as 'proofs'; they are, however, confirmation or corroboration of the basic themes of faith.

Although philosophical textbooks sometimes talk about theologians developing 'proofs of God's existence', a closer examination shows that these were not intended to be thought of as 'proofs' in the strict sense of the word. Certain excellent reasons may be put forward for suggesting that God exists; these do not, however, count as 'proofs' in the sense of 'rigorous logical demonstrations' or 'conclusive scientific experiments'. Anselm of Canterbury (1033–1109) set out what has come to be known as the 'ontological argument', which argued that human ideas of God could be interpreted as an indirect demonstration of the existence of God. Thomas Aquinas set out five ways in which the existence of God could be inferred from examining the world around us. The fifth of these, sometimes known as the 'teleological argument', is of especial interest. Aquinas notes that the world shows obvious traces of intelligent design. Natural processes and objects seem to be adapted with certain definite objectives in mind. They seem to have a purpose, or to have been designed. But things don't design themselves: they are caused and designed by someone or something else. Arguing from this observation, Aquinas concludes that the source of this natural ordering must be conceded to be God himself.

These ideas were developed further by John Polkinghorne (born 1930), one of Britain's leading theoretical physicists with a strong interest in Christian theology. Polkinghorne stresses that

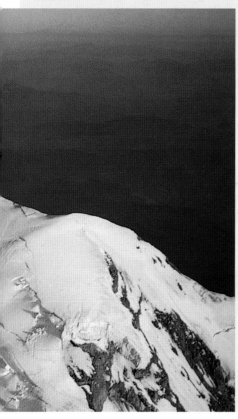

Christianity, like the natural sciences, is concerned about making sense of the world on the basis of the evidence that is available. 'Faith is not a question of shutting one's eyes, gritting one's teeth, and believing the impossible. It involves a leap, but a leap into the light rather than the dark.' Faith is to be understood as 'motivated belief, based on evidence'. It is rigorously based on reflection on the world – on the various 'clues' it offers to its origins and nature. And those clues point to God as their best explanation.

The fundamental point here is that Christian faith is *beyond* reason but not *contrary* to reason. The existence of God is not something that can be proved. Equally, it is not something that can be *disproved*. It is easy to overlook the fact that atheism is also a faith. An atheist believes that there is no God. This belief, however, is just as difficult to prove as the Christian belief that there is indeed a God.

'More lies!' he replies. She runs a videotape of the actual experiment. 'It's amazing what they can do with computer-generated graphics nowadays, isn't it?' he slyly remarks. She calls in technician after technician as eyewitnesses. 'They're all in your pay!' he stubbornly observes.

Finally, Dr Alpha levels what she thinks will be a crushing blow. 'Then do the experiment yourself and see!' 'And be made a fool of?' he retorts. 'Never!' Dr Beta storms out of the lab. He cannot trust, so he cannot learn. (And this is the principle behind the ancient Christian motto, 'faith seeking understanding' and Augustine's dictum, 'I believe in order that I might understand.') In the pursuit of many sorts of knowledge, faith of an appropriate kind is necessary to advance.

Faith and Truth

Religious faith is not completely different from the faith we have discussed so far, but is simply the variety of faith proper to its object. Just as putting faith in a chair is similar to, but also different from, putting faith in a spouse, so is putting faith in a deity both similar to, and also somewhat different from, the other two. We have different warrants for trusting a spouse than for trusting God, for instance. As Christianity teaches, God is normally invisible to us, and so divine activity must be inferred from its results, or believed in on the basis of reliable testimony, while spouses perform a great many actions that we can readily sense. Different stakes are involved in each relationship as well. A husband or wife trusts their spouse with their life, while Christians trust God to guide them and provide for them reliably for their eternities.

So we might arrive at two crucial propositions about the quest for certainty in religious matters: It is impossible, but it is also unnecessary.

We already are accustomed to taking the greatest of relational risks in this life, whether trusting a spouse, or trusting a surgeon, or trusting a rescuer. All we can do is to perform the same exercise of trust in religious matters as well, as human beings who recognize that we do not and cannot know it all before deciding – on *anything*.

At the same time, in our various personal relationships – with friends, co-workers, family members, tradespeople, professionals, and so on – we are wise to trust people neither too much nor too little. We ought to *apportion* our faith, as well as our assent, according to the warrants available. One might trust Mr Atkinson to fix one's car at his garage, but not necessarily to tend one's baby of an evening at home. One might trust one's lawyer to draw up a reliable will, but not necessarily to date one's daughter.

In ultimate relationships, though, we have to make more radical decisions. A fiancée cannot strictly calculate what faith she can put in her groom-to-be and then act proportionately. Maria cannot decide to enter marriage at 60 per cent confidence and therefore get only '60 per cent married', with the understanding that she will proceed to marry her husband 'more thoroughly' as their relationship goes along and her warrants presumably increase. At the altar she has to decide: 'I do' or 'I don't.' She cannot know what her husband will be like in the future. She does not even have complete or certain knowledge of what he has been like in the past. She must, however, enter into a lifetime's commitment, all or nothing, on the basis of what she does know. She must commit herself to trusting her husband. She must exercise faith that day.

Maria must, furthermore, continue to exercise faith every succeeding day of her marriage, for she will never

'The disbelief of Thomas has done more for our faith than the faith of the other disciples. As he touches Christ and is won over to belief, every doubt is cast aside and our faith is strengthened.'

Gregory the Great

Science and Religion

Are the natural sciences and Christian faith opposed to each other? For some, such as the Oxford atheist writer Richard Dawkins (born 1941), the natural sciences lead inexorably to atheism. The sciences not only make God redundant; they eliminate any space for him in the explanation of the world. Yet things are far from being this simple.

One of the most interesting aspects of the history of science is that there are good reasons for thinking that the Christian doctrine of creation was of considerable importance in catalysing the emergence of the natural sciences. If the 'heavens declare the glory of the Lord' (Psalm 19:1), might not studying those heavens help us appreciate God's glory all the more? John Calvin argued that the study of God's creation led to a deepened appreciation of God himself. This idea was further developed through what is sometimes called the 'two books' tradition – namely, the book of Scripture and the book of nature – as proposed in 'The Belgic Confession', a Calvinist document dating from 1561. This argued that knowledge of God could come from two sources – the Bible itself, and 'the universe, which is before our eyes as a most beautiful book, in which all creatures, great and small, are like so many characters leading us to contemplate the invisible things of God'. To study the 'book of nature' was widely seen as a way of coming to a deeper admiration of the God who was made known fully and definitively in Scripture.

Some argue that the natural sciences are, by definition, atheist. As God is not invoked in scientific explanation, the sciences are therefore atheist. This is not the case. A standard Christian approach to this issue reasons as follows. God is the cause of all things. Yet while God must be considered capable of doing certain things directly, God delegates causal efficacy to the created order. For Aquinas, this is expressed in the notion of 'secondary causality'. God does not do everything personally and directly, but can act in and through other causes. Yet these secondary causes must be considered as an extension of, not an alternative to, the primary causality of God himself. Events within the created order can exist in complex causal relationships, without in any way denying their *ultimate* dependency upon God as final cause. The critical point to appreciate is that the created order thus demonstrates causal relationships that can be investigated by the natural sciences and correlated – for example, in the form of the 'laws of nature' – without in any way implying, still less necessitating, an atheist world view. To put this as simply as possible: God creates a world with its own distinct ordering and processes, which the natural sciences can investigate.

A weakness of this approach is that God can be left out of things with alarming ease. As Pierre-Simon Laplace (1749–1827) pointed out in his *Treatise of Celestial Mechanics*, the idea of the solar system as a self-sustaining mechanism eliminated any need for God. But the fact that God does not need to be directly invoked in scientific explanation does not mean that the sciences presuppose or necessitate atheism, or that the existence of God is inconsistent with the sciences.

arrive at full knowledge either of her husband's character or of his activities when he is not in her presence. And we would normally say that she is entirely right to keep trusting him on the basis of her increasing knowledge of him. Indeed, her faith in him properly will grow, just as our faith in God grows into greater strength and sophistication as our relationship with him extends and deepens (Romans 4:19–20; 2 Corinthians 10:15).

We might observe that Maria ought to keep trusting her husband at least until the sad day, if it ever comes, when her faith is overwhelmed by reasons not to continue trusting him. Strange perfume on his shirt, unknown female callers on the phone, loss of affection when he is with her – such data eventually add up. If they add up sufficiently, then we would conclude that she is no longer admirable to keep believing in him, but foolish. She must indeed change her mind, her commitments, and her life accordingly.

So to have faith does not mean to suspend critical thinking in either secular or religious contexts. And it doesn't mean that in the religious sphere, either. You might be entirely entitled to believe in religion X, given what you have learned in life to that point. But the intelligent person who runs up against challenges (what contemporary philosophers call 'potential defeaters'), is obliged to pay attention to them. You don't need to throw your faith aside at the first sign of trouble, of course. That would be as silly as a scientist trashing his years of research whenever a lab result came out 'wrong'. The truly critical thinker, however, pays attention to such difficulties. She tries creatively to see if they can be met within her current scheme of thought, or whether she needs to modify her views, or – in the extreme case – whether she needs to abandon her theory (about this chemical process, about this spouse or

> 'Have you been in a room from which faith has gone? Like a marriage from which love has gone.'
>
> Graham Greene

about this religion) for a better one.

In the Christian religion, faith rests on claims to truth. We believe and trust because of what we have already come to know. Christians believe that their hope is 'sure' because they believe that they have very good reasons to trust God for the future – reasons ranging from historical arguments to personal spiritual experiences to philosophical proofs. Many books have been written through the ages offering evidences for the truth of various Christian beliefs. Millions of people have found such resources to be convincing – while others, to be sure, have not.

In this book, however, we are not arguing for the Christian faith, but explaining it. However, it is worth making this basic observation. The religion of the Old Testament depends entirely upon the following fundamental dynamic: Since God is the God who has been faithful to us in the past, and particularly in the crucial instance of rescuing Israel from Egypt and bringing us into the Promised Land, then God can be trusted for the future – therefore we will obey him now. 'Great is your faithfulness,' proclaims the prophet Jeremiah, even in the midst of his great worry and sorrow over Israel's apparent abandonment (Lamentations 3:21–23).

The Christian faith has exactly this shape: Since God is the God who has been faithful to his people in the past, and particularly in the crucial instance of raising Jesus from the dead in validation of his work and as a sign of universal resurrection to come, then God can be trusted for the future (1 Corinthians 15).

To be sure, this trust in God is often difficult, not least because there are so many occasions and reasons to doubt that God is good, or powerful, or even there at all. The problem of evil – as well as several other challenges to Christian faith – remains a genuine

problem for believers as well as for enquirers and sceptics. Christians cannot properly hope to resolve all of these problems and then repose in complete intellectual certainty. The best minds of the ages have wrestled with these questions and none have emerged with definitive answers that can calm all doubts and resolve all difficulties. Instead, God has offered us adequate grounds for belief, and particularly shown himself to be both entirely good and entirely powerful in the person and work of Jesus. Moreover, Christians enjoy a heartfelt assurance, granted as a gift by the Holy Spirit, that brings them through the worst of life's trials. Thus the Bible tells believers that they can enjoy rest, peace, and comfort even in the valley of the shadow of death (Psalm 23; Matthew 11:28; 2 Thessalonians 2:16–17). But no one has a direct and

unclouded sight of God and his ways that dispels all shadows and renders faith unnecessary. Thus the fundamental posture of Christians is indeed faith, not complete knowledge (2 Corinthians 5:7; Galatians 2:19–20).

Since God has provided humanity with both adequate grounds for faith and the spiritual ability itself to perceive and respond to him in faith, Christians believe God – despite appearances to the contrary and despite their own doubts and fears – and act accordingly. This pattern shows up throughout both Testaments, and is sometimes referred to as the 'indicative/imperative' motif: 'Since X is the case, therefore we ought to do Y.' In both biblical Hebrew and Greek, we find faith and truth connected in just this way. Believing entails doing. One has faith that the other person is faithful and one is thus reciprocally

Jan Brueghel the Elder's painting, *Christ Preaching at the Seaport*, shows Jesus near the start of his ministry.

faithful. Indeed, the word-sets of 'faith' in the ancient languages are often translated 'truth' in English Bibles, much as we say in our everyday speech that 'she is a true friend' and 'I will always be true to you.' So the connection of faith and truth is not just a matter of recalling what one knows about the past in order to come to convictions about the future – that is far too rationalistic. Christian faith is always about the whole person, not merely the mind. Thus we believe that God has been true in the past and will be true in the future, and so we are true to him today – with head, heart, and hands.

Faith and Revelation

If Christian faith were faith in a cosmic principle, then the basis of that faith perhaps would be empirical observation of that principle at work, or maybe rational deduction of the nature of that principle, or even spiritual intuition of the existence of such a principle. Because Christian faith instead is a posture of personal confidence in, and cooperation with, a personal God, the fundamental ground of this faith will be personal revelation. We get to know and trust people not just by amassing information about them from others' testimony, but by observing their actions and listening to their speech. Most importantly, however, we learn to trust them as we actually meet them and then as they go on to relate to us and particularly as they unfold something of their private selves to us.

The basis of Christian faith in God is the observation of the words and deeds of that God as he relates to his creation and particularly to his people. Some people, like the ancient Israelites at the foot of Mount Sinai or the apostles by the shores of Galilee, witnessed God's action and speech directly. Indeed, the centre of God's revelation to humankind is not a

message or a text or a symbol, but a person: the person of Jesus Christ: 'He is the image of the invisible God... In him all the fullness of God was pleased to dwell' (Colossians 1:15, 19). In his earthly career, Jesus not only told humanity about God; he also showed them God since he is himself God. Thus Jesus is called the pre-eminent 'Word', or revelation, of God: 'In the beginning was the Word, and the Word was with God, and the Word was God... And the Word became flesh and lived among us, and we have seen his glory, the glory as of a father's only son, full of grace and truth' (John 1:1, 14). God has met us, walked with us, and unfolded himself to us.

Yet it is only in a secondary sense, it seems, that one can encounter Jesus today. He is, after all, dead and gone – Christians believe, of course, that he has gone to heaven until his second coming. None of us has walked by Galilee with the Saviour. We did not witness the miracles, listen to the sermons, hear the testimony of the apostles, see the prophecies fulfilled, and so on. We instead must believe the authoritative testimony of believers who have come before us. And that testimony has been encoded in several ways to be handed down to subsequent generations: in the 'rules of faith' and other creeds; in the liturgies that direct the church in proper worship; in the sacraments that depict the gospel; and especially in the Bible.

The Place of the Bible

The Bible, like Jesus, is also called the Word of God, albeit in a secondary sense. The Scriptures have been understood by Christians through the centuries as the literary record of both God's mighty deeds through the main plotline of salvation history and of God's own interpretations of those deeds. This record was produced by many people – authors and editors down through the centuries. But the

'O how glorious our Faith is! Instead of restricting hearts, as the world fancies, it uplifts them and enlarges their capacity to love, to love with an almost infinite love, since it will continue unbroken beyond our mortal life.'

Thérèse de Lisieux

The Place of Tradition

The word 'tradition' comes from the Latin term *traditio* which means 'handing over', 'handing down' or 'handing on'. The idea is found at many points in the Bible. For example, the apostle Paul reminded his readers at Corinth that he was passing down to them core teachings of the Christian faith which he had himself received from other people (1 Corinthians 15:1–4). He was handing on to them what had been handed on to him. The term 'tradition' can refer to both the action of passing teachings on to others and to the body of teachings which are passed on in this manner. Tradition can thus be understood as a *process* as well as a *body of teaching*. The three later New Testament letters that are particularly concerned with matters of church order – 1 Timothy, 2 Timothy and Titus – stress the importance of 'guard[ing] the good deposit which was entrusted to you' (2 Timothy 1:14). What has been passed on and entrusted to church leaders – in other words, tradition – must be preserved and defended.

However, the New Testament also uses the notion of 'tradition' in a negative sense, meaning 'human ideas and practices which are not divinely authorized'. Thus Jesus Christ was openly critical of certain human traditions within Judaism (for example, see Matthew 15:1–6; Mark 7:13), which he regarded as compromising the word of God. The New Testament stresses the importance of putting every tradition to the test and keeping only those that are to be trusted (1 Thessalonians 5:20–1).

The importance of tradition first became clear during an important dispute which broke out during the second century. The Gnostic controversy centred on a number of questions, including how salvation was to be achieved. Christian writers found themselves having to deal with some questionable interpretations of the Bible. How were they to deal with these? If the Bible was to be regarded as authoritative, was every interpretation of the Bible to be regarded as of equal value? Clearly the answer was 'no'. But what reason could be given for rejecting certain interpretations of the Bible?

Irenaeus of Lyons, one of the church's greatest earliest theologians, argued that heretics simply interpreted the Bible according to their own taste. What had been handed down from the apostles through the church was not merely the biblical texts themselves, but a certain way of reading and understanding those texts. Tradition is thus the guarantor of faithfulness to the original apostolic teaching, a safeguard against the innovations and misrepresentations of biblical texts on the part of the Gnostics. This development is of major importance, as it underlies the emergence of 'creeds' – public, authoritative statements of the basic points of the Christian faith.

This point was further developed in the early fifth century by Vincent of Lérins, who stressed the need for public standards by which doctrines could be judged. But what standard was available, by which the church could be safeguarded from errors? For Vincent, the answer was clear – tradition. Similar ideas were developed during the Reformation period by Martin Luther, who appealed to traditional interpretations of the Bible in refuting the ideas of some of his more radical colleagues.

Interpreting the Bible

The task of interpreting the Bible (sometimes known as 'hermeneutics') and applying it to the situations faced by the church has long been recognized as being of critical importance. The Bible itself makes it clear that its interpretation is an important issue. For example, the the book of Acts tells of how an Ethiopian reading a passage from the book of Isaiah (Isaiah 53:7–8) recognized the need for an interpreter to understand what he was reading (Acts 8:30–35). Peter's second letter observes that the letters of the apostle Paul contain some difficult passages, which can be misunderstood and misrepresented by the unwary or misguided (2 Peter 3:16).

Three stages are often identified in this process of interpretation. First, there is *exegesis* (a Greek word meaning 'drawing out' or 'exposing'), which can be thought of as extracting meaning from the text. A fundamental theme of biblical interpretation is that our task is to ascertain what Scripture itself is saying, rather than imposing our own preconceived views upon it. In the second place, there is *integration*, in which the interpreter seeks to correlate what one particular biblical passage has to say with other passages, in an attempt to ensure that the entire weight of the biblical testimony is being conveyed. Interpreting passages in isolation or out of context (an approach sometimes called 'proof-texting') is widely regarded as unacceptable. Finally, this leads on to the process of *application*, which aims to bring together thought and action, by allowing our interpretation of the Bible to shape the way we behave.

Discovering what Scripture itself is saying is a key aspect of biblical interpretation.

In the Middle Ages, this approach was consolidated using a scheme sometimes known as the 'fourfold sense of Scripture'. This held that the Bible possessed four levels of meaning: the literal sense of the text, in its original historical context; its application to matters of doctrine; its implications for Christian behaviour; and its relevance for the Christian hope. At the time of the Reformation, other schemes were developed, often involving the recognition of 'literal' and 'spiritual' meanings of the text. More recently, emphasis has been placed on recognizing the literary character of Scripture. Recent writers have stressed the need to treat history as history, and poetry as poetry – rather than reducing all to the same level.

An issue that remains particularly important in contemporary Christianity is which biblical passages should be treated literally, and which metaphorically or symbolically? For example, are the early chapters of Genesis to be treated as scientific history, or as an interpretation of the place of humanity in the universe? Are the prophecies of the book of Revelation to be interpreted literally as providing a timeline for the end of the world, or as reassuring Christians of the ongoing presence of God in the world, despite persecution and tribulation? It is, however, important to appreciate that the debate over how best to interpret a biblical passage has never been seen as undermining the authority of Scripture.

composition took place always under the direction of God's Holy Spirit so that the believing community – Israel in the old covenant, the church in the new – recognized that each finished book of the Bible bears the imprint of God's own approval. This idea of the divine supervision of the production of the Bible is technically known as *inspiration.*

Modern critics of the doctrine of inspiration have pointed out that the Bibles we have today are translations of copies of copies of copies – lines of manuscripts going back into the mists of history. Over the course of time, different words in the same verses have shown up in this or that manuscript – or even in whole 'families' of manuscripts. According to these critics, these 'variants' compromise the authority of the Bible, for no one can say beyond question what the Bible definitively says in this or that instance.

Late in the nineteenth century, some Protestant Christians sought to protect the Bible's authority and the doctrine of inspiration by restricting the phenomenon of inspiration to the actual writings of the biblical authors – whether Isaiah, Matthew, or Paul. These *autographs* were inerrant, as they were guided word for word by God's Holy Spirit. Then, so the argument ran, since we have reasonably close approximations of the originals – according to the historical science of textual criticism that specializes in sorting out these things – we can be confident that the Bibles we have in our hands today are reliable as God's Word.

This argument still has considerable force as long as we qualify it in one respect and apply it carefully in another. The qualification is this: The doctrine of inspiration must apply to the entire process by which the various biblical writings were first composed, and then edited, and then recognized by the people of God in a final, definitive form – or canon. (The word 'canon' means a rule or standard, and thus those items that meet that standard together can be called 'the canon' – of Scripture, in this case.) Christians thus do not have to try to defend, or to mourn the loss of, those original manuscripts. And we need not fret over who wrote which bit of the Pentateuch, or whether there are two or more 'Isaiahs', and so on. These are interesting and important questions that affect our understanding of the Bible. But they do not affect the fundamental questions of inspiration, canonicity, and authority. Instead, we value our translations of Hebrew and Greek biblical texts that are 98 per cent of the canonical versions accepted by Jews in Jesus' day (in the case of the Old Testament) and by the Christians in the first two centuries (in the case of the New).

With this qualification, we then see that Christians must be careful to read and learn as much of the Bible as possible, in order to derive as comprehensive and as balanced a view of God's written revelation as possible. No major doctrine or practice should hang on a single verse – particularly since that verse might be part of that putative 2 per cent of disputable material. Instead, doctrines and practices are best derived from a broad, thorough, and integrative reading of the entire canon of Scripture.

To be sure, Christians have disagreed as to the extent of divine inspiration. The first Christians continued Jesus' practice of accepting the Hebrew Scriptures as God's written Word. As counterpart and fulfilment to those books, called therefore the Old Testament or 'books of the former covenant', the early church added the books of the New Testament. All Christians acknowledge these books as Scripture.

'Sacraments not only presuppose faith, but by words and objects they also nourish, strengthen, and express it. That is why they are called 'sacraments of faith'. They do indeed impart grace, but in addition, the very act of celebrating them disposes the faithful most effectively to receive this grace in a fruitful manner, to worship God rightly, and to practice charity.'

Second Vatican Council

In between these two sets of documents, however, were composed Jewish religious books (known as the Apocrypha) that the early medieval church translated and respected – particularly via the Vulgate, Jerome's estimable, yet not wholly accurate, Latin translation project in the fourth century. Roman Catholics came to believe that Jerome's work itself was divinely inspired and treat the Apocrypha as Scripture, while Orthodox and some Anglican Christians venerate the Apocrypha, and most Protestants ignore it.

Whatever their convictions, then, about whether the books of the Apocrypha belong in the canon of Holy Scripture, all Christians agree on the Old and New Testaments as God's literary revelation, his 'Word', to them. And at the centre of the Bible's story, of course, is Jesus Christ, God's supreme revelation and the basis of the Christian faith – the (personal and definitive) Word about whom the (written) Word testifies.

God has revealed himself in many other times and places through visions, dreams, prophecies, and other means. God has revealed something of himself in his very creation – the natural world and especially human beings – as an artist reveals himself through his work. And God has placed what John Calvin called the *sensus divinitatis* – a 'sense of divinity' – in the hearts of all people, however corrupted or effaced it has become.

All of these revelations, however, do not avail to prompt anyone to saving faith. Sin is too deeply rooted in human hearts. It blinds humankind, deafens them, coarsens them, and maddens them so that they fail to pay attention to what is in their best interests and instead preoccupy themselves with distractions and ephemera. They do not see clearly, they do not think straight, they do not choose wisely, and they do not love

> 'Nothing true or beautiful or good makes complete sense in any immediate context of history; therefore, we must be saved by faith.'
>
> Reinhold Niebuhr

well. So they certainly do not pay proper attention to God's revelation. Indeed, the original call of Christ in the gospel is to *repent and believe* – genuine faith can arise only in the company of genuine penitence (Mark 1:15).

It should also be acknowledged that sin is not the only problem. The claims that Christians make for Jesus of Nazareth are literally cosmic. When the disciples of Jesus were asked by him to report what people were saying about him, they replied that some were crediting Jesus with the highest accolades of the day: Jesus was a great prophet and possibly even an ancient prophet such as Elijah or Jeremiah come back from the dead (Matthew 16:13–17). But when Peter acknowledged that Jesus was in fact the Christ, or Messiah – the long-awaited Deliverer of Israel – Jesus pronounced him 'blessed', and not 'insightful' or 'acute': God himself had shown this truth to Peter. No Jew otherwise could come to such a conclusion, even having witnessed Jesus performing many miracles, because Jesus did not look like the sort of messiah any Jew of that time was expecting. Even more difficult for Jews to accept was the assertion of a crucified messiah, a kind of contradiction that amounted to 'cursed blessed one', and thus was 'a stumbling block' to Jews – as well as sheer 'foolishness' to Gentiles (1 Corinthians 1:23). Ever since that time it has also been true that it requires considerable faith – indeed, a supernatural gift of faith – to believe that this carpenter from the countryside who was crucified as a political irritant centuries ago is in fact the Incarnate Son of God and Saviour of the world.

Christians agree, therefore, that for any person to come to trust Jesus as Saviour and Lord, God's Holy Spirit must perform an act of revelation in that person's heart – showing him or her the truth of the Bible, and especially the truth of its central message about Jesus Christ. Indeed, the Holy Spirit must show him or her even more than the truth of this good news. For, again, the Christian posture of faith is fundamentally one of trust in the person of God, not merely assent to authoritative doctrine or the delegated authority of the church. The true believer must meet Jesus himself in personal acquaintance, in actual spiritual perception of God-in-Christ. Only in this way can a person come to genuine, saving faith *in* God, rather than just coming to a set of true beliefs *about* God (2 Corinthians 4:6).

Indeed, some scholars have seen a linguistic innovation in New Testament Greek – and particularly in John's writings – through the addition of the prepositions 'in' and 'into' to the verb 'believe'. Almost all of these uses are believing 'into Jesus' or 'in Jesus' or 'in Jesus' name' – the only two exceptions being belief in God. Such locutions are reminiscent of Paul talking about Christians being incorporated 'into' the body of Christ so that they are 'in Christ'. And we also recall John's distinctive imagery of 'abiding in' Christ. This language is all deeply personal – even intimate.

It is this experience, this encounter, that the Holy Spirit provides. Indeed, the preposterous division of some modern theology between 'the Jesus of history' and 'the Christ of faith' is thus healed and sealed by the immediate revelation of that one Lord Jesus Christ to each believer by the Holy Spirit of God.

Once again, one can see the marks of personal relationship in Christian faith. And we can see how important it is that we conduct ourselves properly in our relationship with God, even as inquirers, if we hope to obtain a true and adequate revelation of him.

Remember the nervous girlfriend? If she cannot believe anything her boyfriend says without corroboration of, say, a legally-adequate kind ('How do I know you really have the job you say you have? How can I know that you're not a pimp or a bigamist? Can I hire a private detective to watch you for the next month?'), then most of us would pronounce their relationship doomed. For she will never be satisfied – and their love cannot grow – as long as she has these extreme suspicions. She can always twist the evidence to fit her dark fantasies.

Worse than this, however, is the probability that in the face of this suspicion her boyfriend can, and probably will, decide not to reveal any more of himself to her. He simply walks away. He feels insulted, treated with less faith than he thinks he deserves, and wants therefore nothing more to do with this bizarre woman who must decide upon everything for herself. That's what happens in personal relationships. The 'investigated' party can choose whether or not to reveal more to the 'investigator'. And if the investigator fails to move forwards in appropriate increments of faith in her new friend, then she risks losing the relationship entirely under the crushing weight of her arrogant demand to know it all on her own terms.

Positively, however, we can conclude that faith can enjoy a dialectic, an ongoing fruitful conversation, between reason and revelation. Faith receives both as gifts of God with joy and gratitude, and spends time profitably correlating the two to learn everything possible about God and his ways in the world. Faith is cautious, of course, about not allowing human reason to constrain revelation. Nor does faith make too much of any human interpretation of God's revelation. Instead, faith trusts God to guide the believer, the

> 'What we perceive through faith you attempt to establish by arguments, and often you cannot even express that which we see, so it is clear that insight through faith is better and more secure than your sophistic conclusions.'
>
> Anthony of Egypt

What is Theology?

Most technical terms are based on the Greek language. Words ending in '-ology' are based on the Greek word 'logos', which means something like 'talk' or 'discussion'. Thus 'biology' means 'talk about life' (from the Greek word *bios*, 'life'). 'Theology' is thus 'talk about God' (from the Greek word *theos*, 'God'). In one sense, of course, all Christians are theologians, in that they all want to talk about God. Yet theology has come to have a more developed meaning. It can be thought of as the systematic exploration of Christian belief, grounded in the Bible. 'Theology is the *science* of faith. It is the conscious and methodical explanation and explication of the divine revelation received and grasped in faith' (Karl Rahner). Theology is not – and was never meant to be – a substitute for Scripture. Rather, it is a learning aid for reading Scripture. Like a pair of spectacles, it brings the text of Scripture into focus, allowing the reader to notice things which might otherwise be missed, and correctly understand things that might otherwise be distorted. Theology is always 'under' Scripture, its servant rather than its master

A helpful way of thinking of the relation of theology to the Bible was put forward by the great nineteenth-century Scottish preacher Thomas Guthrie (1803–73). He based his approach on the different environments in which flowers grow. Guthrie argued that the Bible was like nature, where flowers and plants grew freely in their natural habitat, unordered by human hands. Yet the human desire for orderliness leads to these same plants being collected and arranged in botanical gardens according to their species, so that they can be individually studied in more detail. The same plants are thus found in two different contexts – one of which is natural, the other of which is the result of human ordering. Theology represents the human attempt to order the ideas of Scripture, arranging them in an orderly way so that their mutual relation can be better understood.

So what does theology do? Two of its functions are of especial importance. In the first place, theology helps us to summarize what we find in Scripture: the immense richness of the biblical witness to God, Jesus Christ, and human nature and destiny. Thus the doctrine of the Trinity can be seen as a summary of the biblical witness to the person and actions of God.

In the second place, theology integrates these biblical ideas, weaving them together into a coherent whole. It brings together biblical statements, and sets out to establish the overall picture to which they point. Individual biblical statements are seen as the bricks which build up the overall picture. They are like brush-strokes, which combine to produce a magnificent picture. Or they can be thought of as pieces of a jigsaw puzzle. As the pieces are set in place, a pattern is disclosed. Theology aims to put the biblical pieces together, so that we can see the big picture. And by doing so, it expands our vision of God, enabling us to know and worship him more effectively.

Christian family, the local church, and other faithful individuals and institutions to that knowledge of him and his will that will equip each of them best to love God and accomplish his work in the world.

Indeed, Christian faith expects God to guide individuals and groups sometimes quite directly, especially on crucial matters. Some Christians believe God does so by way of prophecy even today; others that he does so by less direct but still powerful inward inclinations; and yet others that God leads by guiding their reflection on Scripture and the facts at hand. Some Christians, to be sure, avail themselves of all three modes of receiving God's direction. Faith is more than believing that God once led his people. Faith walks with God in the present and into the future in a truly personal relationship of communication, love, celebration, and labour.

Christian faith, then, is simply the issue of responding to God appropriately as he reveals himself to us. Christians believe that God is great and good and wise, and we human beings in turn are to be humble, grateful, and obedient. They believe that God knows what is ahead and will take them to everlasting peace, while helping them negotiate the tests and obstacles of the present age. They therefore trust him for their future and follow him in the present. They have faith that God is faithful and so they are faithful.

> For nothing worthy of proving can be proven, Nor yet disproven; wherefore thou be wise, Cleave ever to the sunnier side of doubt.
>
> Alfred Lord Tennyson

Theology has been described as the ordering and arranging of the natural and free-growing message of God.

Religion in Human Life

Christians are not the only ones, of course, who put their faith in God or a god. Christians owe a great debt to the God-centred religion of early Judaism and the earlier religion of ancient Israel, whose Scriptures form much of the Christian Bible. And Christians recognize the similarities between their view of God and the view of God in the later religion of Islam – also a monotheism ('belief in one and only one God') with roots in both Christianity and Judaism. Indeed, 'Islam' can be translated both as 'submission' to God and as 'dependence' upon him. Jews,

Led by a Hindu priest, young Newar girls and their mothers make offerings to the gods during a festival.

Christians, and Muslims generally agree, of course, that their views of God are not identical. But each of their religions is a religion that trusts a personal God for gracious deliverance from sin and suffering.

Furthermore, the general pattern of putting one's trust in a deity as the provider of blessings one cannot earn or secure for oneself is found in many of the world's religions. The most popular variety of Hinduism, for example, is *bhakti*, or 'devotion' to a god – whether Vishnu, Shiva, Deva, Ganesh, or one of Hinduism's many other divinities. These gods help their followers attain a spiritual bliss – sometimes called a 'heaven' – beyond

their cycle of reincarnations. The 'great or larger way' of Buddhism, *Mahayana*, features a wide range of buddhas and bodhisattvas ('enlightened ones') who are willing to assist believers on their way to the release of nirvana – a state of perfect happiness. And tribal religions around the world teach of gods – and often of a Supreme God – who will come to the aid of supplicants.

It must be acknowledged that many religions of the world do not feature anything like the dynamic of Christian faith. There is no God or gods in whom believers are to put their trust, and certainly no personal saviour to forgive us our sins and grant us the gift of eternal life. The two other major traditions in Hinduism are 'the way of [correct] action' *(karmamarga)* and 'the way of [correct] knowledge' *(jñanamarga)* – both of which require the Hindu to sort out his own problems as best he can, with the assistance of the teachings and rituals of the community, but with no help from a deity. The early Buddhist 'tradition of the elders' *(Theravada)* also requires religious heroism of all who hope to escape the otherwise endless round of rebirths. Such people undertake the rigour of meditation and asceticism with the guidance of the Buddhist scriptures, the believing community, and the example – but not the actual, personal assistance – of the long-departed Buddha. Generally, then, only monks have any hope of succeeding in this life. Early Daoism and some forms of Confucianism also pay little regard to asking for help from heaven and the gods (although many folk versions of these Chinese religions do ask). And many of the life-philosophies of western culture – which function as religions for many people – also have no concept of a transcendent Being from whom one can ask and expect favours.

We therefore should not continue in the western habit of using the term 'faith' as a synonym for 'religion' (for example, 'the Christian faith,' 'the Buddhist faith') since many religions do not, in fact, practise faith. At the same time, Christians must not perpetuate the common teaching that 'only Christianity preaches "divine grace" which believers receive by faith; other religions preach only "works" by which believers merit divine favour'. We have seen that the Christian understanding of faith includes faithfulness, that is, grateful and trusting obedience. We recognize that Christianity, like Judaism and Islam and other religions too, can devolve into a kind of religious legalism in which people congratulate themselves on their scrupulousness and expect God to do so as well. And we appreciate that many other religions do preach that human goodness cannot suffice to earn God's blessing, but that blessing is received only with supernatural assistance.

Christianity and Other Religions

As Christianity has spread across the world's cultures, therefore, it has had to reckon with these various other religions. Christian missionaries, church leaders, and theologians have debated just what to make of them. Are they genuine quests for God? Are they genuine gifts of God? Are they instead mere human substitutes for true religion, or even perhaps satanically-inspired counterfeits? What, then, is the appropriate Christian response to an encounter with these alternatives?

All Christians agree that religions are a mixture of what God has revealed of his truth to this or that people; of what human beings have made of that revelation (for both good and ill); and what malevolent spirits have encouraged believers to make (and un-make) of that revelation. As such mixtures, religions at their best have helped to foster social order, basic morality, and hope. They have restrained at least some evil and helped at least some good to prosper. At their worst they have legitimized oppression, encouraged violence, and promoted subservience to priests and princes. (Christians recognize that their own religion has produced both kinds of effects.) Christian missionaries typically have tried to commend and to build upon the good that is in this or that religion as they call nonetheless for the conversion of each person, each people, and each culture to the proper orientation of all human existence: faith in Jesus Christ. Indeed, missionaries sometimes have required great discernment to know whether in the case of any particular belief or practice Christianity is coming as replacement, as fulfilment, as corrective, or as complement.

Furthermore, Christians agree, no one is saved by the correct practise of a religion – not even of Christianity. Faith properly trusts the mercy of God, not one's own spiritual accomplishment. Only God can save us, and believers receive that salvation only in the posture of humble, obedient, grateful trust – the posture of faith.

Beyond this consensus, however, Christians have not agreed on precisely what God is doing in and through other religions – if anything. Some Christians believe that people in other religious traditions can, by the grace of God, glimpse God truly, if also distortedly and incompletely, in the teachings of their religion and (more importantly) in the perceptions of their hearts. If, again by the grace of God, such people embrace God as their Lord and cast themselves upon his mercy as their Saviour, then they will, indeed, be saved. Christians who hold this view – sometimes known as

> 'I long to understand in some degree thy truth, which my heart believes and loves. For I do not seek to understand that I may believe, but I believe in order to understand. For this also I believe, that unless I believed, I should not understand.'
>
> Anselm of Canterbury

> 'Faith is the first factor in a life devoted to service. Without it, nothing is possible. With it, nothing is impossible.'
>
> Mary McLeod Bethune

> 'Reason is our soul's left hand, faith her right.'
>
> John Donne

inclusivism – hold with all other traditional Christians the solemn conviction that the basis of salvation is the work of Jesus Christ on our behalf. But such inclusivists believe that – like believers in the Old Testament – a person does not have to have actual knowledge of Jesus to benefit from his saving action. They do, to be sure, have to have genuine knowledge of the one true God and to respond in the only appropriate way – in faith. Hence, Hebrews 11: 6: 'And without faith it is impossible to please God, for whoever would approach him must believe that he exists and that he rewards those who seek him.' But if a person has such faith, then inclusivists are hopeful for his or her salvation.

Inclusivists still believe in the value of missionary work, for they place great value on bringing to all people the benefits of the Bible, Christian tradition, the sacraments, the fellowship of the Christian church, and other gifts of God for the people of God. Inclusivists recognize that the development of mature, pure, and properly-oriented Christian faith – a faith that believes correctly, practises correctly, and loves correctly – can take place only in a Christian context. Every other sort of faith is, even at best, incipient and malformed. So inclusivists gladly and energetically continue in the age-old enterprise of following Jesus' directive to 'make disciples of all nations' (Matthew 28:19).

Most Christians through the ages, however, seem to have held to a

The Human Quest for God

The beauty of the night sky often prompts people to explore questions of faith more deeply.

From the beginnings of recorded history, people have longed to reach out beyond what they can see, feel and touch, and discover whatever lies at the heart of the universe. Contemplating the wonder of the universe raises questions. It is as if there is some inbuilt longing for purpose or meaning which drives us to look for clues to the meaning of the universe. We contemplate the glory of the night sky, wondering if the silent beauty of the stars might cast light on the riddle of human destiny. Is our real homeland out there somewhere, beyond this world? We appreciate the beauty of a glorious sunset, while wondering if the sense of beauty it awakens within us is somehow a pointer to another and more wonderful world that we have yet to discover. The book of Job compares the human quest for wisdom to the mining of precious metals and stones from deep within the earth. They lie hidden from human view, and must be sought out.

Paul seems to have based his proclamation of the gospel on this human longing for meaning when he spoke in Athens (Acts 17). For Paul, Jesus Christ represented the goal of the long, unfulfilled human quest for significance. Paul opened his address on Mars Hill (sometimes known as 'the Areopagus') by noting that the Athenians were renowned for their different view. They have understood the Bible to teach that salvation is restricted to those people who hear the gospel of Jesus Christ and respond positively to at least that minimal narrative about him – thus this position is sometimes called restrictivism. And most of these Christians believe that everyone must hear and decide about Jesus in this lifetime, or be forever lost. (A small minority of Christians believe that God provides everyone with an opportunity to hear this message – whether at the point of death or perhaps immediately thereafter.) This view thus is sometimes known instead as particularism – meaning that salvation can be received only on the particular ground of faith in Christ as response to the gospel message. Mere faith in some

shadowy view of God will not do. Thus missionary work that teaches about Jesus and calls for repentance and faith is the chief and necessary work of the church, whatever else it may do in the world to glorify God and benefit his creation.

Missionaries continue to share the gospel message with people all over the world.

religiosity. They were aware of the spiritual dimensions of life, and as concerned as anyone to find out the meaning of life. Paul drew attention to an altar which he had seen at Athens inscribed with the words 'to an unknown god'. Whoever had constructed the altar was clearly aware of some presence within themselves and nature that could not be known or named. Paul argues that he is able to identify this nameless and faceless god. 'What you worship as something unknown, I proclaim to you.' For Paul, there is a personal presence at the heart of the cosmos, who has created us so that we may enter into a relationship with him.

John Calvin argued that the human quest for God was driven by two things: a 'sense of divinity' which we experience within us, and a sense of wonder at the natural order around us. A similar idea was developed by the philosopher Immanuel Kant (1724–1804): 'Two things fill my mind with ever-increasing wonder and awe: the starry skies above me and the moral law within me.' Both could become pointers to God. As Calvin pointed out, belief in God is one of the most universal characteristics of human nature and culture. Yet Calvin also noted how this could lead people astray. The human quest for God often led to the invention of gods that suited people's needs, or to idolatry. For Calvin, the quest for God should lead us to ask how and where God could be found – and hence to encountering him through revelation.

The God who is known to some limited extent through nature and experience has disclosed himself fully in Christ and through Scripture.

A third view has been held by relatively few Christians through history and many would dispute whether this is even a viable Christian option. It has shown up mostly in modern societies that have been impressed by contact with other religions and are seeking ways of cooperating with believers in those religions. This view sees Christianity as simply one among many forms of authentic and wholesome religion – hence its label, *pluralism*. Other major religious traditions have proven satisfactory to many millions of people, and those traditions have shown themselves to produce people of high moral character. To be sure, pluralism does not simply validate all religions, since some religions have shown themselves to be exploitative and ugly – leading even to human sacrifice of various sorts. But the great religions seem to be as good as each other, and therefore ought to be celebrated as such.

Clearly, in this view, the motif of faith in the mercy of God for salvation has dropped out of sight in favour of a religious dynamic of moral challenge and attainment. And, in particular, the figure of Jesus Christ – supreme in the other two views as the single and necessary Saviour and Lord – steps back into the ranks of the many other noble religious leaders of the world. Thus Christians who hold to the other two views agree that pluralism is not

Modernity

Until very recently, the West was dominated by a world-view that is generally known as 'modernity'. Although the word 'modern' can mean 'very recent', it now also has the more specific sense of 'reflecting the outlook of the Enlightenment'. While sociologists and intellectual historians debate how best to define the characteristics of modernity, a number of features are generally agreed to be characteristic of the movement. In terms of culture in general, the modern period has been shaped by the growth of capitalism, increased specialization and interdependency within society as a whole, and a tendency towards centralization and bureaucracy. It is, however, the intellectual aspects of modernity that are of greatest importance for Christian belief.

One of the leading themes of modernity is the omnicompetence of human reason. The movement known as 'the Enlightenment', which has had a highly significant impact on western thinking since about 1750, argued that human reason was adequate to determine whatever needed to be known about reality. Human rationality was seen as the ultimate basis of both thinking and the organization of society. To its critics, the Enlightenment elevated human reason to the place rightly occupied by God himself. Rationalist writers argued that humanity did not need to be told what God was like; we were able to work this out for ourselves, on the basis of reason.

This new emphasis on reason meant that a number of traditional Christian beliefs were criticized as being illogical or irrational. How could anyone believe in Jesus Christ being at one and the same time God and human? It was a logical impossibility. How could any thinking person believe in the Trinity, when its inner logic is so contorted? However, the belief that was most rigorously contested by the Enlightenment was the resurrection of Jesus Christ. Rationalist writers argued that no one has ever been raised from the dead before (despite the occasional insignificant references to something possibly along the same lines in Egyptian or Nordic mythology) and no one currently alive has ever witnessed a resurrection.

an authentic option – for those whose religion is indeed centred upon faith in God as revealed to humanity pre-eminently in Jesus and whose salvation is won for them alone by Jesus: 'I am the way, and the truth, and the life. No one comes to the Father except through me' (John 14:6).

Thus inclusivists and particularists join together as *exclusivists* – those who maintain the traditional teaching that 'There is salvation in no one else, for there is no other name under heaven given among mortals by which we must be saved' (Acts 4:12). And they therefore work together to spread the gospel and call all people to faith in God.

The Importance of World-Views

Everyone has a religion. Many people don't think that they do, of course. And that's because 'religion' for them means what we might call 'proper-noun' religion – Buddhism, Islam, Sikhism, and so on. But everyone has a central motivation in his or her life and everyone has a map of reality in his or her head, and the combination of motive and map we can call each person's functional *religion*. It's the defining centre of one's life, whether framed by traditions as old as Judaism or Hinduism, or by what one saw on television last night or read on the Internet this morning.

> 'Faith is not belief without proof, but trust without reservation.'
>
> Elton Trueblood

Although Christians claim that Christ's resurrection is unique, logic suggests that this is impossible anyway. Therefore, we must conclude that the resurrection probably did not happen. All these objections are specifically determined by a modernist world-view, which insists that everything conforms to predetermined patterns, laid down by the rational mind.

In recent years, modernity has found itself the subject of relentless criticism. While its merits are conceded, the darker side of the movement has become increasingly evident. Stalin's purges and the Nazi holocaust are regularly cited as indications that modernity's emphasis on rationality merely excluded those who disagreed with its notions, where these could not be enforced. Non-standard elements are thus marginalized, victimized, or eliminated. It is regularly argued that modernism's demands for uniformity and conformity lead to social alienation, a feeling of rootlessness, and loss of shared values. While some critics of modernity argue for a postmodern world-view as an alternative, others long to return to a premodern world. Though both unrealistic and idealized through nostalgia, this latter response is a telling indication of the failure of modernity to meet human needs and longings.

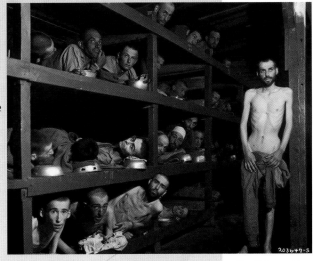

The Holocaust is often cited as an example of rationalist modernity's darker side.

Postmodernity

The term 'postmodernity' is often used to designate the complex, loosely-knit outlook that has developed in western society following the collapse of confidence in modernism. The new world-view can be approached in a number of ways. For example, it can be seen in economic terms as the 'cultural logic of late capitalism', or in more sociological terms of social decentralization and the rising power of the individual consumer. Whatever the difficulties of definition may be, there is little doubt that the cultural mood in the West has changed significantly since about 1980, with the transition being anticipated by a number of earlier developments, whose full significance was not appreciated at the time.

One of the leading themes of the postmodern criticism of the modern world-view is that it offered a 'totalizing' outlook, in which 'the other' was always reduced to 'the same'. This process of reduction can be seen in a number of modernist philosophies, such as Marxism. For Marxism, just about everything could be reduced to socio-economic categories. Postmodernism rejects such totalizing schemes, or 'grand narratives', as they are sometimes known. One of the core reasons for doing so is that such 'grand narratives' are held to lead to oppression or discrimination. One of the leading themes of postmodernism is an aversion to the notion of 'truth', in that a claim to tell the truth is interpreted by postmodern writers – such as Jacques Derrida or Michel Foucault – as a misguided claim to dominate or control others.

While postmodernism is a complex movement, at times difficult to characterize, there is no doubt that it has major implications for Christian belief and practice. One obvious point of tension between postmodernism and traditional Christian belief is the former's criticism of any outlook that claims to have a unique or privileged insight into reality. The idea of divine revelation is seen as inconsistent with postmodernism's emphasis on the individual's right to believe as she pleases: 'I believe as I please.' The easy relativism which attends a postmodern reading of life often reduces to little more than an endorsement of an individual's views without any attempt to evaluate them critically. Christianity's traditional emphasis on truth-telling – evident, for example, in the biblical idea of Jesus Christ as 'the way, and the truth, and the life' (John 14:6) – exists in an uneasy relationship with this more amorphous, individualist approach to the meaning of life.

Perhaps because of the growing important of image-linked technology, such as television and various digital imaging formats, postmodernity has come to value the image over the word. This has caused difficulty for some standard means of presenting Christian beliefs, such as the sermon or the religious book, which are fundamentally word-based. Christian writers and preachers have responded to this development in a number of ways, not least through making increased use of images in worship and sermons, using new digital technology suitable for this purpose. There has been a growing interest in rediscovering the strongly image-based content of the parables, amongst other biblical genres, in response to this cultural development.

These maps and motives are sometimes called 'world-views' (from the German word *Weltanschauung*) – basically, how one sees the world and takes one's place in it. We all have one. Furthermore, it is typical of modern life to encounter a variety of world-views: my university professor might be a feminist; my yoga instructor a Hindu; my banker a Presbyterian; my girlfriend a Pentecostalist; my football teammate a hedonist; and my physician a Darwinist. Indeed, modern people tend to inhabit various world-views temporarily in different social sectors: I myself might think like a feminist at the university, like a Hindu in yoga class, and so on. Many of us find this experience to be bewildering, and we quest after a stable core, a central world-view that can integrate the best of these various options. Some observers believe that a characteristic trait of postmodernity is the effortless switching among these various world-views, a mental incoherence that is not, in fact, a strain but rather a delight.

Christians can rejoice in the excitement and freedom and openness to novelty that is postmodernity at its best. Christians can cheer the undermining and overthrowing of previous hegemonies of ideologies and political structures that stifled diversity and channelled everyone into uniformity easily exploited by powers in government and commerce.

Christians also tend to believe, however, that once the dust has begun to settle from postmodern insurrections, it is good to think integratively once again. It is good to do so as an act of submission to the one God who made us and made all else. For a coherent Christian world-view – beyond whatever satisfaction

Postmodernity argues against 'grand narratives' such as Christianity and instead states that each individual viewpoint is as valid as the next.

and delight it may provide for the intellect – gives believers an interpretive frame within which they have the best opportunity to live as Christians in the most fundamental sense: to discern God's will and way, and thus to respond to him best in faith – in humble, obedient, and grateful love.

Christians believe that, for all its faults, their religion puts first things first – indeed, puts Jesus Christ in the centre, and at the first and the last, where he belongs (Hebrews 12:2). Thus the Christian outlook has the best chance of putting everything else in its proper place as well. Christians believe that they can learn much from people of other world-views. They

have seen things, and heard things, and made things, and felt things that Christians have not. Christian can rejoice in the generous gifts of God to all whom he has created. They believe, however, that the Christian religion offers an integrative world-view that can sort out and draw into a practical arrangement the best insights of feminism, spirituality, physical exercise, financial prudence, and the rest.

In the end, however, it is not world-views, theologies, and other intellectual constructs that matter most to Christians. Abraham is commended for his faith, not for his philosophical sophistication. Noah believed what God said, believed that

Islam

Islam has become an increasingly significant global religious presence, partly through complex patterns of immigration which have led to large Islamic communities settling in many parts of western Europe and North America. It is a variegated movement, with significant variations and distinctions, most notably between the majority Sunni and minority Shia communities. Islam became a significant religious movement amongst the Arab people in the seventh century. A program of conquest was initiated, which eventually led to Arab forces taking control of the entire coastal region of North Africa by about 750. Islamic forces also moved north, posing a serious threat to the great Christian city of Constantinople (modern-day Istanbul). Arab forces laid siege to the city during the period 711–78, eventually being forced to withdraw, having failed to conquer the city. The enforcement of Islam in the conquered regions of the Holy Land led to intense concern in the western church, and was one of the factors which led to the crusades during the period 1095–1204.

Despite such temporary setbacks, the expansion of Islam continued, with the fall of Constantinople (1453) sending shock waves throughout much of Europe. By the end of the fifteenth century, Islam had established a significant presence in several regions of the continent of Europe, including Spain, parts of southern Italy, and the Balkans. This advance was eventually halted by the defeat of the Moors in Spain in the final decade of the fifteenth century, and the defeat of Islamic armies outside Vienna in 1523. Yet European setbacks were countered by expansion elsewhere: the regions now known as Indonesia and Malaysia converted to Islam through contact with Arab traders around this time, and remain significant centres of Islamic thought today. Islam is currently the second largest world religion, and has become an increasingly important dialogue partner and potential rival to Christianity, especially in Africa and Asia.

God would save him, and then did what he was told. But for Christians, thinking itself is only part of what it means to be faithful. At the end of the day, and at the End of Days, what will matter most is not whether Christians have sorted out Christian theology in its wonderful and delicate details: It is whether they will hear this commendation from the Lord in whom they have put their trust: 'Well done, thou good and faithful servant' (Matthew 25:21).

Following the revolution in Iran, Ayatollah Khomeine greets his enthusiastic followers on his return to Tehran in 1979.

Unlike most modern forms of Christianity, which are content to operate within secular world views, Islam sees itself as establishing its own intellectual domains. Islam determines every aspect of life, from politics to personal devotion. It is a world view in its own right, which often sees itself as defined in opposition to the secular ideologies of the West. The origins of this modern Islamic movement can be traced back to about 1875, when Jamal al-Din al-Afghani (1838–97) urged Muslims to resist the growing western influence in the Middle East by a reaffirmation of their Muslim heritage. He encouraged Muslims to believe that, prior to the arrival of the westerners, a golden age of wise Islamic rule held sway. This situation could be retrieved by a return to personal religious piety, a reform and renewal of Islamic *shariah* law, and resistance to western presence and influence in the region. Since then the establishment of the State of Israel has contributed powerfully to the resurgence of Islamic fundamentalism. The Iranian revolution of 1978–79 may be seen as evidence of the importance of this vision.

2 God

GERALD BRAY

'People fashion their God after their own understanding. They make their God first and worship him afterwards.'

Oscar Wilde

At the heart of Christianity lies the belief that there is only one God, who is the creator and redeemer of all things. Nowadays, most people are prepared to accept that the universe is a coherent structure, which implies that it has some kind of unity behind it, whether or not we identify this principle of unity with the God of the Bible. But in the world in which Christianity emerged, belief in the fundamental unity of all things was much less common. There were some Greek philosophers who taught it, but even if they were prepared to speak of a supreme being, they did not call it 'god' in the Christian sense. In their minds there were a large number of 'gods', all of whom had supernatural powers but no one of whom dominated over the rest. Today we call this belief 'polytheism', and in the days when the Christian Bible was written, virtually all religions were polytheistic.

It is therefore understandable why most of the people who became Christians in the early centuries of the church had been polytheists, or at least had been brought up in that environment. In preaching to them, Christians used the words which they were accustomed to when describing divine beings, and did not insist on using a different vocabulary. This is why the word 'god' can be applied to pagan deities as well as to the God of the Bible, even though Christians believe that only the biblical God really exists. The success which Christians had in changing popular perceptions of the divine can be clearly measured by

looking at the way the word 'atheism' has changed its meaning. In ancient times, Christians were accused of being atheists because they refused to worship the gods of Greece and Rome. But that accusation sounds peculiar to us because, for almost everybody today, an 'atheist' is someone who denies the existence of the Christian God.

Pre-Christian polytheism is now dead, at least in western culture, where it is now assumed that if there is any divine being at all, it will be the God revealed in the Bible. Polytheism survives in some countries, particularly in India and other parts of Asia, but it is under pressure from both Christianity and Islam and it is fair to say that the tendency everywhere nowadays is towards a monotheistic definition of divine reality, whether people believe in it or not.

In sharp contrast to the polytheists of ancient times, the Jewish people stood out as unique, because they believed in only one God. This belief is called 'monotheism' and nowadays it is held in common by the three great religions which have sprung from the same ancient Hebrew source – Judaism, Christianity and Islam.

What Do We Mean by 'God'?

In the Old Testament, which is the Bible of Judaism, God reveals himself by different names, of which the most common are *El* (or its plural form *Elohim*) and YHWH. *El* is a general word for a supernatural being, and it can be used to describe other 'gods' in addition to the Jewish one. This biblical precedent gave the early Christians a theological, as well as a practical reason for not trying to impose the use of a distinctive name for God on non-Jewish believers, but to be content to adopt whatever word people normally use for the highest supernatural being in their own languages. Ultimately, this practice is based on the belief that all peoples everywhere have an innate knowledge of the God who created them, and therefore are likely to have a word which they use to describe him, even if they do not always recognize his uniqueness (Romans 1:21). YHWH, on the other hand, is the special name of God, revealed only to the Jewish people. The Hebrew language is written without vowels, which makes it difficult for us to know how this word might have been pronounced, but the best guess is that it would have sounded something like 'Yahweh'. We cannot be sure about this, however, because from a very early time the Jews refused to pronounce the name of God, on the grounds that it was too sacred to be uttered. Whenever they

had to refer to this name, which occurs many times in the Bible, they substituted another word for it, such as 'ha-Shem' ('the Name') or 'Adonai' ('my Lord').

Occasionally the vowels of 'Adonai' would be written below the consonants of YHWH, making it look as though it was to be read 'Yahowah', a word which has been taken into English as 'Jehovah'. It is important to realize however, that this word never existed in that form, and that the use of the word 'Jehovah' is based on a misunderstanding of the way in which the Jews read their Scriptures. Modern-day Jehovah's Witnesses are therefore wrong to say that 'Jehovah' is the true name of God, and to claim that the church has tried to suppress it for hundreds of years. 'Jehovah' is no more than a mistake for YHWH or Yahweh, and although similar forms can be found in Greek and Latin, it never became a name commonly used to describe God in those languages. When the ancient Jews translated their Bible into Greek, they rendered YHWH as *Kyrios*, or Lord, reflecting 'Adonai',

Part of a Parthenon frieze showing Poseidon, Apollo and Artemis. The Greeks, along with the Romans and the inhabitants of the near East, were polytheistic at the time of Christ.

and this usage became standard in the Christian church. Today, many Bibles print LORD or GOD in capital letters when translating the Hebrew YHWH, making it easy for anyone to work out when the special covenant name of God is used in the Old Testament.

Scholars have occasionally debated whether the Jews recognized any significant difference between El and YHWH. Some have claimed that in very early times, the Hebrews accepted the polytheistic view that there were many gods (elohim), even though they worshipped only one of them (YHWH) themselves. Later on, so the argument goes, the Jews concluded that YHWH was the only true God, and began to regard the other 'gods' as figments of the imagination, or perhaps as evil spirits. It is extremely difficult to decide whether there is any truth in this reconstruction of the development of biblical religion, though it can be argued that the evidence of Hebrew names speaks against it. Personal names are usually very conservative in their forms and often reflect meanings of words which have disappeared from ordinary speech. But in Hebrew it is noticeable that 'el' and 'jo' (or 'iah' at the end of the word) are often interchangeable, so that the names Elnathan and Nathanael (also written Nethaneel and Nathaniel) are the same as Jonathan and Nethaniah, all of which mean 'God has given'. This ability to substitute one name of God for the other in personal names must go back to a very early time in the history of Israel, and it argues strongly in favour of the view that the Hebrews were always monotheistic, regarding their God (YHWH) as the only God (El) who truly exists.

In the Bible God is often portrayed in terms which suggest that he is a heavenly man of some kind, but the Jews have always insisted that such language must be interpreted figuratively. Expressions like 'the hand of God' or 'the eye of God' do not mean that God possesses a body comparable to ours, but that he is capable of doing the things which our hands and eyes do. One of the worst sins in ancient Israel was to draw a picture or make a statue of God, because it is impossible to portray him in a human form. Even to make a house for God to dwell in was initially regarded as wrong, because he cannot be limited to a particular place. It is clear that the Jewish people were allowed to erect a Temple at Jerusalem in which to worship God (1 Kings 8:27) once it was understood that this did not mean that the God of Israel was restricted to this specific building.

For similar reasons, it must be said that God is not 'male' in the human sense, even if this is the way he is almost always pictured in the Bible. The language of human sexuality is figurative when it is applied to God, although this does not mean that the figures used are arbitrary. In the ancient world, female goddesses were usually associated with fertility cults of one kind or another, and they often involved ritual prostitution on the part of worshippers. The Jews regarded sexual immorality in the name of religion as an abomination, and God's apparent 'masculinity' was one way of guarding against it. Christians would add to this that when God became a human being, he became a male in Jesus Christ, a fact which makes it necessary to use the masculine when referring to him as God. To suppose that this usage excludes the feminine is wrong, because in most languages, including Hebrew and Greek, the masculine gender is inclusive of both male and female, whereas the feminine is not.

The occasional use of feminine or gender-neutral language by some modern theologians to describe God may be well-intentioned attempts to remind us that God is not a sexual

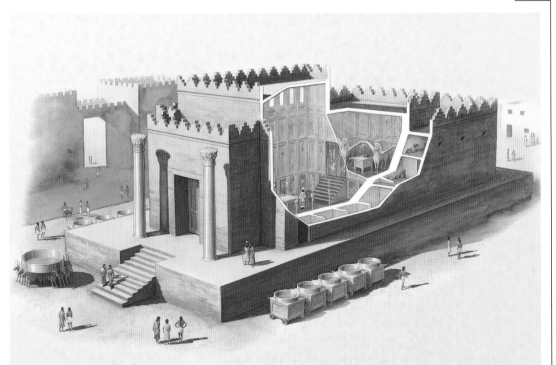

being, but they go against the usage of the Bible and for that reason, Christians have generally been extremely reluctant to adopt such practices. That this is in no sense an attack on women or femininity can be seen from the fact that when the Bible describes the relationship between God and the church, it sometimes uses bridal imagery – Christians are depicted as brides of Christ, even if they are male (Revelation 21:2).

Christians have always claimed the Jewish heritage as their own and have asserted that they believe in the God who revealed himself to Abraham, Moses and the prophets of ancient Israel. Even when they taught that Jesus Christ was God in human flesh, the first Christians claimed that it was the Jewish God who had appeared in this way, and not some other deity. Of course, traditional Jews could not accept this, because they regarded it as blasphemous to suggest that God could appear in a human form. But Christians argued that his coming had been foretold in the Old Testament,

and that Jews who refused to believe that Christ was God were closing their eyes to the truth revealed in their own Scriptures (John 5:39). This difference of opinion could not be overcome, and before long it made Christianity a different religion from its Jewish parent, although many close similarities continue to exist between them.

Muslims also worship one God, and believe that he is the same as the God of both Jews and Christians, but it has to be said that Christians do not usually believe that they have as much in common with Muslims as they have with Jews. The main reason for this is that Islam emerged several centuries later than Christianity, and so there is no mention of it anywhere in the Bible. If Christians lived for six centuries and developed all the essentials of their theology without knowing anything about Islam, it is hard to see how it can make that much difference to them now.

Another problem is that Muslims often claim that their religion has

Solomon's temple could not be built until the people of Israel understood that it would not restrict their God to one place.

> 'In the beginning, God created Adam, not because he had need of human beings, but so that he might have beings on whom to bestow his benefits.'
>
> Irenaeus of Lyons

superseded Christianity in much the same way that Christians say their religion has superseded Judaism. But whereas Christians do not deny anything that the Jewish tradition teaches about the being and nature of God, Muslims quite specifically reject the idea that God became a man in Christ and that he is, in fact, a Trinity of three persons. To complicate matters still further, Christians believe that God revealed himself fully and finally in Jesus Christ, which makes it impossible for them to believe that there has been a subsequent revelation from God of the kind claimed by Muslims. For all these reasons, Christians cannot accept Islam as readily as they can embrace Judaism, though they certainly recognize that there are many important similarities between the two faiths. Odd as it may seem, the monotheism of Islam is closer to that of Judaism than either of them is to Christianity, and in both cases the reason for this is the highly distinctive Christian doctrines of Christ and the Trinity.

The Bible does not argue a philosophical case for God's existence, other than to suggest that the complex harmony of the universe reflects the ordering of a divine mind behind it (Psalm 19). Today this would be called the cosmological argument for the existence of God, or the argument from design. As expressed by the philosopher–theologian William Paley (1743–1805), it is the belief that just as a watch is too complex to have come into existence by accident, so the universe is far too sophisticated for it to have been the chance result of a random process. A watch presupposes a watchmaker, and the universe presupposes a rational creator, whom Christians equate with the God of the Bible.

Other so-called proofs for the existence of God have been put forward from time to time, though with less obviously biblical a foundation. One of them is called the teleological argument, which says that everything which exists was created for a purpose, something which would be impossible if there were no guiding mind behind it all. The teleological argument is really a variant form of the cosmological one, and probably ought to be combined with it. Also popular in the past was the ontological argument, developed by Anselm of Canterbury (1033–1109). This says that everything which exists is a being, and that God is the greatest being of which it is possible to conceive. The main difficulty with this line of reasoning is that while those who believe in God already will accept that it is true, it is impossible to prove his existence merely on the basis of a supposed hierarchy of being. Apart from anything else, how could one know when the top of the scale of being had been reached?

Somewhat similar to this are the moral and aesthetical arguments, which try to show that the human race's innate sense of morality and beauty mean that there must be some standard against which these notions can be measured. Unfortunately for those who think this way, most would now hold that beauty is in the eye of the beholder, not necessarily in the mind of God, and that even morality is perceived differently in different cultural contexts, making it hard to prove that an absolute standard exists anywhere.

Perhaps the best thing to say about these traditional proofs for God's existence is that they all contain an element of truth and, for Christian believers, they can be used as aids to an understanding of who and what God is. Taken together, they make a persuasive case for considering the possible existence of God, and to that extent they may be helpful to Christian philosophers who want to keep the

> 'The will of God is the measure of things.'
>
> Ambrose of Milan

Christians believe that the complexity of the universe is so great that, like a watch, it cannot have come into existence without a rational creator.

idea of theism alive in philosophical discussion. But none of these arguments is foolproof or conclusive, and none is likely to make anyone a Christian believer. In the final analysis, God's existence can be proved only by experience and not by rational argument, however sophisticated it may be.

The Mind of God

Christians have always believed that God has a mind which created and sustains everything that exists. It follows from this not only that God must know everything which will happen in human history, but that he must have ordained it in some way. This is called predestination, and it is one of the most controversial subjects in Christian theology. At one extreme are those who equate predestination

with determinism. Determinism is the belief that not only is everything that happens preordained, but that we can do nothing to escape our fate. Odd as it may seem, many secular philosophies, including atheistic ones, are deterministic. This is true of Marxism, for example, and also of Freudian psychology. Christians do not believe that human beings are the victims of an impersonal fate which has determined the outcome of their existence in advance, and for this reason, many believers reject predestination. To them, all human beings have free will and can decide their fate for themselves. This idea is attractive to many, but it hardly makes much sense when looked at in perspective. None of us has chosen our parents, our nationality, or the period in which we live. We have not chosen

'I can see how it might be possible for a man to look down upon the earth and be an atheist, but I cannot conceive how he could look up into the heavens and say there is no God.'

Abraham Lincoln

our sex (though some people have managed to change it), nor have we decided how tall we will be or what our biological and psychological make-up will be like. Whatever freedom we may have is therefore highly restricted, and can only function within the very narrow parameters laid down by the limitations of our human nature.

The Christian doctrine of predestination accepts that human beings have a will, and that each of us is responsible for our actions, which appear to be free and are usually felt that way by us when we do them. But at a deeper level, the doctrine proclaims that God has a purpose for the lives of his people which he is constantly working out in them, whether they know it or not. Those with no Christian faith do not understand this, but when someone becomes a Christian they begin to see how everything that has happened to them fits a pattern; they start to recognize how God has guided them and protected them even from the time before they were converted. In other words, predestination is something which believers come to understand as the mind of God, and they do this by being admitted into God's presence and associated with the unfolding of his mind's purpose. Far from being the victims of an impersonal fate, Christians discover that by entering the divine counsels, they have become co-creators with God and co-rulers of his universe, as they were meant to be from the beginning of creation. They exercise this privilege by means of intercessory prayer, in which they ask God to do certain things because they believe that they are according to his will. But in the end, of course, Christians recognize that their understanding of that will is imperfect, and if God shows them that they are wrong, they accept his judgment and submit to his will as he has revealed it to them.

> 'God of Abraham, God of Isaac, God of Jacob – not of the philosophers and scholars.'
>
> Blaise Pascal

The mind of God is essentially unknowable, and what he has disclosed to humankind is only a small part of his eternal purpose. Christians believe that God has told them everything they need to know about him in order to be saved from sin and death, and to dwell with him in eternity, but there are still many things which believers do not understand about him. For example, although it is written that those who believe in Christ will be saved, the Scriptures do not explicitly talk about the fate of those who have never had an opportunity to hear the gospel message. One cannot deny that there is evil in the world, but no one knows how it got here, nor can we say why God continues to tolerate its unwelcome presence. It sometimes seems to believers as though what God has promised them is contradicted by what they see around them, particularly when they discover that the wicked are prospering while good people suffer at their expense (Psalm 73). The Bible recognizes this, but says that the problem arises because of humankind's limited perception of God's overall plan, not because there is any inner contradiction in his mind. Believers are told that now they see only part of the truth, but when they go to be with God in heaven, everything about him and his work in the world will be made clear to them (1 Corinthians 13:12). In the meantime, they are expected to trust him in the knowledge that he knows what he is doing, and that in the end everything he does will work out for the best.

Humankind's limited perception of God's purposes also explains why it sometimes seems that God changes his mind. Perhaps the most obvious example of this in the Bible occurs in the book of Jonah, where God decreed that he would destroy the city of Nineveh in forty days (Jonah 3:4).

When the Ninevites heard this, they repented and asked God to spare them, which he did. God's change of plan was contingent on the repentance of the people but, of course, he foresaw that by sending Jonah to preach to them in the first place. It was only in Jonah's eyes that God had changed his mind – much to the prophet's annoyance! Another example can be found in 1 Samuel 15:11, where it is said that God was sorry that he had made Saul king of Israel. This was because Saul had not worked out as he should have done, so God decided to replace him on the throne. But if it is true that God had made Saul king in the first place, he had done so only at the request of the people, and only after warning them that it would not do them any good to have a king. We can therefore say that Saul's failure was part of God's plan from the beginning, and not a sign that he had changed his mind in the true sense.

According to the Bible, all human beings have an innate awareness of God and can see his works displayed in creation, but they cannot come to know him by the kind of intellectual enquiry which is typical of philosophy and the natural sciences. These disciplines have traditionally been considered useful in helping us to understand God better, but they are not a substitute for direct divine self-revelation. God is a personal being, and the only way to know him properly is by having a personal encounter with him. Such a personal encounter is only possible if God initiates it, and both Jews and Christians believe that about four thousand years ago, God did just that when he spoke to a man called Abraham and established an alliance, or covenant, with him. According to this covenant, Abraham was called to worship the one God who controlled everything in heaven and on earth. God would protect him and make his descendants a mighty nation –

promises which both Jews and Christians believe were fulfilled in the creation of the Jewish people. Later, Christians modified this belief by saying that since the coming of Jesus Christ, the boundaries of the nation of Israel have been extended to embrace everyone who believes in him, so that the Christian church today is also part of the fulfilment of God's promise to Abraham.

Several hundred years after the time of Abraham, God gave Moses a comprehensive law for his people. The most famous part of this law is the Decalogue, or Ten Commandments, the first of which reinforces Israel's basic monotheism – you shall have no other gods but me. According to Hebrew tradition, Moses was the first person who wrote down the revelation which God gave him, thereby creating the first five books of the Bible. We do not know how much of the material in these books goes back to Moses himself, but the important thing is that from his time onwards, God instructed his prophets and messengers to commit his words to writing. This is the origin of our Bible, which Christians believe is the written word of God. Through it we gain an understanding of who God is and of what his purposes are, and by obeying its commands we enter into a covenant (that is, a legally binding agreement or promise) relationship with him. Christians accept that God can and does speak to people outside the context of the Bible, but it remains the only authentic touchstone for Christian faith. What God says to an individual must be received by that person, but it does not form part of general Christian teaching unless it is in agreement with what the Bible already says and is accepted by the church as having a significance which goes beyond the particular circumstances of the individual concerned. Even so, it has to be said that Christians disagree

> 'Absolute power turns its possessors not into a God but an anti-God. For God turned clay into men, while the absolute despot turns men into clay.'
>
> Eric Hoffer

A sixteenth-century depiction of Jonah, who found it hard to understand God's purposes for the people of Nineveh.

about the extent to which this happens in actual practice. Roman Catholics have a highly-developed system for determining what is revealed by God outside the Bible and what is not, but other Christians are less certain about this and are usually unwilling to grant such revelations any authoritative status. But whatever position they take on this question, all Christians believe that what the Bible says must be regarded as God's message to his people and obeyed accordingly.

The Creator and the Creation

The world as we know it was created by God and is maintained by him, despite the presence of evil within it. Creation has two dimensions, one of which is spiritual (invisible) and the other material (visible). In the spiritual dimension, God has created beings whom we call angels. From hints found in the Bible, it seems that some of these angels rebelled against him and fell into a state of permanent opposition to his will (2 Peter 2:4). Those angels are headed by one who is commonly called Satan, or the devil, whom the Bible describes as the 'prince of this world' because his sphere of rebellion extends to the material dimension in which we live. The Bible does not explain why the

devil continues to exist, but it is quite clear that he is a personal spiritual agent who can tempt human beings and lure them into disobeying God. Christians, believe that people can be delivered from the power of the devil and become obedient children of God, but they do not believe that even the conversion of every human being would be enough for evil to be eradicated altogether. Christians believe that the rebellion of the fallen angels will continue to affect them as long as they live in the world, and it will not be finally ended until time and the created order are brought to an end. At that point, God will judge the evil powers of this world and deliver his people from them completely (Revelation 20:10). It is not entirely clear whether they will be completely wiped out or condemned to eternal punishment, but whatever the case,

Christians will no longer have to fear that these evil powers will ever attack them again.

In addition to the spiritual creation, there is a material one which we can see all around us. Material things are either animate (animals) or inanimate (plants, rocks, and so on), but they lack the personal quality which applies to the spiritual creation and are therefore incapable of *doing* either good or evil in the moral sense. Christians believe that everything in the material universe was put there by God and is therefore essentially good, although evil forces can use material objects for their own purposes. This happened at the beginning of human history, when Satan tempted Adam and Eve by offering them a piece of fruit which God had forbidden them to eat. It was not the fruit itself which was evil, but the motives of Satan and the disobedient behaviour of the first human beings (Genesis 3:1–7). Of course, all Christians recognize that there are things in the material universe which will harm us if we use them wrongly, and we know that there are creatures such as bacteria and viruses which can cause disease and bring death. But these things are not evil in themselves, even if their effects are harmful. Evil is a spiritual thing and for that reason it can only be discerned and opposed by spiritual means. In the history of the church there have often been well-meaning people who have tried to abolish evil by restricting the use of substances such as alcohol or drugs, but even if they are successful in this, evil continues to exist because it is present in the human heart, from which it can only be dislodged by a spiritual work of God in our lives.

A view from Mount Sinai where God gave Moses the Ten Commandments.

The Place of Humanity in Creation

Human beings form a kind of bridge between the spiritual and the material dimensions of creation because we are the only creatures who have a natural link with both of them. In the material dimension we are very much like the animals and our life cycle is similar to theirs. We are born, we reproduce, we eat food in order to survive and in the end we die, just as animals do. But in spite of these similarities, human beings are not animals. Unlike them, we also have a spiritual dimension, which the Bible describes as 'the image and likeness of God' (Genesis 1:26–27). This

Ways of Thinking About Creation

The doctrine of God as creator is found thoughout the Old Testament. Attention has often focused on the creation narratives found in the first two chapters of the book of Genesis, with which the Old Testament canon opens. However, it must be appreciated that the theme is deeply embedded in the wisdom and prophetic literature in the Old Testament – see, for example, Job 38:1 – 42:6, which highlights the role of God as creator and sustainer of the world.

The Christian teaching that God is creator emphasizes that *nature is not divine*. The Genesis creation account stresses that God created the moon, sun and stars. The significance of this point is too easily overlooked. Each of these celestial entities was worshipped as divine in the ancient world. By asserting that they were created by God, the Old Testament is insisting that they are subordinate to God and have no intrinsic divine nature.

But how are we to understand this idea of 'creation'? What does it mean to speak of God 'creating' the world? Three main ways of conceiving the creative action of God became widely established within the Christian church.

1. *Emanation*. This term was widely used by early Christian writers to clarify the relation between God and the world. The image that dominates this approach is that of light or heat radiating from the sun, or from a human source such as a fire. This image of creation (hinted at in the Nicene Creed's phrase 'light from light') suggests that the creation of the world can be regarded as an overflowing of the creative energy of God. Just as light derives from the sun and reflects its nature, so the created order derives from God, and expresses the divine nature. There is, on the basis of this model, a *natural* or *organic* connection between God and the creation.

2. *Construction*. Many biblical passages portray God as a master builder, deliberately constructing the world according to a definite design (for example, Psalm 127:1). The image expresses the ideas of purpose, planning and a deliberate intention to create. In addition to bringing out the skill of the creator, this way of thinking about creation also allows the beauty and ordering of the resulting creation to be appreciated, both for what it is in itself, and for its testimony to the creativity and care of its creator.

3. *Artistic expression*. Many Christian writers, from various periods in the history of the church, speak of creation as the 'handiwork of God', comparing it to a work of art which is both beautiful in itself, as well as expressing the personality of its creator. This model of creation conveys the idea of God's personal self-expression in the creation of something beautiful – for example, as a sculptor creates a statue, or an artist a beautiful painting. In each, the mind of the artist finds expression in what is actually created.

image is given to both men and women, and means that we have a spiritual character which is part of our created nature and sets us apart from the rest of the material creation. More than that, human beings have been given dominion over that creation, with the right to develop its potential in ways which we call 'culture' or 'civilization'. As God's agents on earth, we have complete freedom to decide how the material creation should be used, and we can even eliminate parts of it if we choose to do so. Sometimes this elimination may be regarded as a bad thing (as when rare species are made extinct), but in other cases, as with the

> 'You have made us for yourself, and our heart is restless until it finds its rest in you.'
>
> Augustine of Hippo

The Bible often depicts God as a 'master builder', who forged the world to a definite design.

eradication of certain viruses, most people believe that it is for the general good of the human race.

Many Christians believe that in the exercise of this dominion, a distinction must be made between the image of God as given to the male (Adam) and the image of God as given to the female (Eve) through the male. This difference is highlighted in the New

The archangel Michael subdues Satan. Christians believe that evil will not be fully overcome until the second coming.

Testament, where it is used to explain why there is a certain hierarchy in the family and in the ministry of the church (1 Corinthians 11:7–9). In recent years, feminist theologians have questioned the validity of this interpretation, but there can be little doubt that the Bible envisages some form of male headship within the human race, however that ought to be manifested in particular circumstances. Disagreement about the consequences of this is likely to continue for some time, but one thing at least seems to be quite clear from the biblical texts. This is that men and women are meant to share the image of God with each other. At a time when there is a tendency for each sex to affirm its own identity, this complementarity needs to

be remembered. God did not intend men to live independently of women, or vice versa. In particular, he did not want human beings to develop same-sex relationships of a kind which are properly intended for the bonding of one sex to the other. The story of Adam and Eve shows quite clearly that heterosexual marriage is an essential part of God's plan for the procreation of the human race, which he laid on them as a duty inherent in their creation mandate. To reject procreation on principle, or to advocate homosexual unions analogous to marriage, therefore goes against the will of God and is a deliberate denial of the meaning of his image and likeness in us.

The spiritual character given to men and women who are made in the image of God cannot be lost or removed, which means that people who have learning disabilities or who have lost the ability to function normally are also creatures with a spiritual dimension and must be respected as such. It is this spiritual dimension which gives us an inbuilt awareness of God and an ability to have a relationship with him. It also makes it possible for us to communicate with angelic creatures, both good and evil. Unfortunately, it was also this ability that caused the first human beings to disobey God's commands, when they listened to the voice of Satan tempting them. Because of that disobedience, the entire human race has fallen under the same condemnation which God has reserved for the disobedient angels. This is the curse of death that cuts every human being off from God, and which, apart from the saving grace of God, cannot be reversed.

The Attributes of God
Recognizing that God is our creator has several consequences for the way in which we understand him. First of all, although the creation reflects

How Can God Be Known Through Nature?

'The heavens declare the glory of God' (Psalm 19:1). At many points, the Bible points to the ability of nature to reveal something of the wisdom and glory of God. If God created the world, we may expect to find at least some aspects of the creator reflected, however dimly, in the creation. So what can be known of God from the created order, and what purpose does this serve? In his letter to the Romans, Paul argues that God has not left himself without witness in nature, so that people have no excuse for ignorance of God's existence (Romans 1). A natural knowledge of God is thus the basis for divine judgment. Elsewhere, Paul appeals to a natural knowledge of God as a means of connecting up with secular wisdom, as may be seen in his famous sermon preached at Athens (Acts 17).

The beauty and design of creation reveals something of the character of God.

One of the most influential discussions of this matter is found in John Calvin's *Institutes*. This important work opens with discussion of this fundamental problem of Christian theology: How do we know anything about God? Calvin affirms that a general knowledge of God may be discerned throughout the creation – in humanity, in the natural order, and in the historical process itself. Two main grounds of such knowledge are identified: one subjective, the other objective. The first is a 'sense of divinity' or a 'seed of religion' which has been planted within every human being by God. The second lies in experience of and reflection upon the ordering of the natural world. The fact that God is creator, together with an appreciation of the divine wisdom and justice, may be gained from an inspection of the created order, culminating in humanity itself.

Calvin makes no suggestion whatsoever that this knowledge of God from the created order is peculiar to, or even restricted to, Christian believers. Calvin is arguing that anyone, by intelligent and rational reflection upon the created order, should be able to arrive at the idea of God. The created order is a 'theatre' or a 'mirror' for the displaying of the divine presence, nature, and attributes. God wills to be known under the form of created and visible things within creation.

Calvin argues that the Bible reiterates what may be known of God through nature, while simultaneously clarifying this general revelation and enhancing it. 'The knowledge of God, which is clearly shown in the ordering of the world and in all creatures, is still more clearly and familiarly explained in the Word.' It is only through Scripture that the believer has access to knowledge of the redeeming actions of God in history, culminating in the life, death, and resurrection of Jesus Christ. God may thus be fully known only through Jesus Christ, who may in turn be known only through Scripture; the created order, however, provides important points of contact for this fuller revelation.

God's power and greatness, there is nothing in it which can be directly identified with him. To worship a creature instead of the creator is idolatry, one of the greatest errors of non-Jewish people in the ancient world and something which is strictly forbidden in the second of the Ten Commandments. To acknowledge God as creator means recognizing that he is not bound by the limitations of time and space which are inherent in creation. God is both eternal and infinite, existing in a dimension of reality which we can only explain by describing what it is not. For example, we say that God is invisible because he has no space-defined body which can be seen by the eyes of a creature. We also say that he is immortal, because he has no time-defined life which will come to an end. We even say that he is impassible (unable to suffer) because no created thing can gain control over him and subject him to its will.

In recent years, some Christians have questioned God's impassibility because they think that if he has established a personal relationship with us, he must be able to feel our pain and suffering as well as experience emotional reactions to our behaviour towards him. Traditional Christianity has never denied that God understands our problems, but this does not compromise his impassibility

> 'Beauty is God's handwriting.'
>
> Charles Kingsley

Creation and Evolution

All Christians are agreed that God created the world, including humanity. However, there has been considerable discussion over how the word 'creation' is to be understood, and the time frame of the creation process. The Genesis creation accounts have been interpreted in a variety of ways throughout Christian history, sometimes to imply an immediate creation of all things in the form we now know

Charles Darwin, the nineteenth-century biologist whose theory of evolution sparked an ongoing controversy over the nature of creation.

them about six thousand years ago, sometimes to imply an extended process of creation over a long period of time. All Christians hold that the created order witnesses to God's wisdom, an idea that is given a particularly high profile by the Intelligent Design Movement.

The debate within Christianity over the origins of life was catalysed considerably in the second half of the nineteenth century by the development of Charles Darwin's theory of natural selection, which proposed that life forms evolved slowly, over very long periods of time. Those theories were set out in two major works: his *Origin of Species* (1859) and *Descent of Man* (1871). Taken together, the two works argue that all species – including humanity – result from a long and complex process of biological evolution. Darwin's theory suggested that humanity emerged gradually, over a long period of time, and that no fundamental biological distinction could be drawn between human beings and animals in terms of their origins and development.

A wide variety of viewpoints on this matter is now encountered within Christian churches, particularly in North America. In what follows, we shall note three of the major positions.

1. *Young Earth Creationism* argues for a literal interpretation of the Genesis creation accounts, including a six-day creation and a global flood over all the earth. The earth is thus held to be about 6,000 years old. The fossil evidence – which points to a much older age for the earth – is understood to have been created in its present form, and does not imply that the earth is as old as the fossil evidence might suggest.

in any way. In ancient times the main intention behind the use of this word was to say that God cannot be harmed or controlled by some power outside himself. Today it is perhaps more helpful for us to think of God as a doctor tending his patients. A good doctor understands what they are going through and sympathizes with them, but does not experience their suffering himself. Christians do not worship a God who shares their weaknesses, but a God who knows what they are and who rescues them from these frailties (Psalm 23).

Closely connected to the idea of impassibility is divine immutability (the idea that God cannot change in any way), which is another characteristic traditionally attributed to the divine nature. For many centuries, immutability was accepted without serious argument, but in the past hundred years it has come under attack because it seems to suggest that God is a static, rather than a dynamic being. It has been pointed out, for example, that his name YHWH can be read as 'he is becoming' as well as 'he is', and that the more dynamic verb gives us a better impression of how the Bible understands God's nature. However, this is a false problem. To say that God does not change does not mean that he is static or inert, but that his character and purposes remain the

> 'God cannot be grasped by the mind. If he could, he would not be God.'
>
> Evagrius of Pontus

2. *Old Earth Creationism* accepts that the earth came into being a long time ago, in line with the fossil evidence. Many within this movement have no difficulty with the findings of modern cosmology, which point to a vast universe that came into being billions of years ago. The critical question concerns how life developed. The Darwinian idea that life forms develop by the essentially random process of variation and natural selection is rejected. Some old earth creationists – sometimes referred to as 'progressive creationists' – hold that God created various living forms sequentially, in the order found in the fossil record.

3. *Theistic Evolution*, sometimes also known as 'Evolutionary Creationism', holds that life did indeed come about by a process of biological evolution. However, it argues that this process of evolution is not to be seen as random, but as guided by God's providential care, with certain definite goals in mind – such as the emergence of humanity. The word 'creation' is here understood to denote God's ability to bring into being a natural order which will develop further, under God's direction.

When did these fossils come into being? Christian thinking has addressed the evolutionary debate in three different ways.

same. Whatever happens to us, he is still the same loving, caring creator and saviour as he always was (Malachi 3:6). His immutability is therefore a guarantee of his trustworthiness, not an assertion that he is effectively dead!

These characteristics of God derive their meaning and their importance from the sharp distinction which the Bible makes between the creation and the being of its creator. One of the problems which arises from the essential difference between God and creation is the nature of the language we use to talk about God. If God cannot be identified with or defined by anything that exists within creation, how can we describe him? The traditional Christian answer to this question takes two forms. On the one hand, Christians believe that God has accommodated himself to human limitations when talking to humanity. Just as an adult will simplify his language when speaking to small children, so God adapts his thoughts to human understanding. This does not mean that what he says is false, but that it is expressed in a way which simple human minds can grasp.

An obvious example of this is the description of the creation in Genesis 1, where it is explained as a six-day process. Some Christians believe that this must be understood literally, but most accept that it is a picture being used to explain a highly complex development in a way which ordinary people can grasp. To read this Bible passage as if it were a scientific account is to misunderstand it, which is why most Christians see no fundamental contradiction between scientific theories and the biblical story. Science and the Bible may be talking about the same events, but they are doing so in very different ways and with different ends in view. To put it simply, the natural sciences are concerned mainly with the 'how' of creation, and try to explain the mechanisms which have produced reality as we know it. The Bible, on the other hand, is concerned primarily with the 'why' of creation, and explains to us what God's purpose was when he put those mechanisms in operation.

Alongside the concept of accommodation there is the principle of analogy, which is used to explain the nature of the language which human beings use when they speak about God. For example, Christians call God 'Our Father' and pray to him in that way, but this does not mean that God is the heavenly equivalent of a human parent. The word is used because there are some aspects of human fatherhood which are similar to God's relationship to his people (or 'children') and which can therefore help them understand more about him. But God is much more than a human father can ever be, and if the analogy is taken too far it will break down. For example, as he grows older, a child's relationship with his human parents changes from being one of dependence to being one of equality, but that never happens in a Christian's relationship with God. Words like 'father' serve a useful but limited purpose in explaining the relationship believers have with God, and Christians have always recognized that there are things about him which they shall never know or be able to describe accurately. Some people find this troubling and may be tempted to speculate about things which are not revealed to human minds, but the best way to deal with this is to remember that a Christian's knowledge of God is part of a personal relationship which they have with him. Personal knowledge is real but it also contains an element of mystery which we cannot fully understand. For example, a mother will see things in her children which she cannot explain, because the child is an independent person whose thoughts and actions

Human Sexuality

God created humanity – male and female – in his own image (Genesis 1:26). The Christian understanding of sexuality is firmly grounded in the belief that both male and female owe their origins to God, and that both bear his image. Sexuality is understood to be an aspect of the created order, not something within God. While the Bible regularly uses both male and female imagery – such as father, mother, and shepherd – to help its readers picture God, these analogies do not imply that God *is* either male or female. The point being made is that both male and female social roles have the potential to model or image God.

The contrast with other religions of the ancient Near East will be obvious. When Israel entered Canaan, it encountered a form of fertility religion which acknowledged various gods and goddesses whose sexuality determined their function, especially in relation to the fruitfulness of the land. The Old Testament avoids attributing sexual functions to God, on account of the strongly pagan overtones of such associations. The Canaanite fertility cults emphasized the sexual functions of both gods and goddesses; the Old Testament refuses to endorse the idea that the gender or the sexuality of God is a significant matter.

The Old Testament stresses the complementarity of male and female in creation, especially in the Garden of Eden (Genesis 2). The creation narrative stresses that it was 'not good' that Adam was alone; Eve was created in order that there might be companionship and partnership between them in the task of tending the creation. Enmity between them is seen as the outcome of the fall (Genesis 3). As Peter Lombard, a medieval theologian of the twelfth century put it, 'Eve was not taken from the feet of Adam to be his slave, not from his head to be his lord, but from his side, to be his partner.'

Christian sexual ethics has stressed the importance of committed relationships between men and women, particularly the importance of marriage as a social institution and as a sanctifying relationship. This has led to tensions with contemporary social norms in the West, especially in relation to growing demands for the recognition of homosexual marriage.

A central theme of the gospel is that there is in Christ no male or female (Galatians 3:28). This does not mean that the genders are somehow abolished, or the distinctiveof male and female eroded. Rather, it is to affirm that all distinctions of race, status and gender are transcended by the unity that believers have in Christ, and the tasks to which he calls them. It is significant that Jesus Christ treated both male and female as partners in sharing the news of the kingdom, and that the evangelistic mission of the early church was undertaken by both men and women. There is an important debate under way at present in many churches over gender issues in ministry. A key issue is which aspects of a person's ministry are shaped by historical, social and cultural, and which by biological, factors. This discussion seems likely to continue in the foreseeable future.

The Image of God in Humanity

Christians have seen the book of Genesis as offering an important insight into the distinct place of men and women within creation: we are created 'in the image of God' (Genesis 1:27). Although humanity is not divine, it possesses a relationship with God which is distinguished from that of other creatures. Humanity bears the image of God; no other living creature shares this privilege or responsibility. So how is this relationship to God to be understood? How can it be visualized? A number of models have been developed within Christian theology, and two are noted in what follows.

One approach is to see the 'image of God' as a reminder of the authority of God over humanity. In the ancient Near East, monarchs would often display images of themselves as an assertion of their power in a region (see, for example,

Unlike the followers of many religions, Christians do not believe that the image of God can be depicted in a physical form.

the golden statue of Nebuchadnezzar, described in Daniel 3:1–7). On this understanding, to be created in the 'image of God' is to be accountable to God. This important point underlies an incident in the ministry of Jesus Christ, recorded in the Gospels (Luke 20:22–25). Challenged as to whether it was right for Jews to pay taxes to the Roman authorities, Jesus requested that a coin be brought to him. He asked, 'Whose image and title does it bear?' Those standing around replied that it was Caesar's. Christ then tells the crowd to give to Caesar what is Caesar's, and to God what is God's. While some might take this to be an evasion of the question, it is nothing of the sort. It is a reminder that those who bear God's image – that is, humanity – must dedicate themselves to him.

A second approach argues that to be created in the 'image of God' is to possess the potential to enter into relationship with God. The term 'image' here expresses the idea that God has created humanity with a specific goal – namely, to relate to God. This theme has played a major role in Christian spirituality. Many Christian writers have argued that we are *meant* to exist in a relationship with our creator and redeemer. As C.S. Lewis pointed out, if we do not do this, there is an absence where there ought to be a presence. There is a God-shaped gap within us, which only God can fill. And in his absence, we experience a deep sense of longing – a longing which is really for God, but which fallen and sinful humanity misreads, accidentally or deliberately, as a longing for things within the world. And these things never satisfy. If we are made for God, and God alone, then there is nothing else that will satisfy. And, as Lewis constantly pointed out, this God-given sense of longing proves to be a key to answering the great questions of life with which humanity has wrestled.

cannot be totally controlled by its parents. So it is in a Christian's relationship with God. He or she knows what to expect from God to the extent that it has been revealed to them, but God cannot be tied down or contained within the limits of human understanding. As he said to the prophet Isaiah: 'My thoughts are not your thoughts, neither are your ways my ways... As the heavens are higher than the earth, so are my ways higher than your ways and my thoughts than your thoughts' (Isaiah 55:8).

But although the creator is above and beyond the limitations of his creation, he is also able to enter into it and operate freely within it, because it belongs to him. We may perhaps begin to understand this by thinking of an aquarium. In an aquarium the fish swim about without any apparent restrictions, but the owner of the aquarium knows that he is ultimately in control of them and can reach into the water whenever he likes to change things around, whether the fish want that or not! In a similar way, God is perfectly able to suspend or alter the apparently 'natural' laws of creation and perform what we call 'miracles', because those natural laws derive from his will and exist only at his pleasure. God is also free to establish relationships with his human creatures, which have to be expressed in terms of time and space because that is the nature of the world we live in, but which are not limited by those constraints. From God's side, this means that he can reveal his will to us in progressive stages, even though that will is eternal and therefore unchanging. This is basically what happened in the course of biblical history, when God gradually made it clearer what his purposes for his people were. The process culminated in the sending of Jesus Christ into the world, an event which the Bible

describes as the unveiling of a mystery which had been hidden from the beginning. In other words, it was always present in eternity, but it was only slowly revealed to God's people on earth.

From the Christian standpoint, this means that we can offer up meaningful prayers to God, which he hears and answers, though not always as expected. The apostle Paul writes about a problem which he describes as 'a thorn in the flesh', which he asked God three times to take away from

God is often likened to a father who continuously watches over and cares attentively for his children.

him. Paul explains that God refused to do this, telling Paul that it was better for him to live with his difficulty, so that God's grace might be revealed in helping Paul to overcome his weakness (2 Corinthians 12:7). On the other hand, there are many people who can testify to prayers which God has answered in wonderful ways, even beyond their expectations. Paul himself experienced this on many occasions, when he was rescued from dangers of one kind or another and set free to preach the gospel to the pagan world of his time (Philippians 1:3–6).

Christians believe that revelation and prayer are the most important ways by which God speaks to his people and by which they relate to him. Knowledge of this revelation, which is contained in the Bible, and the practice of prayer, both privately and in the fellowship of the church, help Christians to establish and deepen their relationship with God and to understand his purposes for them and for his whole creation.

The image and likeness of God in humankind is the means by which this relationship becomes possible. Some Christians have thought that 'image' and 'likeness' are two different things, and that the 'likeness' was lost when the first human beings fell into disobedience. Others have said that 'image and likeness' are really just two names for the same thing, and that when our first ancestors fell the image was corrupted to the point where it could no longer serve as the vehicle of a relationship with God. Today, most biblical scholars agree that 'image and likeness' are indeed one reality, not two distinct things, but they also recognize that the Bible nowhere says that the image was lost or corrupted at the fall. On the contrary, there are biblical texts which clearly assume that the image of God in us is still there, in spite of our disobedience. For example, Genesis 9:6 forbids the murder of another

Humanity as the Steward of Creation

According to the Bible, humanity is the steward of creation (Genesis 2). Adam was placed in Eden in order to tend and nurture the garden. It is sometimes suggested that Christianity is the enemy of the environment, encouraging exploitation of the earth's slender and diminishing resources. The reality is quite otherwise. 'The fundamental relation between humanity and nature is one of caring for creation.' These words, taken from the statement *Renewing the Earth*, issued by the Catholic bishops of the United States of America in 1991, admirably summarize one of the great themes in the Christian understanding of environmental issues, as set out in the Bible and resulting from Christian reflection on the biblical text.

The biblical notion of creation is enormously rich and complex, and offers a number of insights of determinative importance in relation to the issue of the stewardship of creation. Four ideas can be discerned within the biblical account of creation:

Exploitation of the earth goes against central Christian principles about caring for our world.

1. The natural order, including humanity, is the result of God's act of creation, and is affirmed to be God's possession.

2. Humanity is distinguished from the remainder of creation by being created in the 'image of God'. This distinction involves the delegation of responsibility rather than the conferral of privilege, and cannot be seen as legitimizing environmental exploitation or degradation.

All of creation – from the mountain tops to the depths of the oceans – belongs to God, who has entrusted its stewardship to humanity.

3. Humanity is charged with the tending of creation (as Adam was entrusted with the care of Eden – Genesis 2:15), in the full knowledge that this creation is the cherished possession of God.

4. There is no theological ground for asserting that humanity has the 'right' to do what it pleases with the natural order. The creation is God's, and has been entrusted to humanity, who are to act as its steward, not its exploiter.

It is important to notice how the Christian understanding of creation can function as the basis of a rigorously-grounded approach to ecology. Calvin B. DeWitt, a University of Wisconsin professor of environmental studies who founded the Au Sable Institute for Environmental Studies, argues that four fundamental ecological principles can readily be discerned within the Bible:

1. The 'earthkeeping principle': just as the creator keeps and sustains humanity, so humanity must keep and sustain the creator's creation.

2. The 'sabbath principle': the creation must be allowed to recover from human use of its resources.

3. The 'fruitfulness principle': the fecundity of the creation is to be enjoyed, not destroyed.

4. The 'fulfilment and limits principle': there are limits set to humanity's role within creation, with boundaries set in place which must be respected.

If anything can be identified as the enemy of those who care for creation, it is the ruthless human tendency to exploit and the refusal to accept that limits have been set for human behaviour and activity. For Christians, the fundamental element of original sin (as described in Genesis 3) is a desire to be like God, and be set free from all the restraints of 'creatureliness' – including being free to do what we like and as we please with the created order.

> 'God is that than which nothing greater can be conceived.'
>
> Anselm of Canterbury

> 'An atheist may be simply one whose faith and love are concentrated on the impersonal aspects of God.'
>
> Simone Weil

human being on the grounds that all people are created in the image of God, and James 3:9–11 condemns slanderous talk about others for the same reason.

Deciding what the image of God actually is, however, is more difficult. Some have equated it with the human soul and others with the mind, but neither of these analogies really works very well. Nowadays, the soul is usually thought of as the life-force of the body, which dies with it, while the human mind can be damaged without doing injury to God's image in us. It is better to identify the image with the human spirit, which bears witness with the Holy Spirit that we are children of God (Romans 8:16). From this we see that the image of God in us is bound up with our sense of personhood. It is the aspect of our nature which links us most closely to God and which distinguishes us most obviously from the rest of the created order in which we live.

The effect of the presence of God's image in us is twofold. On the one hand, it means that every human being has an innate awareness of the creator, whether we recognize this or not. God holds us accountable for this knowledge, and if we ignore it we are guilty of neglecting his will for us (Romans 1:18–25). In that case, whatever we say or do is wrong in God's eyes, because it is not being said or done in line with the way in which he has made us. Christians believe that this state of alienation from God is universal in the human race, and that only God can change this situation, by reaching out to us and restoring us to his favour. On the other hand, once the broken relationship is restored, the image of God makes it possible for us to know him in a personal way and to grow to be more like him. It is the aspect of our nature which is compatible with his and which gives meaning to an

individual's relationship with him.

This has particular importance for us when it comes to participating in God's own life. Although it is true that many of his characteristics – his invisibility, for example – are beyond our reach, there are nevertheless some things about him which he wants to share with us. The first of these is what the Bible calls his 'holiness'. God is holy because he is set apart from all other beings, but in the context of a fallen world, his holiness acquires a moral aspect, and it is this which he wants us to obtain (Colossians 1:22). Over against the fallenness of the human race, God's holiness appears as both justice and mercy. It is justice, because it demands that the standards required by his holiness shall be respected by his creatures. If they cannot measure up to these, then they must be punished for their sins and corrected. But his holiness also appears as mercy, because God knows that it is impossible for unholy beings to attain the righteousness which he requires. Far from turning against us because of this, God reaches out to us in love and forgives us for the wrong that we have done. In this way his mercy overrules his justice in order for his holiness to be manifested in all its glory.

God's holiness is a special and precious possession which he instructs his people to guard as carefully as possible. This is why the Bible calls him a jealous God (Exodus 20:5). The word 'jealous' does not mean that God envies other beings, but that he wants us to understand that we must treat him properly, as the one and unique source and sustainer of our being. If we fail to do this, we shall suffer the consequences, because God cannot tolerate any abuse of his glory. This may seem arrogant to some people, but we must consider who God is. As the creator and ruler of the universe, his power and majesty must be

What Do We Mean by an 'Almighty' God?

What do we mean when we say that God is 'almighty'? At first sight, what this means is perfectly straightforward. To say that God is almighty means that God can do anything! On reflection, however, it is not that simple. Think about the following question: 'Can God draw a triangle with four sides?' It does not take much thought to see that this question has to be answered with the word 'No'. Triangles have three sides; to draw something with four sides is to draw a quadilateral, not a triangle.

However, on reflection, it is not clear that this question causes problems for the Christian understanding of God. Four-sided triangles do not and cannot exist. The fact that God cannot make such a triangle is not a serious issue. It just forces us to restate our simple statement in a more complicated way. 'To say that God is almighty means that God can do anything that does not involve logical contradiction.'

Yet we need to go deeper than this. To make this important point clearer, let us ask another question. 'Can God break his promises?' There is no logical contradiction involved in breaking promises. It happens all the time. It may be a matter for regret, but there is no intellectual problem here. If God can do anything that does not involve a logical contradiction, surely he can break a promise? Yet for Christians, this suggestion is outrageous. The God who we know and love is one who remains faithful to his promises. If we cannot trust God, who can we trust? The suggestion that God might break a promise contradicts a vital aspect of God's character – his total faithfulness and truthfulness.

There is a tension between power and trust. An all-powerful deceiver can make promises which cannot be relied upon. Yet one of the greatest insights of the Christian faith is that we know a God who *could* do anything – but who *chose* to redeem us. And having committed himself, he remains faithful to his promises. We have the privilege of knowing a God who has chosen to stay with us. The Old Testament expresses this idea in terms of a covenant – an agreement by which God binds himself to be our God, and to care for us.

God has committed himself to our redemption, because he loves us so much. We can rely on him to achieve his purpose. So the word 'almightiness' – as used by Christians – does not mean 'God's ability to do *anything*' but 'God's ability to achieve his purposes'. God does not do things that are logical contradictions or which deny his character. Instead, he works to achieve his purposes. So we are dealing with a God who does not just *promise* us salvation; he has the ability to achieve it. 'The one who calls you is faithful, and he will do it.' (1 Thessalonians 5:24) acknowledged by his creatures – for their own good. We do not put our hands in a fire or touch live electric wires because we know the inevitable consequences if we do so. It is the same principle which is at work in our dealings with God. He is too important to be slighted, and if we fail to respect him we shall feel the effects of our lack of consideration in the way in which he will then proceed to deal with us.

This way is called in the Bible God's wrath or anger, and it too is an essential part of his holiness. God's wrath is not an emotional reaction to our misbehaviour, but a carefully considered response to it. Disobedience to his will has consequences, because God cannot live in harmony with those who rebel against him. Those who persist in their disobedience will be punished for it – a theme which recurs throughout the Bible (Deuteronomy 9:7–8; Romans 1:18). Christians do not fear God's wrath because they know that he has reached out in mercy and rescued them from its consequences. But they believe that those who reject his love will pay the price for their rebellion, which will be eternal separation from his presence. As with the fallen angels, no one knows whether this will take the form of eternal punishment or of annihilation, but it hardly matters; either way, those who spurn God will be cut off from him forever because of their rebellion against him.

Christians are holy because they have the Spirit of God in them, not only teaching them the difference between right and wrong, but also giving them the strength to choose the former and reject the latter. It is the image of God in each Christian which gives them this moral awareness and makes it appropriate for them to share in that aspect of his nature. Another divine characteristic Christians are called to share is love. Love is not a thing in itself, but a quality of

> 'Those persons who best know God are those who least presume to speak of him.'
>
> Angela of Foligno

relationship which God manifests perfectly and which his people are called to reflect. No one can ever attain the fullness of God's perfection of course, but thanks to the presence of his image in them, Christians can respond to his love and imitate it in their dealings with others.

God is Personal

This brings us naturally to a consideration of the personal nature of God's being. It is fundamental to the biblical revelation that God is personal, because it is this side to his nature which makes it possible for him to enter into relationships with humanity – in particular, with us. The personal character of God is so obvious to readers of the Bible that it is easy to forget that many people in the ancient world found such an idea very difficult to accept. Even though they worshipped gods whom they portrayed as supernatural human beings, they almost always made a sharp distinction between those gods, who despite their superhuman powers were nevertheless limited in certain respects, and the supreme being, which they regarded as absolute. The Greek philosophers who spoke of the supreme being usually did so in abstract terms – the supreme being was the Good, the Beautiful and so on, but it was not a person with whom it was possible to have a relationship. To them, what we call personhood – with its implied marks of individual distinctiveness – was itself a limitation, and therefore a sign of imperfection. It also implied the existence of other persons, which meant that the concept could not be applied to the supreme being, which by definition had to be perfect and self-sufficient.

Those who thought about the connection between human beings and the supreme being often considered the latter to be a great mind, of which we share a small portion. Some of them compared it to a cosmic fire, and human souls to sparks which had become detached from it, thereby acquiring a separate identity. The further the spark got away from the fire the colder it became, until it eventually died altogether. The best solution for the spark therefore was to return to the fire from which it came, so that its life could continue, even though its individual identity would be lost in the process.

The early Christians challenged the philosophical concept of the supreme being by saying that this being was not only personal in himself, but that it was possible to have a relationship with him which would give us a share in his eternal life. Christians felt confident in equating the God of the Bible with the supreme being, because they believed that this was implied by the name YHWH, which means 'he who is'. In the gospels, Jesus had called himself 'I am' in what appears to be an absolute sense, and similar ideas are found elsewhere in the New Testament. In fact it is very hard to imagine how any monotheistic religion could not identify its god with the supreme being, since if there were other, independent or superior beings, belief in that god alone would hardly be justified. We can therefore say that even if the Bible does not dwell on the subject very much, the identification of God with ultimate reality is logically coherent and probably inevitable in the long run. But it was still not easy for the early Christians to make out a case for belief in a personal supreme being, something which still remains the greatest single hurdle which any philosophically-based theology has to overcome.

When looking for words to use to describe God, the early Christians quite happily borrowed the vocabulary of Greek philosophical thought and adapted it to their own uses. It is often said that this process led to a corruption of Christianity by the importation of dogmatic categories which were alien to it, but this is an exaggeration. No language is sufficient to explain God fully, but the philosophical concepts which the Christians borrowed were not so narrowly defined that they could not be adapted to Christian use. A good example is the word 'being' which could refer to many things, and which Christian theologians applied to God – allowing them to define what it means in a Christian context. In other words, if God is the supreme being, then the word 'being' must be redefined to fit what we know about God, since God cannot be scaled down to the limits imposed by 'being'. In fact, the more the early Christians wrestled with this, the more they came to appreciate the limitations of human language and the more they insisted that true knowledge of God must go beyond all human categories. Some of them eventually developed a mystical theology of 'non-being' in order to do justice to God's eternal 'otherness'. In this theology, even the highest concepts which we can imagine are inadequate to describe God, and we must seek to transcend them if we are to have a genuine experience of him.

What is particularly telling, however, is that the word 'person' was not used to describe anything in ancient Greek philosophy. 'Person' originally came from the theatre and meant 'mask', because the actors wore masks to indicate which characters they were playing. From there it came to mean 'face', which is the usage we find in the New Testament (see 1 Corinthians 13:12). The Romans took it over and applied it to their legal language, where it came to mean an agent who can take part in a court action. In ancient Rome, not every human being had legal personality – slaves, women and children were all deprived of it. On the other hand, a company could

> 'There are three stages in the work of God: impossible, difficult, done.'
>
> James Hudson Taylor

become a legal person, which is the concept lying behind the modern idea of 'incorporation' – becoming a body. It was from the law courts, and not from any theatrical or philosophical source, that the word 'person' came into Christian theology, because God gave his law to his people and is therefore the supreme agent in any action which might result from that.

If the history of Christian theology can be regarded as a deepening appreciation of the personal character of God, that process can also be regarded as a progressive distancing of theology from any kind of philosophy, in spite of the many attempts which were made over the centuries to reconnect the two disciplines. Christian theology overlaps with different kinds of philosophy in many interesting and important ways, but in the end its doctrine of a personal God sets it apart from any purely human speculation. Philosophers can construct a vision of reality in which a supreme mind rules and governs the rest, but they cannot discover the Christian God without special divine revelation. Christian philosophers construct reality in ways which coincide with the divine self-revelation, so that this supreme mind and the God of the Bible are one and the same being, but when they do this they are harmonizing two different types of knowledge, one of which is the fruit of human reasoning and the other of which depends on divine self-disclosure.

Biblical Images of God

The Old and New Testaments contain a rich range of images of God. Individually and collectively, these build up to give a profound and deeply satisfying vision of who God is, and what he is like. In this study panel, we shall note two of the most familiar, and the insights that they bring us.

Perhaps the most familiar biblical image for God is that of the *shepherd* (for example, Psalm 23:1; 80.1; Isaiah 40:11; Ezekiel 34:12). The first insight that it conveys is that of the loving care of the shepherd for his sheep. The shepherd was committed to his flock of sheep on a full-time basis. The idea is developed very powerfully in the New Testament, especially in the parable of the lost sheep (Luke 15:3–7). Here the shepherd actively seeks out the lost sheep, in order to bring it home.

The second point that this image of God conveys is that of God's guidance of his people. The shepherd knows where food and water are to be found, and guides his sheep to them. It is he who finds the green pastures and quiet waters (Psalm 23:2). To liken God to a shepherd is to emphasize his constant presence with his people, and his gentle guidance as he tries to protect them from the dangers which life offers, and to bring them to a place of plenty and safety (Isaiah 40:11).

A third insight concerns ourselves, as we relate to God. We are the sheep of God's pasture (Psalm 79:13; 95:7; 100:3). It tells us that we are like sheep, incapable of looking after ourselves, and continually going astray. We are not self-sufficient: just as the sheep rely upon the shepherd for their existence, so we have to learn to rely upon God. We may like to think that we are capable of looking after ourselves, but realism demands that we recognize just how totally dependent on God we are from the moment of our birth to our death.

Another very different biblical image of God is the *rock* (Psalm 18:2; 28:1; 42:9; 78:35; 89:26; Isaiah 17:10). This powerful image conveys the security and reliability of God. We may feel that we are being beaten down by a powerful flood, continually threatening to overwhelm and destroy us. And yet, in the midst of this

The Doctrine of the Trinity

In line with the identification which they made between the supreme being and the God of the Bible, the early Christians realized that God did not need relationships with other beings in order to manifest his own nature. If that were the case, God would be dependent on other things in order to be fully himself, an impossible situation which would have compromised his absolute supremacy. For God to be the supreme being, he has to be perfect in and of himself, and so if he has a capacity for personal relationships, these must be fully worked out within his own oneness.

In fact, as the early Christians came to understand, the New Testament tells us that God does indeed have such relationships inside himself. Quite apart from his creation of personal beings in his own image and likeness, the one eternal God is a community of three equally eternal persons. They are not to be regarded as parts of God which can be separated from him, because if that were the case, the divine being would have been impaired when the Son became a man in Jesus Christ. It would be absurd to suggest that the Son is the mind of the Father, if that were taken to mean that the incarnation of Christ caused the Father to lose his mind for a time! However hard it may be to imagine it, each person of the Godhead is fully divine in and by himself, and it is in the fullness of that divinity that they each contribute to that eternal

sea of surging water, there is a place of security – the rock that is God (Psalm 42:7–9). A rock is something firm and immovable, which can survive storms, floods and heat alike. It is a place of refuge. Thus Moses, when criticizing the Israelites for worshipping false gods, points to the close relationship between God, rocks and safety: 'Where are their gods, the rock they took refuge in?' (Deuteronomy 32:37).

The image has, of course, been developed extensively in Christian sermons and devotional writings, and is perhaps best known through the familiar hymn of Augustus Toplady:

Rock of ages, cleft for me,
Let me hide myself in thee.

In thinking about God as a rock, we can think of him as a secure place of shelter from the storms of life, a place of refuge from sin and evil.

God is humanity's rock, able to stand firm in times of trouble.

fellowship which Christians call the Trinity of persons.

It is true that this Trinity can extend its capacity for relationships to include human beings if they have believed in Jesus Christ (the second divine person) and been filled by the power of the Holy Spirit (the third divine person), but important as this is for us, it does not affect the inner balance of Trinitarian relationships in themselves. The doctrine of the Trinity has caused a great deal of perplexity in the history of Christian thought, and there are many people today who prefer to ignore it, because it is so difficult to understand. For this reason, it is essential to realize that the first Christians did not arrive at their belief in the Trinity by a complex process of speculation, but by an examination of their own experience of God. As the apostle Paul put it: 'Because you are sons, God sent the Spirit of his Son into our hearts, the Spirit who calls out 'Abba, Father' (Galatians 4:6). This verse was one of the earliest in the New Testament to be written, and it contains the essence of the doctrine which was later spelled out as the Trinity of persons. It is by the Spirit of the Son that Christians cry to the Father. By preaching this, the early church proclaimed a new faith which was significantly different from its Jewish parent and radically so from anything which the non-Jewish world had to offer.

At first, Christians were not particularly interested in how their beliefs would affect the pagan world, but from the very beginning they were deeply concerned about their relationship with Judaism. Not only were most of them Jews, but they had no intention of breaking their ties to their ancestral faith, which they believed had been fulfilled by the coming of Christ. In effect, these Christians introduced a hermeneutical shift in their interpretation of the Old Testament which may be described in simple terms as going from a perspective which is basically external to one which is basically internal. This is a bold statement, and it has to be expressed and understood with great subtlety. To say that Old Testament Judaism was a religion in which external things were fundamental is not to deny the reality of an Old Testament Jewish spirituality, any more than the affirmation that Christianity is primarily an internal experience of God means that it has no meaningful outward forms of expression. What we are talking about here is a shift of emphasis and perspective within a framework in which both the external and the internal are necessary for the whole reality to be appreciated. But having said that, the difference is sufficiently important for it to have produced a new religion which cannot return to the bosom of the old without losing its essential character.

That Judaism is defined primarily by external criteria appears from the Law of Moses. According to that law, the people of Israel are set apart from the nations by the rite of circumcision, which leaves a permanent, visible mark on the body, and by a whole series of statutes designed to create observable differences between Jews and other people. They are given a specific territory in which to dwell, where their destiny will be worked out in the sight of all other nations. They are told to avoid certain types of food, to restrict their relationships with non-Jews (and in particular to avoid intermarriage with them), and to concentrate their worship in the elaborate sacrificial rituals of the Jerusalem Temple. In biblical Judaism, the Temple was of particular importance, because it was there that God met with his people – albeit in a highly structured way. Once a year, the high priest was allowed to enter the inner room known as the holy of holies, where he offered the sacrifice of atonement for the sins of the entire nation. To do this without authorization was to court disaster, as King Uzziah discovered to his cost. When he tried to offer sacrifices in the Temple, he was struck with leprosy – an object lesson, if ever there was one, in what was and what was not allowed (2 Chronicles 26:19–21).

The Temple was of course only the last and most sumptuous form of the space in which the meeting with God took place. Before it was constructed, there was the tabernacle which followed the people in the desert, and in the tabernacle lay the ark of the covenant, a sacred box which contained the charter instruments of the Mosaic dispensation. The ark was strictly off-limits to the profane – so much so that when a man named Uzzah tried to prevent it from falling to the ground on its bumpy journey across the Judaean countryside, he was struck dead for his pains (1 Chronicles 13:10). In ancient Israel, God dwelt in the midst of his people, but he could not be approached directly, except by the very few people who were authorized by the law to do so. To be sure, the prophet Jeremiah knew that one day God would write his law in his people's hearts (Jeremiah 31:31–34), but this was a future prophecy, and it is symptomatic of the difference between Judaism and Christianity that the early Christians specifically declared that it had been fulfilled in their time (Hebrews 8:8–12). In fact, the more we look at the New Testament, the more we see that it was these symbolic markers of the restrictiveness of Judaism which provoked the most impassioned pleas in favour of the new dispensation brought by Christ.

In that Christian dispensation, there was to be no holy land, no Temple and no ark of the covenant. The ritual of baptism, which has replaced that of circumcision, may be a visible act, but since baptism leaves no permanent mark on the body, it must be regarded as essentially invisible. Like Jews, Christians are required to be careful about the kinds of relations they enter into with non-believers, and this is still seen as problematic, but we are not expected to form a distinct nation in the way that Israel was. The apostle Paul expressed all this quite clearly only a few lines before his Trinitarian statement, when he said that in Christ the barriers between male and female, Jew and Gentile, slave and free man have been broken down (Galatians 3:28). Christians stand in the presence of God, not because they are the *physical* descendants of Abraham, the ancestor of Israel, but because they are his *spiritual* descendants. It is because Christians believe as Abraham believed that they have received the inheritance originally promised to him, and it is also because the Jews have rejected this understanding of the matter that they have been excluded from God's blessing, at least for the time being. In Paul's mind, it is not Christians who have rejected Judaism but Jews who have rejected Christ, and moreover, those Jews were being unfaithful to their own heritage in so doing. Paul always believed that Israel's faith was essentially spiritual, as is that of Christians, and he regarded the Mosaic law as a sort of protective covering, which had to be introduced in order to keep the wayward Israelites on the straight and narrow. Unfortunately, later generations had come to mistake the husk for the kernel, and so they had fundamentally misinterpreted the true meaning of the Bible. The coming of Christ did away with the husk, opening up the kernel to give believers direct access to God (see Ephesians 2:18).

In the words of the gospels, the veil in the Temple was torn in two when Jesus was crucified, and the way into the holy of holies was opened up

'Only God can fully satisfy the hungry heart of man.'

Hugh Black

'We shall steer safely through every storm, so long as our heart is right, our intention fervent, our courage steadfast, and our trust fixed on God.'

St Francis de Sales

Joshua and his trumpeters approach the walls of Jericho carrying the ark of the covenant.

GOD

(Matthew 27:51; Mark 15:38; Luke 23:45). Those who are Christians have gone into that inner sanctum, and in Paul's words, they are now seated in the heavenly places in Christ Jesus (Ephesians 2:6). To put it another way, whereas ordinary Jews were kept out of the holiest place in the Temple, Christians have been admitted into the inner life of God. Only in that context, and based on that understanding, can Christian theology be reconciled with the Old Testament revelation. The God who appears as One to those who view him on the outside, reveals himself as a Trinity of persons, once his inner life is opened up to our experience. The Christian doctrine which has resulted from this is nothing more nor less than a description of what that experience of God's inner life is like, something which becomes clearer as we look at what the Bible has to say about each of the persons of the Trinity individually.

The Person of the Father

The fatherhood of God is a concept so widely accepted in modern times that few people bother to consider what it really means. At one level, it can be equated with God's work of creation, as Paul apparently did when he preached in Athens (Acts 17:28). But it is noticeable that when he did so, he quoted the pagan Greek poet Aratus and not the Old Testament, which seldom if ever conflates these two ideas. The idea that God is *Israel's* father does occasionally occur in the Old Testament (for example, Jeremiah 31:9; Malachi 2:10), but this only occurs in contexts which make it clear that the Father–Son imagery applied to the covenant relationship which the ancient Jews had with God. We have no evidence that it ever extended beyond this, to take in the whole of the created order. But at the same time, if the use of Father–Son language was possible within the covenant context, it was not common, and when Jesus taught his disciples to pray to God as their Father, his command came across, both to them and to others, as something fundamentally new.

Jesus clearly intended his disciples to understand the Father as the God whom they already worshipped, but is it possible to make a simple equation between the Old Testament God and the Father of Jesus Christ? To put the matter a different way, is the God of the Old Testament only the first person of the Trinity, or is he in some sense all three combined? In Galatians 4:6, it is the undifferentiated 'God' who has sent his Son's Spirit into believers' hearts, and it would appear from the context that he must be identified with the Father, especially since the Spirit's mission is to cry 'Abba' in the hearts. Nor does this verse stand in isolation, as there are other New Testament examples which might be quoted in support of the same idea. For example, 2 Corinthians 13:14 says: 'May the grace of the Lord Jesus Christ, and the love of God, and the fellowship of the Holy Spirit be with you all, evermore.' In the context, it is clear that the 'love of God' must be a reference to God the Father, and so the question naturally arises as to whether the Father can be said to be God in a way which the Son and the Holy Spirit are not. If he can, the doctrine of the Trinity will be seriously affected, and may even fall to the ground, particularly in its traditional, orthodox form, and believers may find themselves closer to Judaism than most Christians in the past have imagined.

In point of fact, however, we cannot say that the God of the Old Testament is just the first person of the Trinity without further qualification, because whatever texts like the ones quoted above might suggest, such an assertion goes against other claims which the New Testament makes for Jesus. It would take too long to elaborate on this in detail, but we can grasp the essential point by looking at the term 'creator'. In the opening chapters of Genesis, God appears in this role, and the theme recurs periodically throughout the Hebrew Bible. But in the New Testament the Son is also said to have been the creator of the world (John 1:3; Colossians 1:16), so that to identify the creator with the first person of the Godhead is a form of reductionism which betrays the witness of the New Testament. We must not forget that Jesus claimed to be the uniquely

complete revelation of God the Father (John 14:7) and that later on the apostle Paul would tell the Colossians that in him the fullness of the Godhead dwelt bodily (Colossians 2:9). If it is really true, as Jesus told his disciples, that no one can come to the Father except through the Son (John 14:6), then it must follow that the ancient Jews could not have known God apart from Christ, even though the latter was hidden from their eyes at the time. The Old Testament God must therefore be more than just the Father, even though the two seem to be equated in various parts of the New Testament. How can we account for this?

The answer to this question seems to lie in the assertion, often made in the course of church history, but frequently denied in modern times, that the Father is in some sense the 'anchor person' in the Trinity. The traditional view may be expressed by saying that whereas the Son is the person who became incarnate in Jesus Christ, and the Holy Spirit is the person who dwells in Christians' hearts by faith, the Father is the person who primarily manifests what we now call 'divinity'. He is the reminder that however much God comes to us and reveals himself to us, he remains in a fundamental sense hidden from our eyes, above and beyond our understanding. This view has been criticized in recent years, mainly because it seems to give the Father a special degree of divinity, which makes the Son and the Holy Spirit somehow inferior to him. This is always a danger, of course, but as long as we are careful to recognize it and avoid it when it crops up, we can attribute this special work to the Father, much in the same way as we attribute the work of redemption to the Son, because he alone became incarnate, though, of course, the overall work of redemption belongs to all three persons of the Trinity, each of whom participates in it in his own special way.

Another objection which has been raised is that it is wrong to think of God as a 'substance' when he is in fact a community of persons. The theologians of the early church happily described God as a 'substance' and the term has survived in traditional Christian theology, but it has to be admitted that for many people today, the word conjures up an abstract or materialist scientific theory, and one moreover which is no longer current in the scientific world. This may be true, but we do not have to get into an argument over whether God is properly described as a 'substance' or not, to recognize the Father as the person who manifests the objective being of God in himself, and who in some way gives order and direction to the Trinity as a whole. Certainly, it is perfectly clear from the New Testament that it is the Father who sent the Son into the world to do his will by saving his people from their sins. In this way he can be equated with the God of the Old Testament, because it was precisely this saving will and purpose of God which was revealed to ancient Israel, and which was the ultimate aim of the Mosaic law. Furthermore, if we fail to think of the Father as the person who manifests God's essential divinity, we run the risk of saying that the divine 'substance' or whatever we wish to call his being, is a fourth thing, in addition to the three persons of the Trinity. That accusation has been made in the past, and although it is seldom heard today, (thanks largely to the tendency to dismiss the concept of 'substance' altogether), we cannot be sure that it will not return to the discussion at some future time. If that should happen, we have to be ready to say that the particular work of the Father is to be God simply as God is, remembering that however meaningful

> 'God is sufficiently wise, and good and powerful and merciful, to turn even the most apparently disastrous events to the advantage and profit of those who humbly accept and adore his will in all that he permits.'
>
> Jean Pierre de Caussade

one's experience of divine immanence may be, no one can ever contain the transcendent mystery of deity within the limited horizons of the human heart and mind.

The Person of the Son

Once the person and work of the Father are clear in our minds, we can move on to consider the person of the Son and the theological meaning of 'sonship'. There is a logic in this, because the Son's work stands in dependence on that of the Father, and can only be understood in that light. What that means with respect to the Son's being, in relation to the being of the Father, is more complex, but the names for the two persons as given to us in Scripture would suggest that, however we look at this, the Son stands in second place. At the same time, the Son represents something in the inner life of God which is also true of Christians, in that they too are called to be 'sons' and in some respect share in his 'sonship'. The cry of 'Abba', the Aramaic word for 'father', which the Holy Spirit puts in the hearts of believers, is the cry of the Son, whose relationship with the Father they now share by means of adoption. So characteristic was this of Jesus' teaching that the use of this name became his particular hallmark. When the apostle Paul picks it up and tells his readers that the Spirit of the Son has come into their hearts in order to allow them to cry 'Abba' too, he is telling them that in the Spirit, they have the privilege of being able to speak to the Father in the same way (and therefore with the same authority and assurance) as Jesus did. Our relationship with the Father is directly patterned on that of the Son, so much so in fact that we can almost say that it is assimilated to the Son's relationship within the Godhead.

Let us consider, first of all, the Son as he stands in relation to the Father.

Nowadays, any suggestion of hierarchy or subordination is liable to elicit a strong reaction from those who scent a whiff of Arianism in the air (see page 160), not to mention from those who fear that any compromise on the principle of divine equality among the persons of the Godhead may lead to a denial of equality in human relationships, which they see as being modelled on the inner life of God. In answer to this, we can say that Father and Son imply each other's existence, since the names would otherwise be meaningless. You cannot have one without the other. If there were no Son, the first person of the Trinity would not be the Father – he would have to have some other name which did not imply a parenting relationship. But having said that, we must also say that there is an inner logic in the Father–Son relationship which makes it appropriate for the latter to do the will of the former, rather than the other way round. Why it should be like this is a mystery, but one thing we do know is that the submission of the Son is voluntary, which is why the word 'submission' must be preferred to 'subordination' or 'subjection', both of which imply some form of coercion. This is made clear in Philippians 2:5–11, where the apostle Paul tells us that the Son humbled himself and took on the role of a servant, in order to accomplish the work of our salvation. Only someone secure in his relationship of equality with the Father would do this voluntarily, and so by what may appear to some as a paradox, it is precisely in the Son's abasement that his true glory as the Father's equal is revealed.

Of course, the sonship which believers enjoy in God is not identical to that which belongs to Jesus, although there are significant parallels with it. The essential difference is that whereas Christ is the Son by nature, having been begotten by the Father in eternity, Christians are sons by adoption. What they cannot claim by virtue of their created being, they have been given by grace, so that they too can become 'partakers of the divine nature' (2 Peter 1:4). This somewhat curious phrase means that Christians are given access to the power of God, which they see at work in our lives. As God's sons by adoption, they are gradually (but continually) being transformed into the likeness of God's Son by nature, who remains their model and their goal. But the natural Son of God is not some remote divine being, whom Christians strive in vain to imitate. On the contrary, he became a man in Jesus of Nazareth, and lived the life of a normal man. This incarnation was not an end in itself, but a preparation for the supreme act of God in saving humankind from its sins. Jesus Christ did not just identify himself with us in our humanity; he also became sin for us (2 Corinthians 5:21), and took our place at the judgment seat of God. By dying for us in his human nature – our nature – the only-begotten Son of God paid the price for our sins, in order to deliver us from a burden too great for us to bear on our own. Those who do not understand this, do not understand the gospel, and there is no entry into the inner life of God for those who have not died with him in this way.

This belief, which in theological terms is called 'penal substitutionary atonement' has often been criticized by people who think that it is somehow immoral of God the Father to send his innocent Son to die for the sins of the human race, but these people have failed to grasp the voluntary nature of the Son's substitution. God the Father did not decide to punish his Son on our behalf and then force him into complying with that decision, and given their fundamental equality within the Godhead, he probably could not have done so even if he had wanted to.

> 'God's gifts put man's best dreams to shame.'
>
> Elizabeth Barrett Browning

It was only when he humbled himself and became a servant, in order to accomplish the Father's will, that the Son became a man, since only in that mode could the price of humanity's redemption be paid. If there is any 'injustice' in this, it is not in the Son's voluntary act on the behalf of others, but in the fact that Christians have been redeemed, since they have received something from God which they have done nothing to deserve, and which all their own thoughts and desires make them unworthy to obtain.

commend my spirit' (Luke 23:46). But echoes of this can be found right through the gospels, not least in John, where Jesus is constantly explaining his mission in terms of the Father's will, which he has come to accomplish on earth. The roles of the Father and of the Son may be distinguishable, but they can never be separated, since in the end, the divine work of redemption belongs equally to them both. Yet Christians' experience of that redemption does not come directly from either the Father or the Son.

A twelfth or thirteenth-century Armenian depiction of Christ washing the Feet of the Disciples, when Jesus took the place of a servant.

At the heart of the atonement lies the relationship between the Son and the Father within the Godhead, without which his saving act could not have occurred. This relationship can be seen, first of all, in the words which Jesus uttered on the cross, three of which were addressed directly to the Father: 'My God, my God, why hast thou forsaken me?' (Matthew 27:46; Mark 15:34), 'Father, forgive them; for they know not what they do' (Luke 23:34) and 'Father, into thy hands I

Instead, the apostle Paul tells us that God has sent his Son's Spirit into our hearts, making him, a third person, the vehicle through whom they enter into God's inner life. Who or what is this Spirit, and why should this be necessary?

The Person of the Holy Spirit

It is no exaggeration to say that in the history of Trinitarian theology, it is the way in which different Christians understand the person and work of the

Holy Spirit which has caused the most controversy. Even more basic than that, it is hard to know what to make of the many occurrences of the word 'spirit' in the New Testament, since it is far from clear just how many of them refer to the third person of the Trinity. To go no further than Galatians 4:6, it is not immediately clear from the text that the Spirit of the Son is a distinct person at all. If we knew no more than this, it would be perfectly possible to interpret the phrase simply as a rhetorical device for referring to the Son himself. There are certainly plenty of precedents for this in the Old Testament, where a phrase like 'the Spirit of God' can easily be used in this way, and the word 'spirit' is sufficiently flexible that there are times when it may mean no more than 'attitude'. For example, what did Jesus mean when he told the Samaritan woman that God is a Spirit, and must be worshipped in 'spirit and in truth' (John 4:24)? In the first use of the word 'spirit', it seems probable that it refers to God's non-material nature, but the second occurrence is more puzzling. Does it mean that we should worship him in the power of the Holy Spirit, which seems unlikely in the context, or is the word merely referring to the attitude which should be adopted in prayer? Most interpreters of the Bible think that the latter is more probable and, if so, it is a warning not to read too much into occurrences of the word elsewhere in Scripture if the context does not make a reference to the third person of the Trinity inescapable.

Compared with the Father and the Son, the third person of the Trinity suffers from being in effect anonymous, since both the words 'holy' and 'spirit' can be applied to many different beings, including righteous people who have died and gone to heaven. His personhood has therefore often been in doubt, and even when it is accepted, his precise relationship to the Father

and the Son has long been an area of controversy between eastern and western Christians and remains one to this day. The work of the Holy Spirit may be somewhat clearer, at least in outline, but the means by which he effects it have provided endless fodder for debate within the western church, and have contributed, more than is often realized, to the great divisions between Roman Catholics and Protestants on the one hand, and among different Protestant groups on the other. Indeed, it is probably not too much to say that virtually all the great points of disagreement between the different denominations of western Christendom today come down in the end to different ways of understanding the work of the Holy Spirit both in the church and in individual believers. Why has this complication arisen in Christian theology and brought so much grief in its wake? Do we need a third divine person whose identity is obscure, or can we not make do with the two who so obviously complement one another?

To answer these questions adequately, we have to look at the broader sweep of the New Testament, and in particular at John 14–16, where Jesus explains to his disciples what their experience of God will be like after he has gone away from them. Jesus tells them that he has to go away, because otherwise they will not be able to enter into the fullness of the experience which God has promised them. It is hard to imagine why he told them that there was something more, and indeed better, for them than what he had brought already, but that is what Jesus said. After his departure, he would send another Comforter, who would lead them into all truth, who would enable them to do even greater things than he had done, and who would dwell with them forever. What is more, when the other Comforter came, both he and the Father would come

'Providence is the care God takes of all existing things.'
John of Damascus

'None but God can satisfy the longings of an immortal soul: that as the heart was made for him, so only he can fill it.'
Richard Chevenix Trench

with him, and dwell along with him in their hearts.

From this description of his future activities, it is not difficult to see that the 'other Comforter' of John's Gospel is the same Holy Spirit, whom Paul mentions in Galatians 4:6 as being the Spirit of the Son, sent by the Father. In the fourth Gospel he is specifically defined as proceeding from the Father (John 15:26), and as possessing all the power and authority of Christ himself. Paul's statement is much briefer, but it ties in with John's exposition remarkably well. In Paul's understanding, the Spirit of the Son has the power to enable us to pray as the Son did. For this to be possible, he must have a relationship to the Father which is equal to that of the Son. If that is the case, then the Holy Spirit must be just as much a person as the Son is, since if he were not, any relationship with the Father which he might have would be of a fundamentally different (and necessarily inferior) kind to that which the Son enjoys. To put this a different way, it is the work of the Holy Spirit in our hearts which makes us confess that he is also a person of the Godhead, and indeed the person through whom Christians come to understand and experience the other two. Once again, we see that it is the Christian experience of God which obliges them to develop a Trinitarian confession, since any narrower expression of the relationship between Christian believers and God would be inadequate to explain it.

No one can presume to say why God should have revealed himself to Christians in this way, but it is clear from what Jesus told his disciples in John 14–16 that had the Holy Spirit not been sent into believers' hearts, they would now have an inferior knowledge of God. It is clear from the gospels that the disciples of Jesus had a lesser experience of him before

Pentecost than they were to have later on, even though they were privileged to see the incarnate Son face to face. As in the Old Testament, the God who became incarnate in Jesus Christ dwelt among his people, but not inside them. They could behold his glory (John 1:14) but in some sense it remained alien to their understanding. Neither his teaching nor his miracles were

enough to bridge this gap, and at the end of his earthly life, his disciples deserted him because they believed that his mission had been a failure. Jesus had predicted his resurrection, but when it came it was still a surprise to the disciples, who did not quite know what to make of it. In some fundamental way, Jesus remained external to them, and they would not really understand what was going on until their experience of him and his message was internalized. That happened when the Holy Spirit descended on them at Pentecost, and since then his indwelling presence has been the common possession of the church.

The Holy Spirit works in many different ways, but his overall purpose

Calvary by Andrea Mantega. Jesus' death made full and final atonement for those who believe in him.

The Charismatic Movement

The charismatic movement, which places an emphasis on such spiritual gifts as speaking in tongues, is often traced back to the opening years of twentieth century. The African-American preacher William J. Seymour (1870–1922) opened the 'Apostolic Faith Mission' at 312 Azusa Street, Los Angeles in April 1906. Over the next two years, a major revival broke out at Azusa Street, characterized by the phenomenon of 'speaking in tongues'. The term 'Pentecostalism' began to be used to refer to the movement, taking its name from the 'Day of Pentecost' – the occasion, according to the New Testament, when the first Christian disciples had that same experience (Acts 2:1–4).

In terms of Christian belief, Pentecostalism is quite traditionalist. It distinguishes itself from other forms of Christianity by the emphasis that it places on speaking in tongues, and its forms of worship. These are strongly experiential, and involve prophesying, healings, and exorcisms. The worship style and lack of intellectual sophistication of the movement led to its being ignored by mainline denominations and the academic world. Yet after the Second World War, a new phase of its expansion began, which paved the way for its massive growth in the second half of the twentieth century.

Pentecostalism came to attention in Van Nuys, California, in 1960, when the rector of the local Episcopalian church, Dennis Bennett, told his congregation that he had been filled with the Holy Spirit and had spoken in tongues. It soon became clear that others in the mainline denominations had shared Bennett's experience. By the late 1960s, it was evident that some form of renewal based on charismatic gifts (such as 'speaking in tongues') was gaining a hold within Anglican, Lutheran, Methodist and Presbyterian circles. Perhaps most importantly of all, a growing charismatic movement began to develop within the Roman Catholic Church. Using the term 'Pentecostal' to describe this now became problematic, as this term was used to refer to a family of churches – such as the Assemblies of God – which placed particular emphasis on 'speaking in tongues'. Accordingly, the term 'charismatic' was used to refer to movements within the mainline churches based upon the ideas and experiences of the Pentecostalist movement. Charismatic renewal within the mainline churches has led to new and informal worship styles, an explosion in 'worship songs', a new concern for the dynamics of worship, and an increasing dislike of the traditionalism of formal liturgical worship.

The charismatic movement is now one of the most significant elements of twenty-first century Christianity. It is now estimated that there are 500 million Pentecostalists and other charismatics in the world, with a very wide geographical distribution. Although the movement may be argued to have its origins primarily within African-American culture, it has taken root in South America, Asia, Africa and Europe. It is clear that the movement is here to stay, and is likely to be a major force in shaping Christianity in the emerging and developing world in the future.

is to build up the body of Christ so that believers may come to the fullness of the perfection which God wants for his saints. That is a tall order and it will never be perfectly realized in this life, but the Bible makes it clear about what that perfection must be based on. It is rooted and grounded in a series of characteristics which are known collectively as 'the fruits of the Spirit' (Galatians 5:22–23). The first and greatest of these fruits is love. So important is this that without it, whatever Christians do is a complete waste of time (1 Corinthians 13:1). The other fruits (joy, peace, patience, and so on) are also universal qualities which every Christian is expected to manifest. In addition to these are the special gifts of the Spirit, which are listed in 1 Corinthians 12 and in a shorter form in Romans 12:6–8. Paul tells believers that they are all given different spiritual gifts, according to the grace of God at work in them, and their responsibility is to use these gifts in the most appropriate way. To some extent there is a hierarchy of gifts, with the apostles coming first and speakers in tongues bringing up the rear (1 Corinthians 12:28), but too much should not be made of this. The context was one in which too many people wanted to speak in tongues and were disturbing the good order of the congregation, so Paul does his best to put that in the proper context and encourage his readers to seek the 'higher gifts'. However, the overall thrust of the passage suggests that every gift has its place and must be recognized as coming from God; nobody has the right to despise a fellow Christian on the grounds that he or she has received a lesser gift of the Spirit.

The fruits and gifts given to individuals are important, but they must be placed in the context of the Holy Spirit's wider purpose, which is to edify the church as a whole (1 Corinthians 14). If a particular gift is not particularly useful at any given time, then it should not be used. In other words, Christian believers have the power to control the use of their gifts; there is no suggestion that a speaker in tongues or a prophet is someone 'possessed' by the Holy Spirit. The needs of the church are paramount, and it is here that the major differences between most forms of Protestantism and Roman Catholicism appear most clearly. The Roman Catholic Church tends to believe that the Holy Spirit works primarily through the ministers and sacraments of the visible church community. At the head of that community is the bishop of Rome (the pope) whose authority descends from the apostle Peter and who is regarded as infallible when speaking officially about matters of faith and doctrine. The Spirit empowers the ministers of the church (bishops and priests) to perform the sacraments, which also take effect when they are properly administered. Thus, a person who has been baptized is a Christian whether he or she has professed faith or not, and if that person shows no subsequent sign of spiritual life he or she will probably be regarded as a 'lapsed Catholic' rather than as a non-believer.

Most forms of Protestantism place much less emphasis than Roman Catholics do on the church's official ministers or on visible signs like the sacraments, even though they usually make good use of them. Protestants tend to believe that the Holy Spirit works primarily in the heart through faith, so that it is impossible to become a Christian merely by being baptized. The ritual itself can do nothing without the presence of faith in the heart of the recipient, and unless there are signs of such faith, most Protestants would be reluctant to accept that a person who has merely

'I love to think of nature as an unlimited broadcasting station, through which God speaks to us every hour, if we will only tune in.'

George Washington Carver

Charismatic worship can be very enthusiastic and experiential.

gone through the official motions can reasonably be called a Christian. The key element here is the work of the Holy Spirit in the heart and mind of the believer. As Paul put it in Romans 8:16: 'The Spirit himself testifies with our spirit that we are God's children.' Without this spiritual concordance between God and the believer, there can be no faith, and without faith there can be no true church of God. It is true that Protestants differ among themselves about what can be considered 'faith' and about when and to whom the sacraments should be given, but on the necessity of heartfelt faith they are generally agreed. It is not by external acts performed by the church but by an internal work of God's Spirit leading to conversion and a changed life that a person truly comes to faith in Christ.

All Christians agree that the Holy Spirit inspired the texts which we now call the Bible (2 Peter 1:21) and believe that they were given to the church for the purposes of teaching, discipline and edification (2 Timothy 3:16). But Eastern Orthodox Christians see the Bible as part of a wider tradition which includes a number of unwritten beliefs, and

Roman Catholics agree that there is a body of traditional beliefs and practices which shares equal authority with the Bible when it comes to deciding matters of faith and morals. Roman Catholics also believe that the papacy has been given to the church in order to continue the work of divine revelation when doubtful matters arise. This has led to the proclamation of the bodily assumption of Mary the mother of Christ into heaven, as well as to the declaration that she was born without original sin, both of which are required beliefs in the Roman Catholic Church but are either unknown to, or denied by other Christians. Protestants believe that the church continues to be guided by the Holy Spirit, but they rely on a consensus of biblical interpretation when it comes to deciding what the Spirit is actually saying to the church, and they refuse to accept any doctrine which is not based on the clear teaching of the Bible.

Matters are further complicated because some Christians also believe that the Holy Spirit speaks to the church through the great social and political issues of our time. Thus there have been many theologians who have said that Marxism was a work of the Spirit, despite its antagonism to traditional Christian beliefs. More recently, much the same thing has been said about changing patterns of human sexual behaviour, which some people believe the church must adopt even though the Bible points in a very different direction. A more moderate view is that God may indeed be speaking to the church through these things, but that his message may not be one of simple approval for whatever the spirit of the age is suggesting. On the contrary, it may be a wake-up call to the church which is in constant need of challenges to its faith, partly to avoid an unwarranted complacency and partly to help Christians clarify matters which might otherwise remain obscure (1 Corinthians 11:19). That view would appear to be more in line with what the Bible teaches, and it gives Christians both a mandate to be involved in the social and political concerns of the day without being submerged by them in the process.

Whatever their differences on this important subject, all Christians are united in affirming that the primary work of the Holy Spirit is to bring glory to God in Christ. In other words, it is Trinitarian in conception and in fulfilment. The ultimate touchstone of whether something is of the Spirit or not must be this – does it further the cause of Christ or not? Remarkably enough, even divisions and hostility among Christians may be used as vehicles of the Spirit's work, despite the less than ideal circumstances. That was the case, for example, when Paul wrote to the Philippians, pointing out that there were many preachers of the gospel whose motives were unworthy, but that as long as Christ was preached it did not matter all that much (Philippians 1:15–18). Paul was not

really tolerant of strife and division in the church, but he recognized that the work of the Holy Spirit could not be thwarted by the evil intentions of mere human beings.

Models of the Trinity

Having considered each of the divine persons individually, we must now look at how they come together in the Trinity. We have already seen that it is best to regard the work of God in the Old Testament as a Trinitarian one, even though the distinctions of the three persons were not fully revealed at that time. Some Christians have claimed that the Old Testament does in fact reveal the existence of the Trinity in God, but the evidence which they offer to support this assertion is ambiguous and must be treated with the greatest caution. For example, when God says: 'Let us make man in our image' (Genesis 1:26), there have been those who have understood this as the Father talking to the Son and the Holy Spirit, and they have even gone to the point of trying to find Trinitarian elements in the image itself. The great proponent of this way of thinking was undoubtedly Augustine of Hippo (354–430), one of the greatest theologians of the western church whose fifteen books on the Trinity remain a classic exposition of the subject. Augustine believed that it was possible to look at the human mind and find in it three dimensions (memory, intellect and will), which could be compared to the Trinity in God.

Just as the three aspects of the mind are different but need each other to be able to function, so Augustine claimed that the Father, Son and Holy Spirit were also different but could not function without each other. He even took the word 'conception' and pointed out that it has two meanings – one physical and the other mental. To say that the Father conceived (and gave birth to) the Son is to use a physical term for what is really a mental process, and if it is understood in this way, there will be no problem in understanding why the Son's generation must be eternal. The mind cannot exist without some thought,

The Holy Trinity by Mariotto Albertinelli. Artists have often attempted to convey the mystery of the Trinity through their work.

and in the perfect mind the thought will also be perfect. But if the perfect mind contemplates the perfect thought, then that thought must correspond to the original perfection of the mind and be equal to it. Hence, for Augustine, the Father and the Son are co-equal and co-eternal of necessity, since otherwise the divine

mind could not be itself. Augustine's speculations are the work of a genius and they have continued to find admirers and followers over the centuries, but speculations are what they remain and it is hazardous to claim that they are the teaching of Scripture as such. To be fair to their author, Augustine himself understood this and warned his readers not to confuse his theories with what the Bible specifically reveals about the mind of God.

A helpful way of thinking about the Trinity is found in the Old Testament text describing the appearance of the three men or angels to Abraham and Sarah at the oak trees of Mamre (Genesis 18:1–15). In this story, Abraham greeted the three men in the singular, apparently calling them all 'Lord', a curiosity which was noticed by the Jewish commentator Philo of Alexandria (died AD 50). Philo, who knew nothing of Christianity, nevertheless speculated that here we have a revelation of God as a trinity – three distinct beings who could nevertheless be addressed in the singular. Philo was not trying to prove the divinity of Christ, but probably something quite different. It was the belief of many ancients that three was the perfect number, and for Philo, a perfect God had to manifest this perfection somewhere in his being. The appearance of these heavenly beings suited his purposes ideally, and he interpreted it as an epiphany of God himself. The New Testament makes no mention of this, but it appealed to a number of Greek theologians in the early church, who took it up and called it the Old Testament Trinity. Nowadays, this belief is less common in theological circles, but it can still be found in the iconic tradition of eastern Christian art, where the Old Testament Trinity has been a standard theme for many centuries.

Less serious from the theological

point of view, but still well known and sometimes quoted, is the belief that the words 'Holy, holy, holy, Lord of Hosts', which the prophet Isaiah heard when he had a vision of God in the Temple (Isaiah 6:3), are an indication of the Trinity because the word 'holy' is repeated three times. This verse was sometimes quoted in the early church as a way of proving the absolute equality of the three divine persons and of explaining how each of them could manifest the fullness of the Godhead (holiness) without detracting from the other persons. In modern times, it has become famous thanks to Reginald Heber's hymn 'Holy, holy, holy', which sets this theory to music. However, it must be said that it is now well known that the ancient Hebrews used repetition to signify greatness or intensity, and no theologian today would use this verse as evidence of the existence of a Trinity of persons in God.

The main objection to such theories is that they read back into the Old Testament something which was only revealed by the coming of Christ. Nobody in New Testament times thought to refer to such passages as proofs of the Trinity, despite their apparent convenience for such a purpose. Jews (with the possible exception of Philo) have never read the texts that way, and reject such interpretations as invalid. Even Christians have to admit that they are not always very satisfactory; for example, when God speaks in the plural ('let us make') there is nothing to indicate that there were three – and only three – divine persons doing the talking. There could have been many more, or perhaps only two! The conclusion must be that to read the Old Testament in this way is to impose on it a doctrine which can only be known from the New Testament revelation, and which therefore cannot

be determinative of its interpretation. Augustine and Philo may have been right, but we cannot be sure about this, and it is better not to place too much reliance on theories which are ingenious but not entirely convincing.

More promising than any of the above are some passages in the Psalms where it appears that the king is referred to as 'god'. In Psalm 45:6–7, for example, it seems that God has raised the king up and given him a throne which will last forever and ever. In Psalm 110:1, we find that the Lord says to 'my lord': 'Sit at my right hand until I make your enemies a footstool

for your feet.' In both these cases it appears that the king is somehow being elevated to the status of God himself. It was usual in the pagan cultures of the ancient Near East to do this kind of thing, and it is possible that the Hebrew psalmist derived this picture from there, but the imagery does not fit the strict monotheism of

Andrei Rublev's painting of the three angels who visited Abraham is often interpreted as an icon of the Trinity.

How Muslims See the Trinity

The three great monotheistic faiths of the world – Judaism, Christianity and Islam – share a belief that there is only one supreme being, the Lord and creator of the universe. 'Hear, O Israel, the Lord our God is one Lord' (Deuteronomy 6:4). Islamic critics of Christianity regularly criticize Christians, however, for deviating from this emphasis upon the unity of God (often referred to by the Arabic word *tawhid*) through the doctrine of the Trinity. This doctrine is argued to be a late invention, that distorts the idea of the unity of God, and ends up teaching that there are three gods. The teaching of the Qur'an on what Christians believe is not quite as clear as might be hoped for, and has led some Christian interpreters of Islam to suggest that it believes that Christians worship a Trinity consisting of God, Jesus and Mary (*The Qur'an*, 5:116). Although there are reasons for suspecting that Mohammed may have encountered heterodox forms of Christian belief in Arabia, including unorthodox statements of the Trinity, it seems more likely that the doctrine has simply been misunderstood as implying that Christians either worship three gods, or that they worship a single God with three component parts.

The Christian doctrine of the Trinity is rigorously grounded both in the Bible and in reflection on its implications. Historically, the starting point for Christian reflection on the doctrine of God has been the divinity of Christ – something that Islam rejects. For Christians, God is known fully and directly through Christ. Where Islam holds that one may know the will of God but not the face of God, Christianity holds that both have been fully and definitively revealed in Jesus Christ. Mohammed is seen as one who wrote down the revelation entrusted to him by the angel Gabriel; Jesus is one who was himself the definitive revelation of God. As God incarnate, Jesus reveals God and makes restoration to him possible through his saving death and resurrection. Underlying the Islamic criticism of the doctrine of the Trinity is a more fundamental concern about the identity of Jesus Christ himself. For Islam, Jesus is a prophet – and not God incarnate.

Having established the divinity of Christ, Christian theology then asks: 'What sort of God makes himself known and available in this way?' In other words, how are we to think about God, to do justice to the biblical revelation of God as the one who created us and the world, who redeemed us in Jesus Christ, and is present now in the world through the Holy Spirit? The doctrine of the Trinity has never been seen as compromising or contradicting the unity of God. Christians believe in one God, and one God only – but a God whose revelation discloses him to have a certain specific character and nature, which they must faithfully reflect in their teaching about him. Far from teaching that there are three gods – whether God, Jesus and Mary, or any others – Christianity proclaims that there is only one God, who became incarnate in Christ.

The Trinity, to put it as simply as possible, is simply the summary of the Bible's immensely rich teaching about the nature of God. Christians have always seen it as being more important to do justice to God than to produce a doctrine of God that may be easy to understand, yet in the end fails to do justice to God as they know him in Christ.

Israel. Furthermore, in the New Testament, the writer to the Hebrews picks up these verses and applies them to Jesus Christ, which shows us that the identification of the king with God was intended to be a prophetic revelation of him. Even so, we must be careful about pressing such texts too far. Jesus was the divine son of David, the one who fulfilled the Old Testament promises made to that king about the survival of his dynasty, and it is natural to see this assimilation of the Israelite kingship with God in his person. But although this chimes in very well with the idea that there is a Trinity of three persons in the Godhead, it does not prove this any more than other such passages from the Old Testament do. What we have here are hints and figures which are brought out in the New Testament and shown to refer to the Son of God in his Trinitarian glory, not proofs which would lead us to establish such a doctrine independently of the revelation which has come to us in Christ.

In the end, Christians have generally recognized that they must find their models for understanding the Trinity in the New Testament, not in the Old, because it is in the New Testament that this great mystery has been clearly revealed. This revelation comes to them in two ways. First of all, as we have already seen, the New Testament speaks clearly about the persons of the Father, the Son and the Holy Spirit, indicating that all three are God. But the New Testament also says that there is only one God, which means that the task of the Christian theologian is to explain how the three divine persons can be accommodated within that fundamental unity. All theories which would make one of the persons more fully God than the other two must be rejected because they deny the basic principle that each of the persons is fully God in himself. A trio of God plus two inferior divine beings would not be

a Trinity, but something else altogether, and the doctrine would not exist if that were the case. There are however more subtle ways in which the persons of the Trinity can be subordinated to, or even subsumed in, the divine unity, and we must consider them briefly before looking at how the tri-unity of the Godhead can be expressed adequately.

One of the most subtle errors is to think that the words 'Father', 'Son' and 'Holy Spirit' are simply different names for the same being, with no real distinction between them. According to the context, God may appear to us as a father, or as a son, or as a holy spirit. He is a father when he stands over us in judgment, a son when he stands alongside us in sympathy and a holy spirit when he dwells inside us as a comforter and defender against evil. In other words, the names attached to God depend on whatever function it is that he is performing at the time. They do not in any way affect his being, which remains one and indivisible.

The main difficulty with this idea is that it does not do justice to the many New Testament passages where Jesus distinguishes quite clearly between himself and the Father. Perhaps the clearest of these is in John 17, where Jesus prays to the Father on behalf of his disciples, and makes it quite clear that the Father has a responsibility for them which is distinct from (though analogous to) his own. Failure to distinguish the persons adequately also makes a nonsense of what Jesus has to say in John 14–16 about the coming of the Holy Spirit. Why should he tell his disciples that he must go away before the Spirit can come, and that the Spirit will do greater things than he has done, if in fact the Spirit and the Son are one and the same? To believe that is actually harder than to believe in a divine Trinity, which appears simple and logical by comparison.

Another subtle error, closely related to the previous one, is to tie the

> 'Holiness is doing God's will with a smile.'
>
> Mother Teresa of Calcutta

persons of the Trinity to the ages of salvation history. In such a scheme of things, the Father would be the God of the Old Testament, the Son the God of the Gospels and the Holy Spirit the God of the church since Pentecost. Ideas like this one floated about in the early church but they were eventually discredited because, like the functionalist scheme outlined above, they make it impossible to account for the relationships which we observe within the Godhead. The Son could hardly converse with the Father if the latter had only existed in an earlier dispensation!

Viable models of the Trinity cannot be limited to divine functions or to periods in the history of revelation, but must explain the mutual relations of the persons within the Godhead, which are simultaneous and which encompass all the divine activities. The most common way of doing this has been to start with one of the persons and develop the Trinitarian framework by explaining how he is related to the other two. Not surprisingly, the earliest attempt to do this took the Father as the link person in the Godhead and connected both the Son and the Holy Spirit to him, and it is this model which is dominant in the Eastern Orthodox churches. This was done by saying that the other two persons were related to the Father as effects are related to their cause. According to the testimony of John's Gospel, the Son is begotten (John 1:14) and the Holy Spirit proceeds from the Father (John 15:26). These two distinct relationships of 'causation' were then held to define the distinct identities of the second and the third persons, and by negation, of the first person as well, since he was both unbegotten and non-proceeding. This model of the Trinity has the advantage of appearing to be very close to the New Testament, where the Father is often referred to as God in an undifferentiated sense, and no one can deny what the fourth Gospel (John) says about the other two. But it also has significant weaknesses which must be taken into consideration before adopting it uncritically as the best model of the Trinity available.

The first weakness is that the notion of 'cause' inevitably suggests that the Father is somehow superior to the Son and the Spirit, and this in turn raises fears that this model hides a latent Arianism (see page 160). Theologians who have considered the two causations have always maintained that they are different from one another, so that the Holy Spirit cannot be regarded as the Son's twin brother; but they have never been able to agree about how the Son and the Holy Spirit are related to each other. Some have thought that the Spirit proceeds from the Father through the Son, a solution to the problem which preserves the

The Baptism of Jesus by Joachim Paternier. It was at his baptism that Jesus openly received the Father's gift of the Spirit's unlimited power.

Karl Barth, Swiss theologian, regarded by many as a modern day 'Church Father'.

ancient sense that there is a hierarchy of persons in the Trinity, but others have claimed that the baptism of Jesus gives us the best clue about this. According to them, when Jesus was baptized, the Holy Spirit descended on him like a dove (Matthew 3:16). This is supposed to be a manifestation of the eternal relationship which exists between the two persons. The Holy Spirit proceeds from the Father and rests on the Son, acting as his illumination and glory. Only by experiencing the Spirit is it possible to see the glorified Christ, and it is in his glorified state (that is, through the Spirit) that Christ now acts in the world. Neither of these theories has ever received official acceptance, however, and the question of the precise relationship of the Holy Spirit to the Son remains unresolved.

A second model, which has generally been associated with the western churches, sees the Holy Spirit as the link person in the Godhead. According to this model, God is a God of love (1 John 4:16) and love requires both a lover and a beloved. Jesus Christ is the beloved Son (another echo of his baptism) and the Father is the one who loves him. But the love of the Father for the Son and of the Son for the Father acquires an identity of its own, which is the Holy Spirit, the bond of unity between the other two persons. It is the Holy Spirit who dwells in our hearts by faith, and when he comes into our lives, the Father and the Son come with him (John 14:23). He bears witness equally to the other two, and for this reason must proceed from them both in equal measure, since otherwise there would be an imbalance in God's love. This model of the Trinity resolves the problem of how the Son and the Holy Spirit are related to each other, but it creates another difficulty which is not hard to spot. The personhood of the Father and the Son are both

clearly preserved, but to all appearances the Holy Spirit is reduced to an impersonal force – a thing, rather than a person. Various stratagems have been employed as ways around this difficulty, but they cannot be said to have been very successful, and it must be admitted that the creation of a depersonalized Holy Spirit is a very real danger when this model is uncritically adopted.

A third model, which did not appear in the early church but which seems to have been proposed for the first time by Karl Barth (1886–1968), puts the Son at the centre of the Trinity and explains the Father and the Spirit in relation to him. Barth starts from the revelation of God in Christ, which is undoubtedly the main theme of the New Testament, and argues that everything we know about the Father and about the Spirit we know because of his teaching. In other words, it is in and through the Son that the other persons are revealed to us, and it is only with reference to him that they can be understood. Barth's view has great appeal if we start with the teaching of Jesus, but it also has the defect that Jesus revealed that the Father was greater than he was (John 14:28) and that it was the Father who would in due course send the Holy Spirit. To follow Barth's model to its logical conclusion therefore is to overturn it, because it becomes clear as we sift the New Testament data that Jesus is revealing a structure of divine relationships in which he plays a vital but not a commanding role.

The truth seems to be that the inner relations of the persons of the Trinity are too subtle to be reduced to any model which takes only one of them as the link person and tries to explain the others in the light of that. What we have to do is remember that all three persons establish their own identities within the Godhead, and therefore establish the Trinity of personal relations. No one of them can claim precedence over the others, and no one of them is subordinated to the others. Each of the models outlined above helps us to see some aspect of this, but none is able to explain the whole, because God remains in essence a mystery which we can observe but never fathom. That is the measure of his greatness, and a reminder that Christians can do no more than fall down and worship the one who is their Lord, Saviour and their God.

3

Jesus

PETER WALKER

'Christianity *IS* Christ.' This pithy statement, that emphasizes the centrality of Jesus within Christian belief, contains a key insight. There never has been, nor could there be, any version of Christianity that did not give a key role to the person of Jesus Christ. He stands at the heart of the faith. He is its indispensable centre. Take away Jesus and you are left with nothing that deserves the name 'Christian'.

Why is this? After all, in some other faiths or world-views we could imagine the 'movement' continuing to be a powerful force within the world even if we suddenly discover that the original 'founder' of the movement may never have existed. For what counts in these movements is the *teaching* associated with the founder – the ideas that he or she is thought to have fostered. But if Jesus never existed, the Christian faith immediately falls apart.

THE IDENTITY OF JESUS

The existence of Jesus is crucial because the teachings *of* Jesus contain so much *about* Jesus. We cannot separate out those things that he said about other matters (for example, about God and faith, about good and evil) from those things he said about himself. In a subtle way (see page 145), Jesus made his own person integral and essential to all his teaching and ministry. For example, he spoke much about the 'kingdom of God', but gave ample hints that he saw himself as its king. So we cannot love his preaching without also dealing

> 'He is the image of the invisible God, the firstborn over all creation. For by him all things were created: things in heaven and on earth, visible and invisible, whether thrones or powers or rulers or authorities; all things were created by him and for him.'
>
> Paul (Colossians 1:15)

squarely with his person. Sooner or later we are faced with the same question that he so pointedly asked his followers, 'who do *you* say that I am?' (Mark 8:29).

Or, to put it another way, Christian faith has always involved not just emulating the faith *of* Jesus, but also exercising faith *in* Jesus.

In other words, within the essence of Christian belief, Jesus is far more than just a religious teacher or a great example. He is both these things, but also much, much more. For example, according to the New Testament, he did not just speak about God, he actually in some way brings God to humanity – he did not just show us the way to God, he himself is the Way. Or again, he did not just speak the word of God, he himself is the ultimate Word from God – he said what was true, but in his own person he embodies the Truth. Perhaps above all, he did not just talk about spiritual life, he is the very source of that Life.

These may seem absurd claims, but they are an essential part of the Christian faith examined in this book. So we would do well to be aware of them at the very outset. Whenever people look seriously at the life of Jesus, the 'stakes are high' – higher than many of us might hope. Yes, there have of course been many who have tried to lower the stakes, to suggest that you can be a 'Christian' without accepting these high claims for Jesus himself. Yet no 'Christian' denomination or church has publicly renounced these high claims for Jesus and then successfully built itself on these lower foundations.

ROOTED IN HISTORY
Christianity, then, is rooted in the person of Jesus. *His* identity is fundamental to *its* identity. This also means that Christianity is rooted in history, because it is necessarily rooted in *his story* – the real-life story of Jesus. Again, we cannot separate out the ideas of Jesus from the concrete events of his life. Jesus' purpose was not just to speak, but also to act; he came not just to impart a few truths but truly to bring about and effect something extraordinary in the real world of space and time.

In particular, the events associated with his last days in Jerusalem are vital. Why did he die? And is it true that he was raised by God from the dead three days later? The earliest Christianity that we know asserts that Jesus' death and resurrection are essential to the message and are of 'first importance' (1 Corinthians 15:3). So, if we are going to understand the Christian faith, we are going to be faced very soon with questions about history. Again, Christianity cannot be reduced to a set of ideas – it is rooted in the identity and the story of Jesus. Who was he? And what actually happened?

Perhaps the best place to start looking for some answers is with two key introductory issues:

1. If the story of Jesus is rooted in history, then what are the documents that take us back into that history? Are they themselves reliable historically?

2. How does the story of Jesus fit into that which went before? We must briefly set Jesus within his own historical context (that of first-century Judaism) and ask: how does the story of Jesus fit into the longer storyline of the Bible as a whole?

New Testament Accounts of Jesus

THE 'GOSPELS' AS GOOD NEWS
The New Testament is a collection of 27 short books written by Jesus' first followers in the second half of the first century AD. These writings complement those of the Old Testament but describe how God's purposes towards humanity were taken forward through Jesus into the era of a new covenant. (A covenant is a solemn and binding agreement like a 'last will and testament'.) Hence the title later given to these books – the 'New Testament'.

Amongst these 27 books there are broadly four different types of literature. A substantial part is made up of letters (or 'epistles') written to the young churches around the Mediterranean (many of these are by Paul, but there are also a few by Peter, James, John and others). There is an account of the early church's history (the book of Acts). There is also an extended prophecy or 'apocalypse' (the book of Revelation), which uses colourful imagery to 'unveil' or reveal the spiritual realities that lie behind and beyond this present world. But, at the very beginning of the New Testament are the 'Gospels' – four accounts of the life of Jesus (by Matthew, Mark, Luke and John). These four books are our chief sources for the story of Jesus.

But what exactly is a gospel? The word 'gospel' is derived from Anglo-Saxon and simply means 'good news'. It reflects the opening sentence (or title) of Mark's account: 'The beginning of the *good news* about Jesus Christ, the Son of God' (Mark 1:1). Mark's Greek word for 'good news' (*euangelion*) had itself been used before in translations of the Old Testament: 'how beautiful... are the feet of those who bring *good news*, ...who proclaim salvation, who say to Zion, "Your God reigns"' (Isaiah 52:7).

The Birth of Jesus in Christian Art

The 'nativity' – that is, the birth – of Christ has long played a central role in Christian iconography. Christians have always appreciated the theological and spiritual importance of the birth of the saviour, and have found picturing this event to be helpful to personal and corporate devotion. The incarnation declares that God, the creator of the world, chose to redeem it by entering it in the form of a human being. God descends into this sinful world, so that he might raise us up to the heavenly places. The more Christians are reassured that God really did enter into our history in this way, the more they can be reassured that they shall be raised up into those heavenly places in which the Christ-child now reigns in glory.

Sandro Botticelli's *Mystic Nativity* (c.1500) was painted for his own private devotions.

In the West, the dominant approach to depicting the nativity is to set Mary and her child at the centre of the picture. An excellent example of this approach can be found in *The Mystic Nativity* by Sandro Botticelli (1447–1515). In this work, executed around the year 1500, Mary is depicted in terms appropriate to the era of the painter, rather than the New Testament. Botticelli here follows other Renaissance painters of the fourteenth and fifteenth centuries, who portrayed Mary dressed as a noblewoman of their time. The point being made is that Christ's entry into history is of importance to all ages, not simply the Palestine of the first century. Representing Mary as a lady of the Renaissance was a means of emphasizing the transformative potential of the Christ-child for the Renaissance, as well as for all ages.

Botticelli follows a long-standing tradition in including an ox and ass in the nativity scene. Yet a quick reading of the gospel nativity accounts soon discloses that no mention is made of either animal. So why are these traditionally included in the scene? From the second century onwards, commentators on the birth of Christ linked the scene with Isaiah 1:3, which speaks of the ox and the ass knowing their true master and his crib. It seems that this prophetic passage was then linked with the birth of Christ, thus reminding us that the whole of the created order is involved in the birth of Christ, and the new creation which will result from his incarnation, death and resurrection. Botticelli follows this tradition, and portrays the angels in heaven as rejoicing over the transformation of the created order that will take place through Christ. Indeed, in the lower section of the painting, angels are even depicted as dancing with humans, as they celebrate the possibility of a new heaven and a new earth.

Rembrandt van Rijn's *Adoration of the Shepherds* (1646).

In some cases, the themes of Christmas and Epiphany are merged. For example, in Rembrandt's *Adoration of the Shepherds*, we see the first visitors to the newborn king – the shepherds from the fields around Bethlehem, together with some of their sheep. These are sometimes joined by the three 'wise men' or kings from the East, who brought the newborn child the exotic and costly gifts of gold, frankincense, and myrrh. Traditionally, it is assumed that each 'wise man' brought one of the three gifts; the Gospels do not tell us how many 'wise men' actually came.

This means that the gospel writers (or 'evangelists', that is, announcers of the *euangelion*) were concerned not only to relate the story of Jesus as a matter of history but also to show how this story was indeed good news – indeed the best news in the world. In the imagery of Isaiah they could well have seen themselves as heralds announcing the news of victory, the fulfilment of hopes, the offer of safety and peace, and the arrival of a king.

The gospels are therefore a unique genre (or kind of literature). They are not seeking to be comprehensive biographies (in the modern sense). For example, they do not describe what Jesus looked like nor give many details of his family background and upbringing; in fact they skip over the majority of his life and give a disproportionate focus to the days leading up to his death. Instead, they are clearly selective, highlighting those things which show how the coming of Jesus is good news. At the same time, however, precisely because (as we have seen) this good news of Jesus is not good news if it is not true and rooted in real history, they are still clearly concerned to offer as accurate an account as possible. This is history, they claim, but more than mere history – this is a message with a meaning. They have been selective in order to make the good news as clear as possible to as many as possible.

FOUR DIFFERENT ACCOUNTS

But why do we have four accounts, rather than just one? The initial answer from history must simply be that four different writers felt the need to give an account of Jesus' life and teaching and that, when the four of them began to circulate, the early church decided that this was no problem. In fact around AD 160 someone called Tatian did try, without much success, to condense them into just one account. It became evident, however, that each gospel had an important contribution to make, giving us a different (but equally valid) perspective on Jesus. Perhaps after all, this unique historical character was a little 'larger than life' – certainly more than could be conveyed in just *one* account.

Some commentators (for example, Irenaeus, about AD 190) thus defended the four gospels by comparing them with the 'four corners of the earth' (the number four signified the universe in some biblical thought) or even the four animal-figures found in Revelation 4:7 (ox, lion, man and eagle). To the modern mind, these may appear somewhat fanciful, but they do reflect a feeling, certainly not unique to the period, that there is something very appropriate about the fourfold nature of the gospels.

INTRODUCING THE GOSPELS

It will be useful to note the different perspective each has on the story of Jesus. The first three are commonly know as the 'synoptic' gospels, because they 'view things together' from very similar perspectives.

A page from a rare Dzruchi Gospel depicts Mark, author of what many consider to be the earliest Gospel.

The Parables of Jesus

Jesus taught 'many things in parables' (Mark 4:2) These parables – earthly stories with heavenly meanings – are usually simple word-pictures drawn from everyday life, with the capacity to illuminate the good news of the coming of the kingdom. These stories challenged Jesus' audiences to rethink and rediscover the nature of God, and the promised kingdom. Many of them begin with the words 'the kingdom of God is like…', followed by a description of an event, a natural phenomenon, or a story. The unknown is thus presented in terms of the known, the new in terms of the familiar.

Most of the parables draw on the everyday experience of people in rural Palestine – for example, sowing seeds, fig trees that bear no fruit, lost animals, burst wineskins, hiring workers, and wedding parties. They relate immediately and naturally to their audiences. The parables often involve an element of surprise, an unexpected twist in a story, or a shrewd observation. Just as in order to own a pearl of great value it is worth selling lesser possessions, so it is worth giving up everything for the kingdom of God (Matthew 13:45–46). Just as a small amount of yeast can raise a large amount of dough, so the kingdom of God, though small, can exercise its influence throughout the world (Matthew 13:33). Just as a shepherd will go out and look for a sheep that has got lost, so God will seek out those who have wandered away (Luke 15:4–6).

Sometimes, the parables are more complex. The Parable of the Prodigal Son (Luke 15:11–32) is an example of this more developed type of parable, particularly associated with Luke's Gospel. It tells of a son who decides to leave his father's home and seek his fortune in a distant land, only to realize that this new life turns out not to be as rosy as he had expected. He longs to return home to his father, but is convinced that his father will have disowned him and will no longer wish to acknowledge him as his son. The parable is clearly intended to be interpreted along the following lines. The father represents God; the son represents those who have sinned, or turned their backs on God. The message of the parable is therefore simple: just as the father was overjoyed at the return of his son, so God will be overjoyed at the return of sinners.

Yet the meaning of parables is often far from straightforward. The word 'parable' draws on an older Hebrew word meaning 'riddle' or 'dark saying'. At several points, Jesus indicates that parables are capable of concealing truth, as much as revealing it. When speaking to his disciples about his use of parables, Jesus tells them that only some will be able to discern their true meaning. 'To you it has been given to know the secrets of the kingdom of God; but to others I speak in parables, so that "looking they may not perceive and hearing they may not understand." ' (Luke 8:10). Those whose minds are closed to the values and ideals of the coming kingdom cannot grasp the meaning of the parables about that kingdom.

The 'synoptic' gospels

Many consider the Gospel of Mark to be the earliest of the four. It is certainly the shortest, written in the roughest Greek, and with a great sense of urgency. It does not refer at all to Jesus' birth or childhood but starts with the ministry of John the Baptist. In describing Jesus' own public ministry Mark immediately focuses on Jesus' teaching authority (1:22) and his astonishing power over disease, nature, sin and even death itself (1:21–2:12; 4:35–5:43). Some stories he tells in quite some detail, with vivid description and characterization. After a mid-point climax, when Peter, the leader of Jesus' disciples, declares that Jesus is the Messiah (8:27–30), Jesus repeatedly teaches about the necessity of his coming death. So the final half of the Gospel focuses on Jesus' last journey to Jerusalem and his suffering

A representation of Matthew from *The Book of Kells,* c.800. Matthew wrote from a Jewish perspective, urging his own nation to find Jesus as their Messiah.

there (the 'way of the Cross' and the 'Passion narrative'). Mark concludes with a brief account of Jesus' resurrection which seems to have been interrupted in mid-sentence.

Almost certainly it was written by John Mark, a man who had lived in Jerusalem (see Acts 12:12) and had perhaps been in the garden of Gethsemane when Jesus was arrested (14:51). He writes the Gospel in Rome about thirty years later (about AD 65), probably putting on paper some of the personal memories of Peter (see 1 Peter 5.13). The fact that Christians in Rome were being persecuted around this time (Peter was martyred in Rome a few years later) may well explain its urgent tone, its focus on Jesus' suffering and its abrupt ending. In any event, Mark writes with great passion to encourage believers to hold on to their faith in Jesus.

Throughout his account Mark is appealing urgently to individuals. He wants them to respond to this unique Jesus, the Messiah (see page 134) and Suffering Servant (8:29; 10:45); to join in their own personal declaration that Jesus is truly the 'Son of God' (1:1; 15:39); and to follow Jesus, taking up their cross too in the service of him who suffered for them (8:34–38). It is an urgent call to discipleship.

The Gospel of Matthew is much longer and is written in a tighter, more condensed style. It is masterpiece of organization, using Mark's outline (with its single journey to Jerusalem) and much of his material, but drawing on other sources too. Compared with Mark, he includes much more of Jesus' actual teaching (conveyed in five long teaching-blocks, perhaps echoing the first five books of Moses in the Old Testament). Here we find Jesus' teaching about the 'kingdom of heaven' and many of his sternest warnings to the people of his day.

For Matthew, Jesus' coming must be understood in the light of God's previous relationship with the nation of Israel. Thus many events in Jesus' life are shown to fulfil Old Testament prophecies. We hear Jesus being given more Jewish titles ('Son of David', 'Immanuel' or 'God with us': 1:1; 1:23) and see him portrayed as the truly faithful Israelite (2:15; 4:1–11). Because he is tragically being rejected by his own people, Jesus warns Israel of a judgment to come (23:35–36), but also hints that non-Jews will soon be gathered into his kingdom (21:43). This good news will go out to 'all nations' (28:19), whilst some of 'those who should be in the kingdom will be thrown into the darkness, where they will cry and grind their teeth' (8:12).

Matthew is writing from a consciously Jewish perspective, as a 'teacher' to his own nation (13:52; 23:34), urging them to find in Jesus their true Messiah. Quite possibly he had lived in Jerusalem but had recently fled to Syria (4:24) at the time of the Roman siege upon Jerusalem (see Jesus' warnings in 24:4–25). If so, he may be writing just after the fall of Jerusalem (AD 70), keenly aware of the tragedy that has overtaken his own people. He knows that he (like Jesus) may himself be rejected for his message, but writes to encourage Christians (Jewish believers, but probably Gentiles too) to hold onto their faith. He wants them to see themselves as the true remnant within Israel and to ensure they do not make the same mistakes as did his own nation. No, they must fulfil the new Law introduced by Jesus, obeying all his teaching and doing good in his name (28:19; 5:20; 7:15–23). For if you disobey Jesus, your house will be like one built on sand (7:24–27). This Gospel is an urgent plea to Israel and all people to note what God has done in sending Jesus, the true Messiah.

Luke's Gospel has a quite different

A twelfth-century representation of Luke. His Gospel shows both Jesus' humanity and his role as the Saviour of all.

feel. Luke is the only New Testament writer who is not Jewish but a 'Gentile'. He had been a companion to Paul (the 'apostle to the Gentiles') and possibly researched his Gospel whilst Paul was in prison in Caesarea for two years (c. AD 57–59: see Acts 24:27). So his first drafts may have been written before Mark's and probably before the fall of Jerusalem.

With this Gentile background, Luke was fascinated by how the good news of this Jewish Jesus had now reached out to the whole world and brought people like himself into God's kingdom. Thus he emphasizes that Jesus was truly the 'Man for Others', the person who welcomed outsiders into the kingdom of God. Jesus' good news is for both men and women (see, for example, 15:1–7, 8–10), both for Jews and Samaritans (10:25), for those inside Israel and those beyond its borders (4:25–27), for the rich (19:1–10) but especially for the poor (4:18; 6:20; 7:22).

So Jesus in Luke is seen as a very approachable human being – accessible to all. We see more of him spending time at parties (14:1–24); we have a unique story of him when aged twelve (2:41–52); we see Jesus

'We profess to think Jesus the grandest and most glorious of men, yet hardly care to be like him. When we are offered his Spirit, that is, his very nature within us, for the asking, we will hardly take the trouble to ask for it.'

George MacDonald

weeping over Jerusalem (19:41–44). And Luke selects from Jesus' teaching some parables with a great deal of human warmth – especially the story of the Prodigal Son being embraced by his father (15:11–32). Jesus comes across in a compassionate way as truly one of us. He is also a man of prayer, who is uniquely filled with joy and with the Holy Spirit (see 10:21).

Yet none of this denies that Luke also saw Jesus in more than human terms. More often than in the other gospels, Jesus is presented to us as the 'Lord' (2:11; 7:6; 10:1; 24:3); he is transfigured in glory (9:29); he is the 'Son of God' (10:22); he is the 'Son of Man' whose coming will be like the 'lightning that lightens up the sky from one end to the other' (17:24).

A favourite word for Luke is 'salvation' (or safety). People need rescuing by God – in other words, they need the 'forgiveness of their sins' (see 1:77; 24:47). And Jesus is the one they need. He is the Saviour for all people (2:10–11); for 'the Son of Man came to seek and to save the lost' (19:10). This Gospel offers everyone a warm welcome, to come inside and find safety and security in God and in his new family.

John's Gospel

Finally there is John's Gospel. The other three gospels follow a similar structure with much material in common, but with John we seem to enter into a different world.

It is clearly the same story, however, John has chosen not to repeat the other gospels but rather to draw on a different selection of material. We see Jesus in Jerusalem on several occasions (not just at the end of his life); we see Jesus in conversation with a religious Jew named Nicodemus (3:1–15) and then, by contrast, with an unnamed woman from Samaria (4:7–26). We have extended debates with the Jewish leaders (7:14–52; 8:13–59), the miracle of Lazarus' being raised from the dead (11:43), and five chapters focused on Jesus' last evening with his close followers (13–17).

John also has some distinctive features. Jesus' miracles are 'signs' that point to Jesus' glory (2:11; 4:54). There are frequent references to themes such as 'eternal life', 'light' and 'darkness' (for example, 1:3–5). John's descriptions of Jesus' discourses are more meditative, showing us what was truly in Jesus' heart. He includes the famous 'I am' sayings (see John 6:35; 8:12, 58; 10:7, 11; 11:25; 14:6; 15:1) in which Jesus alludes to one of the Jewish titles for God ('I am who I am' in Exodus 3:14). And he teaches quite clearly that Jesus existed before he was born: as the eternal Word, he shared in God's work of creation (1:1–18) and will be the world's true judge (5:27).

So John's Gospel gives us a quite different angle on Jesus. Some have called it a 'spiritual Gospel'. Undoubtedly John believes in Jesus'

A ninth-century representation of John. It is strikingly different from the other Gospels and the early church leaders labelled John as the 'spiritual' Gospel.

The 'I am' Sayings of John's Gospel

John's Gospel is particularly noted for its seven 'I am' sayings, which are found on the lips of Jesus in this Gospel alone. Each of the sayings picks up some major themes from the Old Testament (such as Israel as a vine, Moses as the giver of the bread from heaven, and God as the shepherd of Israel), and applies them directly to Jesus. The form of these sayings is grammatically unusual, making them stand out from the remainder of the text. This point is probably a little difficult for readers unfamiliar with Greek to appreciate; however, the importance of the point is that there is a direct similarity between these sayings and Exodus 3:14, in which God reveals himself to Moses as 'I am who I am.' There thus seems to be an implicit declaration of divinity on the part of Jesus within each of these sayings. The seven 'I am' sayings in John's Gospel can be set out as follows:

6:35   The Bread of Life

8:12, 9:5   The Light of the World

10:7, 9   The Gate for the Sheep

10:11   The Good Shepherd

11:25   The Resurrection and the Life

14:6   The Way, the Truth and the Life

15:1, 5   The True Vine

In John's Gospel, Jesus represents himself as the true vine, on which the faith of God's people will flourish.

So how does meditating on Christ as 'the true vine' or the 'bread of life' help us to understand Christian beliefs about the identity of Jesus?

The first of these sayings is found at John 6:35, in which Jesus speaks the following words: 'I am the bread of life.' This immediately suggests the idea of being nourished; of meeting the specific human need of hunger. We are immediately reminded of our spiritual emptiness. We may find that we are satisfied physically, but a deeper hunger remains – a hunger for meaning, for immortality, for something that is profoundly satisfying. To speak of Christ as bread is to establish a connection with human hunger and emptiness. What humanity needs, Christ provides.

The main point to notice here is the form which these statements take. Christ is not represented as saying 'I show you the way' or 'I make it possible for you to have life', or even 'I teach you the truth'. The statements are emphatic: it is Christ himself who *is* the way, the truth and the life. He is not merely the agent though whom certain benefits are gained, wonderful though those benefits may be. He is the bread of life, who meets human hunger. The 'I am' sayings proclaim the utter inseparability of giver and gift, of person and benefit. Who Jesus *is* determines what Jesus *gives*.

full humanity (see 1:14; 4:6; 11:35), but he has given us clearer hints as to Jesus' divinity. Yet, even though Jesus is presented in such exalted terms, there is also great simplicity here. John's Greek is uncomplicated and Jesus comes across straightforwardly as a knowable person that the believer can now meet and grow to love (see, for example, 10:14–15, 27–28; 17:3).

Although it is hotly debated, John himself was almost certainly 'the disciple whom Jesus loved' (20:2; 21:20). He writes at the end of his long life (about AD 85–90), after many years of prayerful meditation on his own relationship with Jesus. And as the one who had been so close to Jesus in the Upper Room (see 13:23), he now wants his readers to be brought into the intimate circle of Jesus' 'friends' (15:14–15). The Gospel is written so that 'you may believe that Jesus is the Christ, the Son of God, and that by believing you may have life in his name' (20:31). It is written by Jesus' special friend to invite you too to enjoy a special relationship with this unique Jesus.

FOUR GOSPELS, ONE JESUS
The gospels thus give us four different – but ultimately complementary – portraits of Jesus. Some (as noted above) have seen this fourfold presentation of Jesus as a problem. By contrast, we might treat it as a rare gift. Indeed many students of the ancient world would rejoice to have four such detailed accounts of the person they are studying. So, even if some scholars may speak of the 'synoptic problem' (as they try to solve which came first), we might think instead in terms of a synoptic *bonanza*. In fact the four presentations, when combined, give us a well-rounded picture of Jesus. We do not have, as it were, a flat photo of Jesus but an almost three-dimensional portrait of a real person.

Moreover, we have a Jesus who can make connections with a wide variety of people. In terms of modern 'personality types', Mark might appeal to those who love colour and stories, Matthew to those who like order and rational argument; Luke might appeal to those interested in human emotions and characters, John to those who are intuitive and like to dream and ponder. Thus all types of people are able to access Jesus through the lenses provided by the character and interests of the four different evangelists.

Another way of summarizing their different viewpoints is as follows:

Mark, the Gospel for the individual, presents Jesus as the Suffering Servant;

Matthew, the Gospel for the Jewish nation, sees Jesus as the fulfilment of Israel's ancient promises and hopes;

Luke, the Gospel for Gentiles, portrays a very human Jesus with a heart for all people;

John, the Gospel for the whole world (indeed for the *cosmos*), sees Jesus the Eternal Son, come from the Father's heart, and as God incarnate coming down into his world.

THE RELIABILITY OF THE GOSPELS
These different perspectives, however, raise in an acute form the issue of the gospels' reliability: can we trust them? Yes, it may be much better to have four gospels rather than just one (for that would then be an easy target to criticize); this forces us to take very seriously the reality of Jesus as a historical figure. Yet what if those four accounts show significant inconsistencies with each other? And doesn't the fact that they are evidently *evangelists* (and not mere 'historians') mean they are thoroughly biased?

Not surprisingly, then, the gospels have been subjected to an immense barrage of criticism during the last 200 years. At one level this is, of course, a perfectly valid exercise in historical criticism. Yet it is worth noting at the outset the high stakes that are involved; and also how it is possible for personal agendas to colour the task. For if the gospels could be 'deconstructed' and shown to be unreliable, that would mean historians no longer having to deal with the stark claims of Jesus contained in the gospels. Indeed Jesus could now be 'reconstructed' in their own image. No one, of course, dares to criticize Jesus himself directly, instead they criticize the gospel writers so that they can then rewrite Jesus according to their preferences.

BIASED AUTHORS?

This may seem harsh, but it helpfully alerts us to the reality that there is no such thing as detached and 'objective' history. Everyone has a personal interest in this Jesus – for or against. And the same was true when the gospels were written. We would not necessarily have had a more 'historical' account of Jesus if the writers had been his enemies rather than his friends and followers. The fact that the gospel writers themselves believe in this Jesus as the truth (they are therefore personally committed) does not in itself prevent them from writing what is true. Indeed it may have given them the strongest incentive to check their facts and to ensure that they did not make claims for Jesus which he himself would have denied. After all, this story was not good news if it was untrue, based on lies and fabrication. So there are good reasons for presuming the evangelists were aiming to speak the truth. Their personal commitment to that truth does not undermine this, but rather undergirds it. Their supposed 'bias', then, is not in itself a problem.

CONTRADICTORY ACCOUNTS?

The issue of possible discrepancies between the four accounts, however, requires some more detailed response. Our overview (above) has shown that there are clear differences in emphasis between them. Yet such differences are not necessarily discrepancies. Nor should we assume that a particular 'angle' seen in one gospel is a sign of the evangelist's invention; it could be a sign of his selectivity of his sources.

Other factors that must be borne in mind here include the following. Firstly, different versions of Jesus' teaching may not be variants of one particular 'sermon'. On the contrary, Jesus will have spoken for hundreds of hours on many different occasions, sometimes using slightly different words. What is recorded in the gospels amounts to only about three hours of his teaching. It is also a Greek translation of Jesus' original Aramaic. The gospel writers never imagined they were passing on Jesus' exact words, only their 'dynamic equivalent' in a different language.

Secondly, something similar can be said of Jesus' actions. Where there are discrepancies in the gospel accounts, we may be dealing with different (but similar) events in Jesus' life. After all, the evangelists did not promise to recount every event in exactly the right order – their work is more of an 'anthology' than a sequential recording. And where they clearly *are* recounting one and the same event, good modern historians work first at harmonizing their material before dismissing it out of hand. For some people the existence of what appear to them as minor discrepancies between the gospels only strengthens their conviction in the gospels' overall reliability. For if they were all identical, we would be far more suspicious of their writers 'cribbing' from one another and of an agreed 'party line'. In this way their apparent differences may in fact only serve the truth.

'Not only do we not know God except through Jesus Christ; we do not even know ourselves except through Jesus Christ.'

Blaise Pascal

> 'I search in vain in history to find the similar to Jesus Christ, or anything which can approach the gospel. Neither history, nor humanity, nor the ages, nor nature, offer me anything with which I am able to compare or explain it.'
>
> Napoleon Bonaparte

PROBLEMS OF TEXT OR TIME?

There are therefore good reasons for accepting the general reliability of the gospels. Few scholars now have any doubt that the Greek text we now have is virtually identical with what the evangelists wrote. In contrast to other classical texts like Tacitus' *Histories* there are thousands of hand-written manuscripts of the gospels – many from the fourth century, but with some fragments from as early as AD 125. So the text itself is considered very reliable.

Meanwhile the elapsed time between the gospels' composition and the events of Jesus' life (25–50 years) is not as problematic as people often suppose. There may have been some earlier brief written accounts (see Luke 1:1), such as what scholars refer to as the 'Q' source (supposedly seen behind both Luke and Matthew). Yet, even if not, it is clear that in 'oral' cultures, people can exercise incredible powers of memory. This can be seen in Jewish or Arabic culture to this day, but was even more so in the ancient world – for example, neither Homer's *Iliad* nor Buddha's *Tripitaka* were written down for over four hundred years! How much more, then, might the sayings of Jesus (whom his followers believed to be risen from the dead and the unique teacher sent from God) be lovingly preserved over the course of just one generation. Quite probably each Sunday, as his followers gathered, they recited and pondered his words and deeds. It was then the role of the gospel writers to organize this material and write it down for future generations.

Jesus and the Religious Movements of His Day

First-century Palestine was a volatile place. By the time of Jesus various religious groups had emerged in response to Judaism's various crises. The Jewish historian, Josephus, lists four different such groupings – or, as he calls them, 'philosophies' (*Antiquities* 18:1:2–6). The majority of ordinary people did not belong to any of these 'parties', but they would have known well what they stood for.

The Pharisees were well respected, being the largest religious group within Judaism. They were particularly strong in Galilee, the area of Jesus' early ministry. They fostered a vision for a distinctively Jewish life amongst those who lived far from the Temple. They were involved with the local synagogues, ensured that the commands of Torah (Law) were applied closely to daily life (for example, ritual purity and tithing) and they valued oral traditions (in addition to the Bible) which offered guidance on these matters.

This quest for holiness was driven by a strong hope that God would one day act to vindicate his people – that is why people needed to be visibly 'separate' from those outside the true 'people of God'. This future hope increasingly involved a belief in resurrection–God physically raising his people in the 'age to come'. Yet they were not 'other-worldly'; no, physical resurrection was a hope for *this* world, causing some of them (especially in the more conservative Shammaite wing) to be ardently nationalistic and anti-Roman.

In Jerusalem the predominant group was the Sadducees. They were more 'establishment' figures, involved with the Sanhedrin (Judaism's ruling council). They were eager to defend the *status quo* with the Romans and therefore wary of nationalistic or revolutionary tendencies. Their beliefs matched this. They played down this hope of God's future vindication, denied the doctrine of resurrection,

CONCLUSION

It seems that the four gospels can adequately bear the weight that is pressed upon them. Although we know from Jewish and pagan sources that Jesus was a historical figure, we are indeed dependent solely on the gospels for any real detail about Jesus' life, character and teaching. This they achieve with remarkable success. Though they have been studied and analysed on an almost daily basis for nearly 2,000 years, they show remarkable resilience. They still have the capacity to fascinate and refresh, to frustrate sceptics and to foster faith, a capacity which they probably derive from the very person they are describing – Jesus himself.

The Jewish Background to Jesus

Any examination of Jesus' life must consider the issue of his Jewish background and understand the context of first-century Judaism in which he lived.

This is true with any such investigation. With any historical figures we are bound to appreciate their goals and achievements better if we understand something of their historical setting. Without this we can straightforwardly misinterpret some of their sayings and many of their actions.

JESUS IN HIS BIBLICAL CONTEXT

In the case of Jesus, however, we may need this context more than we realize. For one of the dangers with people accessing the story of Jesus many centuries later is precisely that it 'universalizes' so well. In other words, there is something so trans-cultural

> ''Twas a thief said the last kind word to Christ: Christ took the kindness and forgave the theft.'
>
> Robert Browning

and only accepted the authority of the Pentateuch (the five books from Genesis to Deuteronomy in the Bible) – thus omitting the prophetic writings that stirred popular hopes for a better future. Many High Priests (such as Caiaphas) were Sadducees.

The Essenes were quite different. Some 200 years earlier, perhaps led by a Temple priest (whom they called the 'Teacher of Righteousness'), they had split away from the Jerusalem Temple authorities, setting up alternative communities that could embody the best values of the Temple in worship and lifestyle. The most famous of these to date was discovered over the years 1946–57 on the shores of the Dead Sea at Qumran. The Essenes were highly ascetic, frequently celibate, and committed to a close reading of all the Scriptures (hence the biblical commentaries amongst the so-called Dead Sea Scrolls, found near Qumran). Yet they were politically quietist, preferring to wait 'in the desert' for God himself to act against the 'sons of darkness'.

The Zealots, however, could not wait. They preferred to fight, not retreat. Although the term 'Zealot' may not strictly have been coined till the AD 60s, there were numerous violent uprisings throughout this period (e.g. in 4 BC and AD 6, culminating in the two Jewish Revolts of AD 66–70 and 132–35). For Zealots, Jews had no 'king' but God, and the pagan overlords must be removed.

Qumran, where a community of Essenes live, is close to where the Dead Sea Scrolls were found.

about Jesus' message, that we can easily ignore the task of setting it within its original culture. Christians can be too quick to think we know what he meant.

In part, of course, this is precisely because of the Christian belief that in Jesus it is possible to see the entrance of God himself into our world, so that what is revealed through him was always intended to be universal for all people and for all time. This is quite true (and the fact that Jesus' story translates so well across time and culture only serves to supports this claim). Yet it can mean that Christian believers set Jesus' coming, as it were, only against a spiritual or heavenly backdrop rather than against a historical one. They can see Jesus' coming as a sudden invasion from outside (a 'vertical drop'), rather than also as something that arises up from within the timeline of history (along the 'horizontal').

Yet that previous history is vitally important. Indeed, according to Christian assumptions about God's purposes throughout the Old Testament period, it has a strong and equal claim to be seen as reflecting the purposes of God. If the coming of Jesus can (rightly) be seen as the action of God, suddenly stepping into his world, it can also (just as rightly) be seen as the divine fulfilment of that which God had been patiently promising to his people throughout the previous centuries.

Thus the story of what God had been doing in and for the nation of Israel is a vital backdrop for truly understanding the story of Jesus. Without it we may miss out on much of what God was doing through Jesus. And we will certainly find it difficult to build an appropriate theology that is true to the Bible *as a whole*. We cannot ignore the Old Testament, for this is the God-given preparation for the good news as then revealed in Jesus.

For obvious historical reasons we need to set Jesus against the background of the Old Testament as well as within the first-century context of Palestinian Judaism. Consideration of both the biblical background and the Jewish context will enormously enrich our grasp of the Jesus story. Indeed, what makes Jesus' story so electric is precisely the way he interacts with the Judaism of his day. Yet the process also works in reverse: the story of Jesus can also shed its light on those earlier stories, giving them too new significance.

THE QUESTIONS OF FIRST-CENTURY JUDAISM
So where had the biblical storyline progressed to by the time of Jesus? And what were the concerns and hopes of people in the nation of Israel in his day? One of the best ways to get inside the mindset of other people is to press them for their answers to some of life's key questions. So, to discover the world-view of Jesus' contemporaries, it will be helpful to draw out the kind of answers they would have given to the following four questions.

WHO IS OUR GOD?
For Jesus' contemporaries the answer to this was clear: the God of Israel was the one true God, the creator and sustainer of the world. Each day a devout Jew would recite the *Shema*: 'Hear, O Israel, the Lord is our God, the Lord alone. You shall love the Lord your God...' (Deuteronomy 6:4). Jews were thus ardent *monotheists* – believers in but 'one God'.

This was quite extraordinary at the time. The surrounding nations were *polytheistic* (that is, believing in 'many gods'), but the Jewish people would not compromise: their god was not just one among many, nor could he be identified with the chief god in other systems (such as Zeus). No, these other 'gods' were no gods at all; they were man-made 'idols' (see, for

'Today Jesus Christ is being dispatched as the Figurehead of a Religion, a mere example. He is that, but he is infinitely more; He is salvation itself, He is the Gospel of God.'

Oswald Chambers

example, Psalm 135:15–18). The god of Israel was the God of creation, who had created the world and all its people – so everyone should worship him alone. 'God' was not then to be identified with the natural order (as in *pantheism*), nor with something created like the sun (as in some forms of *paganism*). No, the true God was one God, separate from his creation. But he was also the God of providence, actively involved with his creation and reigning over the affairs of Israel and the nations.

As for his character, first-century Jews (inspired by texts such as Exodus 34:6–7) would have described him as 'abounding in love and faithfulness', a 'compassionate and gracious God', full of forgiveness but also majestically holy and opposed to sin and all that was evil. His character was summed up in his special name – 'Yahweh', meaning something like, 'I am who I am' or 'I will be who I will be' (see also pages 56–58 in 'God'). He was unchanging and true. He was also a speaking God, who had revealed himself to his servants and who kept his promises.

But how then might one explain the existence of evil within this world? This leads on to the second question.

WHO ARE WE?

First-century Jews believed that one of God's major strategies in combating evil was his choice of his people, Israel. This is known as the doctrine of *election* – the belief that they were God's 'elect' or chosen people. This election was then ratified by God's making a special covenant (or agreement) with Israel.

Although, of course, this belief could (and often did) lead to arrogance, they were reminded that God's choice of them was because of his great love, not because they deserved it (Deuteronomy 7:7–8). And there was also a strong understanding that this election was somehow for the blessing of others. God's calling of 'Abraham and his seed' was a divine response to the problem of human sinfulness and would be for the 'blessing of many nations' (Genesis 12:1–3). Abraham had been called precisely in order to undo the sin of Adam. So behind God's particular election of Israel was his universal intention to bless all the peoples of the world.

Jesus' contemporaries would thus have seen themselves as God's chosen people, in a special 'covenantal' relationship with him. They had a responsibility to withstand evil and to preserve the 'boundary-lines' around God's people. Sometimes this opposition to the 'nations' (the 'Gentiles') would boil over into a vindictive spirit, looking for God's judgment on the pagans. But deep down there was also this awareness that God somehow would use Israel to be a 'light to the nations' (see Isaiah 49:6), the means by which God would overcome the evil in the world.

WHAT HAS GOD GIVEN US?

To help Israel in this task, first-century Jews would say that God had given his people some special gifts. The most important of these was the Law or *Torah* (which means 'instruction'). This was a gift for the people he had already chosen – just as the Ten Commandments were given to those whom he had already rescued from Egypt. Obeying *Torah* was thus not a way of *joining* God's people but a sign that you already *were* the people of God.

By the time of Jesus (and especially now that they were under Roman occupation) three aspects of the Law had taken on a particular importance: circumcision, the Sabbath and the food laws. These were vital safeguards of Jewish national identity and helpful 'boundary-markers' to delineate who truly belonged to God's people – those whom one day God would vindicate. In a frontier situation like Galilee where Jews were in frequent contact with non-Jews, any compromise on these issues would meet with fierce opposition.

Israel also prized two further gifts – the land and the Temple. Although because of their sins God had sent their forebears into exile far away, the land was still seen as part of God's covenant gift. But right now the Roman occupation effectively rendered it 'unclean' – it was as though they were in 'exile' in their own land.

Meanwhile the Temple in Jerusalem was understood as God's dwelling-place and the place for appointed sacrifices. There were three festivals each year (including Passover), but the highpoint of the year was the Day of Atonement (*Yom Kippur*). Some Jews were critical of the present Temple for various reasons, but deep down there was a conviction that it was a gift from God that he would eventually use to accomplish his purposes.

WHAT IS GOD GOING TO DO?
Beliefs such as this could not be sustained without hoping that God would soon act decisively to clear up the many ambiguities that they raised. By the time of Jesus the Temple was being rebuilt by pagan King Herod; the

A model of King Herod's Temple. Despite his rebuilding of the Temple, the Jews felt that they were in exile in their own land because of the Roman occupation. Herod's Temple was destroyed by the Romans in AD 70 and has never been rebuilt.

Old Testament Prophecies Concerning Jesus Christ

The New Testament sees Jesus Christ as fulfilling the great hopes and expectations of the Old Testament. The promises made by God to Israel were brought to completion, and extended to all nations, through the life, death and resurrection of Jesus Christ. This can be seen by considering the gospel accounts of the life and death of Jesus Christ. The Gospel of Matthew sets out some reasons why we should draw the conclusion that Jesus was the Messiah, the long-awaited descendant of King David who was expected to usher in a new era in the history of Israel. The Gospel opens with a list of Jesus' forebears (Matthew 1:1–17), which establishes that Jesus was legally the son of David – as the Messiah was expected to be. In his account of the birth of Jesus, Matthew draws his readers' attention to the remarkable parallels between the circumstances of that birth and the prophecies of the Old Testament, drawing our attention to this point no less than five times in his first two chapters (Matthew 1:22–23; 2:5–7; 2:16; 2:17–18; 2:23).

Mark's Gospel opens by focusing our attention on the figure of John the Baptist. John is the long-expected messenger who prepares the way for the coming of the Lord (Mark 1:2–3). Having established this, Mark records John the Baptist's statement that someone even more significant will come after him (Mark 1:7–8). And who is it who comes on to the scene at once? 'In those days Jesus came from Nazareth of Galilee and was baptized by John in the Jordan' (Mark 1:9). The conclusion Mark wishes us to draw is obvious.

The gospels also note the important parallels between the 'Righteous Sufferer' of Psalm 22 and Christ's passion. Jesus' words 'My God, my God, why have you forsaken me?' (Matthew 27:46) draw our attention to this mysterious Psalm, and particularly to its descriptions of the mode of death of the 'Righteous Sufferer'. This figure is mocked by those who watch him die (Psalm 22:6–8), as is Jesus (Matthew 27:39–44). He has his hands and feet pierced (Psalm 22:16), as would most victims of crucifixion, including Jesus. He sees his tormentors casting lots for his clothes (Psalm 22:18), as does Jesus (Matthew 27:35).

Perhaps most important of all is the remarkable parallel between the crucifixion and the account of the 'Suffering Servant' of Isaiah 53, which Luke notes explicitly (Luke 22:37). This great Old Testament prophecy speaks of a suffering servant of God, who was 'wounded for our transgressions, and bruised for our iniquities' (Isaiah 53:5). This servant is to be 'numbered with the transgressors' (Isaiah 53:12), which is clearly understood by the Gospel writers to be fulfilled in two ways. First, Christ died by crucifixion, which was a mode of death reserved for serious wrongdoers. In other words, Christ was identified with sinners by the manner of his death. Second, Christ was not crucified alone, but along with two convicted and condemned criminals (Matthew 27:38). In this, and in other ways, the coming of Christ was seen to fulfil the great hopes of the old covenant, and bring the knowledge of God to all peoples on earth.

land was occupied and ruled by Romans; the evil in the world showed no signs of abating; and his chosen people were under continual pressure to compromise. How long could all this continue? When was God going to do something?

This introduces us to a third major stream within Jewish thought. First-century Jews did not believe only in monotheism and election: they also believed in *eschatology*. This was the hope that at the *end* of the ages (the *eschaton*) God would bring into this world a new state of affairs – the 'new age' or the 'age to come'.

In contrast to some pagan systems (where history seemingly went round in circles) the Old Testament portrayed an active God who was taking history forwards towards his goal. Hence its emphasis on prophecy. There were scriptural promises that spoke of Israel being restored, the Temple being purified and the nations coming to acknowledge the truth of Israel's God. When would these be fulfilled, and how?

There were also two further hopes. Firstly, there was a growing consensus that God would send an 'anointed one' (a messiah), who would deliver God's people. Just as Israel's kings had been 'anointed', so many expected this messiah to be a new king descended from great King David; others expected him to be a military figure, driving out the pagans; others thought he would be a priest, restoring true worship, or else a prophetic teacher.

Secondly, they hoped that the exile would at last be over. In one sense, of course, the exile had come to an end some six centuries before Jesus (when the remnant of those exiled in Babylon had returned to Jerusalem). But, with much of the land now settled by non-Jews, the returning exiles had complained: 'We are slaves today, slaves in the land you gave our fathers'

(Nehemiah 9:36). It was in this sense that the exile was not over. Surely one day God would act to 'restore' the fortunes of his people more fully, bringing his people truly out of exile. Then at last would be fulfilled the grandiose prophecies about the Temple, the return of exiles and the 'ingathering of the nations'.

In fact, many of these hopes were clustered together in the prophecy from Isaiah which spoke of the good news: 'How beautiful on the mountains are the feet of those who bring good news, … who say to Zion "Your God reigns!"'… When the Lord returns to Zion, they will see it with their own eyes. Burst into songs of joy together, … for the Lord has comforted his people, he has redeemed Jerusalem… all the ends of the earth will see the salvation of our God' (Isaiah 52:7–10). When these things came to pass – the arrival of God as King, the Lord's return to Zion, the redemption of Jerusalem, and salvation going out to the world – then, and only then, would the prophecies have been fulfilled and Israel's state of 'exile' brought finally to an end. This would indeed be good news.

No wonder, then, first-century Jews were on tenterhooks – eager to see God act to bring this painful drama to its appropriate resolution. This state of tension is confirmed when we are introduced in the New Testament to people who are 'waiting for the 'consolation of Israel' and looking forward to the 'redemption of Jerusalem' (Luke 2:25, 38) – clear echoes of the prophecies of Isaiah. A first-century Jew hearing these Old Testament texts would be perfectly entitled to ask the question: just when is this ever going to happen? When will the Lord, our covenant-keeping and gracious God, finally bring about what he has promised to his people?

'I believe there is no one lovelier, deeper, more sympathetic and more perfect than Jesus – not only is there no one else like him, but there could never be anyone like him.'

Fyodor Dostoyevsky

THE ARRIVAL OF JESUS AND JOHN THE
BAPTIST

This was precisely the tense, hope-driven context in which Jesus had to minister. Here was an age-long story in search of an ending.

In the first century various other groupings had appeared within Judaism, each with their own convictions about how the story was supposed to end. The Sadducees were trying to play down these prophetic hopes of the populace. The Pharisees expected God to act only when his people had properly sanctified themselves. The Essenes were awaiting the overturning of the Temple cult and the Jerusalem hierarchy. Meanwhile the revolutionaries were beginning to decide that, if God would not act himself, then they had better take the law into their own hands, ridding the land of its pagan overlords once for all.

Jesus in his ministry would have to steer a straight path through the midst of all these competing options. In fact he walked into this situation and proposed a quite different end to the story – a resolution that revolved around himself and promised to fulfil the prophecies.

Now we can begin to glimpse the significance of Jesus' ministry in its own day, within its original Jewish and biblical context. In fact his ministry may be seen as an intended fulfilment of the hopes engendered by Isaiah's prophecy: the good news of the exile's end, the coming of God as King, the return of the Lord to Zion, and the conquest of evil. Not for nothing did he launch his public ministry in Galilee with that compelling announcement – 'the kingdom of God is near!' This was precisely the news that his contemporaries were longing to hear!

Meanwhile, further to the south, in the Judean desert near the River Jordan, there is a 'voice crying in the desert'. Suddenly, in the months before Jesus himself comes on the scene, the nation of Israel is stirred to life by rumours of an unusual figure out in the wilderness. His clothes are 'made of camel's hair' and his food is 'locusts and wild honey' (Mark 1:6). 'All the people of Jerusalem', we read, 'went out to him' (1:5). They were intrigued. They wanted to know if this strange figure might be the One (Luke 3:15; John 1:19–24). Was he the Messiah? If not, was he Elijah (who was expected to precede the Messiah)? Or perhaps the prophet (predicted by Moses in Deuteronomy 18:15)? Once again we sense the anxious questions and eager expectations of first-century Jews.

This figure was, of course, the person we now know as John the Baptist. He was the son of a priest called Zechariah, and Jesus' own (slightly older) cousin (Luke 1:36). His ministry was indeed a dramatic moment in the history of Israel. Ever since the ministry of Malachi some 400 years before, the voice of authentic prophecy had not been heard in Israel. But now many were convinced that John was indeed a 'prophet' like those of old (Mark 11:32). At long, long last God was on the move, acting to redeem and bless his people.

Yet, if so, God was acting in a strange way. What John was offering was a message of 'repentance for the forgiveness of sins' (Luke 3:3). That in itself was not perhaps surprising – perhaps the Pharisees and the Essenes were right that God would only act when first his people turned towards his holiness in repentance. Jesus too would issue a call to 'repentance' (Mark 1:15). What was more strange was that John's call to repentance was joined with a call to be 'baptized', going down into the waters of the River Jordan.

Many of John's audience would have associated a ritual 'baptism' like this with what was required, not of Jews, but of Gentiles. This was what Gentiles

The Judean desert where John the Baptist had his ministry which prompted Jewish hopes of the imminent arrival of the Messiah.

had to go through if they wished to become 'proselytes' and join themselves to Israel and the people of God. By insisting on baptism John was therefore effectively telling the people of Israel that they too needed to re-enter the people of God. Their membership was 'up for renewal' and they had to re-subscribe from scratch.

Not surprisingly many were offended at this call to be baptized – after all, 'we have Abraham as our father'. But John's reply was stern: 'Don't say that: For I tell you that out of these stones God can raise up children for Abraham' (Luke 3:8; Matthew 3:9). It was a tough message. God was now reconstituting his people. Relying on previous privileges would no longer suffice. A new day had dawned in God's purposes – where the ground was potentially level beneath Jews and Gentiles. If it was God's

appointed time for the restoration of his people, it was clearly also a time for his judgment.

What is also intriguing about the ministry of John the Baptist is that it too can be seen as a fulfilment of prophecies in Isaiah. All four gospel writers explicitly make the link between John and Isaiah 40:3: 'A voice of one calling in the desert, "Prepare the way for the Lord" ' (Matthew 3:3; Mark 1:3; Luke 3:4; John 1:23). This text (which comes from the chapter that begins with the famous words 'Comfort, comfort, my people') was, like Isaiah 52, all to do with God's promise to restore his people from their exile. So John's ministry was seen as an announcement that the exile was over. Or, as some scholars have termed it, this was a time of 'restoration eschatology' – God's new age when he was renewing his people in accordance

was not unfounded, but the gospel writers are clear in their conviction that this hope was fulfilled not at Qumran but through what John was doing a few miles to the north. Down near the Dead Sea, a place of death and the lowest place on face of the planet, God was at work to renew his world and bring new life to many.

Finally, of course, John the Baptist is remembered as the 'forerunner', the one who pointed away from himself to Jesus. 'One more powerful than I will come, the thongs of whose sandals I am not worthy to untie. He will baptize you with the Holy Spirit and with fire…' (Luke 3:16; see also Mark 1:7–8; Matthew 3:11; John 1:26–27). He was like the 'best man' at a wedding who takes second place once the groom has arrived (John 3:29–30). It was a humble calling. It would involve him in times of questioning when Jesus' ministry seemed to be not quite what he was expecting (Luke 7:18–23). And in due course he would be imprisoned and then put to death at the whim of Herod Antipas (Mark 6:27). But Jesus publicly commended him – as a 'prophet and more than a prophet' (Luke 7:26). He was, so Jesus asserted, the 'messenger' whom Malachi had predicted would precede the coming of the 'Lord' (Malachi 3:1 in Luke 7:27); or, as in Isaiah's words, the one who 'prepared the way for the Lord' (Isaiah 40:3 as above).

The stage was thus set for the arrival of Jesus – the one whom the evangelists from the very outset want us to consider as none other than the 'Lord'. It is an awesome prelude to the ministry of Jesus.

with his promises. And Luke (with his Gentile concerns) cannot help going on to point out how Isaiah's prophecy had continued – with a clear prediction that this restoration of Israel would be the time when the Gentiles would come in to enjoy God's blessing: 'And all mankind will see God's salvation' (Isaiah 40:5 in Luke 3:6).

Some have wondered if John was associated in any way with the Essenes, whose monastic centre was only a few miles away – at Qumran on the north-western shores of the Dead Sea. There are some similarities in their thinking, but also significant differences, so John was almost certainly independent of them. Yet they too had been inspired by this text in Isaiah 40. They saw themselves as those waiting 'in the desert' in preparation for the day of God's vindication and rescue. Their hope

The Mission and Aims of Jesus

So Jesus had to carry out God's work in a time of great tension, upheaval and ferment. Politically the Palestine of his day was like a box of fireworks waiting to explode. Elsewhere in the

> 'If Christians would really live the teachings of Christ, as found in the Bible, all of India would be Christian today.'
>
> Mahatma Gandhi

The Quest for the Historical Jesus

The 'Quest for the Historical Jesus' is a way of describing the activity throughout the last 200 years of those scholars who seek to reconstruct a portrait of Jesus without assuming the general reliability of the gospel accounts. Prior to the eighteenth century the church, of course, believed in the historical Jesus (not just some 'spiritual' Jesus), but was convinced that the true Jesus of real history could be discovered through the New Testament accounts.

This assumption was overturned in the so-called 'Enlightenment' – the era of both rationalism and deism (the belief that God, if he exists, cannot be involved in human affairs). So in the 1770s a German called Reimarus argued that Jesus had performed no miracles, was never raised from the dead, and did not see his death as a sacrifice for sins. He wanted to find *Jesus as he really was* – without the 'falsifying' lens of the early church's faith and the later developments of church doctrine.

Throughout the nineteenth century there were many such 'historical' portraits of Jesus (for example by Paulus, Strauss and Renan), which were sceptical about many things related to the 'traditional' Jesus: his virgin birth, his predicting his own death (or his second coming), his miracles and so on. In 1910 Albert Schweitzer, however, effectively ended this 'quest'–through portraying Jesus as a mistaken Jewish prophet predicting the world's imminent end. If true, Christian faith was better off ignoring this 'historical Jesus'.

In the 1950s a 'New Quest' was launched, which has led to various fresh portraits: Jesus was a wandering philosopher, a charismatic Jew with miraculous powers, a social prophet (promoting peace and justice) or a radical liberationist (seeking to overthrow the Romans). Indeed, since the 1980s there has been a so-called 'Third Quest'. This has picked up one major aspect of Schweitzer's challenge (Jesus only makes sense within his native Judaism), but reinterpreted Jesus' eschatology: he predicted the 'age to come', but this did not mean the end of this space–time universe. This re-affirmation of Jesus' Jewishness is vitally important. Sometimes scholars, to their loss, have seen it instead as something almost embarrassing.

In all such quests the gospels are put under the closest scrutiny – often (unlike other ancient texts) being presumed 'suspect' until proven otherwise. Distinctive criteria (for example of 'multiple attestation' or 'dissimilarity') are set for determining whether individual gospel statements are authentic – often with nit-picking results. Far more helpful is the application of the historian's normal procedure: suggesting a hypothesis and then seeking to test it against all the available evidence. When seen in this light it is remarkable how the gospels' portraits of Jesus begin to make eminent sense.

Historical research is vitally important – and significant advances have been made. Yet too often the 'historical Jesus' is subtly reduced to the bare minimum that historians are confident is assuredly historical. But what if the 'Jesus of real history' was more than this? And there is always the real danger of so-called 'historians' unwittingly creating 'Jesus' in their own image. They look down the well of history in order to see Jesus (as one critic observed in the early twentieth century), but they end up seeing the reflection of their own faces.

JESUS

Roman empire there might be some benefits from the so-called *Pax Romana* (the 'Roman peace'), but not here. The might of Rome sought to keep a lid on the box, but the more pressure they applied the more they kindled Jewish resistance – fuelled by religious hope and a sense of painfully unfulfilled divine destiny. It would not take many sparks before the whole thing went up in flames.

And that is what happened. Within just forty years of Jesus' ministry, Jerusalem was burnt to the ground. Jesus predicted as much (see Luke 19:41–44; 21:20–24). Seen in this light Jesus' whole ministry was conducted at the 'eleventh hour', offering a last call to Israel before it was too late, a final means of escaping the crisis and coming through to the other side. He had come just 'in the nick of time'.

When looking at Jesus' public ministry and, in particular, examining the goals of his mission, it is important to remember this urgent context. Too often Jesus is cast as the 'teacher of timeless truths', but in a sense that was not what the Israel of his day was looking for. If that was all that he was, then he would have made few connections with the aspirations of his people. No, they needed their God to be acting within time and within their history-line in order to bring history itself to a turning-point from which they could then be propelled into the 'new age' – the promised time of God's kingdom. And this is precisely what Jesus offered – only it did not look, at first glance, to be in quite the way that the Jews were expecting.

Jesus shared this biblical hope, but he had a different understanding about what God was going to do next – and also about his own place in the scheme of things. In short, Jesus' aim was to place himself in the storyline of Israel and then to move the plot forwards into its crucial and long-awaited next

phase. When he did so, God's long-term plan to 'bless the nations' (as announced in Genesis) would also come to pass.

So what were the goals of Jesus' ministry? There were three overarching aims, each of which is authentically Jewish but also startlingly original. And each of them would get him into trouble.

1. 'THE KINGDOM OF GOD IS HERE'

Jesus was an itinerant preacher. Unlike many rabbis he had no fixed address ('nowhere to lay his head': Luke 9:58), though for a while he was based in Capernaum on Lake Galilee (Matthew 4:13). It was an unconventional lifestyle; but he also had a surprising message.

From the outset Jesus set about proclaiming the 'kingdom of God' (Mark 1:15). Each of the 'synoptic' gospels contains numerous references to this theme (though Matthew,

Capernaum, on the shores of Galilee, where Jesus lived during much of his ministry.

because of Jewish sensitivities about using the divine name, speaks of the 'kingdom of heaven'). Despite some misunderstandings in later Christian history (seeing this as a heavenly, other-worldly reality), the 'kingdom of God' in Jesus' day meant, quite simply, that God was at last *becoming king* in his world and over his people – precisely the 'good news' prophesied in Isaiah. Israel's God would be vindicated as the true Lord of the world and the exile would now properly be over. For Jesus' hearers this was just the news they had been waiting for – the long-awaited day had dawned!

The wrong kingdom?
However, it soon became alarmingly clear that Jesus' kingdom did not involve the commonly expected outcome – the removal of the pagan Romans from the land, giving Israel its independent sovereignty (perhaps under a newly enthroned Jewish king). Jesus' announcement, we might say, 'pressed the right buttons' in terms of faith but the wrong ones in terms of politics.

For a start, he did not propose any military action against Rome, but spoke in positive terms of the Roman forces. He commended the Roman centurion for his faith, indicating that such pagans would have a welcome, perhaps even a priority, in this kingdom (Matthew 8:10). 'Render to Caesar', he said, 'the things that are Caesar's' (Matthew 22:21). If a Roman soldier 'forces you to go one mile, go with him two miles' (Matthew 5:41) and 'Blessed are the peacemakers' (Matthew 5:9).

The wrong people?
Jesus' kingdom also welcomed the wrong people. When he spoke in the synagogue in his hometown Nazareth, he indicated that his Spirit-filled programme would bring blessing to those outside Israel – like Naaman the Syrian in days past (see 2 Kings 5). This got people angry. So they tried to throw him over one of the nearby cliffs (Luke 4:16–30).

Even the hated Samaritans were not outside its scope (hence his parable of the good Samaritan: Luke 10:25–37). God's kingdom was indeed focused on Israel, but would also be for the blessing of the nations. Indeed, judging by those Jesus kept company with, it would seemingly include some most unlikely people – a mixed bag of the unimpressive, the religiously 'unclean' and the socially outcast (see Mark 2:15). Jesus frequently upset society's conventions, ignoring the barriers erected between those of different class, sex or religion. Evidently status and respectability did not count much in Jesus' kingdom; indeed one of his slogans was 'the last will be first' (Matthew 19:30; 20:16). This kingdom was indeed seemingly 'upside-down'.

The wrong shape?
Other things were odd about Jesus' kingdom. It would not look as impressive as people might hope, but would grow from small beginnings (hence his parable of the mustard seed: Mark 4:31). It would not lead immediately to the eradication of evil (hence his parable about the wheat and weeds: Matthew 13:24–30). Its final consummation might be delayed beyond people's expectation (hence his parable about the 'foolish bridesmaids' caught out by the delay of the bridegroom: Matthew 25:1–13).

Worse still, the arrival of God's kingdom would involve judgment. Israel had experienced this in the exile and longed for the cloud of God's judgment to pass them by. But now this kingdom-prophet implied that Israel was facing another moment of judgment. As in the days of Amos, they longed for the 'day of the Lord', but it would be a day of darkness (see Amos 5:18). There are at

Jesus and the poor

One of the most distinctive features of the ministry of Jesus is the fact that he welcomed and embraced those who society regarded as outcasts or untouchables for physical or cultural reasons – such as prostitutes, women, tax collectors, those with leprosy, Romans, and Samaritans. One of the most important marginalized groups to be embraced by Jesus was the poor.

The gospel accounts of the life of Christ constantly stress his identification with the poor, and his critique of those who are wealthy. This can be seen in the sermon preached in the synagogue at Capernaum, which inaugurated his ministry. Here, Jesus declared that he had been sent to 'preach the gospel to the poor' (Luke 4:18). We find this theme reflected in the words and deeds of Jesus throughout his ministry.

In the first place, Jesus exalts and commends the poor. He himself, like so many poor, had no permanent home (Matthew 8:19–20). When a poor widow visits the Temple and can only afford to give 'two very small copper coins' to the treasury, Jesus insists that 'she has put in more than all the others' (Luke 21:1–4). The poor woman has given all that she had to live on, in contrast to the rich. It is the poor who will inherit the kingdom of God. This is made especially clear in the story of the rich man, clothed in purple and fine linen, who is contrasted with the poor and homeless Lazarus, whose open sores are licked by dogs (Luke 16:19–22). When they die, it is Lazarus who is carried by the angels to sit beside Abraham in heaven. The rich man, in marked contrast, ends up tormented in hell.

In the second place, Jesus asked that the situation of the poor should never be overlooked or forgotten. This is clearly seen in the gospel incident concerning a rich young man, who asked Jesus what he must do in order to be saved (Matthew 19:16–26). After establishing that the young man has kept all the commandments from his youth, Jesus tells him that there is one more thing that he must do: sell everything, and give the money to the poor. This demand to care for the poor is supplemented by the transformative impact that Jesus has upon people, when he encounters them. Zacchaeus (Luke 19:1–10) is described as being a wealthy tax collector. On being accepted by Jesus, Zacchaeus declares that he will give half of his goods to the poor, and make good any wrong he has done in the past.

This especial compassion for the poor does not mean that it is impossible for the rich to be saved, or that the wealthy lie beyond the love of God. It is part of the inversion of the values of the world that is so characteristic of the preaching of Jesus concerning the kingdom of God. Jesus offers a new vision of the world, in which the mighty will be cast down, and the poor raised up. In the kingdom of God, the first shall be last. Riches can easily become a barrier between an individual and God on the one hand, and between an individual and others in society on the other. In a world in which poverty remains a serious issue, Jesus' special concern for them must challenge us to value the poor, and seek to do something about their plight.

'Christ is the great hidden mystery, the blessed goal, the purpose for which everything was created.'

Maximus the Confessor

least thirty-four occasions in the gospels where Jesus threatens the people of his generation with judgment. No wonder some compared him to Jeremiah (Matthew 16:14) – for, like Jeremiah, Jesus predicted the imminent destruction of Jerusalem (Matthew 24:15–16).

Jesus was giving solemn warnings to his contemporaries about the impending national disaster. He was offering Israel a last call, warning what would happen if they did not repent: 'Unless you repent, you too will all perish...' 'Daughters of Jerusalem, do not weep for me; weep for yourselves and for your children' (Luke 13:5; 23:28). Jesus shared with John the Baptist the conviction that Israel was now entering the most crucial phase in its history, and warned of a national disaster.

Jesus was consciously connecting with the strong feelings aroused by Israel's hopes, but then giving a shocking 'sting in the tail'. He was being thoroughly Jewish, but subversively so, retelling Israel's story in an unwanted direction. The kingdom was coming, but it would be full of surprises.

A prophet at last?

So Jesus was an 'eschatological prophet', called by God to proclaim the arrival of God's kingdom which fulfilled the divine promises for the 'last days'. But his word would be a last word. In this sense Jesus put himself in a different category to John the Baptist (Matthew 11:11–13). Jesus would be the last prophet of this kind. And, if Israel was like a vineyard, then Jesus was the one sent by its owner 'last of all' (Mark 12:6).

Although these passages also hint that Jesus saw himself as *more* than a prophet, we can be sure that his contemporaries would have categorized him first and foremost as a 'prophet' announcing God's

kingdom (Luke 7:16). As with John the Baptist, this sudden reappearance of prophecy after centuries of silence was quite enough to cause people to sit up and take notice.

2. 'THE KING IS HERE'

But Jesus had not just come to announce the kingdom; he was inaugurating it. *His* arrival was *its* arrival. Jesus comes with the kingdom and the kingdom comes with Jesus – the two are inseparable. Surrounded by Pharisees on one occasion, he dared to state that 'the kingdom of God is in the midst of you' (Luke 17:21). The kingdom had arrived because Jesus himself had arrived. Unlike John the Baptist, he saw himself not just as the herald of the kingdom, but as the king himself.

This is where Jesus' miraculous works of power fit in (see page 146). His power over nature and even death were all dramatic signs that God's kingly rule was at work in a powerful new way. So when John the Baptist had questions about Jesus' kingdom, Jesus answered by sending back a report about his miracles – these showed the arrival of God's kingdom in and through Jesus.

The king in the kingdom

This explains a great paradox in the gospels. Jesus' talk about the 'kingdom of God' sounds so self-effacing, drawing attention away from himself and on to God. In fact, however, he is using this as a cryptic way of pointing to himself. He is daringly egocentric.

For example, on one occasion, he is asked a question about who will be 'saved' and enjoy the 'feast in the kingdom of God'. He answers with a story about 'the owner of the house' closing the door on people who wish to come in (Luke 13:22–30). Clearly the 'owner' represents God, the king in the 'kingdom of God'. But the story continues. The people outside the

---

JESUS

'Christ is the Son of God. He died to atone for men's sin, and after three days rose again. This is the most important fact in the universe. I die believing in Christ.'

Watchman Nee (note found under his pillow after his death)

Jesus is shown acting with messianic authority in Jan Brueghel's *Christ Driving the Traders from the Temple*.

door complain, 'We ate and drank with you, and you taught in our streets.' Suddenly Jesus is talking about his *own* contemporaries and warning that having *Jesus* teaching in their streets will not be enough to save them when they meet again at the door of *God's* kingdom. 'Away from me all you evildoers!' Jesus is identifying himself with the owner of God's house. He is the king in this kingdom! Christians believe that an individual's response to *him* determines whether they enter the kingdom of *God* and that to accept him is to accept the One who sent him (Matthew 10:41).

There are many other examples of Jesus obliquely focusing attention on himself. For example, he holds the keys to the 'mystery of the kingdom' (Mark 4:11). He is the 'bridegroom' at the messianic banquet (Mark 2:19). His eating meals with sinners is intended to symbolize God's welcome to the people of *Jesus* at the messianic banquet (Luke 14–15). He tells a parable about himself dividing the sheep from the goats, but then starts talking about 'the king' (Matthew 25:31–46). This kingdom-talk is evidently designed to help people 'swallow the hard pill' of his own identity as the king.

Other hints

Unashamedly, then, Jesus was aiming to hint at his own mysterious identity and such hints can be seen elsewhere in the gospels on many occasions. His action in the Sabbath cornfields suggests he has a greater authority than great King David; indeed he is the 'Lord of the Sabbath' (Mark 2:23–28). He dares to forgive the paralytic his sins, when this is the prerogative of God alone (Mark 2:1–12). He refers to himself as the 'Son of Man' (Mark 2:10, 28), but this apparently neutral term turns out (in the light of Daniel 7:9) to speak of an exalted figure, the one appointed to represent Israel before the 'Ancient of Days'.

Then, at the end of his ministry, he enters Jerusalem on a donkey, but this fulfils a prophecy about 'Zion's *king*' (Zechariah 9:9) – a staggering claim, given that, in biblical thought the true king of Zion is God himself. He cleanses the Temple with messianic authority, quoting some words from Isaiah 56:7 ('*my* house shall be called a house of prayer') as though he owned the place (Mark 11:17). And when he goes on to tell the parable of the vineyard he casts himself in the role of the vineyard owner's 'son' (Mark 12:6). Jesus is dropping hints everywhere as to his mysterious identity.

The alternative messiah

The category uppermost in the minds of his contemporaries was that of 'messiah'. Palestine had a string of messianic claimants (from Judas the Galilean in AD 6 through to Bar Cochba in 135). Since 'messiah' was a royal title (suggesting an anointed 'king' of some kind), it would not be long before the inevitable question was raised: was this kingdom-announcer himself the awaited messiah–king?

The evidence above (for Jesus as the 'king of the kingdom') suggests Jesus indeed saw himself in this way. Others too claimed to be the messiah (after all, no one expected the messiah to be a *divine* figure), so no one could have considered there was anything strange about Jesus thinking this of himself. But he did need to be careful. For Jesus' messiahship (like his kingdom) was radically different from popular expectations. If people hailed him as messiah, they would then either try to squeeze him into their job description for the messiah, or else they would very quickly become disillusioned and turn against him.

Jesus' only strategy was what is now known as the 'messianic secret' – hinting at his messiahship and asking those 'inside' the secret to keep it to themselves (see, for example, Mark 4:11). Only so could he gradually advance his claim to be the true, but different, Messiah. Effectively he had to 're-invent the term', accepting the title but giving its meaning a whole new content.

So Jesus' second aim was gradually to reveal his identity. This would include building the case for his own alternative messiahship but also dropping hints of an even closer relationship to God than had previously been imagined. Not surprisingly the mid-point climax of Mark's Gospel is Peter's hesitant but clear confession: 'You are the Messiah!' (Mark 8:29).

3. THE KING MUST DIE

Peter soon found, however, that this messiah had a quite different agenda. Jesus started predicting that he would 'suffer many things' and be killed (Mark 8:31–34). Just moments before, the disciples might have been preparing themselves for a great revolutionary march towards Jerusalem, now it seemed more like a funeral procession. What was going on?

Jesus had found in the Scriptures a deeper, more mysterious, theme. In Isaiah, intertwined with those passages about Israel's restoration, there were others about a *suffering* servant who by his death would bring about forgiveness for 'many' (Isaiah 53:11). Jesus now interpreted this passage in a bold new way. He brought together this servant motif (the innocent sufferer) with the messiah (the royal conqueror) and moulded them into a strange unity. The messiah would 'give his life as a ransom for many' (Mark 10:45) and would win Israel's battle but it would be through apparent defeat. And that person was... himself!

In so doing, Jesus has clearly reconfigured the Jewish hopes in some radical ways. Instead of seeing Rome as the enemy that must be defeated in God's name by the messiah, Jesus focuses on the problem of fallen human nature. Instead of thinking that Israel's exile was the problem, he focuses on what had caused that exile in the first place – human sinfulness. This was where the true battle needed

JESUS

to be fought. And instead of imagining that the nation of Israel might somehow be the 'light to the nations' and so solve the problem of the world's rebellion, he accepts that Israel has failed and offers himself as a new, faithful Israelite to take on the issue single-handedly – like a new David fighting Goliath.

So Jesus was taking up where Israel had left off, to do *as* and *for* Israel what she herself could not do. If sin and rebellion must lead to God's judgment, then Jesus would now enter that judgment himself. He would bear the 'curse' of God's wrath, so that sin could be put away. Only in this way could the exile caused by sin be brought to an end and the good news of God's forgiveness be published to the world.

This is all deeply mysterious. Yet it explains what can be seen happening in Jesus' ministry. He was announcing the coming of divine judgment upon evil and on Israel's sin in particular;

but he also saw it as his messianic role to bear that judgment in his own body on a cross. Only so could Israel's sin be removed and its exile ended. Indeed only so could the sin of the world be dealt with and the Evil One defeated. Only then could the good news of divine forgiveness go out to the world because God himself would have truly dealt with human sin (Luke 24:46–47).

The suggestion that Jesus intended to die and saw his death as linked to the problem of sin and evil is often attacked, dismissed as an idea invented later by the church. Yet, once Jesus is seen set firmly within his Jewish context, it is possible to understand how Jesus himself could have viewed the situation. He would be the one who, through his death, would bring Israel and the whole world into the promised 'new age' of the kingdom.

For Jesus himself this was an agonizing and lonely vocation. It would

Christ Preaching by Giuseppe Bartomeo Chiari. Jesus' teaching often posed challenges for his hearers.

require incredible courage and involve the ultimate risk. It was the third and most vital part of his mission. But what if he was wrong?

The Ministry and Teachings of Jesus

This focus on Jesus' purposes and mission is essential in order to understand his teaching. In some ways his words are but a commentary on his actions. It is only by understanding what Jesus was doing himself (his agenda for his own life) that one can begin to understand what he wants Christians to do for him (his agenda for *their* lives). And his teaching poses a number of challenges.

1. FOLLOW THE KING

The most obvious thing about Jesus' teaching, then as now, is its amazing authority. 'The people were amazed at his teaching, because he taught them as one who had authority, not as the teachers of the law' (Mark 1:22). These other teachers presumably focused on rules and precedent, leading to ever more subtle distinctions and regulations that frequently left ordinary people bewildered. Jesus, however, cut through this with clarity and authority, boldly declaring the will of God. Unlike other teachers, when he spoke about God and his kingdom, he seemed to know both who and what he was talking about.

This contrast with the religious leaders of his day can be seen in numerous ways. Jesus focused, not on ritual cleanness, but on the uncleanness that comes from people's thoughts (Mark 7:14–23). Rather than worrying about precise observance of the Sabbath, Jesus used this day to heal people, teaching that this day was for human blessing, not religious bondage (Mark 2:23–3:6). Instead of discussing which oaths were permissible or the possible grounds for divorce, Jesus called for simple

truthfulness (Matthew 5:33–37; 23:16–22) and declared God's purpose that marriage not be broken at all (Mark 10:5–9). And 'love your neighbour' did not excuse people from not loving anyone else – instead Jesus' call was to 'love your enemies' (Matthew 5:43–48).

Jesus here was not, of course, opposed to all rules and regulations, nor the serious quest for holiness of life. As he made plain at the start of the Sermon on the Mount (Matthew 5–7), what he was looking for was even more demanding – a 'righteousness' that 'surpasses that of the Pharisees and the teachers of the law' (Matthew 5:20). For he was getting behind the rules to the deeper motivations of the heart, replacing mere external regulations with searching spiritual principles, desiring new attitudes and values deep within the heart.

Yet this authority in his teaching, exposing the human heart, also begged the question of his own identity. Who did he think he was to say such things? Six times in Matthew 5, he dares to say: 'You have heard it said to you... But now *I* say to you'. How could he set himself up in this way, to speak with an authority that matched or even exceeded that of the Old Testament or of Moses?

So the teaching of Jesus, sooner or later, always raises questions about Jesus. Jesus wanted people to be asking, 'Who is this?' And then he wanted them to act. People must recognize the kingship of God, but also follow the king. That's why Jesus posed his disciples the question: 'Who do you say that I am?' (Mark 8:29). If the kingdom of God has arrived, then 'repent' and 'come, follow me!' (Mark 1:15, 17).

This purpose is implicit in all the passages where Jesus is hinting at his identity (see page 132, 134), both to his own disciples and to a wider

> 'Jesus Christ is to me the outstanding personality of all time, all history, both as Son of God and as Son of Man. Everything he ever said or did has value for us today and that is something you can say of no other man, dead or alive. There is no easy middle ground to stroll upon. You either accept Jesus or reject him.'
>
> Sholem Asch

audience. It is there in almost every 'miracle' (for Mark 5:41; Luke 7:16). The gospel writers see almost every story as an invitation to puzzle over Jesus' identity. To be a follower of Jesus is to recognize his unique authority and to commit yourself to finding out more about who he is.

In the context of Israel's hopes and longing, this would mean at the very least being convinced that he was the one in whom Israel's God was now uniquely at work. People were to give up their own agendas for solving Israel's problems and recognize Jesus as the one with the answers.

There is therefore no following of Jesus that does not involve adopting some form of personal loyalty to Jesus himself. In fact, Jesus' challenge to any would-be disciples is stark. They must love him more than their parents (Matthew 10:37); indeed it is more important to follow Jesus than to bury one's father (one of the most important commandments: see Luke 9:60).

And it will be costly. Jesus' true followers must be ready to 'take up their cross daily and deny themselves' (Luke 9:23); as Jesus himself meets opposition, so they too must expect rejection, 'persecutions' and being 'hated for his sake' (Mark 10:30; Matthew 10:18–25). But ultimately they will be the ones to be congratulated or 'blessed' in God's sight (Matthew 5:1–12).

This comes to a head at the Last Supper, where Jesus gives his followers a meal which they are to repeat in the future. They are to do this 'in remembrance of me'. Jesus himself (and now, too, his death) are to be at the centre of his followers' life and thought. Jesus' words and actions consistently point back to himself. If you like, he is not just a man with a message; the man *is* the message – follow *me*!

2. JOIN HIS NEW COMMUNITY

So Jesus was looking for committed followers. He did not want people to pick up a few interesting ideas from his teaching and then incorporate them into some other system. He wanted to be at the centre. A corollary of this was that he wanted his followers to form a new and distinct 'people'. He was founding a new messianic renewal movement with himself as its head.

A new people of God

But how would these followers of Jesus relate to the wider people of God, the nation of Israel? The devastating answer was that Jesus was reconstituting Israel around himself. In his own person (as the Messiah, the king, the Son of Man) there were important senses in which *he himself* was the representative of the nation and *was himself Israel*. But now by extension his followers were to be 'Israel'. Thus he was gathering together a new community, which would be the true embodiment of Israel.

What reveals this most clearly is his choice of 'twelve' disciples (or apostles) to be his 'inner cabinet'. Why the number twelve? Because the people of Israel had originally consisted of twelve tribes (see Matthew 19:28). Jesus now, in both symbol and practice, began the reconstitution of Israel. Picking up the idea of the faithful 'remnant', he tells his disciples that they are God's 'little flock' to whom God has given the kingdom (Luke 12:32).

Jesus, then, was not just challenging individuals in their response to him. He was also calling forth a new community. He was casting a vision for a new people of God, which had himself at its very centre (not the Law, not the Temple, but Jesus). He claimed to have the authority to refashion Israel around himself. In just the same way that John's call to baptism

'God heals the sicknesses and the griefs by making the sicknesses and the griefs his suffering and his grief. In the image of the crucified God the sick and dying can see themselves, because in them the crucified God recognizes himself.'

Jürgen Moltmann

required Israelites to reapply for membership, so now Jesus was calling Israel to start again. Israel was being restored by Jesus – being reconstituted around its messiah.

Who was welcome?

But here Jesus' vision for this new people was so startling. As we saw earlier (page 130), his kingdom seemed to be open to all the wrong people. The Twelve included a tax collector, Levi, who then invited Jesus to a party thronged with other tax collectors and notorious 'sinners'. When people complained, Jesus replied: 'I have not come to call the righteous, but sinners' (Mark 2:17). Jesus touched 'untouchable' lepers and let himself be touched by a woman who was known to have 'lived a sinful life' (Luke 7:37–50). He talked freely with a Samaritan woman (John 4:7–26).

According to Jesus, this reflected the intention of Israel's God: the master of the messianic banquet wanted invitations to go out to the 'good and bad' alike, to the 'poor, the crippled, the lame and the blind'; this God welcomed back the 'prodigal son' and rejoiced over just 'one sinner who

Jesus and Women

Christianity is often portrayed as hostile towards women. Although such attitudes did become commonplace within early Christianity, these appear to result from the assimilation of Jesus' radical views on the role and place of women to the more

patriarchal views of classical pagan culture. Women were an integral part of the group of people who gathered round Jesus, and were affirmed by him, often to the dismay of the Pharisees and other religious traditionalists. It is possible that apostolic Christianity attracted women in part because of the new roles and equal status they were granted in the Christian community. In contrast, Judaism offered women proselytes a circumscribed place at best, for they were faced with Jewish restrictions that limited their participation in religious functions. There were many pagan cults in Greece and Rome that were for men only or, at best, allowed women to participate in very limited ways.

The gospels certainly bear out this respect for women. Not only were women witnesses to the crucifixion; they were also the first witnesses to the resurrection. The only Easter event to be explicitly related in detail by all four of the gospel writers is the visit of the women to the tomb of Jesus. Yet Judaism dismissed the value of

Cariacci's *Holy Women at Christ's Tomb* reminds us that women were the first witnesses to the resurrection.

repented' (Luke 14–15). The new people of Jesus was open to all. As we have seen, its moral challenges ultimately went deeper than those of the 'teachers of the law', but its initial welcome was universal.

Badges of belonging

And how would this new people be recognized? Judaism had defined itself by some boundary-markers which made it quite clear who truly belonged to Israel – especially Sabbath observance, Jewish food laws and circumcision, but also their commitment to the family, the nation and the Temple in Jerusalem. These were the very things, however, that Jesus so frequently challenged (see, for example, Mark 3:31–35; 11:17). In this era of fulfilment God was doing a new thing. So some of the old boundary-markers would become redundant – not because they had been bad, but simply *because their time had come*. These would no longer be the hallmarks of God's people, as refocused on Jesus.

It was a daring strategy, easily misconstrued as disloyalty or dangerous radicalism. In fact Jesus here was being thoroughly Jewish,

the testimony or witness of a women, regarding only men as having significant legal status in this respect.

In recent years, there has been much interest in rediscovering Jesus' attitudes towards women within the church. The following points are worth careful study.

1. Throughout his ministry Jesus can be seen engaging with and affirming women (see, for example, John 4:7–26). He treats women as human subjects, rather than as objects or possessions – often women who were treated as outcasts by contemporary Jewish society on account of their origins (for example, Syro-Phoenicia or Samaria) or their lifestyle (for example, as prostitutes).

2. Jesus refused to make women scapegoats in sexual matters – for example, adultery (John 8:2–11). The patriarchal assumption that men are corrupted by fallen women is conspicuously absent from his teaching and attitudes, most notably towards prostitutes and the woman taken in adultery.

3. The traditional view that a woman was 'unclean' during the period of menstruation was dismissed by Jesus, who made it clear that it is only moral impurity which defiles a person (Mark 7:1–23). Women could not be excluded from acts of worship for this traditional reason.

4. The traditional Judaism of the period ordained that only male children could receive the initiation rite of the people of God – circumcision (Genesis 17:1–14). However, Christian baptism was for all. The early history of Christianity makes it clear that both men and women were baptized, in line with this fundamental teaching.

It is sometimes difficult to appreciate how novel these attitudes were at the time. Jesus' ministry represents an attempt to reform the patriarchalism of his day, and permit women to hold a new kind of authority in religious matters.

'A man who was merely a man and said the sort of things Jesus said would not be a great moral teacher. He would either be a lunatic – on a level with the man who says he is a poached egg – or else he would be the Devil of Hell. You must make your choice. Either this man was, and is, the Son of God; or else a madman or something worse. You can shut Him up for a fool, you can spit at Him and kill him as a demon; or you can fall at His feet and call Him Lord and God. But let us not come with any patronizing nonsense about His being a great human teacher. He has not left that open to us. He did not intend to.'

C.S. Lewis

Facing page:
Jesus preached
the Sermon on
the Mount on
the shore of Lake
Galilee close to
where the Church
of Beatitudes
now stands.

'When I was
abandoned by
everybody, in
my greatest
weakness,
trembling and
afraid of death,
when I was
persecuted by
this wicked
world, then I
often felt most
surely the
divine power
in this name,
Jesus Christ...
So, by God's
grace, I will
live and die for
that name.'

Martin Luther

but subversively so. He was announcing the new age in which the 'people of God' would be redefined around the Messiah. He was also implying that Israel should have been the 'light to the nations' (Isaiah 42:6), but through these boundary-markers she had been keeping her light 'under a bowl'. Jesus' disciples would now instead be the true 'light of the world' (Matthew 5:14).

Not surprisingly, people objected to Jesus' teaching, both about his own identity but also about Israel's destiny – that is why he was later charged with 'misleading our nation' (Luke 23:2). Not surprisingly too, for it was only some twenty years later that the early Christians were insistent on this point: those who truly belong to God's people are those who have faith in Jesus as Israel's Messiah, not those who merely fulfil the former 'works of the law'. Jesus' new people are to be recognized not by things such as food laws or circumcision but by faith in him alone. And what matters is not racial background, but a repentant heart before God's king. The true 'people of God' will no longer be a nation but a community drawn from all nations. This idea was radical at the time, but Jesus' followers got it from the teaching of Jesus himself. He wanted people to join his new community, focused on him.

3. LIVE HIS NEW LIFE
But how was life to be lived in this new Jesus-centred kingdom? Jesus' ethics – his practical teaching on godly living – have been studied in great detail elsewhere, so this is a brief overview.

Jesus' ethics are without parallel. His teaching is breathtaking in its simplicity and its depth. No other 'philosopher' has answered the basic questions of human meaning and action in the same way as Jesus. So they have inspired thousands of people through the ages – even those who

have rejected other parts of the Christian faith.

Yet, strictly, we cannot separate out Jesus' ethics from his teaching about himself and the kingdom of God. For, as we have seen, the primary focus of Jesus' teaching was not ethics, but eschatology – he wanted people to recognize what God was doing *through him* in fulfilment of his promises.

This means that the Sermon on the Mount, for example, cannot be put into practice without responding to Jesus and his God. For this was Jesus' kingdom-manifesto at the launch of his campaign – his challenge to those who would be *his* disciples. It teaches them that Jesus' way is the 'narrow way' (other agendas are 'building on sand'). It shows them Jesus' urgent challenge to Israel to adopt Jesus' way for being God's people. This kingdom, he says, belongs not to the self-confident but to the 'poor in spirit', to the peacemakers, to those who 'thirst for righteousness' and who know the meaning of mercy. The secret inner motivations of the heart will be examined. And this kingdom necessarily involves calling Jesus 'Lord', as well as doing 'the will of my Father in heaven' (Matthew 7:21).

God's holiness and love
Jesus' ethics are thus rooted in the kingdom and in the character of God.

On the one hand, the God of Jesus is clearly the 'Holy One of Israel' – Jesus never corrects the revelation of God's awesome character in the Old Testament. He prays that God's 'holy name' be 'hallowed' (Matthew 6:9). And people need to reckon seriously with the justice of God – both Israel as a nation (Luke 19:44) and as individuals (Luke 13:5). God's words to the 'rich fool' in Jesus' parable, for example, are chilling: 'You fool! This very night your life will be demanded from you' (Luke 12:20). Jesus is

warning that God's holiness is real and that his people must be holy. 'Be perfect, therefore, as your heavenly Father is perfect' (Matthew 5:48).

On the other hand, Jesus clearly teaches the incredible nature of God's love. He shared his table with anyone. The new 'people of God' is not to be marked by a self-righteous dismissal of those outside – for 'God causes his sun to rise on the evil and the good'. Since God is love, Jesus gives his followers this command: 'Love your enemies… that you may be sons of your Father in heaven' (Matthew 5:44–5). The God of Jesus is indeed the 'prodigal father' (see Luke 15:20).

Those who accepted Jesus' call were thus challenged to live in the light of these awesome realities, coming to know and then to imitate the God of perfect holiness and love. It was a staggering calling, then as now. Jesus' followers are to be signs of the reign of God in a broken world. But with the calling comes divine aid. For Jesus' God is also the generous and gracious God who 'gives good gifts to those who ask him' (Matthew 7:11).

The ethics of the kingdom

Jesus' teaching, of course, covered many other areas: revenge and hypocrisy, sexual practice and divorce, prayer and fasting, money and children, dealing with worry and criticism, practising forgiveness and obedience, mission and final judgment. The list goes on. Yet in each area it can be seen how these are ethics of the kingdom, ways of living for those who chose to come under God's rule in Jesus. Jesus is not teaching general, timeless truths. His teaching may appear simple but it is penetratingly deep and is truly theological – it makes no sense without the reality of God and his kingdom. Jesus is thus giving us a vision of human life as lived under God's rule and calling his followers to live this new life of the kingdom. His

ethical teaching turns out to be an outline of what it means in practice to follow Jesus the King.

Jesus in John's Gospel

It is now time to draw upon the witness of John's Gospel, as virtually all the discussion above was drawn exclusively on the 'synoptic' gospels (Matthew, Mark and Luke). This omission is certainly not because John's account is unreliable; nor that he gives a very contradictory presentation of Jesus' life. Far from it. What John has done is consciously to pass on *other* material about Jesus which was in danger of being lost (there was no point in repeating yet again what the synoptics had done so well). But he writes in a more reflective and meditative style, focusing on quite a small selection of material but in greater depth.

THE FORGOTTEN WITNESS?
This then has caused some people to be slightly suspicious of John. They wonder if he has projected back onto the Jesus of history many things that would not have been seen or sensed at the time. In particular, John presents readers with a Jesus who is constantly challenging people with his unique identity – indeed his identity as the 'Son of God'. Perhaps, they ask, the real Jesus never did this in his actual ministry?

But even in the synoptics' account, the identity of Jesus has been shown to be central to so much of his teaching. The idea that the synoptics do not present readers with a unique, or even divine figure, is simply not true. They just have a different, perhaps more subtle, way of conveying it. In a sense, their portrait of Jesus is consciously painted from the perspective of how he might have appeared *at the time* and within the horizontal storyline of Israel. What John then has done – with equal validity – is portray Jesus with the advantage of hindsight. Thus, for example, the glory of the resurrection is allowed to shine retrospectively back onto Jesus' earlier ministry. Or again, because John is convinced of the incarnation (that Jesus was truly a coming of God into his world) he sets Jesus' coming against a more 'vertical' backdrop' – a descent from God into our world.

Of course, if these things turned out to be true (that Jesus was raised from the dead and that he had truly come from God in a unique sense) *then they were also true at the time of Jesus' ministry* – but people at the time would not have been able to recognize it or truly account for it. If so, however, then John was not being untrue or even 'unhistorical' in portraying these events with the wisdom that comes from 'after the event'. There truly was a lot more to Jesus than first 'met the eye'!

John's goal is to make this plain to us. He is revealing the hidden meaning within the historical events. John's Gospel then is an exercise, not in falsely imposing later ideas on the original events, but rather in drawing out their authentic reality. It can be seen not as invention but as elucidation.

Looking through some of what John has chosen to highlight in Jesus' ministry one can see that John's material clearly matches that of the synoptics – they are simply viewing things from a different vantage point. If Jesus really is the one in whom the human and divine meet, in whom the historical and eternal come together, then this is precisely what should be expected.

THE KINGDOM OF GOD

Jesus' teaching about the kingdom is a case in point. This theme, which is so dominant within the synoptics, seems at first sight hardly to appear in John. It only occurs (twice) in Jesus'

conversation with Nicodemus: 'No one can enter the kingdom of God unless he is born again' (John 3:3, 5). Yet this is a key reference near the start of the Gospel, bluntly alerting the reader that this is Jesus' chief concern for people – that they should enter the kingdom. It was clearly at the heart of his message.

Moreover, John's great emphasis on 'eternal life' is almost certainly another way of speaking about the kingdom. His words for 'eternal life' could equally well be translated as 'the new life of the age-to-come'. When we remember that the 'kingdom of God' was precisely a way of speaking about the long-awaited new age or 'age-to-come', we sense that the two ideas are not so far apart. The synoptics say that Jesus announces and brought in the kingdom; John that he announced and brought to us 'eternal life'. Later Christians may have interpreted John's words in a more 'spiritual' sense, but set back within their original Jewish context, they give a better idea of what John saw in Jesus. In fact he is neatly complementing the synoptics, perhaps making Jesus' words more easily understood by those outside Judaism for whom the 'kingdom' language was confusing or misleading.

THE SPIRIT OF GOD

John too has some different teaching about the Holy Spirit. He traces this as quite a major theme throughout Jesus' ministry. Jesus discusses the Spirit with both Nicodemus and the Samaritan woman (John 3–4) and it will be a major topic in the Upper Room (John 13–16) when the Spirit can be seen as a person and also as 'another Jesus' who comes to take Jesus' place after he has gone. Meanwhile (back in John 7), Jesus promises that 'streams of living water' will flow from each believer: 'by this,' John comments, 'he meant the Spirit, whom those who

'In his own lifetime Jesus made no impact on history. This is something that I cannot but regard as a special dispensation on God's part, and, I like to think, yet another example of the ironical humour which informs so many of his purposes. To me, it seems highly appropriate that the most important figure in all history should thus escape the notice of memoirists, diarists, commentators, all the tribe of chroniclers who even then existed.'

Malcolm Muggeridge

New Testament Titles for Jesus

Christ Jesus, being in very nature God, did not consider equality with God something to be grasped; ... being found in appearance as a man, he humbled himself and became obedient to death... Therefore God exalted him to the highest place... that at the name of Jesus... every tongue confess that Jesus Christ is Lord (Philippians 2:6–11).

God has spoken to us by his Son, whom he appointed heir of all things, and through whom he made the universe. The Son is... the exact representation of his being, sustaining all things (Hebrews 1:2–3).

Jesus Christ is the same yesterday and today and forever (Hebrews 13:8).

He is the image of the invisible God... All things were created by him and for him. He is before all things, and in him all things hold together... He is the beginning and the firstborn from among the dead, so that in everything he might have the supremacy. For God was pleased to have all his fullness dwell in him (Colossians 1:15–19).

What extraordinary things were being said about Jesus so soon after his resurrection! These texts come from the New Testament 'epistles' (or letters) that were written *before* the gospels were written down. Indeed in Philippians Paul may be quoting an earlier 'hymn' (possibly dating from the 40s). Here we see Jesus presented to us as 'in very nature God', the 'fullness' of God, the one who gives an exact image of God; the Creator, Sustainer and 'Heir' of the universe; the unique Son of God who is eternal and is the 'Lord'. There are other places too where Jesus is effectively identified with God himself (see texts such as Romans 9:5; 2 Corinthians 4:6; Colossians 2:9).

These are remarkable statements from convinced monotheistic Jews: they identified a human being, who had recently lived and died in Jerusalem, with the God of Israel and worshipped him as Lord. 'Lord' was already a distinctive title for Israel's sovereign God. Yet the earliest Christian creed was a bold statement that 'Jesus is Lord' (Romans 10:9; 1 Corinthians 12:3). Jesus is regularly referred to by three titles: 'Lord', 'Christ' and 'Son' of God. 'Christ' focuses on him as Israel's anointed 'Messiah' (or royal king), but in some instances it has almost become a 'proper name' for Jesus. And, although all believers can be adopted as God's children, 'Son' is used of Jesus to give him a clearly distinctive status (see, for example, Romans 1:3; Galatians 1:16; 4:4).

Other exalted descriptions given to Jesus include the great High Priest, Holy One, Word, Lamb of God, Lord of Glory, Mediator, Sovereign, Lion of Judah, Last Adam, Judge, Head over all, Saviour, Shepherd, Living Stone, Seed of Abraham, the First and the Last. He is also seen as greater than anyone or anything known in the Old Testament – whether Abraham, Moses, David, or the Temple. He is our peace, life, hope and chief cornerstone, our brother and husband. In all these ways the New Testament makes it quite clear that Jesus is seen as unique.

believed in him were later to receive. Up to that time the Spirit had not been given' (John 7:39). This is one of the clearest verses where John shows how he is looking back at Jesus' life with hindsight. He and his readers now know full well about the gift of the Spirit; what John is drawing out are the hints given in advance by Jesus as to this forthcoming spiritual reality.

Yet none of this conflicts with the synoptics. In all of them Jesus is announced by John the Baptist as the one who in due course will 'baptize with the Holy Spirit'; the Spirit is manifested at Jesus' baptism and leads Jesus into the desert; he is the source of Jesus' power against Satan. Luke portrays Jesus as the man anointed with 'the power of the Spirit' (Isaiah 61 in Luke 4) and filled with 'joy through the Holy Spirit' (10:21). There may not be the Johannine reflection on the nature of the Spirit in the life of the believer; yet there is no doubting that Jesus' kingdom-announcing mission is all empowered by the Spirit of God.

JESUS' IDENTITY

Like the synoptics, John focuses on the question of Jesus' true identity, but he does so in a different way. In Mark, for example, the reader is kept in some suspense, joining the puzzled disciples on their slow discovery as to who Jesus is (the 'messianic secret' takes a while to be solved). John, however, cannot hold himself back. The truth of who he believes Jesus to have been tumbles out immediately. Thus even by the end of John chapter 1, the reader has already heard the following titles associated with Jesus: Word of God, Truth, Light, Lord, Messiah, Lamb of God, Baptizer with the Holy Spirit, Rabbi, Prophet, king of Israel, Son of God. When characters within the narrative use these titles, they may of course not have known at the time the full import of what they were saying; but John wants his readers straightaway to know who this Jesus is.

The synoptic writers, however, are not so different. The opening chapters of Matthew name Jesus as the Messiah, son of Abraham, Son of David, 'God with us', Saviour, king of the Jews, shepherd of Israel and God's 'Son'; he is conceived by the Holy Spirit of a Virgin and fulfils numerous prophecies. In Luke he is 'Son of the Most High', seated on David's throne, Lord, Saviour, Messiah. Even in Mark (who omits the narratives of Jesus' birth) the opening verse announces that Jesus is the 'Christ, the Son of God'. This title may have been added after Mark's first edition, yet the discerning reader of Mark chapter 1 can still see that for Mark Jesus is Lord, the baptizer with the Holy Spirit, the beloved Son, the bringer of the kingdom, the Holy One of God, and the worker of miracles. Thus the evangelists may have slightly different ways of dealing with the tension between what the characters in the story knew at the time and what they as writers now believe about Jesus, but they all 'spill the beans' quite quickly.

But what about Jesus' 'divinity'? Has not John presented us with quite a different Jesus from what is found in the other gospels? In John Jesus comes across as a superhuman figure and is described so frequently as the 'Son of God' or simply 'the Son' (more than one hundred times). In particular there are the famous 'I am' sayings. These are not in the synoptics and in several cases suggest that Jesus was identifying himself with God (whose name had been revealed to Moses as 'I AM'). Is this not completely different to the synoptics?

Yet again, however, the contrast is more apparent than real. For a start, John's Jesus is clearly fully human: tired, hungry, thirsty, weeping, and dying. At the same time the synoptics have far more indications of Jesus' divinity than some might think.

This is seen in many of the titles we have just listed from their opening chapters – titles that are then repeated throughout their narratives. 'Lord' may sometimes just mean 'master', but on other occasions its use is forcing readers to see a dramatic link between Jesus and Israel's God, known as the 'Lord'. 'Saviour' is significant because of the Jewish belief that only God can save ('Jesus' means *God* saves'; see Matthew 1:21). Likewise when Jesus is portrayed as the judge, or the one who forgives sins, or as the instant calmer of a violent storm, he is doing what it was expected *only God could do*.

The title 'messiah', it is true, does not imply divinity (no one was expecting a divine messiah). But then when Jesus enters Jerusalem on a donkey as the 'King of Zion' and is portrayed as the king in the kingdom of God, these are clear hints that something unexpected is happening. On occasions (see Luke 11:31) Jesus even speaks as though he is the embodiment of Wisdom (a figure associated in the Old Testament with God himself).

Then there are the revelatory moments at Jesus' baptism and at the transfiguration when the divine voice speaks of his 'beloved Son'. All the synoptic writers (in particular, Matthew) go on to have other references to Jesus as the 'Son' of God – clearly understanding this as applicable to Jesus in a new and unique sense.

Finally, there is this significant verse in both Matthew (11:27) and Luke (10:22): 'All things have been committed to me by my Father. No one knows who the Son is except the Father, and no one knows who the Father is except the Son and those to whom the Son chooses to reveal him.'

With its focus on the Father and the Son this verse sounds as though it is from John's Gospel, but it is not. The synoptic writers evidently know too the same Jesus of whom John speaks.

There is no doubting, then, that the synoptic writers share with John this belief in Jesus' unique identity as the Son of God. They may present Jesus more from the perspective of how he would have been *perceived at the time*; they may also not ponder much about his pre-existence and what it was like for him then to enter our human world, but they are in no doubt that Jesus has truly come from God.

THE MIRACLES OF JESUS

There are apparent differences, too, in John's presentation of Jesus' miracles. Partly this is because he includes a different selection: three healings (of the centurion's son, the paralytic at the pool of Bethesda, and the man born blind), the changing of water into wine at Cana, and the raising of Lazarus from the grave. Unlike the synoptics there are no exorcisms (though he sees Jesus' death as the time when the 'prince of this world' is cast out: John 12:31). Even so, there is one miracle that is found in all four gospels – the feeding of the 5,000.

More importantly, however, John sees these miracles not as 'mighty works' or 'wonders', but rather as 'signs'. So the Cana miracle was 'the first of his miraculous signs... he thus revealed his glory, and his disciples put their faith in him' (John 2:11). For John, Jesus' 'signs' are signposts pointing to his unique identity, moments when the inherent 'glory' of Jesus is unveiled, and opportunities given so that people may be moved to put their faith in him. It is not enough for people to marvel or 'wonder', they must now trust.

Yet this is not so different to the synoptic miracles, which all point in

Jesus performed his first miracle, the changing of water into wine, at the wedding at Cana depicted in this German painting.

different ways to Jesus' identity. In the synoptics there are other levels of meaning: Jesus' responding with compassion, or the in-breaking of God's longed-for kingly rule (fulfilling a prophecy such as Isaiah 35). John's focus is more single and pointed. He is fixated with Jesus' glory and wants others to see this too. The language of 'signs' enables him to do this. It also will give colour to his account of Jesus' death – this too is a 'sign' that also, despite its shame, reveals his true glory.

All four evangelists are well aware, of course, that what they are describing here are unusual events. Yet they were working with a biblical vision of a God who is well able to work within his world. They were not deists (believing in God as an absent 'referee') or pantheists (identifying God fully with the natural world) but Jewish monotheists believing in the God of creation and providence. They would have recognized the normal 'laws of nature' but not seen these descriptions of normal life as setting a bar on what the Living God could do according to his will. Their God was one who had frequently acted through the medium of history and human beings, but could also on occasions work outside these channels (for example in the days of Elijah). And this was what they came to believe he had done in Jesus – not only in his particular 'miracles' but also in the very act of sending Jesus into the world. What John has done is simply to see Jesus' acts of power more directly as an indication of this second, much larger miracle (that of God becoming human in Jesus). They point to the awesome miracle of the Incarnation; they are truly 'signs' of his 'glory'.

THE GLORY OF JESUS

John's Gospel is thus an account that deliberately focuses on Jesus' glory – where the glory, as it were, keeps breaking through. Jesus seeks to 'glorify' God (12:28), but God then glorifies him (12:23, 28). Through Jesus' signs people see 'the glory of God' (11:40), but also Jesus' glory. In fact Jesus' own glory is eternal – it was even seen by Isaiah, says John (12:41). So Jesus prays that his disciples may 'see my glory, the glory you have given me because you loved me before the creation of the world' (17:24).

glory and majesty of Jesus are seen at last within the synoptic account. At the time it was a private revelation, but now the reader is allowed into this awesome secret.

Yet, strangely, John's Gospel omits this account of the transfiguration. But this is precisely because he has let the transfiguration flood all his account. The whole gospel is a transfiguration, an unveiling of the true Jesus. It is all his way of publicising what he had been privileged to see in private – the

Mount Hermon where Jesus' transfiguration is believed to have taken place.

What has caused John to write in this way? According to his own claim it is because he himself was an eyewitness of this glory: 'we have seen his glory' (1:14). Although this can be read in a weaker sense, it is almost certain that this is an allusion to that moment in the gospel story when, as the synoptic writers agree, Jesus' glory did indeed break through. Peter, James and *John* were on the side of a mountain when they suddenly saw Jesus 'transfigured' in 'glorious splendour' (Luke 9:31; Matthew 17:2; Mark 9:2). Here the

inherent, eternal glory of Jesus.

At this point, then, one can sense one of the chief differences between the synoptics and John. The synoptics have deliberately restrained themselves, dropping clear hints as to Jesus' identity, but all the time keeping the perspective of those who watched Jesus with a degree of distance. John has simply been unable to do so: it is the account of someone who knew him intimately and who wants this previous secret to be published throughout the world.

The transfiguration effectively marked the end of Jesus' ministry in Galilee. It was the occasion when

JESUS

Jesus' identity (now glimpsed by his disciples) was confirmed; when Jesus was affirmed by his heavenly Father; when Moses and Elijah discussed with him the next, most critical phase of his mission – the 'exodus' (or departure) that he would 'bring to fulfilment at Jerusalem' (Luke 9:31). From this moment on, as soon as he leaves this mountain-top experience, Jesus will 'resolutely set out for Jerusalem' (Luke 9:51). It is the 'calm before the storm'.

Jerusalem and the Crucifixion of Jesus

'When [Jesus] came near the place where the road goes down the Mount of Olives, the whole crowd of disciples began joyfully to praise God in loud voices for all the miracles they had seen: "Blessed is the king who comes in the name of the Lord!"' (Luke 19:37).

ENTERING THE CITY
Jesus' 'triumphal entry' into Jerusalem is one of the climaxes in each of the evangelists' accounts. For Galilean pilgrims, tired after their journey from the north, the moment when they arrived at last and suddenly saw Jerusalem's magnificent Temple spread out in front of them, would always be an electric moment. But on this occasion, there was extra cause for rejoicing. At last this messianic claimant, himself from backwater Galilee, was making his public bid for the capital's attention. There were even rumours going round that this man's arrival would cause the 'kingdom of God' to 'appear at once' (Luke 19:11).

Jesus had carefully prepared this moment. Unlike other messianic claimants, he did not arrive on horseback, boasting his military power. Instead he came seated on a donkey. This clearly was sign of peace – he was a messiah with a different agenda. Yet it also sent out another, deeply subversive signal. For, according to a prophecy in Zechariah (9:9), the one who came 'seated on a donkey' was 'Zion's *King*'. Jesus was claiming to be the fulfilment of this prophecy. He saw himself as Jerusalem's true king, entering his capital and seeking his throne.

This was a dramatic claim indeed – and all the more so, when it was remembered that in some biblical passages the true King of Zion was ultimately *God himself*. Moreover, that important prophecy about the 'good news' (in Isaiah 52:7–8) had spoken about the 'Lord himself returning to Zion'. Could Jesus be hinting that he was the Lord? Was the Lord returning to Zion *in* and *as* Jesus? Was God at last becoming King through the arrival of this Jesus in Jerusalem?

It was the beginning of a dramatic week in Jerusalem. Many had been wondering what would happen when this forthright prophet spoke out in the nation's capital. And what would happen in the Temple, given that Jesus' actions had challenged the Temple in so many ways? Sparks were set to fly.

CLEANSING THE TEMPLE
The next day, after retiring for the night to the home of his friends in Bethany, Jesus indeed returned to the Temple. And this time he made his presence felt in no uncertain terms. 'He began driving out those who were selling. "It is written", he said to them, 'My house will be a house of prayer'; but you have made it a 'den of robbers'." (Luke 19:45–46). Evidently, like Jeremiah before him (Jeremiah 7:11), he was radically opposed to many of the corrupt practices in the Temple.

Yet there was more than a hint too that, as in Jeremiah's day, Jesus was also using this prophetic action to warn of the Temple's imminent destruction. So, when alone with his

'When Plato says that it is difficult to see the maker and Father of the universe, we Christians agree with him. And yet he can be seen, for it is written: "Blessed are the pure in heart, for they shall see God." Moreover, he who is the image of the invisible God has said: "He who sees me, has seen the Father."'

Origen

> 'Jesus whom I know as my Redeemer cannot be less than God.'
>
> Athanasius

Jesus washing the disciples' feet before the Last Supper is depicted in this eleventh-century Italian fresco.

disciples, he explicitly taught that 'not one' of the Temple's stones would be 'left upon another' (Luke 21:6). He also used his strange cursing of a fig tree as a sign that the Temple was now under God's curse – because it was failing to bring God the desired fruit (Mark 11:12–14, 21). His 'cleansing of the Temple' was, more accurately, a portent of destruction. Jesus, with prophetic and political insight, can be seen as warning how this beautiful building would look like within a generation – when it would be demolished and burnt by Roman armies under Emperor Titus in AD 70.

At some point later in the week, when seated on the Mount of Olives, he would warn his disciples of horrendous days ahead for Jerusalem, which would all be connected in some way with his own vindication as the 'Son of Man' (Luke 21:7–36). That's why, on first seeing the 'city of peace',

he had wept over it: 'if you had only known what would bring you peace… Your enemies… will encircle you… on every side… because you did not recognize the time of God's coming to you' (Luke 19:41–44). This was a critical hour for Jerusalem, the moment of its destiny, but it did not know it.

So this powerful act in the Temple was deliberately symbolic. It was also deeply controversial, inevitably bringing Jesus into trouble with the Temple authorities. They were soon asking 'by what authority' he had done this (Luke 20:2). At the time there were widespread beliefs that the Messiah would have royal authority over the Temple – indeed that he would 'restore' and purify it. Was Jesus implicitly claiming to be the Messiah? And if he was, why was he hinting at the Temple's destruction, not its restoration? Jesus, however, sidesteps

their question by quizzing them about the 'authority' of John the Baptist. He then continues teaching daily in the Temple courts, fielding more awkward questions, until some time on the Thursday.

EATING BREAD AND DRINKING WINE

After sundown Jesus meets his disciples in an Upper Room somewhere in Jerusalem's 'Upper City'. Taking a towel he teaches them the importance of humility and service. A little later, however, taking some bread and wine, he teaches them the most important lesson of all: that he is about to give his body and blood for them in a costly death which from then onwards must always be at the very centre of their lives. 'This is my body… this is my blood… Do this in remembrance of me.'

This Last Supper of Jesus is deeply shocking. For Jesus' disciples, whose

Jewish religious traditions forbade them from drinking blood, it was a macabre command – almost sacrilegious, indeed seemingly cannibalistic. But Jesus insisted. Just as Peter had to have his feet washed by Jesus (otherwise he would have no part with Jesus), so the disciples, if they wished to continue as Jesus' followers, had to eat and drink.

It was the Passover season, when Israel looked back with thanksgiving to God's rescue from Egypt and to the way God's judgment had 'passed over' their families through the shed blood of a lamb. It was a time too when they prayed that God would deliver them again from their pagan oppressors. Jesus, however, adapting the Passover liturgy and altering its symbolism, now places himself and his own death into the heart of this story. God will accomplish a new 'exodus' through Jesus, the real enemy will be overthrown, Jesus' people will come through the judgment to safety – and all this, because of the shedding of *his* blood.

The disciples might also have sensed a contrast with Jesus' prophetic action in the Temple a few days earlier. There he had overturned the tables, symbolically bringing the Temple sacrifices to a halt. Now he is establishing a different table and speaking of a new, different sacrifice. Could it be that the Temple's days were numbered, not just because of its present corrupt practices, but because this Jesus would himself render it obsolete? For in his own person he seemed to be everything that the Temple was meant to symbolize (God's presence on earth) and his own death would be a costly sacrifice dealing with the sins of God's people. So the Temple could effectively be 'relocated'; for Jesus was both the 'Lord of the Temple' and its ultimate sacrificial offering.

Such ideas might have been too

'Socrates dies with honour, surrounded by his disciples listening to the most tender words — the easiest death that one could wish to die. Jesus dies in pain, dishonour, mockery, the object of universal cursing — the most horrible death that one could fear. At the receipt of the cup of poison, Socrates blesses him who could not give it to him without tears; Jesus, while suffering the sharpest pains, prays for His most bitter enemies. If Socrates lived and died like a philosopher, Jesus lived and died like a god.'

Jean-Jacques Rousseau

much to consider just at that moment, but in due course, when they looked back on what Jesus had been doing in these important symbolic actions in Jerusalem, they would begin to make eminent sense. Certainly the New Testament writers will not be slow to draw these conclusions in due course: Jesus himself was the true Temple (John 1:14; 2:21) and his death finally ended the need for any of its animal sacrifices (Romans 3:25; Hebrews 10:10).

All this (and much more besides) is packed into Jesus' famous words at his Last Supper – words that have been repeated by Jesus' followers ever since as they celebrate this special meal in his name. For now we note simply that Jesus here is clearly resolved to die. He is planning for it and making arrangements for after his death. That is why the mood in John's extended account is so solemn; the disciples' hearts are grieving because Jesus is talking so much about his 'departure' (John 13–17). What this then means is that we have to reckon very seriously with the fact that Jesus positively intended to die. It was no accident but a conscious part of his purpose. And he wants his death to be right at the very centre of his followers' attention from now on.

AWAITING ARREST

At some point in the meal one of the disciples, Judas Iscariot, leaves. He makes his way to the nearby house of Caiaphas the high priest. Jesus knows full well that he has been looking in recent days for an opportunity to betray him over to the authorities. Now he has his opportunity. For Jesus' talk of his own death gives Judas the necessary assurance that Jesus will not put up a fight. In fact, Jesus has announced his intention to leave shortly for a place that will be ideal for him to be arrested discreetly – an enclosed olive grove called

Gethsemane outside the city at the foot of the Mount of Olives. The key question now becomes one of timing: can Jesus be put to death before the start of the Sabbath at sundown the next day? This will require urgent consultation amongst the leaders – and perhaps even a late night visit by Caiaphas to the Roman governor. Jesus himself seems to have set the timetable – and it is extremely tight.

Once in Gethsemane, Jesus prays alone in agony. It was one thing to talk about your own death, quite another to go through with it. But Jesus' trust in God shines through: 'not my will, but yours be done' (Luke 22:42). He resolves to drink the 'cup' (an Old Testament reference to God's judgment). There is a long delay – perhaps till around two o'clock in the morning (the disciples fall asleep *three* times); but Jesus does not flee over the hillside to Bethany. Instead he waits, intent on accomplishing his God-given, unique mission. Then, at last, the search party arrives and Jesus is led back into the city to be interrogated by the high priest.

STANDING TRIAL

It will be a long night with no sleep. During the next eight hours, Jesus will be 'tried' by several judges: Annas and Caiaphas, the Jewish Sanhedrin, Herod Antipas and Pontius Pilate (the Roman governor). The religious authorities, fearful that Jesus will incite the populace against them and perhaps envious of his evident authority, will come up with a charge of 'blasphemy'. They begin with questions about his actions in the Temple. (What did he mean when he spoke about 'destroying' the Temple and 'rebuilding it in three days'?) Then they press the question of his identity, placing him under oath. Jesus responds, speaking of himself as the 'Son of Man sitting at the right hand of the Mighty One' (Mark 14:62). This is an enormous,

> 'Learn to know Christ and him crucified. Learn to sing to him, and say, "Lord Jesus, you are my righteousness, I am your sin. You have taken upon yourself what is mine and given me what is yours. You have become what you were not so that I might become what I was not."'
>
> Martin Luther

preposterous claim. In their sight, Jesus has clearly condemned himself out of his own lips.

The problem is, only the Roman governor can issue the death sentence and he may not be too bothered by this charge of 'blasphemy'. So Jesus' 'crimes' are now dressed up in a more political garb: opposing taxes to Caesar (a lie) and claiming to be the 'king of the Jews' (true, but not in that sense). After some hesitation, initially declaring Jesus to be innocent of these charges, Pilate is persuaded – fearful perhaps of how the emperor would view his tolerating this supposed 'king'. He commands that Jesus be flogged and then crucified.

COMPLETING THE TASK

So Jesus is led out to Golgotha, the 'place of the skull' to be crucified between two bandits. Crucifixion was reserved for just such people – for political rebels and for slaves. It was widely agreed to be the most terrible way to die, barbaric in the extreme. Victims had nails hammered through their forearms into a wooden beam and then were lifted up on another wooden stump. Eventually (and sometimes it could take days, not hours) they died of suffocation, unable to pull themselves up sufficiently to breathe.

Jesus, in fact, died more quickly than some. For those of his followers watching (especially his mother), it was a harrowing event, a tragedy of infinite proportions. Despite its emotional and spiritual significance, however, the gospel writers are remarkably restrained in describing the crucifixion. Through mentioning those who cast lots for his clothing, they give

The Mount of Olives where Jesus was arrested after Judas had betrayed him in the Garden of Gethsemane.

a hint that Jesus would of course have been naked on the cross – something deeply shameful in Jewish thought. They also recount some of the key things he said in his agony, in particular: 'Father, forgive them, they know not what they do'; 'My God, why have you forsaken me?'; 'Into your hands I commit my spirit'; and 'It is finished!' Some of these are words of forgiveness and trust; others speak of the torment he was enduring, but also of his sense that he had finally achieved what he had set out to do.

As sundown approached, the soldiers checked the victims were dead. Joseph of Arimathaea (a member of the Sanhedrin but an admirer of Jesus) got permission to take Jesus' body and place it in his nearby tomb, while some of the women, who had travelled with Jesus from Galilee, looked on.

For most people it was the end of another ordinary day. Jesus' enemies will have gone off to their family Passover celebrations. Others, more sympathetic to Jesus, will have been sickened to see someone they admired put to death so cruelly – when would the Romans go away? When would God send a true Messiah? But priests in the Temple were in for a shock – the curtain covering the holy of holies had been torn from 'top to bottom'. And there was at least one Roman soldier who knew there had been a gross miscarriage of justice: 'Surely this man was the Son of God!' (Mark 15:39). His words were truer than he knew.

The Crucifixion in Christian Art

Christ suffered and died upon the cross in order to bring about the salvation of humanity. Christian writers and artists have always been aware of the need to reflect on this pivotal event, and its life-changing implications. Churches, private chapels, and houses were often decorated with depictions of the crucifixion as a means of encouraging personal devotion. Unlike the Docetic heresy (which held that Jesus merely had the 'appearance' of humanity, and did not really suffer), Christian orthodoxy stressed both the reality of Christ's agony on the cross, and the salvation which it achieved. Visual representations of Christ's suffering on the cross thus served to stress the costliness of humanity's redemption, and to deepen Christians' appreciation of what he achieved for them. The more they appreciate the pain he suffered, the more they shall adore him for what he did for all.

Depictions of the passion of Christ often show different emphases. Some depict Christ as raised up on this cross, high above the crowds around him. This is meant to focus our attention on the way in which Christ was 'raised up' on the cross, so that we might in turn be 'raised up' to heaven by his cross and resurrection. Others focus on the crowds around him, sometimes depicting the rage and fury on the faces of those who mocked him. The point being made here is that those who crucified Christ were actually quite ordinary people, just like us. On a Christian understanding of human nature, our natural instinct is not to adore Christ but to crucify him. It is a telling reminder of the power of sin to distort and destroy, and an equally powerful reminder of our need for redemption – the redemption, of course, that Christ brought by death on the cross.

Others images focus on those who are standing around the cross. An excellent example of this is provided by Matthias Grunewald's famous altarpiece at Isenheim, completed in 1515. To the left of the cross, three people mourn the dead Christ: Mary, the mother of Jesus; John, the beloved disciple, and Mary Magdalene. This is intended to help us appreciate the appalling impact that Christ's death had on his

Matthias Grunewald's *Crucifixion* includes many symbolic images.

disciples. In the case of Mary, we are invited to imagine how she must have felt when her son – the one whom she held in her arms as an infant – was taken away from her, and spread out on the arms of the cross.

To the right of the cross, we see John the Baptist. Grunewald wants to remind us of the words of John on seeing Jesus: 'Behold the lamb of God, who takes away the sin of the world.' The death of Christ is the means by which the sin of the world was removed. By pointing to the crucified Christ, John proclaims that this Christ is the lamb of God, whose death purges us of our sins. In case we miss this allusion, Grunewald includes a lamb in the lower part of the picture, along with a cross and chalice to point to the importance of its saving death. John the Baptist also symbolizes the continuity between the Old and New Testaments. For Grunewald, Jesus is to be seen as the fulfilment of the great Old Testament prophecies of redemption – the one by whose stripes humanity is healed, and whose wounds bring salvation (Isaiah 53).

DYING FOR OTHERS

Jesus' followers ever since have wanted to understand in more detail what was going on in this seemingly disastrous event. For the evangelists, committed to recounting the story without giving great theological explanations, the key points that emerge from the story are these.

Jesus' death was no accident but a conscious part of his purpose. He had alluded to it many times and clearly predicted it. 'The Son of Man must be… killed' (Mark 8:31). Their narrative shows how Jesus, rather than escaping, calmly engineered his own demise.

Jesus himself was innocent – both of the political charges made against him, but also in terms of any personal sin. His death was therefore undeserved at every level. It was clearly not for his own sins, but somehow for the sins of others. So, picking up the motifs of the innocent Suffering Servant, Jesus said that he had come to 'give his life as a ransom for many' (Mark 10:45). His blood would be poured out 'for the forgiveness of sins' (Matthew 26:28).

These two key insights, rooted in the Jesus of history, will then be the bedrock on which other New Testament writers build their theology of the cross (see page 176). It is a powerful story in its own right, but it is also one that needs further explanation – not least in the light of what followed. For the crucifixion, central as it is, can never be understood without noting what happened three days later. Jesus said he would rebuild the Temple 'in three days'. What exactly did he mean?

The Resurrection and Kingship of Jesus

'Dead men do not rise from the dead.' The ancient world knew this bitter truth just as much as we do – perhaps more. Yes, of course there were various views about a possible 'after-life' in another world or for the soul, but the pagan world knew one thing for certain: 'Once a man has died, and the dust has soaked up his blood, there is no resurrection' (Aeschylus, *Eumenides* 647). The Greek word here for 'resurrection' is *anastasis* (literally, a 'making to stand upright'). Everyone knew this physical 'raising' of dead bodies never happened.

At least, almost everyone. In the centuries before Jesus a major strand within Judaism had begun to develop a belief in 'resurrection' – but it was what God would do for *all* his faithful people at the dawn of the *very end* of the age. No one, not even the Pharisees who espoused this view most strongly, expected it could happen to *one man* in the *middle* of human history.

Yet this is precisely what is claimed for this one man, Jesus of Nazareth. Jesus' followers stuck their necks out – defying everyone, both pagan and Jewish – with this stark claim: on the third day after his crucifixion, Israel's God had raised Jesus from the dead. Their word for this was none other than *anastasis*. They were not talking about some spiritual, invisible event for Jesus' soul; they were not talking about resuscitation after a period of sleep. They were making a claim for his corpse: it had been truly dead, but now it had been raised 'from the dead' (literally 'from among the corpses').

Such a claim would have met with mirth and derision. It flew in the face of what everyone knew to be true. What could possibly have led them to this absurd belief?

Only one thing: the event itself. They were confronted with a fact. They were presented not with an abstract theory, nor a tentative possibility, nor even some wishful thinking of their own, but with an empty tomb, a missing body and a risen Jesus who met them, talked with them and ate with them.

The story is well known. Most of Jesus' disciples had fled to Bethany from Gethsemane and were not there to see Jesus die. It was only Peter and John (who had followed him into the city for this trial), together with the women in their party, who saw the tragic events of the Friday. And of these it was, not unnaturally, the women who resolved (once the Sabbath was over) to return at first light on the Sunday morning to complete the job that had been done so hastily late on the Friday afternoon – the anointing of Jesus' body for a proper burial.

They make their way to Jesus' tomb (in a 'garden' area just outside the city walls), but they never achieve what they set out to do. The grave has been disturbed. Within a matter of minutes they are running back to Peter and John with a startling tale: first, they had seen that the stone at the tomb's entrance had been rolled away; then that Jesus' body had been stolen; and, finally, a strange figure had spoken to them with some unlikely words about Jesus meeting them again in Galilee. 'He is not here; he is risen!', he had called after them – but they were fleeing from the site in complete panic and disbelief.

Peter and John run to the tomb, and see the grave-clothes still there. Who would have stolen a naked body? Indeed the separate head-cloth is lying there – as it were, in its original position. It is enough to start John believing in an act of God – it is as though Jesus' body has simply left its grave-clothes behind! And then Mary Magdalene, loitering in the garden, actually sees Jesus himself. She thought the person near her was the gardener, but he calls out her name with a knowing love that she instantly recognizes. 'Mary', he says. 'Master!', she cries.

The accounts of that first Easter Sunday, found in each of the four gospels, tell this surprising story with a rough, artless simplicity. They are not polished into one 'sanitized' or 'authorized' account. They show all the signs of people describing bewildering events that made no sense at the time and which all happened so quickly. They go on to speak of other appearances of the risen Jesus to his followers: some later that day (to Simon Peter, to some of the women, to the pair walking to Emmaus, and to the disciples re-gathered in an upper room), some in the following few weeks (on a mountain in Galilee, by the lake and on the Mount of Olives).

Each account has freshness about it, pulsating with excitement. An unheard of thing has happened. A dead man is now walking. A crucified man is showing his wounds. The man who made messianic claims has been raised by God from the dead!

But there came a time when these resurrection-appearances came to an end. After a period of around forty days, during which Jesus had given 'many convincing proofs that he was alive', the risen Jesus met his followers somewhere on the Mount of Olives, not far from Bethany. Jesus taught them and blessed them (Acts 1:1–11). Then a cloud hid him from their sight, and he was gone – taken back into the very presence of God. In due course they

When Peter and John found the stone moved from the front of Jesus' tomb and his body gone, they were at first uncertain whether to believe in his resurrection.

return to Jerusalem and to the Temple – praising God for what they have seen, and waiting (as Jesus had told them to) for the next instalment in this extraordinary sequence of events.

Matthew chooses to finish his Gospel with Jesus' appearance to his disciples on a 'mountain' in Galilee and with some words that set the seal on all that Jesus had said and done: 'All authority in heaven and on earth has been given to me. Go therefore and make disciples of all nations, baptizing them in the name of the Father, the Son and the Holy Spirit, and teaching them to obey everything that I have commanded you. And remember, I am with you always, to the end of the age.' (Matthew 28:18–20).

For Matthew (as indeed for all the evangelists) the resurrection shows that Jesus is the true Messiah, God's appointed king, the divine Son with unique authority. This message of Israel's king, however, is not only for Israel. Jesus now commissions his followers to take this message to 'all nations', bringing them too under the rule and authority of this king. And, although he is no longer walking this earth, he is no absentee ruler, but through his Holy Spirit he is able to live in and amongst his people, who can say, 'truly God is with us'.

This message has gone around the world from that day till now. The kingdom of God spreads as people are brought under the rule of this King Jesus, acknowledging who he is and learning to do what he commands. It is a message that in one sense is very narrow – it focuses on this unique Jesus. And yet it is universal in its range and appeal. All people can be brought within this kingdom. 'Christians' are simply those who confess that Jesus is the 'Christ' – that is, the Messiah or king. The question that is posed to all of us through the resurrection and the ascension of Jesus is simply this: will we have this person to be our king?

> 'Christianity without discipleship is always Christianity without Christ.'
>
> Dietrich Bonhoeffer

The Incarnation and Revelation of Jesus

Like any 'thriller' or detective story, the story of Jesus only makes sense in the light of its end. Now we have witnessed the resurrection, now that we have seen where the story was going, we are in a far better position to understand what it was all about. We can go back and find the clues that were there all along.

As we have seen, this was one of the major factors that explains the differences between the gospels: the synoptics writers tend to tell the story 'forwards' from the 'front', whereas John's Gospel has simply told the story in the light of its end, drawing out for his readers the clues they might otherwise have missed. The rest of the New Testament, of course, joins John at this point, basing all its teaching on the full picture of Jesus – seen in the light of his resurrection.

JESUS' IDENTITY: OTHER NEW TESTAMENT TEACHING

We can see from page 144 some of the immense things that the New Testament writers conclude about Jesus' person. The Resurrection is not just an amazing event in itself for what it reveals about God's plans for the world (for example, the transformation of our physical bodies, the renewal of creation, the promise of eternal life). It also gives the proper grounds for a whole new revelation as to who Jesus was – and *is*! Jesus is Messiah, Son of God, King, and Lord. He is the 'Alpha and the Omega', the 'Lamb that was slain from the creation of the world' (Revelation 13:8); he is the 'firstborn of creation', the 'Head of the Church which is his body' (Colossians 1:15, 18); he is the 'great high priest' who, though fully human, enjoys a status with God far above that enjoyed by angels (Hebrews 4:14).

The New Testament simply cannot

say enough about Jesus. It stretches language to breaking point, adapting available concepts in order to pour into them a whole new meaning. For example, the title 'Son of God' was already in use within biblical thought, but it referred to the Davidic king or perhaps to Israel as a nation. Now it was used to refer to Jesus in a unique and new sense. Yes, he was the true king and the embodiment of Israel, but he was also one who had enjoyed with God a unique and eternal relationship.

One of the remarkable things about this New Testament teaching is just how early it is. The opening verses of Galatians (1:1–3) are probably the first words of the New Testament to be written. Yet, without apology or embarrassment, they say the most outrageous things about Jesus. Thus Paul claims to be an apostle sent not by men, 'but by Jesus Christ and God the Father'. He is clearly bracketing Jesus not with human beings, but with God. 'Grace and peace to you', he then continues, 'from God our Father and the Lord Jesus Christ'. Again Jesus is bracketed with God; he is the 'Lord' (the name previously associated exclusively with Israel's God); and God himself is now defined in a new way as the 'Father' – precisely because Jesus is his Son in some unique sense. All this is written around AD 49 (under twenty years since the crucifixion) to people who had been converted by Paul's preaching several years before *that*. So here is clear evidence from the very earliest days that the apostles are proclaiming Jesus as the Divine Son. There never was a preaching of the gospel, nor an authentic version of Christianity, that did not take this as its basic starting point.

This teaching about Jesus is also remarkable because all the New Testament writers (with the exception of Luke) are Jewish. Trained in monotheism, raised with the

conviction that there is but 'one Lord', they yet proclaim that 'Jesus is Lord'. This was the earliest Christian 'creed' or statement of faith. That then is why the earliest Aramaic-speaking Christians prayed, '*Maranatha*', which means, 'O *Lord*, come!' (1 Corinthians 16:22). It also explains an extraordinary passage in 1 Corinthians, where Paul writes: 'for us there is but one God, the Father, from whom all things came… and but one Lord, Jesus Christ, through whom all things came' (1 Corinthians 8:6). In other words, Jesus serves a parallel role to God. If Jews confessed 'one *Lord* and *God*', Jewish believers now confessed *God* as the Father and Jesus as the *Lord*. Jesus is, as it were, right there in the heart of the one God of Israel.

These texts then dismiss any idea that it was only Gentiles (non-Jews) who proclaimed Jesus as a divine figure. This argument is put forward frequently in some circles. The first followers of Jesus, so it is claimed, presented him as a (merely human) messiah; only when the good news went out to non-Jews, did anyone start identifying Jesus with God. Such a thing, it is said, would have been unthinkable for good Jews.

Yet Paul the rabbi clearly disagreed. So too did the writer of Hebrews, arguably the most Jewish writer of the New Testament. In his opening verses he proclaims Jesus as the 'Son, whom [God] appointed heir of all things, and through whom he made the universe. The Son is the radiance of God's glory and the exact representation of his being, sustaining all things by his powerful word' (Hebrews 1:2–3). No, Jesus is not the 'son' of some semi-pagan god, but the Son of the one true God of Israel. People may try to soften this teaching or explain it away, but the New Testament is unashamed. Thus it is entirely fitting that John at the climax of his Gospel has doubting

Jesus in Early Christian Thought

We can learn much about the significance of Jesus from the history of the Christian church in the first few centuries of its existence. One of the most interesting historical observations is that the early Christians had no hesitation in worshipping Christ as God. This practice was noted by a Roman official, the younger Pliny, in his famous letter of AD 112 to the Emperor Trajan, in which he reports that Christians sang hymns to their Lord 'as God' (*quasi deo*). These ideas were the common currency of the early Christian communities. Clement, a first-century writer, insisted that Christians 'think about Jesus as we do about God' (2 Clement 1:1–2). Other writers stressed that only God could reveal God. The Christian belief that Jesus revealed God fully and definitively was fundamentally linked with the fact that he was God incarnate – in other words, that God had entered into human history as a human, in order to make himself known and available to humanity.

The Arian controversy of the early fourth century was of especial importance in clarifying the identity of Christ. Arius, while giving Christ precedence over all of God's creatures, insisted that he was still nothing more than a creature, rather than God. Although Jesus was to be treated as first among human beings, he was still only a human, and nothing more.

Responding to this, Athanasius argued that Arius was making the entire church guilty of worshipping a creature, rather than God. Only God could be worshipped, argued Athanasius, and as Christians had worshipped Christ from the beginning of the Christian era, this meant that Christ had to be regarded as divine. But who must Jesus be if he can be worshipped legitimately in this way? Athanasius also argued that only one who *is* God can be worshipped, in that only God is *entitled to* worship. We can see here an argument progressing from Christ's function (as an object of worship) to his identity (as God, who alone may be worshipped).

Athanasius followed this up by pointing out that created beings cannot be saved by another created being. Only God can save – and as Christ saves those who trust in him (which Arius did not, incidentally, dispute), he must be treated as God. Once more, we can see a direct argument from Christ's function (as Saviour) to his identity (as God). If Jesus Christ really does save believers, this implies that he is none other than the saviour God, who has come into our history to redeem us.

The early Christians, then, worshipped Christ as a fully divine saviour, regarding this as the obvious interpretation of the New Testament material. This basic understanding of the identity and function of Jesus Christ has remained characteristic of Christianity since then, despite a number of challenges to this understanding from within, as well as outside of, the Christian church. The Council of Chalcedon (451) may be regarded as laying down a controlling principle for classical Christology, which has been accepted ever since as definitive within Christian theology. The principle in question could be summarized like this: Provided that it is recognized that Jesus Christ is both truly divine and truly human, the precise manner in which this is expressed or explored is not of fundamental importance.

Thomas say to Jesus, 'My Lord and My God!' Thomas may not have thought through all the implications of those few words, but they are an entirely understandable response from someone who is encountering the risen Jesus. The risen Jesus forces everyone to rethink their views both of him and of his God.

JESUS' IDENTITY: CREEDAL REFLECTION

Classical Christian belief (see page 159) has therefore developed certain concepts to define who Jesus truly is. In particular in the creeds (derived from the early church) Christians declare their faith in the 'incarnation', in Jesus being 'of one substance/being with the Father' and in God as 'Trinity' (Father, Son and Holy Spirit).

These concepts and phrases can quickly be dismissed by some as 'non-biblical' (on the grounds that these precise words do not appear in the biblical texts). Perhaps, it is suggested, they are another sign of later developments in Christian faith, which take us yet further away from the original (merely human) Jesus?

Yet, as can be seen from our survey (above) of New Testament texts, the deity of Jesus Christ is clearly taught in the Bible. What these later concepts are doing is simply trying to summarize or elucidate the teaching that is already there in the New Testament – though it used some other words. The truth of God as Trinity, for example, is there in numerous texts (such as Matthew 28:18–20; 1 Corinthians 12:4–6; Romans 8:9–11; Ephesians 4:3–6; John 14–16). Similarly, the 'incarnation' is only a *noun* coined to express what John had taught (using a *verb*) when he said that in Jesus the 'Word became flesh' (John 1:14).

What is true, however, is that later Christians were forced to explain the identity of Jesus within a pagan culture that was more concerned (than was Hebrew culture) with difficult concepts like the 'being' of God – hence the awkward phrase 'of one being with the Father'. By and large, the biblical writers did not use this language (though John 1:1–18 comes close). Hebrew thought tended not to meditate on the conundrum of God's divine *being* (or, what is called, 'ontology') but rather on his divine *actions*. This meant that, when the New Testament writers wanted to assert the deity of Jesus, they tended instead to talk of his sharing in the *activities* that were normally reserved for God alone. Thus, for example, he is described as the one who 'created' the world (John 1:3; Colossians 1:15–16; Hebrews 1:2–3) and who will be our judge (2 Corinthians 5:10; John 5:27.). And Old Testament verses that spoke of God's actions were now seen as fulfilled in Jesus. Thus, for example, Isaiah had predicted that everyone would one day 'bow the knee' before Israel's God (Isaiah 45:23); but now an early Christian hymn said 'every knee will bow before *Jesus*' (Philippians 2:10–11).

In the New Testament, then, *Jesus is God at work*. Yet, to say this (that Jesus shares in the very *actions* of God) is itself to say something startling and extraordinary. It is hardly much less than saying that he shares in God's eternal being – that *Jesus is God* (full stop). The New Testament in fact teaches the latter as well (see John 1:1; 20:28; also perhaps Romans 9:5; Acts 20:28). All that the Creeds have done is to make this plain. They press through behind the actions of Jesus to see the true identity of Jesus. If Jesus was *God at work*, then he must also, in some sense, *be* God.

So the resurrection triggers off a whole process of re-evaluating who Jesus must have been. The earliest Christian preaching declares that Jesus, because now raised, has been established by God as 'Lord and

Christ' (Acts 2:36); and the worship of the first Christians included the radical (and 'blasphemous') innovation of worshipping Jesus (see Philippians 3:3; cf. Revelation 22:9). So it would not be too long, as we have seen, before the apostles were proclaiming that this Jesus had come from God in a unique sense.

JESUS' LIFE AND BIRTH

Of course this conviction about the resurrection and Jesus' divine identity can shed new light on other parts of Jesus' life. For example, Jesus' concern for the poor and marginalized can be recognized as a sure sign of God's love. Jesus' suffering and association with those in trouble begins to reveal the sympathy and presence of God in difficult circumstances. Jesus' authoritative teachings become the very words of God. Jesus' mission (proclaiming and introducing the kingdom of God) now shows the essence of God's purpose for all time. And Jesus' arrival in the storyline of Israel can now be seen as the most important moment in the whole drama of the Bible. For this is the arrival of Israel's God amongst 'his own'. This actor, who comes on stage in the middle of the drama, turns out to be none other than its author.

The Virgin Mary in Christian Thought

As the mother of Jesus Christ, Mary has long had a particularly important role in Christian devotion. Luke's Gospel stresses the importance of Mary's obedience to God in giving birth to the Messiah. Without in any way underplaying the importance of the Holy Spirit in the conception of the Saviour of the World, Luke clearly brings out the critical role of Mary's trust in God's promises, and obedience to his will. Many early Christian commentators highlighted these virtues, and argued that Mary should be a role model for all Christians in both respects. Like Mary, Christians should trust and obey God – even when what was promised or demanded seemed far beyond what humans could expect or deliver.

In the course of Christian history, the role of Mary has undergone significant developments. During the fourth century, the divinity of Christ became a matter of theological debate. The Arian controversy forced the church to revisit the biblical witness to Christ. In the end, the church reaffirmed the divinity of Christ, and developed a series of 'slogans' or theological formulae to defend it. One of these involved referring to Mary as *Theotokos*, 'bearer of God'. To affirm that Jesus was God was to imply that Mary was the 'mother of God'. Although some of the church's theologians were unhappy about this trend, it became increasingly important, and continues to this day.

In the Middle Ages, Mary began to assume a new role in Christian devotion. The official teaching of the church often made Jesus seem remote from ordinary people, and presented him primarily as judge, and secondarily as saviour. Reacting against this, popular piety began to find Mary a much more accessible and approachable figure. Mary increasingly became the focus for the needs, aspirations and prayers of the faithful. Although the medieval church valued all the saints, both as role models and as intercessors, Mary came to be seen as supreme among them. Although the official teaching of the church allowed only that Mary should be 'venerated' (treated with the greatest of respect) rather than 'worshipped' (something appropriate only to God or Christ), there is ample evidence that the devotional lives of many ordinary Christians – both male and female – centred on Mary as a source of encouragement and consolation.

The list could go on, but it is important to return now to the very beginning of Jesus' life. In the light of the resurrection one can understand why the New Testament writers insist that Jesus was not born in the normal human way. For Jesus was not just an ordinary human being who was 'promoted' to divinity only at some later point in his life. No, from the outset he had truly been the God–man – indeed he had been in existence long before that as well. But if so, how could he enter into our world? What would be the appropriate means for God to 'bring his firstborn into the world' (Hebrews 1:6)? The New Testament answers that Jesus was born from a virgin without the involvement of a human father (Matthew 1:18–25; Luke 1–2; see also Galatians 4:4).

The virgin birth has always been subjected to criticism – as a 'fairytale' miracle, useful perhaps for children at Christmas time. But, viewed in the light of the whole of Jesus' life, it now falls into its proper place. It is actually what you would expect. The story that ends so dramatically necessarily had a dramatic start. Not unnaturally the Virgin Mary did not draw attention to all this at the time; instead she 'treasured' all the things that happened and 'pondered them in her heart'

A theological development of the Middle Ages should be noted here – the idea of the 'immaculate conception'. In this view, Mary was born without sin, and was thus able to give birth to a sinless Saviour. Although the origins of the idea can be traced back to the thirteenth century, it only became the official teaching of the Roman Catholic Church in 1854, with the proclamation of the dogma of the immaculate conception. Protestants and others have serious misgivings about this notion, which seems to be unwarranted by any statements in the Bible, or the teachings of the early church. The Second Vatican Council (1962–65) preferred to stress the humanity of Mary, emphasizing that she sought to obey God, rather than displace him.

'I am a Jew, but I am enthralled by the luminous figure of the Nazarene… No one can read the Gospels without feeling the actual presence of Jesus. His personality pulsates in every word. No myth is filled with such life.'

Albert Einstein

An eighteenth-century Ethiopian depiction of the Madonna and Child.

How Muslims see Jesus

The growing global importance of Islam makes the question of how Muslims view Jesus of increasing significance to Christian apologetics and evangelism. Islam acknowledges that Jesus was a prophet, and a messenger of God. The name 'Jesus' (Arabic *isa*) is used twenty-five times. In most cases, his name is linked with the title 'Son of Mary' (*ibn Mariam*), although it is less frequently linked with that of Moses. Although the New Testament makes it clear that the name 'Jesus' means 'God saves' (Matthew 1:21), the Qur'an offers no explanation of the name *isa*. The related term 'messiah' (*al masih*) is also used in the Qur'an. Again, the rich Old Testament association of this term as 'God's anointed' is not noted or understood. It is not clear why the Qur'an should refer to Jesus as the 'son of Mary'. This title is used very rarely in the New Testament (Mark 6:3). It is also unusual (but not unknown) in the Semitic world for any major figure to be named after his mother, rather than father. The Qur'an also refers to Jesus using quite elevated language. Thus Jesus is referred to as the 'word of God' and 'spirit of God', giving him a place of honour within the Islamic understanding of the progression of revelation, which is held to reach its definitive climax in the revelation to Mohammed, committed to writing in the Qur'an.

The Islamic view of the significance of the death and resurrection of Jesus is somewhat complex. Although there are points where the Qur'an refers to the death of Christ, indicating that this was in accordance with the will of God, the precise manner and significance of his death remains unclear. One passage seems to teach that Jesus was neither killed by the Jews, nor crucified by his enemies 'although it seemed so to them' (*shubbiha la-hum*). Rather, Jesus was translated to heaven, with some other unnamed person taking his place on the cross. The phrase 'it seemed so to them' would thus bear the sense of either 'the Jews thought that Jesus died on the cross' or 'the Jews thought that the person on the cross was Jesus'. The mainstream Sunni position thus allows for some form of divine exaltation of Jesus, either as resurrection or ascension. Although the Qur'an itself does not mention any hope of Jesus' return to earth before the final judgment at the end of history, such ideas are found in at least some popular Islamic writings. It is probable that this idea may have developed in the post-Qur'anic era, possibly as a result of growing familiarity with Christian views of the end of time.

Perhaps most significantly, the idea of the incarnation is completely unacceptable to Islam. The Christian belief that Christ is the Son of God is seen by Islamic writers as a reversion to some form of paganism, characterized by the idea of God having physical children. The distinctively Christian understanding of what the phrase 'Son of God' entails appears not to have been fully understood at the time of the composition of the Qur'an.

(Luke 2:19). But it did mean that she was given a privileged window into the identity of Jesus. Unlike others she could watch the story's progress with an insider's knowledge – with foresight, not hindsight. However, there was a cost. She was warned that a 'sword' would 'pierce her soul' – for she would see her son Jesus nailed to a cross (John 19:25). Yet finally there was joy: she was there to share with the disciples in the joy of the resurrection (Acts 1:14).

From then on, no doubt, she began to share her secret. For truly, through her, God himself had chosen to enter the world. This was not a myth invented by an impressionable teenager (despite her critics, ancient and modern), but the awesome never-to-be repeated reality of the incarnation. This was God's chosen way of becoming one of us – of being truly Immanuel, God 'with us'. How else could it be?

JESUS' DEATH AND RESURRECTION

The resurrection also gives us a whole new perspective on Jesus' crucifixion. We can now see this not as a tragedy but as a victory; if it is a place of shame, it is also a place of glory. It is no accident, but reveals the immense depths of God's purpose. Without the resurrection we might never even have heard of this messianic claimant from Nazareth – those crucified on Roman crosses were clearly failed messiahs. With the resurrection, however, we see the cross as his greatest 'messianic' achievement – entering the 'messianic woes' to rescue God's people on the day of judgment.

The various Christian interpretations of the cross (in the New Testament and later writers) are summarized elsewhere (see page 176). All of them, however, only make sense in the light of the resurrection. If Jesus' death is seen as something he set out to achieve, only the resurrection shows that he was successful – his mission was accomplished. If the cross is seen as a sacrifice for sins, the resurrection shows that this sacrifice was accepted. If the cross is seen in more legal terms, then it is through the resurrection that we are 'vindicated' or justified (Romans 4:25). The cross makes no sense without the resurrection. With it, we see the cross as the very heart of what Jesus came to do.

The resurrection gives new meaning to the cross, however, in another vitally important way. For the resurrection, as we have seen, was the trigger for the discovery of Jesus' divine identity. Once one is convinced that Jesus on the cross is somehow *God at work*, then inevitably the cross becomes yet more powerful. For at the cross many find themselves being confronted with the mystery of God himself in the person of his own Son suffering and dying for his world. They begin to see it as an act of divine self-sacrifice. What amazing love their God has shown.

And this is what the New Testament clearly teaches. In fact it is only because Jesus can be identified with God in some way that one can see in the cross of Jesus the love of God. If Jesus was just a human being on the cross, then either his work would have been in vain (how could a mere human save others?); or else his God would be guilty of sheer barbarism – making an 'innocent third party' suffer and die for others. But if Jesus is God (and this was the whole reason the early church had to focus in the creeds so much on the identity of Jesus), then the cross becomes a wonder of divine love.

This is then exactly the note of wonder expressed by the apostles as they speak of the cross. 'This is love: not that we loved God, but that he loved us and sent his Son as an atoning sacrifice for our sins' (1 John 4:10). 'God demonstrates his own love for us in this: while we were still sinners,

Christ died for us' (Romans 5:8). 'God was in Christ reconciling the world to himself' (2 Corinthians 5:19).

The logic of these verses falls apart if Jesus cannot be identified in some way with God himself. Access to God's heart of love is cut off if Jesus is not divine. The *work* of salvation is thus dependent on the *person* of the Saviour. Realizing *who* Jesus truly is, evokes wonder at *what* it is that he has done.

The Uniqueness of Jesus

Christians, then, are those who are convinced that they live in a world both visited by God and rescued by God. The incarnation (God becoming human in Jesus) and the work of redemption (Jesus dying on the cross for humankind) fill their sights and become the bedrock on which they build their lives.

If God has visited this world in Jesus, a new view of the world and our own human existence is possible. Despite its tragedies and sin, this world is loved by God; he is working towards the renewal of his creation; the material world is not to be despised or abused. And each of our human lives is given immense dignity and value. Human beings truly bear the 'image of God'. There is nothing wrong

How Buddhists see Jesus

Buddhism is the body of teaching that originated with Siddhartha Gautama, who lived in northern India in the sixth century before Christ. At the age of 29, Gautama renounced his wealth and all his worldly possessions in order to begin the quest for spiritual enlightenment. He developed a series of practices which he believed helped achieve spiritual transformation, which allowed his followers to place themselves beyond being affected by suffering. Buddhism is best seen as an outlook on life which cultivates the state of enlightenment that results from following the teachings and practices of the 'Buddha' (a title, meaning 'enlightened one' or 'awakened one').

The central themes of Buddhism can be summed up in the 'four truths' that lie at its heart. First, the true nature of human existence can be summarized as *dukkha* – a word that conveys the ideas of suffering and dissatisfaction. Our lives are transient, and characterized by suffering. Second, the cause of this suffering and dissatisfaction is our longings and cravings (*tanha*). This leads to the third point – namely, that the cessation of these cravings can only be achieved when their cause itself is eliminated. The fourth point sets out the eightfold path by which these longings can be purged from the soul, and enlightenment achieved.

So how does Jesus fit into this scheme of things? What might a Buddhist make of Jesus? There are some obvious difficulties here, chiefly relating to the historical fact that the Buddha lived and taught six hundred years before Christ, and hence makes no reference to him. However, later Buddhist writers have explored this issue in some detail.

The most common way of understanding Jesus within Buddhism is to see him as a Buddha-figure, and thus to speak of him as 'enlightened' or even 'close to Buddhahood'. There are indeed certain, although limited, elements of Jesus' teaching which resonate strongly with Buddhism. For example, Jesus' insistence that we must die to ourselves in order to find God has important parallels with the Buddhist idea that we are to empty ourselves, losing our individuality in order to find ultimate reality. This Buddhist vision of leading an 'ego-less life' parallels both Jesus' own teaching about the kingdom of God, and also the New Testament developments of this idea – for example, Paul's notion of 'crucifying the self' and in being human and enjoying human life – for God himself has been one of us. Thus the problems with our world are not due to our being human, but to our being sinful.

Then again, if God has visited this world in Jesus, a whole new view of God and of Jesus is possible. God is not an absentee God, far removed from the cares of his creation; he knows what suffering is like, as it were, 'from the inside'; he is clearly at work in his world and seeking to bring about his resurrection-purposes in the many 'deaths' that we face. Meanwhile Jesus himself is seen as quite unique. Unlike any other religious leader, this one can

claim to be the embodiment of truth in personal form, the one who does not just speak about God but actually brings God to his people. For some, this then poses questions about their own response to him and what they are doing to bring this unique person to be known throughout his world.

Finally, Christians believe that if God was also rescuing the world (when Jesus died on the cross), then the world needs to know this urgent message. There are dangers from which humanity needs to be rescued. For the gospel writers, human sin and divine judgment are sombre realities, which cannot be ignored. But those

Elements of Jesus' message can be seen as close to some Buddhist teaching although his role in the salvation of humanity has no equivalent in Buddhism.

'dying to sin'. Again, Jesus' ministry to the poor and outcasts parallels the Buddha's compassion for those marginalized or excluded by the caste system of the time. The Buddha's inclusion of such people in the *sangha* is seen as comparable to Jesus' inclusion of these groups in the kingdom of God.

Despite these important similarities, many Buddhist writers recognize that Jesus cannot really be described in the conventional categories of their tradition. Among the aspects of the New Testament accounts of Jesus that are more difficult to assimilate to Buddhist categories, the most striking is the emphasis placed by the New Testament upon the saving death of Christ. The New Testament portrays Jesus as one who brings salvation not only through his teaching and personal example, but by his death on the cross. This notion of Jesus being the ground of salvation has no real equivalent within Buddhism.

How Hindus see Jesus

Hinduism is the general name given by westerners to the traditional religious beliefs of the Indian subcontinent, dating back more than 3,000 years, grounded in the *Upanishads*. So great is the diversity of belief and practice within the movement that it is difficult to lay down precisely what gives Hinduism its distinctive identity. Core beliefs include a strong sense that ultimate reality (*Brahman*) is something unseen, rather than what is seen. All human beings have the capacity to seek and find God, even though this process may be long and difficult, involving many births and rebirths.

Hinduism has known of Jesus Christ for some considerable time. Christianity became established in the Indian subcontinent at a relatively early stage. Traditionally, it is believed that the apostle Thomas founded the Indian Mar Thoma Church in the first century; even allowing for a degree of pious exaggeration here, there are excellent reasons for believing that Christianity was an indigenous element of the Indian religious scene by the fourth century. We find a rich and complex range of attitudes to Jesus within Hinduism, ranging from an outright rejection of Christ as an intrusive western influence (which has become increasingly influential with the rise of Hindu nationalist parties in India), to a sympathetic reception of Christ as the fulfilment of Hindu aspirations. In what follows, we shall consider some representative views of Jesus from within Hinduism.

Rammohun Roy (1772–1833) was born of a Brahman family in Bengal. He concluded that Hinduism was corrupted, and needed to be reformed. His growing alienation from orthodox Hinduism led to an increasing interest in Christianity. In his *Precepts of Jesus* (1820), he argued that Jesus embodied a moral code that would be acceptable to right-thinking Hindus. However, he insisted that this positive attitude towards Jesus did not require him to accept a Trinitarian concept of God. Furthermore, it was possible for sins to be forgiven without the need for the atonement of Christ.

Aspects of Rammohun Roy's understanding of the relation between Christianity and Hinduism were criticized by other Hindus who had converted to Christianity. Thus the Bengali writer Krishna Mohan Banerjee argued that there were close affinities between the Vedic idea of Purusha sacrifice and the Christian doctrine of atonement, thus challenging Rammohun Roy's view that there were radical differences at this point.

An approach to understanding the relation between Christianity and Hinduism was developed by Keshub Chunder Sen (1838–84), who argued that Christ brought to fulfilment all that was best in Indian religion. Unlike Rammohun Roy, Keshub embraced the doctrine of the Trinity with enthusiasm. He argued that although *Brahman* was indivisible and indescribable, it could nevertheless be considered in terms of its inner relationships of *Sat* ('being'), *Cit* ('reason') and *Ananda* ('bliss'). These three relationships paralleled the Christian understanding of God the Father as 'Being', God the Son as 'Word', and God the Holy Spirit as 'comforter' or 'bringer of joy and love'. This allowed Jesus to be seen in much more exalted terms than Rammohun Roy allowed. A related idea has been developed more recently by Raimundo Panikkar in his *Unknown Christ of Hinduism*, in which he argued for the hidden presence of Christ in Hindu practice, especially in relation to matters of justice and compassion.

same gospel writers proclaim that in Jesus that cloud of judgment can pass over those who acknowledge who Jesus is and what he has done for them. As John put it, when explaining the essence of the good news: 'God so loved the world that he gave his one and only Son, that whoever believes in him shall not perish but have eternal life' (John 3:16).

4 Salvation

GRAHAM TOMLIN

One of the most important themes – indeed, some would say, the central theme – in Christianity is that of salvation. Of course Christianity is not alone in having ideas about salvation – most religions have some notion of it, although what they think it means varies greatly, from the Islamic vision of a paradise where all spiritual and carnal desires are fulfilled, to the Hindu picture of a long series of reincarnations, or the Buddhist vision of 'enlightenment'. It is not only religions that aspire to 'salvation' either. Secular programmes such as Marxism or even psychotherapy offer forms of 'salvation' whether individual or social. Salvation is a word that has

> 'The beginning of atonement is the sense of its necessity.'
>
> Lord Byron

What is Sin?

Sin is about the breaking of a right relationship between the height of God's creation – humanity – and the creator. Although the word 'sin' is often regarded as equivalent to 'evil', it has a quite distinct meaning. It refers to the broken relationship between humanity and God, which affects every aspect of human relationships. As a result of sin, we have an innate tendency to want to go on our own way, construct our own worlds, and invent gods of our own making. The Genesis account of the fall of Adam and Eve (Genesis 3) vividly depicts this human questioning of the wisdom of God. We are not prepared to accept our God-given place in creation, and instead wish to be like gods, deciding what is right and wrong, and rebelling against any who seek to limit our actions.

The fundamental effect of sin is to separate humanity from God. This separation operates at a number of levels. It cuts us off from his presence. Sin corrupts our relationship with God, other humans, and our environment. In the first place, sin disrupts the vital relationship between humanity, as the height of God's creation and the one who bears the image of God, and the creator. We are alienated from God's love and presence. Instead of worshipping God as creator, we show a disturbing tendency to worship the creation instead. At its heart, idolatry is the sinful human inclination to worship and adore what we have made, rather than the one who has made us. In the second place, sin disrupts our relationship with other human beings. The book of Genesis makes the point that the sin of Adam and Eve led to the first murder (Genesis 4). Instead of being and behaving as brothers and sisters, we act as rivals. Instead of joyfully serving each other, we instead seek to enslave and exploit others. And in the third place, we have ruined our relationship with the environment. Instead of 'tending Eden' (Genesis 2), we exploit the earth for our own ends. Our current ecological crisis reflects this human determination to exploit God's gifts for our own ends, instead of tending and caring for them as stewards, who must pass them on to those who succeed us.

passed into much wider usage in contemporary society, to refer to almost anything which improves one's life and well-being!

Why does Christianity, or any other faith for that matter, place such emphasis on salvation? At the most basic of levels, salvation is necessary because of the common perception that things are not as they should be. If we believed that the world was just about as good as it could ever be, that there was nothing seriously wrong with life, the planet or the people who live upon it, then there would be no need for salvation. Christianity however, in common with many other religions, does not think this is the case. There is a deep sense shared by many people (not only Christians) that good as life is at times, it could be a great deal better. Things are somehow not as they should be, or as Shakespeare famously put it, in the words of his tragic hero Hamlet, 'the times are out of joint'. There is something wrong with the world which needs fixing. Salvation is a central part of Christian theology because in some way or another, the world needs saving.

Many people, when asked what salvation means in Christianity, would suggest that it is about 'going to heaven when you die'. Yet a Christian understanding of salvation is much richer and fuller than this. Some theologians would describe the Bible

The Fall from Grace; detail from the Verdun Altar by Nicholas of Verdun. Adam and Eve's sin and disobedience ruined humanity's relationship with God.

Christian theologians have tried to distinguish different aspects of sin. Augustine of Hippo is an excellent example of a writer who sets out to identify the many facets of this complex notion. For Augustine, two of its many aspects are of especial importance. In the first place, sin is about guilt – moral disorder in the face of a holy and righteous God. It needs to be forgiven and purged, in order that our relationship with God might be renewed. In the second place, it is about being infected with a disease that we are unable to cure. Individual acts of sin are like symptoms of this malaise. It is the disease itself, not just its symptoms, that needs to be healed. Christ is the great physician, who alone is able to heal humanity from sin.

The fall fractured the harmony and order of all God's creation.

as 'the story of salvation', so to fill out this picture of what salvation means in Christian theology, it is worth tracing the story of the Bible itself, in particular to draw out the idea that salvation in the Bible concerns the restoration of the creation – the dawn of a new age.

The Dawn of a New Age

The Bible's description of the creation of the universe is not an exact minute-by-minute account of the formation of matter, but a poetic account of the origins of the created order. The story is there to help us understand some basic things about the universe – that it came about not by accident, but as the result of the will of a good and creative God, and that humanity is called to a special role within that creation – of caring for it in the name of God himself. Very soon, the narrative of 'the fall' follows on. Encapsulated in the story

of the disobedience of Adam and Eve, this conveys the idea that although the created order was originally 'very good', that goodness has been fractured and disrupted, primarily as a result of humanity's unwillingness to play the role of 'God's caretakers', instead wanting to rule, dominate and exploit creation for our own purposes and glory.

This fundamental rupture at the heart of the harmony of creation has led to incalculable pain and disorder – like a computer virus, it means that nothing quite works in the way it should. Humankind is estranged from God and from one another, humanity's relationship with the planet itself has been damaged, so that it no longer cooperates, but only yields its fruit 'by the sweat of your brow' (Genesis 3:19), and even human self-consciousness is damaged – shame enters into human experience, as Adam and Eve, the two representative human figures use fig leaves to cover their embarrassment and disgrace.

The rest of the Old Testament contains evidence of this deep rift in creation, in its stories of sin, injustice, warfare and evil. It also, however, contains hope of a different future – glimpses of a new order, or a new age to come, in which all thing will be set right again. The prophecies in the book of Isaiah in particular focus on this expectation, for example (Isaiah 65:17, 20, 21, 23):

'Behold, I will create
new heavens and a new earth…
Never again will there be in it
an infant who lives but a few days,
or an old man who does not live out
his years…
They will build houses and dwell in
them;
they will plant vineyards and eat
their fruit…
They will not toil in vain
or bear children doomed to
misfortune;
for they will be a people blessed by
the Lord,
they and their descendants with
them.
Before they call I will answer;
while they are still speaking I will
hear.
The wolf and the lamb will feed
together,
and the lion will eat straw like
the ox,
but dust will be the serpent's food.
They will neither harm nor destroy
on all my holy mountain,'
says the Lord.

This is a picture not so much of people 'going to heaven when they die', but instead of the whole created order renewed and restored, with the close, intimate harmonious relationships between humanity, God, and the earth itself, the animate, non-human creation all restored and refreshed.

With the coming of Jesus, a new stage in the story is reached. The main theme on his lips was that of the 'kingdom of God'. The background to Jesus' teaching on the 'kingdom of God' is the story of Israel in the Old Testament: since the nation was overrun by the Assyrians and Babylonians in the ninth and sixth centuries BC, God's people had been in exile. From that time, and especially in Jesus' day there was intense desire to see the exile brought to an end – God's people brought home, the true Temple re-built, the messiah coming to deliver them – in short, God becoming king again over his people – the coming of the kingdom of God.

As the gospels tell the story, Jesus is the Messiah (the Greek word is *Christos*, or 'Christ') who brings in God's kingdom. This 'new age' is now here, at least in part, so that we can for once begin to see, and not just imagine, what life is really like when God has his way. This is the significance of Jesus' miracles and healings – these are the kind of things that happen in the 'new age', the kingdom of God – the time when God will again have his way on the earth, when God becomes king once and for all.

At the climax of the story of Jesus comes his death and resurrection. The resurrection in particular is seen in the New Testament as a foretaste of this 'new age' to come. Jesus does not simply 'come back to life again', as if he has been resuscitated from a near-death experience. Instead he passes through death and comes out the other side. We are given a glimpse of new 'Resurrection Life' on the other side of death, like a sneak preview of the end of the story, right in the middle of it. Some recent theologians, such as the German

> 'A man must be set free from the sin he is, which makes him do the sin he does.'
>
> George MacDonald

The Suffering of Christ and the Problem of Pain

Suffering is a real problem for many. So what can we say about it? Of the many proposed answers to this enigma during the long history of human thought, five have endured. First, suffering is merely an illusion. It simply is not there, but is imagined. If we concentrate hard enough, the illusion will vanish, and our bewilderment and pain will end.

Second, suffering is real. However, it is something that intelligent people ought to be able to rise above and recognize as being of little importance. We are to cultivate an attitude of disdain and indifference to our sufferings, and refuse to allow them to get in the way of the important business of life. Third, while suffering is real and is not going to go away, we can take comfort from the fact that life does not go on forever. In the end, we will die, and once we are dead, suffering ends and we shall eventually have peace. Suffering is temporary, not eternal. Fourth, (a more optimistic answer) human progress will eventually eliminate pain and suffering from the world. Some new social policy, or improved economic throughput, or further advances in drug research, will finally conquer pain. Yet somehow, the promises keep on coming, and there is no sign of the sorrow of the world being alleviated. It seems to be here to stay, despite the promises of those who believe we can change things.

The Christian has a fifth answer: God suffered in Christ. He knows what it is like to be human – an astonishing, and comforting, thought. We are not talking about God becoming like us, just as if he was putting on some sort of disguise so that he could be passed off as one of us. We are talking about the God who created the world genuinely and really entering into our fallen and suffering world, as one of us and on our behalf, in order to redeem us. God has not sent a messenger or a representative to help us. He has involved himself directly, redeeming his own creation, instead of getting someone else to do it for him. God is not like a general who issues orders to his troops from the safety of a bomb-proof shelter, far away from the front line, but one who leads his troops from the front, having previously done all that he asks them to do in turn. God therefore knows what it is like to suffer.

The letter to the Hebrews talks about Jesus being our 'sympathetic high priest' (Hebrews 4:15) – someone who suffers along with us, which is the literal meaning of both the word 'sympathetic' (from the Greek word *sumpatheia* – 'with feeling') and the word 'compassionate' (from the Latin word *compati* – 'suffer with'). God the creator enters into his creation – not as a curious tourist, merely passing through on his way to somewhere more interesting and important, but as a committed saviour, who values us and our world. He did not need to suffer to know what it was like. He chose to suffer as a public demonstration that he knows suffering at first hand.

Wolfhart Pannenberg (born 1928) and N.T. Wright (born 1948) have emphasized the central significance of the resurrection as the in-breaking of the future into the present, an anticipation of the coming age into the world as it is now. The book of Revelation at the end of the Bible completes the picture. There, the story ends with a vision of the creation renewed (Revelation 21:1–5):

Then I saw a new heaven and a new earth, for the first heaven and the first earth had passed away, and there was no longer any sea... And I heard a loud voice from the throne saying, 'Now the dwelling of God is with men, and he will live with them. They will be his people, and God himself will be with them and be their God. He will wipe every tear from their eyes. There will be no more death or mourning or crying or pain, for the old order of things has passed away.' He who was seated on the throne said, 'I am making everything new!'

Here is a vision of the 'new heaven and new earth' (2 Peter 3:13) – not a disembodied state somewhere in the clouds, but a new order here on earth, where all sickness, pain, sin and death are things of the past.

This biblical storyline tells us a number of vital things about the Christian understanding of salvation. As well as the expectation of the whole created order being transformed, it embraces the rescue

God suffered through Christ's crucifixion on the cross in order to redeem his own creation.

and redemption of individual people. It is a vision of a renewed humanity, a renewed society and even a renewed earth.

The Christian understanding of salvation also raises some questions which have been debated at great length in the history of Christian theology. If the coming of Jesus anticipates a new age to come, it leaves open the question of to what extent that 'new age' has come, and how much of it still waits for revelation in the future. At times, Jesus spoke as if the kingdom of God had come in his own ministry. At other times, his words imply that it still lies in the future. Some Christians will emphasize the former, expecting the signs of the new age, such as healing, deliverance from evil spirits, even the possibility of a sinless human life here and now. Others will emphasize the latter, claiming that we are not to expect too much of the signs of the age to come here and now, and stressing the ongoing effects of sin in human life and society.

A further question concerns the role of the church in the coming of this 'new age'. Is the church to work actively towards the kingdom, bringing it about by acts of social justice and compassion? This is a position taken by many within the 'social gospel' movement of the late nineteenth and early twentieth centuries. Or is the kingdom something which God alone can bring in, in his own time, and to which the church's work of social action and transformation simply bear witness, pointing towards it, rather than making it happen? Either way, the biblical theme of God ushering in a new age in Christ both for people and for the planet is of huge significance for Christian understandings of salvation.

> 'The glory of Christianity is to conquer by forgiveness.'
>
> William Blake

The Meaning of the Cross: Atonement

It is an indisputable fact of history that Jesus of Nazareth was executed by the Romans in or just outside Jerusalem, sometime in the early AD 30s. The event is confirmed not just in the Christian gospels, but also by external sources outside early Christian circles. In some ways, this was just one of many such deaths. Death by crucifixion was a common and particularly gruesome way to end a human life. It was especially reserved for criminals, runaway slaves and political opponents of the Roman empire – in other words those the regime wanted to make an example of. Many others were crucified in the same way, and even on the day of Jesus' execution, two others were strung up alongside him at the same time.

Yet in other ways, this death was different. And the reason why it was seen as different is clear – the stories of Jesus' resurrection made his disenchanted and disappointed followers begin to see his death in a new light. If God has raised this man from death, then that death cannot be an unfortunate accident, the final defeat of a failed messiah; it must have a greater significance. If he was indeed the Messiah, the long-awaited representative of Israel, and if resurrection, which all Jews expected to take place at the end of time had now happened in the middle of history, then surely his death must play some part in the drama of salvation. So what did this death mean, and what was its significance?

At a fairly early stage in Christian thinking, Jesus' death began to be understood as connected with God's plan to deal with human sin once and for all – it was the means of 'atonement' – the way in which reparation for sin was made. In the

'Connecting up' with the Cross

How do people benefit from the cross? What needs to be done if we are to 'connect up' with the cross and receive the benefits that this brings? This question is of considerable importance to both Christian evangelism and spirituality. The basic Christian answer is framed in terms of two ideas: *repentance* and *faith*. 'Repentance' expresses the idea of a 'turnaround'. The Greek word *metanoia*, found in the New Testament, means 'a change of mind'. It refers to a total reorientation, in which a person turns away from the world and towards God.

This naturally leads to the idea of 'faith'. In Christian thinking, 'faith' means more than just 'accepting that something is true'. It has the more fundamental sense of 'trust'. To believe in God is to trust in God, and in what God promises. Martin Luther often pointed out how the essence of faith was trusting in a God who made promises, and thus receiving what God promises. Faith, for Luther, was like a hand reaching out to receive the benefits that God offered.

Faith can thus be thought of as entry into the promises of God, receiving what they have to offer. Having recognized that the promises exist, and that they can be trusted, it is necessary to act upon them – in other words, to enter into them, and benefit from them. Someone may believe that God is promising them forgiveness of sins, and they may trust that promise; but unless they respond to that promise, they will not receive forgiveness. The first two stages of faith prepare the way for the third; without it, they are incomplete.

A medical analogy is often used to emphasize the critical importance of faith in connecting up with the cross. Consider a bottle of penicillin, the famous antibiotic identified by Alexander Fleming (1881–1955), which was responsible for saving the lives of countless individuals who would otherwise have died from various forms of potentially fatal infection. Imagine that someone is suffering from blood poisoning. A bottle of penicillin sits on their bedside table. That person may accept that the bottle of penicillin exists. They may trust that it is capable of curing their illness, which will otherwise probably kill them. But their poisoning will never be cured unless they act upon that trust and take the penicillin. Acceptance and trust thus prepare the way for the final component of faith – entering into the promise, and receiving what it offers. In the same way, it is only by taking the last step that one can receive the benefits of Christ.

It is this third element of faith which is of vital importance in making sense of the cross. Just as faith links a bottle of penicillin to healing blood poisoning, so faith forges a link between the cross and resurrection of Jesus Christ and the situation in which we find ourselves. Faith unites us with the risen Christ, and makes available to us everything that he gained through his obedience and resurrection – such as forgiveness, grace and eternal life. These 'benefits of Christ' become ours through faith. They are not detached from the person of Christ, as if they could be received in isolation; rather, they are given together with his real and redeeming presence within us, brought about by faith.

'God creates out of nothing. Wonderful you say. Yes, to be sure, but he does what is still more wonderful: he makes saints out of sinners.'

Søren Kierkegaard

AD 50s, when the apostle Paul wrote his first letter to the Corinthians, the tradition was already well established that at the heart of the Christian gospel lay the belief that 'Christ died for our sins according to the Scriptures' (1 Corinthians 15:3). The phrase is significant. The early Christians looked back into the Hebrew Scriptures to find models to help them understand the meaning of the death of Jesus, and there were plenty to be found.

One fruitful set of ideas was the elaborate sacrificial system by which the sins of the people of Israel could be removed. In particular, language derived from the Old Testament 'Day of Atonement', the instructions for which were laid down in Leviticus 16, became a model for understanding the significance of the death of Christ.

Salvation and the Defeat of Demons

An integral part of the biblical world view is that of a 'spiritual realm' within the created order. In creating the world, God established both material and spiritual domains. The Bible regularly speaks of both 'angels' and 'demons' as personal spiritual beings, and hints that the latter may even be fallen angels (2 Peter 2:4; Jude 6). The New Testament uses the Greek word *daimon* to refer to such evil spiritual beings. Although some older translations of the Bible – such as the King James Bible – sometimes translate this word as 'devil', this is unhelpful and inaccurate. The Greek word was widely used in the pagan world to refer to lesser deities, and clearly bears this meaning at points in the New Testament itself (for example, Acts 17:18). Although the Greek word can signify both good and evil minor divinities, it is used almost entirely in a negative sense in the New Testament. Here, we find a wide

The victory of the risen Christ over demons carries powerful resonances for believers in African religions which are often populated by malign spirits and gods.

Bulls and goats were sacrificed or banished into the desert, with the sins of the people confessed over them (and thus 'carried' by the animals), and in this way, the sins of the people were removed. Similarly, the death of Jesus was seen as a sacrifice, removing sin decisively. The book of Hebrews elaborates on the idea that whereas animals had repeatedly to be offered for the sins of the people,

Christ has now died once and for all, so that the sacrificial system is no longer necessary in the new covenant. Jesus had from early days been referred to as the 'Lamb of God' (see, for example, John 1:29, Revelation 5:13) and this idea again picks up the Old Testament concept of the lamb who is sacrificed for the sins of the people.

At this time, the cross of Christ also

> 'The Blood deals with what we have done, whereas the Cross deals with what we are. The Blood disposes of our sins, while the Cross strikes at the root of our capacity for sin.'
>
> Watchman Nee

variety of activities attributed to demons, including afflicting individuals with various physical and mental ailments – such as being dumb, blind, deaf or insane (Matthew 9:32–3; 12:22; Mark 5:2–5; 9.25; Luke 13:16) – and leading individuals astray (1 Timothy 4:1). Demons are depicted as inhabiting wild, lonely places – such as mountains, tombs, and dry, waterless places (Mark 5:2, 5; Luke 11:24).

The ministry of Jesus included acts of healing and exorcism, which involved the expulsion of demons from individuals (Luke 4:33–7). The New Testament attributes supernatural gifts to demons, including that of discernment. The recognition of Jesus as the Son of God by the demons (Matthew 8:29; Mark 5:7) is seen as especially important. Even spiritual powers are forced to recognize and acknowledge the true identity of Christ and the authority he possesses over the spiritual world. Jesus' healing ministry thus extended to both the material and spiritual orders. His authority extended to every aspect of the created world. As the apostle Paul observes, Christ openly triumphed over the 'principalities and powers' of the present age, making them subject to his authority (Colossians 2:15).

Christ's victory over demons has played an important role in Christian thinking about the atonement – in other words, the significance of Christ's death on the cross and resurrection. For many early Christian writers, such as Athanasius of Alexandria, Jesus was raised up on a cross so that he would be brought into direct contact with the realm of the demons, and do battle with them. The same Christ who disarmed demons during his ministry thus went on to battle decisively with the demonic realm on the cross, and vanquished them. Believers need no longer fear the demonic, whose power has been broken by the death and resurrection of Christ.

This theme remains of great importance today. Many traditional African religions believe in a universe which was created and is animated by various gods and spirits, who often exercise a malign influence on individuals. The spirits of ancestors are often understood to haunt the living, imprisoning and oppressing them. The proclamation of the victory of the risen Christ over all spiritual powers and authorities thus carries immense weight in the traditional African context. Christ liberates the living from the fear of their ancestors and breaks the power of evil spirits.

began to be understood through a number of other images. For example, Paul writes of Christians' participation in Christ's death, so they might also participate in his resurrection. Their pre-Christian 'old self', which was prone to sin, decay and death, has now been put to death through the cross of Christ, so that a 'new self' can arise with Christ in his resurrection (see Romans 6:5–10). The image of the law court has also often been used, whereby humanity is the guilty party, condemned for having broken the divine law. Jesus Christ, however, voluntarily pays the price, takes the penalty upon himself, the

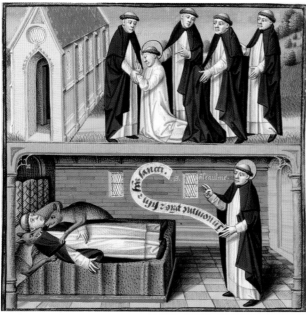

Scenes from the life of Anselm, who believed that the purpose of the incarnation was to enable God, through Christ, to offer forgiveness.

penalty of the death which sin always deserves, in order that humankind might go free. In Mark's Gospel we find Jesus himself using the image of his death as a ransom for many (Mark 10:45), paid to win the release of those held hostage.

The idea, that humankind is held hostage to sin and death until the Son of God gives up his life to secure their freedom, was taken up and developed in subsequent patristic theology. The difficulty came when theologians tried

to tie down exactly to whom the ransom was paid and the exact terms of the deal. If the ransom is envisaged as paid in some way to Satan, does that mean Satan has some kind of rights over God? Is not giving into unjust hostage-takers immoral and a sign of weakness anyway?

In any case, this merely highlights the central issue. In the New Testament and subsequent theological reflection upon it, we find a number of images used to convey the meaning of the death of Christ. The final result is clear – that the death of Christ decisively deals with sin, the obstacle which keeps humanity from God, and effects reconciliation between God and his rebellious creatures – 'we were reconciled to him through the death of his Son' as Paul puts it (Romans 5:10). Some might even say beyond this that central to all these images is some kind of 'substitution' – whereby Christ dies on behalf of and in the place of sinners.

However, we are dealing here with the way language works and how ideas are conveyed, the relationship between fact and meaning. It is perhaps better to speak of 'metaphors' of the atonement rather than 'theories'. Precisely how the cross deals with human sin is not tied down with any one single absolute theory, but we are given a number of models or metaphors from a law court, a ransom case, the Old Testament sacrificial system, a broken relationship. 'Change the metaphor and you change the world,' wrote the novelist George Eliot (1819–80), highlighting the power of metaphor, and these images conveying the central idea of the cross of Christ, that it effects the reconciliation of God and humanity, have echoed powerfully across the ages as Christians have sought to understand, celebrate and remember the death of Christ on their behalf.

As we discover with some of these metaphors (as with almost any metaphor) if you push them too hard in the wrong direction, they begin to strain and break, and even to mislead. Some theologians have pointed out the difficulty, not to say the immorality, of any theory whereby an innocent victim is put to death on behalf of a guilty party. Even beyond this, the idea that Jesus dies to satisfy the judgment of an angry God against sin, or that he is like a sum of money paid by the father to some metaphysical hostage-taker, can paint Jesus as the kind, sacrificial one, and God the Father as some kind of malicious vengeful tyrant. Even the idea of salvation through a death – God working through violence – has come under fire.

In all of this, it is important to place the cross of Christ in two key contexts. One is the doctrine of the Trinity. Several theologians, such as the German Jürgen Moltmann (born 1926), have insisted on the cross as an event within the life of the Trinity. This means that we must always see what is happening on the cross as involving the whole Trinity working together, not separately or in opposition to each other. Despite Jesus' desperate cry, 'My God, my God, why have you forsaken me?' (Mark 15:34), the New Testament does not encourage us to think of Jesus and the Father in opposition to each other, even on the cross. 'In Christ God was reconciling the world to himself' (2 Corinthians 5:19) is the characteristic note, and even Jesus' cry of dereliction points to the fact that this is something that takes place between the Father and the Son, within God himself. It is not Jesus placating a bitter and unforgiving Father (that again is one of the misleading effects of pushing a metaphor too far). It is instead God himself overcoming the powers of sin, death and hell, which bind and tyrannize humanity, through his own self-offering for our sakes.

The other context is that of a sinful, violent and suffering world. The Christian doctrine of sin is brutally realistic about the effect of human pride, jealousy and selfishness on the created order and social relationships. The Christian idea of atonement claims that God enters into precisely this broken and painful world, experiencing the worst of that anguish himself, in order to redeem and rescue it. That is why violence and pain is involved in God's redemption of the world. The cross precisely says that God is no stranger to the common human experience of abandonment and despair. Instead, he not only enters into that suffering himself, he transforms it, offering forgiveness, redemption and reconciliation.

Victory over Death and Satan

According to classical Christian theology, the human race is caught in a battle between good and evil, God and Satan. It is a critical insight in the Christian understanding of the relationship between good and evil, however, that this conflict is set in what is often called an eschatological context – in other words, the world was originally created good and will one day return to that state. Evil is essentially a foreigner, an alien intrusion into a good world, not an inevitable part of existence. It was only in early heretical fringe sects such as the early Manichee movement that the idea of good and evil as eternally coexistent realities was entertained. In mainstream Christian theology, these are not two eternal principles constantly at war with each other. Instead, God is the creator of all that exists, and evil is a derivative force, sometimes depicted as embodied in the concept of a fallen angel, Satan, or Lucifer. The basic

'Men do not differ much about what things they call evils; they differ enormously about what evils they will call excusable.'

G.K. Chesterton

ideas contained in such personification are important – that evil is real and malevolent, and that it only comes about because part of God's good creation chooses to turn away from him, not because evil was there in the beginning with God.

Before that final expulsion of evil, however, the cosmos is the battleground for a huge conflict between God and the powers of evil. And the events of the death and resurrection of Christ have often been seen as the decisive battle of that long war, in which sin, death and the powers of darkness are dealt a fatal blow from which they can never recover. This conflict and the precise nature of the forces involved have been described in a number of different ways in the history of Christian theology.

Traditionally, Christian approaches to the doctrine of the effects of the death of Christ have been grouped into two main categories: objective and subjective. The first type of approach stresses that Christ's death on the cross objectively changed the relationship between humankind and God, achieving something direct and clear, external to human consciousness. The second approach claims that the effects of Jesus' death are not to be seen as changing anything in God or the universe, but instead it brings about subjective and inward changes to our perception of him and ourselves. These two types of theories were usually seen as championed by the medieval theologians Anselm (see page 186) and Abelard respectively. It is worth noting that understandings of the death of Christ, which focus on his victory over powers that threaten humankind, have tended to fall into either one or the other of these categories.

In the patristic period, especially in eastern forms of Christian theology,

this idea of a cosmic conflict between God and Satan (or the devil) took centre stage. In the cross and resurrection, Jesus won the decisive battle over objective powers of sin, death and Satan which held humanity in their grip. In some of these theories, the devil was thought to have acquired rights over humanity due to Adam's sin, so that we were now under his control and rule. Irenaeus of Lyons stressed the idea of Christ's death as a ransom payment (taking his cue from Mark 10:45) which frees sinners from their bondage. The question remained, however, of who was the recipient of this payment, and the answers differed.

Gregory of Nazianzus (329–389) for example claimed that the payment was due to God the Father, while his close colleague Gregory of Nyssa (c. 331–395) argued that it was paid to the devil. Gregory of Nyssa in particular developed the idea that the devil was thought to have in some way been tricked into forfeiting his rights over humanity. Christ's human nature made him seem to the devil as subject to death and hell just like any other human. Under the cloak of his humanity, however, lay his sinless divinity, so that when Satan claimed him through death he somehow exceeded his rights over humanity – thus forfeiting them altogether and allowing humankind to be freed from his evil control. Gregory likened the idea of Christ's humanity to bait which concealed the hook of his divinity – the devil was deceived into taking the bait and hence, like a huge evil fish, was captured by the divine fisherman. However, to many, Gregory's idea of God tricking the devil was morally questionable and seemed to make God seem uncomfortably deceptive.

In the Middle Ages, the general idea of the victory of Christ over the powers of sin, death and hell became

' "Out, damned spot!" That is the true cry of human nature. That stain cannot be removed without blood, and that which is infinitely more, and deeper, and profounder, and more terrible than blood, of which blood is but the symbol – the suffering of Deity.'

G. Campbell Morgan

very popular and influential. The idea of Christ storming the gates of hell after his death to release the captives held there (often known as the 'harrowing of hell'), became the subject of many a medieval woodcut or painting. (The idea was based loosely on a rather enigmatic passage in 1 Peter 3:18–22.)

In the eighteenth-century Enlightenment period, such speculation fell under suspicion for a number of reasons. Scepticism about the idea of a personal devil, and increased confidence in the moral and rational capacity of humanity led to a diminishing sense of the reality of objective evil in the world, and hence the theme of conflict and victory became less pronounced.

In the twentieth century and especially in the aftermath of the First World War, the notions of apocalyptic conflict and real naked evil began to be taken more seriously again. In 1930, a small but rapidly influential book was published which returned the notion of the victory of Christ to

A fourteenth-century altarpiece depicting Christ's descent into limbo to rescue lost souls.

prominence in Christian views of the death of Christ. Gustav Aulén (1879–1977) claimed in his book *Christus Victor* (rather exaggeratedly, it must be said) that the classic view of the atonement held throughout Christian theological history was the idea that in the death and resurrection of Christ, God has won the victory over the powers of evil, bringing about new potentialities for human life. Aulén seemed to offer what was at the time an attractive theory which avoided some of the difficulties of other theories of the atonement. On the one hand, the Latin, 'objective', legal theories of the atonement originating with Anselm raised questions about the morality and the suffering of an innocent victim. On the other, 'subjective' understandings of the atonement, which seemed to suggest that the only change effected by the cross of Christ was in our perception of him, seemed somewhat limp and ineffective in the face of real evil and suffering. Aulén's theory seemed to offer a middle way between these, as it put forward an objective atonement without a questionable legal framework.

Patristic writers had seen the powers of evil as both objective and personal. Aulén still thought of evil as objective, but impersonal. Other twentieth-century theologians began to develop notions of the victory of Christ as overcoming powers of evil which were now more subjective and impersonal. For Paul Tillich (1886–1965) for example, the cross represents God's victory of being over non-being. The cross simply demonstrates and actualizes the divine eternal victory of existence over non-existence. The resurrected Christ is the 'New Being' who brings about cosmic healing, reconciliation and escape from the common human experience of estrangement and alienation. The atonement therefore is described as 'the description of the effect of the New Being in Jesus as the Christ on those grasped by it in their state of estrangement'. This was a restatement and development of the *Christus Victor* theme in the language of 1960s existentialism, with the older ideas of personal evil 'demythologized' into notions of inauthentic existence and alienation. Although Tillich claimed to combine objective and subjective understandings of the atonement in his theology, critics have pointed out that, for him, the cross really only manifests a principle of victory over non-being. It points to an existing state of affairs, rather than bringing about a new one, and locates the achievement of the cross primarily in human consciousness.

Subsequent theologians have put forward other conceptions of the evil overcome by Christ on the cross. For some, especially those working with a model of liberation theology, Christ's death represents his victory over the oppressive regime of the Roman empire, symbolizing repressive social and political forces across the world. For others it is a victory of faith over unbelief, or courage over cowardice. In more recent years, New Testament theologians such as N.T. Wright have understood the whole of Jesus' ministry in these terms, returning to such biblical themes as the kingdom of God to argue that in Jesus and in particular on the cross, God becomes king again over his world, winning the crucial victory over the powers of death, hell and evil.

Despite the different ways it has been understood, the notion of the death of Christ as the victory of God carries a number of valuable insights. The idea upholds the continuity of the death and resurrection of Christ more successfully than some alternative approaches. The resurrection is here seen as the vindication and victory of Jesus of Nazareth after having

> 'Whatever weakens your reason, impairs the tenderness of your conscience, obscures your sense of God, or takes off the relish for spiritual things then it is sin for you, however innocent it may be in itself.'
>
> Susanna Wesley

submitted himself to the powers of death and evil on the cross. It also points clearly to the idea that in his death and resurrection it is God who achieves the victory on the behalf of humanity (although this is clearer in the earlier, more objective versions of the idea).

The idea of the death of Christ as the victory of God is also a powerful idea for human life and hope, especially when seen in the eschatological context with which this section began. Although evil still exists all too visibly in this world, this strand of Christian theology claims that the decisive battle has already been won. Death, sin and evil are alive, but not well. Looking back on the Second World War with hindsight, the British forces and their allies won the decisive victory in the 1944 D-Day landings on the beaches of Normandy. That was the key moment which turned the tide of the war. Once that battle had been won, in a sense the rest of war was simply the clearing up of resistance, the hastening of an inevitable final triumph. In the same way, the cross of Christ can be seen as the crucial battle in the great battle between good and evil, life and death. There, Christ won the decisive victory, and even if we still experience the painful reality of death and evil here and now, they are already defeated and broken enemies, one day to come to an end when the kingdom of God comes in all its fullness.

The Forgiveness of Sins

The New Testament affirms that forgiveness of sins comes through Christ and specifically through his death on the cross (Matthew 26:28; Ephesians 1:7; Hebrews 9:22). This idea is linked closely to the Israelite sacrificial system in which sacrifice was offered for the forgiveness of sins. Nevertheless, the theme has been a rich source of subsequent Christian reflection, exploring why forgiveness is necessary and how it happens, especially for Gentiles without a background in Old Testament sacrifice.

To say that forgiveness is necessary implies that there is something fundamental to forgive. It points directly to the notion, perhaps surprisingly when you think about it, that divine forgiveness of human sin is somehow central to redemption of the whole creation. But that begs the question of who is to blame for sin, or quite simply who needs forgiveness?

Putting it bluntly, there are really only three possible culprits for the fractured and broken nature of the world as we experience it – God, the devil and humanity – and in early Christian theology each had its advocates. Perhaps it is the responsibility of God for creating a faulty world? The Gnostics of the second century roughly held this view – that the creation was the defective handiwork of a lesser divine being who had emanated from the true God. Creation as we know it is therefore not 'good' in any real sense, and salvation consists of escape from creation into another spiritual sphere through special knowledge ('*gnosis*' in Greek). This solution was roundly criticized by such second-century theologians as Irenaeus of Lyons, who argued for the essential goodness of creation, that the created order existed precisely at the will of God himself, not some incompetent divine junior, and that salvation consisted not in escape from the created order but its restoration, or 'recapitulation'.

If it was not God's fault, perhaps it was the fault of the devil? Maybe sin is the result of an evil power which has invaded God's world causing havoc to the divine order? This was an approach favoured by the Manicheans, a group taking their name from Mani, a Mesopotamian

> 'Union with Christ is really the central truth of the whole doctrine of salvation not only in its application but also in its once-for-all accomplishment in the finished work of Christ. Indeed the whole process of salvation has its origin in one phase of union with Christ and salvation has in view the realization of other phases of union with Christ.'
>
> John Murray

prophet who developed a complex mystical mythology in the third century AD. This group was fashionable for a time on the fringes of early Christianity, and even attracted the allegiance of the young Augustine (later the great Augustine, bishop of Hippo). It was he in fact who eventually fatally undermined this idea within Christian theology, with his own growing doubts about it. Augustine came to believe that the Manichean God was so weak and impotent as to be hardly worth worshipping. It seemed to him that this view of evil as the outcome of satanic power in the world gave a dualistic solution, implying there were two centres of power within the world, God and the devil, who were somehow equal with each other, fighting on like two wrestlers locked in combat, neither being quite able to overcome the other. Moreover the active energetic, forceful character in this drama seemed to be not God, who was somewhat pathetic, unable to do anything about this incursion of evil into the world, but the devil himself.

It was Augustine himself who (at least, in western Christianity) helped establish the third explanation for sin and evil – that it is essentially the fault not of God, nor ultimately of Satan, but of humankind. Although he saw salvation as a longer-term process of healing of the human spirit, the very first step in this restoration is the need for forgiveness, which for Augustine was won through the cross of Christ, and bestowed through the sacrament of baptism. Forgiveness is thus not the whole of salvation but it is the beginning of it. Humanity's sin lies at the heart of the disorder of creation, and therefore the first step towards its remedy must be the forgiveness of that sin.

Some of these ideas were given greater focus in the eleventh century by Anselm (1033–1109), an Italian who became one of the great medieval archbishops of Canterbury. In a book called *Cur Deus Homo*, (*Why God became Man*), Anselm argued that the purpose of the incarnation was that God, through Christ, might be able to offer forgiveness, while at the same time satisfying and not offending against his own strict justice. For Anselm, sin is an offence against God, and therefore requires some kind of payment in return (he may have got this idea from the feudal requirements of guilty peasants to their lords in medieval society, or simply from the penitential practice of the church at the time). Humanity cannot pay this debt, as the price demanded is the forfeit of life itself ('the wages of sin is death': Romans 6:23). So Christ as the divine human both has the divine ability and the human obligation to pay the debt and enable satisfaction to be made.

Anselm's doctrine can be criticized for casting the relationship between God and humanity in too strictly legal rather than personal terms. The problem Anselm sets out to solve is how sin can be forgiven without compromising God's justice. However, if we think of our relationship to God as primarily personal, with imagery taken more from marriage than the law courts then we might ask why God doesn't simply forgive sins without requiring any kind of 'payment' or 'satisfaction' – after all, isn't that what most of us do all the time? If someone steps on my toe or crashes my car after I have loaned it to them, I do not demand some kind of payment, I must simply choose to forgive and let it go. Especially when we consider Jesus' command to 'turn the other cheek', then it can seem that God is not following his own advice! In subsequent years, there were further criticisms of the Christian idea of guilt and forgiveness, particularly during

What Are the 'Benefits of Christ'?

'To know Christ is to know his benefits.' These words, written by the German writer Philip Melanchthon in 1521, emphasize the importance of knowing and experiencing the difference that Christ makes to human existence. It is not enough simply to understand what Christ achieves: Christians must share in these 'benefits', and be transformed by them. So what are these benefits? How can they be summarized? The New Testament offers a number of approaches, which have been explored and developed by Christian theologians down the ages. We shall now explore several:

1. Being liberated from fear of death. Through Christ's death and resurrection, Christians are set free from the oppression of death. One New Testament writer describes how Christ's death sets 'free those who all their lives were held in slavery by the fear of death' (Hebrews 2:15). This theme is often emphasized in Christian funeral services. For Christians, death marks the end of a believer's earthly existence, which is seen as a preparation for eternal life, setting believers free from the pain and sorrow of life, and bringing them safely into the presence of God.

2. Being forgiven. Christian understandings of the cross draw attention to the human need for forgiveness and renewal. Human nature is flawed, disfigured and distorted by sin. So how can sin be neutralized? How can its guilt be purged, and its power broken? In many of his hymns, Charles Wesley pointed out how the death of Christ can be seen as God's remedy for human sin. Written in 1739, his hymn *O for a thousand tongues to sing* explains simply but powerfully the significance of the cross of Christ in the following way:

He breaks the power of cancelled sin,
He sets the prisoner free;
His blood can make the foulest clean,
His blood availed for me.

3. Being transformed by divine love. The New Testament often points out how Christ's death demonstrates the love of God for the world (John 3:16). Many Christian writers – such as the twelfth-century theologian Peter Abelard – have pointed out the transformative potential of this divine love. To encounter the love of God is to be reshaped and renewed. Knowing God's love evokes a response of love for God, and for his world.

4. Being liberated from oppression. The death and resurrection of Christ have the potential to set Christians free from spiritual oppression. In the early church, particular emphasis was laid on liberation from satanic forces. Christ is the one who breaks the power of Satan, enabling believers to live in the 'glorious freedom of the children of God' (Romans 8:21). This continues to be a major theme in Christian preaching and spirituality: Christ sets us free from the baleful influence of ancestors and other spiritual forces.

Yet other sources of oppression are also understood to be challenged by Christ's cross and resurrection. In Latin America the movement known as 'liberation theology', which flourished in the closing decades of the twentieth century, stressed the power of the gospel to achieve social transformation. The cross brings transformation, not simply to individuals, but to the societies in which they live.

the Enlightenment, when the notion of individual guilt was questioned, or under more recent Freudian psychology where guilt was understood more as a psychological neurosis than any objective reality. In addition, when recent penal theory tends to see justice as restorative in its intention rather than retributive, the idea of God demanding retribution before he can forgive seems to many to be crude and immoral.

On the other hand, implicit in Anselm's analysis of sin and forgiveness is the importance of distinguishing between offences caused between two human agents and between humans and God. Human sin against God is not a mere trifle, a minor mistake which can easily be glossed over. Instead it causes an elemental fracture to the fabric of the universe – the rebellion of the creature against the creator. Sin is a fundamental problem hence it needs a fundamental solution.

Moreover, the reason I must simply

The Return of the Prodigal Son by Rembrandt van Rijn. This parable of Jesus illustrates the reconciliation of humanity with God.

forgive and not demand any recompense for sins committed against me is precisely because I have no right to judge my neighbour. I am a sinner just as much as the one who has sinned against me, and so I must simply forgive, just as I would hope that he would forgive me. With God, however, it is different – he has the right to judge. He does not stand alongside us as a fellow sinner, but above us as our judge, and for Anselm at least, divine justice and the moral structure of the universe must be upheld. In response to the Freudian critique, some theologians have pointed out that while there is such a thing as imaginary guilt and unhealthy neurotic remorse, this does not remove the possibility at the same time of objective guilt. If I steal my neighbour's car, I may feel guilty for having done it, but I am also objectively guilty of having broken not only my relationship with him but also the law of the land, as well as God's command to love and not take advantage of my neighbour.

It is important to hold together Anselm's legal framework with the more personal character of the divine–human relationship we find in Augustine. A sole emphasis on legal or penal language loses the sense of intimacy in the Christian understanding of the relationship between humanity and God. A broken human relationship still needs forgiveness if it is to be healed – as an essential step towards full reconciliation. It should not be surprising if the same were true of our relationship with God. At the same time, losing the legal or objective framework can make God seem just like one of us, with no sense of transcendence or divine faithfulness to his law or holy character.

As a last word, it is important to grasp that Christian forgiveness is not the same as forgetting. God does not 'forget' human sin in the sense of saying that it doesn't matter, simply because it *does* matter. Sin is as serious as disease to the human body or crime to the fabric of society. Instead, God looks squarely at sin and the damage it has caused, and says, 'This is now dealt with, forgiven and it shall not come between us.' This is vital not only theologically but also pastorally. The Christian art of forgiveness is not the ability to somehow forget or ignore the fact that someone has offended or hurt us. It is instead the ability, while fully and even painfully aware of that hurt, to still say that 'it shall not come between us'. For this reason, forgiveness is a crucial skill for a healthy human life and society. Broken relationships cannot be restored without it, and human transformation in relationship with God must also begin with the forgiveness of sins.

Restoration to God

As we have seen, Christianity holds that humanity is cut off from its intended relationship with God. We have been created by God in order that we may relate to him; yet this life-giving relationship has been sundered and ruined by sin. A central theme of the Christian proclamation is that the death and resurrection of Christ make restoration to God possible. The narrative of the fall (Genesis 3) speaks of sin in terms of both a broken relationship with God and removal from his presence. Adam and Eve, originally able to walk with the Lord in the cool of the day, are expelled from Eden. As the 'second Adam', Christ makes possible a reversal of this situation. What humanity lost in Adam, can be regained through the saving death of Christ. Believers are restored to fellowship with God and, one day, they shall be restored to his presence in heaven.

It is helpful to consider the importance of this theme of restoration to God by exploring some of the images that the New Testament uses to set out the difference that Christ makes to the human situation. The first of these is the idea of being ransomed by Christ. As he neared the end of his ministry, Christ told his disciples that he had come 'to give his life as a ransom for many' (Mark 10:45). This is a powerful way of making sense of the meaning of the cross. It immediately conveys the idea of *liberation*. We have been set free from prison or bondage, and restored to fellowship with God. Through Christ's death, believers have been set free from bondage to sin and the fear of death, and allowed to enter into the glorious liberty of the children of God. The gospel declares that God is, in the first place, determined to save us, and in the second, prepared to pay the price salvation entails. Paul reminded his Corinthian readers that they had been bought at the price of the death of the Son of God (1 Corinthians 6:20; 7:23). God values us so much that he gave his own Son that we might be set free, and restored to a right relationship with him.

A second image is that of reconciliation, which is central to Paul's reflection on the meaning of the cross. 'All this is from God, who reconciled us to himself through Christ...' (2 Corinthians 5:18). To be reconciled is to be restored to fellowship with another. The parallel between the reconciliation of two individuals on the one hand, and between God and sinners on the other will be obvious. God is treated as a person, someone to whom we can relate. Our relationship with him, once close (as in Eden), has been seriously disrupted to the point where it exists in name only. We are, and will always remain, children of God. We were created by God. Sin does not destroy

> 'Nothing hath separated us from God but our own will, or rather our own will is our separation from God.'
>
> William Law

that relationship between the creator and his creatures. Yet it devastates it, by robbing everyone of the closeness that once went with it. The biblical story of Adam and Eve in the Garden of Eden makes clear that the closeness and intimacy of that original relationship with God has been forfeited through sin. It is no accident that the New Testament speaks of salvation in terms of a 'new creation' (2 Corinthians 5:17), or of the need for people to be 'born again' (John 3:1–16) if they are to see the kingdom of God.

Reconciliation involves the making real of what had only been notional. The prodigal son remained the son of his father even when he set off, to live independently, confident that he could live without his father's continual presence and oversight. But that relationship exists in name only. One party to the relationship acts as if it was not there. Reconciliation takes place when both parties to a relationship take that relationship with full seriousness, and acknowledge their mutual love for each other and the obligations which they have towards each other. The son returns to his father, and they embrace – the relationship becomes real.

In discussing the New Testament understanding of how humanity can be restored to God, it is important to notice its emphasis upon the divine initiative. God is the one who restores our situation – not humanity. It is God who reconciles humanity to himself, not the other way round. God approaches humanity, and calls them to respond to this initiative. It is God who takes upon himself the pain and the anguish of broaching the situation of human sin, attempting to let us know of the great distress which sin causes him, and the barrier it places between him and us. 'Your iniquities have made a separation between you and your God,' in the famous words of the prophet (Isaiah 59:2). Our love of God is a result of his love for us, not the other way round: 'In this is love, not that we loved God, but that he loved us, and sent his Son to be the propitiation for our sins' (1 John 4:10).

The image of reconciliation is also important in illuminating the unique role of Christ in our salvation. 'God was in Christ reconciling the world to himself ' (2 Corinthians 5:19). So how is Christ understood to be involved in the reconciliation between God and sinners? There are two ways of looking at this question. First, the phrase 'God was in Christ' can be taken as a reference to the incarnation. Christ as God incarnate makes his reconciling appeal to humanity. He takes the initiative in proclaiming the overwhelming love of God for his creatures and the divine wish that all should be reconciled to him. In proclaiming the need and possibility of reconciliation to God, Christ addresses humanity as God and on behalf of God.

The phrase 'in Christ' can also be understood in a second way. It may reflect a Hebrew grammatical construction with which Paul would have been familiar, which would be better translated as 'through Christ'. In other words, 'God was through Christ reconciling the world to himself.' Christ is understood as the agent of divine reconciliation, the one through whom God reconciles us to him. The following remarks from the letter to the Colossians are instructive: 'And you, who were once estranged and hostile in mind... he has now reconciled in his body of flesh by his death' (Colossians 1:21–22). The ideas of 'estrangement' (or 'alienation', as it could also be translated) and 'hostility' are used to refer to the alienated human relationship with God, which is transformed through the death of Christ into reconciliation.

A further consequence of the reconciliation of God and sinful humanity through the death of Christ is peace. Reconciliation means the end of hostility and the beginning of peace. Through Christ, God was pleased 'to reconcile to himself all things... by making peace through his blood shed on the cross' (Colossians 1:20). Elsewhere, Paul states that one of the direct results of justification is peace with God (Romans 5:1). Christ is seen as a mediator between God and ourselves, pleading God's case to us, and our case to God. Through reconciliation, the hostility between God and humanity is abolished, and a new relationship of peace and harmony established. Christ, and Christ alone, is the mediator between God and humanity, who both makes this alienation known and offers its abolition through reconciliation.

The idea of Jesus being the one and only mediator between God and us is deeply embedded in the New Testament. 'For there is one God, and there is one mediator between God and humanity, Jesus Christ' (1 Timothy 2:5). Paul talks about God 'reconciling' us to himself through Jesus Christ (2 Corinthians 5:18–19). What is particularly interesting is that in this passage Paul uses exactly the same Greek word to refer to the restoration of the relationship between God and humanity that he had used earlier to refer to the restoration of the relationship between a man and his wife who had become alienated in some manner (1 Corinthians 7:10–11). Christ is clearly understood to act as the go-between, restoring the relationship between God and humanity to what it once was.

This go-between must represent God to us, and us to God. He must have points of contact with both God

Christ as the Representative of Humanity

Christianity has always seen Jesus of Nazareth as a representative figure for the whole human race. By dying on the cross and being raised again, Jesus achieves something that benefits humanity as a whole, if they respond in faith. Jesus makes possible a new situation for the human race. 'For our sake he made him to be sin who knew no sin, so that in him we might become the righteousness of God' (2 Corinthians 5:21). Paul here speaks of some kind of transference, by which he takes away our sin, and gives us his righteousness. Martin Luther referred to this as a 'marvellous exchange'.

So how are we to make sense of this? How can we think of Christ as a representative human being, capable of changing the human situation as a whole through his death and resurrection? A key theme here is that of the incarnation. In that Jesus is God, he is able to deliver humanity from sin; in that Jesus is a human being, he is able to 'connect up' with humanity as a whole, acting as a channel through which God's salvation is made accessible to people. Christian theology has developed three ways of conceiving of Christ's role in mediating salvation to humanity, each of which illuminates the rich New Testament teaching on this question. Each answers the simple yet fundamental question: how can humanity as a whole benefit from this one individual, Jesus of Nazareth?

1. *Christ as our substitute*. Christ is here understood as the one who goes to the cross in the place of sinful humanity. We ought to have been crucified, because of our sins; Christ is crucified in our place. God allows Christ to stand in our place, taking our guilt upon himself, in order that his righteousness – won by obedience upon the cross – might become ours. The central theme here is that of one who takes our place, in order that he might bear our sin and bring us his righteousness.

2. *Christ as representative*. Christ is here understood to be the covenant representative of humanity, who wins certain benefits for those he represents. Through faith, we come to stand within the covenant between God and humanity. All that Christ has won for us through the cross is available to us, because of the covenant. Just as God entered into a covenant with his people Israel, so he has entered into a covenant with his church. Christ, by his obedience upon the cross, represents his people, winning benefits for them as their representative.

3. *Participation in Christ*. Through faith, believers are 'in Christ', to use a phrase that is often found in the writings of Paul. 'If anyone is in Christ, there is a new creation' (2 Corinthians 5:17). Faith allows believers to participate in Christ – to be caught up in his person and his achievements – and thus to share in all the benefits won by him through the cross. Participating in Christ thus leads to the forgiveness of our sins, and sharing in his righteousness.

and us, and yet be distinguishable from both. In short, the traditional idea of the incarnation, which expresses the belief that Jesus is both divine and human, portrays Jesus as the perfect mediator between God and us. Christ is like us in every way, except that he does not share our need to be redeemed. If Christ were like humanity in every way, he would be part of the problem, not its solution. Christ's capacity to restore us to God both demonstrates and depends upon his identity as God incarnate, the sinless representative of sinful humanity. Christ possesses a unique ability to redeem us, because of his identity as the Son of God. He is thus able to relate to us on the one hand, and redeem us on the other. All of this points to the close relationship of the person and work of Christ. Who Christ is determines what Christ does. If Jesus were not truly divine and human, reconciliation would be an impossibility.

Justification

For the sixteenth-century German reformer Martin Luther, justification was 'the article by which the church stands or falls'. Many of the Protestant denominations in the world today trace their origins back to the time of the Reformation, and the cracks which began to appear in the medieval church surfaced just over the place where this doctrine lay. So why was it so important?

The doctrine of justification, as it has usually been understood in Christian theology, can be said to concern the way in which sinful human beings are restored to a right relationship with God. And of course that question goes to the very heart of the Christian doctrine of salvation. It does not encompass the whole of it; justification tends to refer mainly to human reconciliation with God, rather than the whole of the creation. At the

Reformation, however, the doctrine of justification lay at the heart of the doctrinal battles which convulsed the church. We might even go so far as to say that the western church began its divisions into many different fragments over differing views of justification. Why then was it so important?

A key point to grasp early on is that both the Latin and Greek words used for justification may be translated into a wide range of English words. Our words 'justice', 'justification', 'righteous' and 'righteousness' all come from the same Latin and Greek root, and all convey a similar range of ideas. The origins of the doctrine lie in the Bible itself. In the Bible, justification generally refers (in the noted English New Testament scholar Tom Wright's words) to 'God's declaration from his position as judge of all the world, that someone is in the right, despite universal sin'. More specifically, the Greek term we usually translate as 'justification' meant not so much how you entered into a right relationship with God, as how you could tell whether someone was or was not in such a relationship. It was mainly about who was included within the true 'people of God'. So, for example, the discussion of justification in Paul's letter to the Galatians concerns the issue of whether or not Jews can eat at the same table as Gentiles in the Christian church – it is about who counts as a true member of God's new people. The position of 'justification by works' which Paul criticizes is not so much the idea that people can get to heaven by trying hard to be good. Instead his target is the notion that the Jews are 'justified', or identified as God's people, by their religious 'works' (circumcision, food laws, Torah-keeping and the like). He claims that as God has acted to defeat sin and death in the person of Christ,

'Our method of proclaiming salvation is this: to point out to every heart the loving Lamb, who died for us, and although He was the Son of God, offered Himself for our sins… by the preaching of His blood, and of His love unto death, even the death of the cross.'

Count Zinzendorf

Martin Luther was concerned that the church had lost sight of the doctrine of justification by faith.

own to do anything about their sin. They were in fact helpless. Sin has so affected human desire, that humankind can no longer choose what is good. We do not desire God, the highest good of all, and our wills are always inclined more towards the evil rather than the good. For Augustine, justification is by grace. We are made good not by our own effort, but by God's work. First, through his 'operative grace' he releases our wills to be able to choose the good. Then, through his 'cooperative grace', he helps Christians to grow in love for God and the good until we are brought to full perfection and righteousness.

Of course, this process could not be considered complete by the end of a normal human lifetime, so the doctrine of purgatory began to be developed as a way of envisaging this process as continuing after death. Purgatory was a state into which most Christians entered after death, where they were assured of entering heaven, but only after many years of enduring the punishments deserved by sin in this life.

In the medieval period, this basic understanding that justification is a process rather than a pronouncement, a being 'made righteous' rather than 'declared righteous' remained intact. As the Middle Ages progressed, in popular Christianity at least, Augustine's stress on the priority of grace and the initiative of God in justification began to fade. Instead, the assumption began to grow that justification was dependent on the performance of a set of religious actions, having a good intention, or simply doing one's best. This was not helped by the fact that there was little or no official teaching on the doctrine of justification. No church council or pope issued an official statement on the church's view of justification for centuries, until the middle of the

justification now comes through faith in Christ, not through adoption of the marks which distinguish Jews from Gentiles.

In the early church, the doctrine of justification began to take a different turn. Under the influence of Greek notions of virtue and character, it began to be understood not so much as God's declaration of someone being in the right, as a description of the process by which a person becomes good. In particular, Augustine decisively shaped the way the doctrine was understood. Augustine insisted that fallen human beings did not have power on their sixteenth century, some years after the Reformation had begun and the fracturing of European Christendom was already under way.

Although there was little real consensus on the issue, generally speaking, most medieval theologians thought that justification was the result of a long process of interaction between God's grace and human cooperation. No medieval theologian thought that anyone could get to heaven by their own works – all of them believed that God's grace was necessary in this process. In that sense, no medieval theologian believed in justification by works alone. They all thought that we had to do our part, as God did his, in the process of justification. And that process was only ever complete when sin was entirely purged from a human life, which in turn could only be after a long process of refinement in purgatory. However, some medieval schools, especially the one in which the young Martin Luther learned his early theology, taught the notion that 'God will not deny his grace to those who do their best.' In other words, grace is still needed for justification to be complete, but the central hinge upon which the doctrine turns is whether or not people 'do their best'. This appeared to Luther and to others to give strong support to some of the more questionable practices of late medieval Christianity which encouraged people to think that their salvation was essentially in their own hands.

Luther eventually developed a new (although he claimed it was rediscovering an old) doctrine of justification. In one sense, he recovered Augustine's insistence on the priority of God's initiative. We are not free to 'do our best', even if our best was good enough. And in any case, that is not the way in which God chooses to justify us. Instead, humankind is *entirely* dependent on God's grace to justify them. More radically still, Luther broke from the idea of justification as a process of being made good or righteous, a view which had remained unchanged through the writings of Augustine and the medieval period. Instead he returned to a view which perhaps has more in common with biblical ideas of justification, namely the idea that justification refers to God's pronouncement that the one who simply trusts God's word or promise is in the right with him, despite the presence of sin.

In other ways, Luther's doctrine of justification is different from the apostle Paul. When Luther opposes 'justification by works', he has in mind the popular medieval assumption that Christians are meant to try to perform religious or other good works that will set them on the path to heaven. Paul doesn't seem to have this in mind at all. As we have seen, for him, 'justification by works' refers to 'works of the law' – the marks of Jewish identity which made Israel the chosen people instead of Gentiles. In subsequent theology, Paul has sometimes been misunderstood on this point by being read through the eyes of Luther. However, Luther's return to the idea of justification as God's declaration that someone is in the right, brought forward from the end of time to the present, is still much closer to Paul's view than the notion of justification common since the early years of post-biblical theology.

The questions Luther primarily addressed were these: 'On what basis are people justified?' and 'To whom is justification given?' The usual medieval answers to these questions were that justification was granted to those who have acquired enough merit through the performance of meritorious actions – normally

> 'It is not thy hold on Christ that saves thee; it is Christ. It is not thy joy in Christ that saves thee; it is Christ. It is not even thy faith in Christ, though that be the instrument; it is Christ's blood and merit.'
>
> Charles Haddon Spurgeon

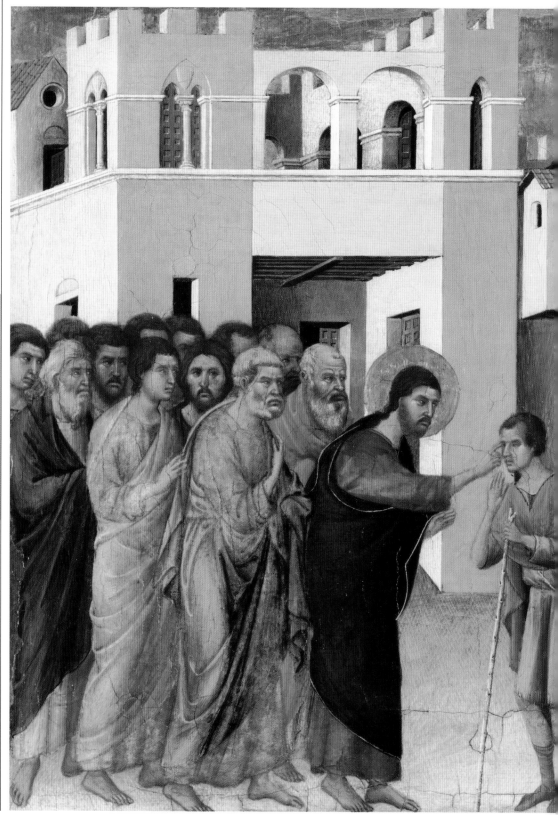

understood as freely-chosen acts of
goodness, performed with the help of
God's grace. Justification was
conferred on the person who had
become good, or righteous through a
long process of transformation,
usually including a lengthy period in
purgatory. Luther departs from these
ideas altogether. He insists that
believers are justified, not on account
of their own merits, but on the merits
of Christ. Christians were never
meant to acquire and accumulate
their own righteousness for God to
confer justification on them as a kind
of prize at the end of the race.
Instead, they are justified by the
righteousness of Christ – an 'alien' or
'external' righteousness, as Luther
used to put it. He used the image of
placing a cloak around his young son
Hans before he left the house on a
cold winter's day to convey this idea:
in the same way, God cloaks, or
covers Christians with his
righteousness to shield them from the
consequences of our sin and final
judgment.

In this fourteenth-century painting by Duccio di Buoninsegna, Jesus' healing of a man born blind symbolizes the opening of people's eyes to the worship of God.

Moreover this righteousness of
Christ is received not by those who
are fully contrite for their sins, or who
have a good intention, or who 'do
their best', but instead, by those who
simply trust the promise of God that
he justifies sinners through his sheer
goodness and grace. In other words,
justification for Luther is by 'faith
alone'. Hope and love, the two other
great Christian virtues, flow out of
faith – once believers know that God
is gracious and kind, forgiving and
justifying them despite their sin, they
naturally and spontaneously act in
love and hope towards their
neighbours, freed from the burden of
having to perform all the religious
activities which the medieval church
seemed to demand. When Christians
know they are justified on account of
Christ, through faith, then the process
of healing, and of transformation

(what later Protestant theologians usually called 'sanctification') can follow on.

After Luther's epoch-making claims, which eventually drove a wedge through the middle of the European church, the Roman Catholic Church, through the Council of Trent (1545–63) still insisted that justification is a process not an event, and while it is received by faith, that must be a faith which is also seen to be active in hope and love. More recent times have seen significant work done on the doctrine of justification in both Protestant and Roman Catholic circles. These discussions have shown that Protestant and Catholic interpretations of justification are not as far apart as they once seemed, and that while there are still significant differences, they do still have much in common.

Although they have differed over the years on how justification takes place and how it is received, the vast majority of Christian theologians have claimed that it is dependent on God's grace. Despite humanity's deliberate disobedience, our failure and turning away from God, he graciously picks us up, turns us back to him and sets us in the right place again, able to relate to him, receive his gifts and love him in return. It describes the Christian experience of being accepted by a God who overlooks and forgives a person's sin and rebellion, because of what Christ has done for them, not because of what they can do for him or for themselves. To that extent, despite the battles which have been fought over it through the years, justification still stands at the heart of the Christian proclamation of God's love for a sinful world.

Healing

Healing was a central aspect of the ministry of Jesus. Wherever Jesus went – in the countryside, in villages or in towns – people were laid out so that he could touch them and heal them (Mark 6:56). Jesus healed the sick, both as an indication of his own identity as the one who had God's authority to transform human life, and to demonstrate that the coming kingdom of God would be a realm of restoration. At the opening of his ministry, Jesus declared that he had come to proclaim 'recovery of sight for the blind' (Luke 4:18). Jesus' ministry is not to be seen as that of a wandering healer, but rather as one who ushers in the coming kingdom of God and the changes that it will bring about.

This theme of healing can also be found in the New Testament's reflections on the difference that Jesus Christ makes to the human situation. Perhaps the best way of appreciating this is to reflect on the word 'salvation'. The most important associations of 'salvation' are those of deliverance, preservation, or rescue from a dangerous situation. The verb 'to save' is used outside the New Testament to refer to being saved from death by the intervention of a rescuer, or to being cured from a deadly illness or a dangerous situation. The word 'salvation' ('to be saved') is used in this sense by the Jewish historian Josephus to refer to the deliverance of the Israelites from their captivity in Egypt at the time of the Exodus. In much the same way, Christ is understood to deliver humanity from the fear of death and the penalty and power of sin. The name 'Jesus' means 'God saves'; it is clear that the New Testament understands this to mean 'saves from sin' (Matthew 1:21 should be noted here). Christ's death is the means by which the penalty due for sin is paid – a penalty that no one could hope to pay themselves. However, there is more to the idea of salvation than this.

> 'Christianity is a religion of rescue. It is designed for the desperate. It is for people who have a craving for something more than they can eke out of life by themselves.'
> Walter Henrichsen

It is important to realize that the biblical understanding of salvation is enormously rich, and also includes the ideas of 'wholeness' or 'health'. There is a very close relation between the ideas of salvation and wholeness. In many modern languages, the words for 'health' and 'salvation' are one and the same. Thus it is sometimes difficult to know whether a passage should be translated in terms of salvation or wholeness. An example of this can be seen in the account of Jesus healing the woman who had been subject to bleeding for twelve years (Mark 5:25–34). Jesus speaks to the woman and she is healed (Mark 5:34). But should those words of Jesus be translated as 'Your faith has made you whole', 'Your faith has healed you', or 'Your faith has saved you?' The Greek word used here can bear all three meanings. Again, consider the gospel account of the healing of blind Bartimaus (Mark 10:52), where precisely the same issue arises.

When someone who has been ill is healed, he or she is restored to their former state of health and wholeness. We can see this in the gospel story of the raising of Jairus' daughter (Mark 5:35–43). Death, which the Bible sees as destroying the integrity of creation, is reversed. By raising Jairus' daughter from the dead, Jesus restores part of creation to what it should be. The creation stories of Genesis make it clear that God created humanity in a state of wholeness, and that this wholeness was lost through the fall. Just as healing involves restoring someone to health, so salvation involves restoring believers to wholeness, to the state in which God first created humankind. Paul draws attention to the relation between the first and the second Adam (Christ): through Adam, humanity lost its integrity before God; through Christ, that integrity can be regained and restored.

Christ can thus be thought of as having undone all that Adam did. One of the most thoughtful Christian writers of the second century, Irenaeus of Lyons, would often point out some significant aspects of the parallelism between Adam and Christ. In each case, there is a parallel or symmetry between the fall through Adam and redemption through Christ. Two of the parallels are of especial interest. First, Adam's disobedience took place in a garden (Eden); Christ's obedience took place in another garden (Gethsemane). Secondly, through Adam, the tree of life became the tree of death; through Christ, the tree of death became the tree of life. In each case, Irenaeus pointed out how the work of Christ went over the same ground as Adam, undoing the original harm done. (Irenaeus uses the term 'recapitulation' to refer to this going over again.) The restoration of humanity to spiritual health involves confronting the original cause of sin and death, in order that these can be neutralized through Christ's obedience.

'Only the wounded physician can heal.' The truth about this statement concerning the medical profession may well be a matter for debate. But it does highlight the fact that we are able to relate better to someone who has shared our problem – someone who has been through what we are going through now, and triumphed over it. It is often difficult to relate to someone who hasn't shared our problem. One way of dealing with this is through 'empathy'. You *empathize* with the other person's problems and fears. Even though you haven't shared them – and may not even be able to fully understand them – you try to think yourself into their situation, so that you can tell them that you

> 'Our salvation comes from something small, tender, and vulnerable, something hardly noticeable. God, who is the Creator of the Universe, comes to us in smallness, weakness, and hiddenness.'
>
> Henri Nouwen

understand exactly how they must be feeling. It works splendidly, provided the person you're trying to help doesn't start asking awkward questions, which expose your lack of first-hand experience of their situation! The incarnation speaks of God sympathizing with our sufferings – not empathizing, as if he himself hadn't experienced them at first hand. God sympathizes, in the strict sense of 'suffers alongside', with us. In turning to God, we turn to one who knows and understands.

This aspect of the work of Christ remains an important part of the ministry of the church. The Christian community has often seen itself as a place of healing, where broken and wounded individuals can find acceptance and restoration. Many Christian writers have seen this ministry reflected in the parable of the Good Samaritan (Luke 10:25–37).

John Newton and 'Amazing Grace'

John Newton (1725–1807) was the main author of the *Olney Hymns*, a remarkable collection of songs of praise, many of which are still widely used today. As a young man Newton spent some time involved with the slave trade and, although there is ample evidence that he disliked this and had considerable empathy for those who he transported to the Americas, he still went on to become the captain of his own slave ship. In 1748, at the age of 23, he underwent a religious conversion, which led him to fully realize the inhumanity of his actions. He left his life as a slave ship captain, and settled down as a 'surveyor of tides' at the port of Liverpool. He was ordained as a priest in the Church of England in 1764, and served in the village of Olney. That same year he published his *Authentic Narrative* which detailed his exploits commanding a slave vessel.

In 1779, he published the collection of hymns for which he is best known. In his preface to this work, Newton explained his objectives in writing these hymns – to 'promote the faith and comfort of sincere Christians'. The most famous of these hymns celebrates the theme of God's grace.

Amazing grace! How sweet the sound
That saved a wretch like me!
I once was lost, but now am found;
Was blind, but now I see.

'Twas grace that taught my heart to fear,
And grace my fears relieved;
How precious did that grace appear
The hour I first believed.

Through many dangers, toils and snares,
I have already come;
'Tis grace hath brought me safe thus far,
And grace will lead me home.

The Lord has promised good to me,
His Word my hope secures;
He will my Shield and Portion be,
As long as life endures.

When we've been there ten thousand years,
Bright shining as the sun,
We've no less days to sing God's praise
Than when we'd first begun.

Although the primary focus of the parable is the kind action of the Samaritan towards a Jew (the two communities generally avoided contact with each other in the time of Jesus), its secondary focus is on the action of the Samaritan in entrusting the wounded man to the care of an innkeeper, and meeting the necessary costs. For Augustine of Hippo, this parable offered a model for the church as a healing community. The church was a hospital, full of wounded individuals who were loved and cared for. And, gradually, they were recovering.

Augustine also develops this idea to make the point that salvation is a process, not simply a one-off event. Salvation is about a past event, a present process, and a future hope. For Augustine, Christ died in order that the process of healing might begin, so that Christians might have

---

It is impossible to read this hymn without connecting it with Newton's own life-experience. There is no doubt that he hated both the slave trade and those who promoted it – including himself. How could God love such a degraded and vile person? Why would God want anything to do with him? In this hymn, Newton tries to express the great paradox of grace – that God loves sinners, even before they have repented of their sins. The hymn reflects Newton's own amazement that he could know and serve God, and write songs of praise dedicated to him.

A similar theme is explored in his hymn 'Praise for the Fountain Opened', based on Zechariah 13:1. In this hymn, Newton again explores the way in which the death of Christ is sufficient to pardon, purge and purify even a sinner such as himself.

There is a fountain filled with blood
Drawn from Emmanuel's veins;
And sinners, plunged beneath that flood,
Lose all their guilty stains.

The dying thief rejoiced to see
That fountain in his day;
And there have I, as vile as he,
Washed all my sins away.

John Newton, slave trader turned abolitionist and the author of 'Amazing Grace'.

the hope of one day being fully healed from their sin, guilt and mortality. Yet these do not cease to be realities in the experience of believers. They need to think of themselves as people who are under the care of a good physician. They are in the process of being healed, but not yet completely well. They live in the hope of healing and restoration, in that God has begun a process which they believe he will see through to completion. As Paul put it, Christians can be 'confident that he who began a good work in you will carry it on to completion until the day of Christ Jesus' (Philippians 1:6).

The Concept of Grace

Grace can seem a simple idea. It points us to God's sheer goodness, and in particular, his glad and free welcome to sinners, despite their failure and sin. It is deceptively simple, however, and the theologians of the church have spilled many gallons of ink exploring the ramifications of grace – how God can be gracious without compromising his nature as pure, how grace operates on people, and what part they play in the reception of God's grace.

The theological attention of the Christian church in its first few centuries was largely taken up by issues surrounding the doctrines of Christ, the nature of God and the Trinity. The theology of grace did not receive a great deal of explicit attention until the early fifth century, during a fierce debate involving one of the church's most influential and important thinkers, Augustine, bishop of Hippo in North Africa. In his doctrine of 'original sin' Augustine taught that the brokenness of the world was at root the result of human rebellion against the creator. Adam's sin in disobedience to God's command released sin and evil into the world and into the human soul like an infection. The result was that sin

twists human desire, warping our will so that we yearn for the wrong things – as Augustine put it, 'we look for happiness, not in you, but in what you have created'. In turn this then affects human thinking – our desires are so strong for such idols as wealth, sex or power that we do not think straight and cannot see the world in its true perspective and value. This in turn leads to damaging behaviour, when, lusting after what is not good for us, we would do anything to get it.

The effect of all this is that we cannot help ourselves. The human will is drawn towards things it thinks will satisfy but which never can, because the human soul was made for God alone. Like a heroin addict who is unable to kick his addiction, since sin entered the world through humanity's primeval act of disobedience, we are unable on our own to kick the habit of sin, always turning to the creation rather than the creator for satisfaction. What is needed is God's grace.

Augustine's understanding of grace emerged in its sharpest form during a debate with a British-born and Rome-based theologian called Pelagius. Worried by the lukewarm forms of Christian life he encountered in Rome, Pelagius wanted to emphasize the responsibility of Christians to take their faith seriously, work hard at it and not just wait around for God to do everything. He and some of his more hardline followers began to teach that from birth humans had a perfectly balanced will, poised between good and evil, and hence were able freely to choose either. God helped us to choose good by giving his grace, which for Pelagius consisted of the ability to choose the example of Christ and the instruction of the divine law. He took issue with Augustine on these grounds, thinking that Augustine's emphasis on humanity's inability to help themselves actually encouraged sloppy Christian passivity.

Augustine also thought that the solution to the human condition was divine grace. Yet as he saw the problem differently, he naturally understood the solution very differently too. And, of course, this led to a very different understanding of grace. Augustine agreed that God had given his law and the example of Christ, but for him, these were God's gifts in nature, not grace. And in particular, they did not help if people's wills were ultimately enslaved by the power of sin and simply unable to imitate Christ's example or obey the law. Grace was something else. For Augustine grace is an internal power which God gave over and above the gifts he had already given in nature. This power gradually frees our enslaved wills to begin to choose the good. It releases us internally so that we can obey him, and produce good works, or to use another image, it heals us slowly but surely from the contamination of sin which affects every aspect of human experience and will. Grace gradually liberates us from wrong desires, and restores within us a desire and longing for God.

For Augustine, there were three main kinds of grace. 'Prevenient Grace' indicates that God's grace is active even before one is aware of it, in both predestining some to salvation and preparing the soul for conversion. 'Operative Grace' refers to God's grace operating directly on us to remit or forgive sins without any help from our side. 'Cooperative grace' is where God cooperates with us, to gradually fix our desires on God rather than other things.

Augustine's teaching on grace was hugely influential throughout the Middle Ages. Medieval theology developed a complex and intricate vocabulary of grace trying to describe its different aspects, as Augustine had begun to do in the three distinctions mentioned above.

Thomas Aquinas (1225–74), in particular, developed a distinction between 'actual grace' (God's activity on human nature 'from outside' as it were) and 'habitual grace' which referred to God's instilling within believers a 'created habit of grace' which 'heals and justifies the soul'. This was a kind of supernatural presence planted by God within the human soul, which was then understood as the basis on which God can justify us. He also viewed grace as perfecting human nature – on our own we can be virtuous to a point, but to become truly God-like, requires God's specific help, the help of grace.

Augustine's notion of grace as a kind of internal force, followed by theories such as Aquinas's 'created habit of grace' led in some circles to the idea that grace was a kind of divine substance injected into humanity like an antidote to a disease. This seemed confirmed by some of the language of the Vulgate, the church's official Latin version of the Bible (see page 16). For example it referred to Mary, Jesus' mother as *plena gratia*, 'full of grace' which made her seem like a vessel filled with this substance called grace. This was reinforced in medieval theology by such notions as *gratia infusa* or 'infused grace', referring to the help God gave to struggling sinners to do good.

The Reformation saw a significant shift in the understanding of grace. Luther disliked what had become a rather mechanical interpretation of grace, where God was obliged to bestow it on those who did their best to please him. This was in fact precisely what some theologians at the time taught – that God had entered into a covenant or agreement whereby he would guarantee the gift of grace to those who did their best, and that grace would enable them to perform

> 'Three things are necessary for the salvation of man: to know what he ought to believe; to know what he ought to desire; and to know what he ought to do.'
>
> Thomas Aquinas

actions which were truly worthy of salvation.

Although originally an enthusiastic exponent of such ideas, Luther increasingly found this notion problematic. It still seemed to put the onus on the sinner to love God, hate sin, to do their best. But what if he didn't 'do his best'? What if his motives for performing good acts were mixed – done out of desire for his own salvation rather than pure love for God? It was as a response to this very personal dilemma that Luther developed his theology of justification by faith alone. In the course of this, he also developed a new understanding of grace, which

John Calvin, one of the chief architects of Reformation theology.

became widespread amongst most of the Reformation theologians. Grace began to be conceived of not so much as a divine substance or internal power, but instead as God's good favour towards humankind.

The key question was how God viewed his sinful human creation in general and individuals in particular. Did he regard us as sinners worthy of judgment, or was he well-disposed towards us, considering us worthy of the gift of Christ and salvation? God's

grace was now understood as his unmerited good will towards humankind, referring to the conviction that God's favour extended to sinners. Salvation was here conceived not so much as a process whereby God's grace infused into a human life gradually freed the Christian to perform good actions leading towards gradual transformation. Instead, grace was increasingly seen as the attitude of God which lies behind his declaration that the sinner who puts his faith in Christ is in the right before God. There is a process of gradual change and transformation into Christ-likeness which follows, but this process of 'sanctification' as it was called in subsequent Reformed theology, was very distinct from the original 'justification' out of which it flowed.

In Reformed Protestantism (the kind that emerged primarily from John Calvin in Geneva) grace began increasingly to be inseparably linked not so much to justification as to predestination. In other words, God's grace was principally seen as expressing God's unconditional choice of particular individuals for salvation at the beginning of time. This idea of course excludes any possibility of human merit or deserving of grace whatsoever, and magnified the power and initiative of God as the sole source of salvation, at the risk of making God seem arbitrary and despotic.

It is not only in Christian theology that grace is central. Although Christian life is meant to be lived in the context of God's grace, his free love, favour and goodness towards his creation, it is not to be sentimentalized. In the twentieth century, Dietrich Bonhoeffer (1906–45) highlighted the danger of what he called 'cheap grace' – a form of Christian life which enjoyed the benefits of Christian civilization and belonging, without the 'costly grace' involved in true discipleship. It is an important note to sound at the end of a discussion of theologies of grace – ultimately, grace is not the subject of a theological game, but brings the equally comforting and challenging call of God to live in a new way, in harmony with and expressing God's costly love for his creation.

Predestination and Human Freedom

One of the most important debates within Christianity is how God's sovereignty and human freedom interact. This is often discussed specifically in relation to the question of predestination. This is a somewhat controversial topic, which needs to be considered carefully. In what follows, we shall explore some of the biblical themes involved, and their implications for Christian thought.

We have already noted the importance of God's will in thinking about 'the mind of God' (see page 61). A central theme in the Bible is that God's choice of peoples or individuals is not determined by their merits, but by God's love and through God's will. This can be seen particularly in God's decision to choose Israel as his people. The Old Testament regularly affirms that Israel was chosen, not because of anything it had to offer, but solely because of the grace of God and by his sovereign choice (Deuteronomy 7:7; Isaiah 41:8–9; Ezekiel 20:5). This, of course, does not cancel Israel's duty to live up their responsibilities as God's people. Many of the Old Testament prophets stressed the *conditionality* of Israel's election. Unless Israel behaved in ways appropriate to the identity and calling as God's chosen people, that status would be revoked.

The New Testament regularly uses the language of 'predestination.' Thus Paul stresses that believers have been chosen by God from the foundation of the world (Ephesians 1:5, 11). Their new birth is not an accident, nor an unwelcome development. Paul clearly sees individuals as having been chosen by God. Paul's extended discussion of God's relationship with Israel (Romans 9–11) stresses that God must be free to do with his creation as he pleases. Although Paul makes this point specifically in relation to the rejection of Israel, many of his interpreters have seen this discussion as having wider significance, including the predestination of individuals.

To explore this point further, we may return to consider Augustine's ideas on grace. As we saw earlier, a central theme of Augustine's thought is the fallenness of human nature. This imagery of 'the fall' derives from Genesis 3, and expresses the idea that human nature has 'fallen' from its original pristine state. The present state of human nature and creation is thus not what it is intended to be by God. The created order no longer directly corresponds to the 'goodness' of its original integrity. It has lapsed. It has been spoiled or ruined – but not irredeemably, as the doctrines of salvation and justification affirm.

According to Augustine, it follows that all human beings are now contaminated by sin from the moment of their birth. Augustine portrays sin as inherent to human nature. It is an integral, not an optional, aspect of our being. In that all are sinners, all require redemption. In that all have fallen short of the glory of God, all need to be redeemed. For Augustine, left to its own devices and resources, humanity could never enter into a relationship with God. Nothing that a man or woman could do was sufficient to break the stranglehold of sin.

Grace is the unmerited or undeserved gift of God, by which God

> 'Salvation is from our side a choice, from the divine side it is a seizing upon, an apprehending, a conquest by the Most High God. Our "accepting" and "willing" are reactions rather than actions. The right of determination must always remain with God.'
>
> A.W. Tozer

> 'Primarily, God is not bound to punish sin; he is bound to destroy sin. The only vengeance worth having on sin is to make the sinner himself its executioner.'
>
> George MacDonald

voluntarily breaks the hold of sin upon humanity. Redemption is possible only as a divine gift. It is not something which we can achieve ourselves, but is something which has to be done for us. Augustine thus emphasizes that the resources of salvation are located outside humanity, in God himself. It is God who initiates the process of salvation, not men or women. But this raises a critical question. If we are totally dependent on grace for our salvation, and grace is not given to everyone, is not God determining in advance who may be saved? This leads us to the famous debates over predestination, some aspects of which are explored in what follows.

Two main positions have developed within the Christian tradition, and they can be illustrated by considering some controversies within Protestantism in the late sixteenth and early seventeenth centuries. While related debates have taken place in other sections of the Christian church, the controversy between Calvinists and Arminians helps to clarify the issues.

The Calvinist position was set out by the famous Protestant reformer of Geneva, John Calvin, especially in his *Institutes of the Christian Religion* (1559). Calvin's thought reflects a concern with human sinfulness and divine omnipotence, a concern which finds its most complete expression in his doctrine of predestination. As we are sinful creatures, we can have no meaningful role in our own election or calling. As God is the sovereign creator, he alone has the right to do with his creation as he pleases. Is not the potter at liberty to do what he likes with vessels that he has made from clay?

There is an important difference between Calvin and Augustine at this point. Augustine uses the term 'predestination' to refer to God's action in giving grace to some. It designates the special divine decision and action by which God grants his grace to those who will be saved. But what, it may be asked, happens to everyone else? God passes them over, according to Augustine. He does not actively decide that they will be damned; he simply omits to save them. Predestination, for Augustine, refers only to the divine decision to redeem, and not to the act of abandoning the remainder of fallen humanity.

For Calvin, however, logical rigour demands that God actively chooses to redeem or to condemn. God cannot be thought of as doing something by default: he is active and sovereign in his actions. Therefore, predestination has two aspects: a decision to save, and a decision to condemn. On this view, God actively wills the salvation of those who will be saved, and the damnation of those who will not. Predestination is thus the 'eternal decree of God, by which he determined what he wished to make of every individual. For he does not create all in the same condition, but ordains eternal life for some and eternal damnation for others.'

Scholars have found it helpful to distinguish the ideas of 'single predestination' and 'double predestination'. The former refers to a single, saving decision on God's part. Humanity is perishing because of sin; God therefore resolves to save some. This is the basic position outlined by Augustine. Calvin's position is better described as 'double predestination', in that it involves two decisions – a decision to save, and a decision to condemn. From the beginning of the world, Calvin argues, God has determined who will be saved, and who not.

The Protestant alternative to Calvinism at this point is known as 'Arminianism', after Jacobus Arminius (1560–1609). Arminius argued that predestination did not involve God's decision to determine which specific individuals would be saved, but rather which groups of people would be redeemed. God determined from all eternity that those who had faith would be saved. But it was up to the individual to come to faith. Where Calvin saw faith as a gift of grace, given only by God, Arminius regarded it as a human decision. Christ died for all people, making salvation a universal possibility. It was up to humans to respond to this possibility, by responding through faith.

These debates continue to this day. Arminianism continues to be widely held within Wesleyan Methodism, whereas more Calvinist positions are found within Reformed groups. A particularly interesting example of these tensions can be seen in the great evangelical revival in England during the eighteenth century. John and Charles Wesley were both Arminian in their theological outlook, whereas their co-worker George Whitefield took a Calvinist stance. Interestingly, the three were able to collaborate on a major programme of reform and renewal, despite their differences on this point.

In this section, we have considered how salvation is understood within Christian thought, and how it is related to the death and resurrection of Jesus Christ. Salvation emerges as a complex, rich idea, embracing believers' past forgiveness, their present transformation, and their hope of entering heaven to be with God. All of these are the 'benefits of Christ' (as Philip Melanchthon wrote in 1521), won for humankind on the cross, and appropriated by faith.

5

The Church

CHRISTOPHER WRIGHT

Facing page:
An illuminated
manuscript page
showing God's
descent on a
ladder to witness
the building of
the tower of
Babel.

If we think of the church as the community of people who confess Jesus of Nazareth as Lord and Saviour, and who seek to live as his followers, then the historical origin of that community, defined in relation to Jesus Christ, must be traced back to the New Testament. The day of Pentecost in Acts 2, when the Holy Spirit was poured out on the small community of the first followers of Jesus, is commonly spoken of as the birth of the church for that reason. However, Christians believe that the church is essentially a community that has been called into existence by God, a people constituted by God for his own purpose in the world. And the roots of that calling and constitution go much further back than Pentecost.

If we want to understand what happened at and after Pentecost, or indeed what went before it in the gospel stories themselves, we have to set this New Testament story in the light of the people of Israel in the Old Testament. Indeed we cannot understand Jesus, let alone his church, without seeing both in terms of this people who traced their own origin back to Abraham in the book of Genesis. And then we shall discover that we cannot understand Abraham either unless we set him in the context of all that happened before him. So all in all, it really would be best to start at the very beginning – not with the birth of the church, but with the birth of the world. We need to look briefly at Genesis 1–11.

The Origin of the Church

The Bible begins with the story of creation. Christians believe that the universe we inhabit is the creation of the one, living, personal God, who made it 'good'. He created us in his own image, to rule over the earth on his behalf, with a coherent set of spiritual and moral responsibilities: to love and obey God, to love and serve one another, and to enjoy and care for the rest of creation. However, with the entrance of sin and evil into human life, all of these dimensions of our existence have been fractured and distorted. We chose to rebel against our creator, and substitute our own moral autonomy for his authority. We live with all manner of personal and social sin – fear, anger, violence, injustice, oppression and corruption. And we exploit, pollute and destroy the earth he told us to care for.

The climax of this sad catalogue of human sin comes with the story of the tower of Babel in Genesis 11. To prevent a unified humanity acting in total arrogance, God divides human languages with the resultant confusion of communication. But the further result is that by the end of this part of the biblical story, we find a humanity that is fractured, divided, and scattered over the face of an earth that is under God's curse. Is there any hope for the world – specifically for the nations of humanity?

God's answer to the question posed by Genesis 1–11 is the story contained in the rest of the Bible, from Genesis 12 to Revelation 22. It is the story of

Propterea babilonia contigit vocari civitate. babel. ip. hebrei confusione vocant: de campo ū seinaar in regione babilonis meminit sibilla dicēs: Turris au altitudo cui causa divise st lingue. duo milia cētum septuaginta. iiij. tenere dicūt passuū: paulatī altiū angustior coartata erat ut ponds imminēs ēt aliꝰ sustetaret.

Hanc turrē. nembroth gigas construxit. Cum q confusione lingua rū migravit ide ad psas. eosqꝫ igne colere docuit.

gentes. ꝙ divisio terrarū facta: phalec gemini rea ꝉ rogau. qui saruch. qui nachor. qui regina filiū cuius duos Sinule filios. saba. ꝙ dadan iosephꝰ ūdic. saba. ꝙ iuda.

God's work of redemption within history. It centres on the cross and resurrection of Jesus Christ. And its climactic finale will be the return of Christ and his reign over the new creation. The remarkable thing is that this whole Bible story begins and ends with the nations of humanity. In Genesis 11 they were united in arrogance, only to be scattered under judgment. In Revelation 7:9 they will be gathered as 'a great multitude that no one could count, from every nation, tribe, people and language'. This final picture of the nations in Revelation, however, is actually a portrait of the church – the multinational community of God's redeemed humanity. And its multinational nature goes back to the covenant promise God made to Abraham, that through him all nations on earth would be blessed (Genesis 12:3).

So in a sense the church, considered as the community of God's people throughout history, fills the gap between Babel and the new creation. This is the community that begins with one man and his wife (Abraham and Sarah), becomes a family, then a nation, and then a vast throng from every nation and language. This is the church in its fully biblical perspective.

What can we learn about this community from the account of its earliest beginning in the call of Abraham? Three things stand out in the promise and narratives of Genesis, three things that should be marks of the church as the people of God in any era: blessing, faith and obedience.

A COMMUNITY OF BLESSING

Blessing is a word we might have thought never to hear again by the time we reach Genesis 11. Yet it was in fact God's first word, as he successively blessed his own acts of creation in Genesis 1. After the flood, God blessed Noah and made a covenant with all life on earth. But

repeated sin and failure seemed to reinforce only the language and reality of God's curse. Where can blessing be found? God's answer is to call Abraham and to promise to bless him and his descendants. So this new community stemming from Abraham will be the recipients of God's blessing. There is a fresh start here, for humanity and creation. But blessing is not just passively received. Abraham is also mandated to 'be a blessing' (Genesis 12:2). The bottom line of the covenant promise God makes to him is that all nations on earth will find blessing through him. It will take the rest of the Bible to show how this can be fulfilled, but it does mark out this community as those who both experience God's blessing and are the means of passing it on to others. Blessing received and blessing shared, is part of the essence of the church.

A COMMUNITY OF FAITH

'Abraham believed God, and it was credited to him as righteousness,' says Paul (Galatians 3:6), echoing Genesis 15:6. The New Testament book of Hebrews also strongly highlights Abraham as a man of faith (Hebrews 11:8–19), having earlier said that 'without faith it is impossible to please God' (Hebrews 11:6). So the community that stems from Abraham must be marked as a people who trust in the promise of God, rather than trusting in their capacity to build their own future security (as they tried at Babel). This is why one common name for Christians is particularly appropriate – they are simply 'believers'.

A COMMUNITY OF OBEDIENCE

Because of his faith, Abraham obeyed God; he got up and left his homeland at God's command. And when he faced the supreme test of sacrificing the son who embodied all God had promised him, he was willing to obey even then, though God intervened to stop him. So at the climax of that narrative, God reconfirms his promise to bless all nations because of Abraham's obedience (Genesis 22:15–18). So Hebrews 11 and James 2:20–24 set Abraham's obedience alongside his faith as proof of his authentic relationship with God.

The church, then, in tracing its roots back to God's call and promise to Abraham, finds here some of its key identity marks (we shall see more of this later). It is the community that not only experiences God's rich *blessing* but also is commissioned to be the means of blessing to others. It is the community that lives by *faith* in the promise of God, and proves that faith by practical and sometimes sacrificial *obedience*.

The Church in the Old Testament

If the church as the biblical people of God began with Abraham, then it is necessary to give some attention to the Old Testament part of its story. An examination of the whole history of Israel before Christ is not essential, but it will be important to see how some of the things that Israel believed about themselves in their relationship with God and the world are strongly reflected in what the Christian church thinks of its own existence and mission in the world. The following explanatory list of some of the key concepts that governed Israel's sense of identity in the Old Testament shows how the New Testament church has inherited the same self-understanding.

ELECTION

The foundation of Israel's faith was that God had chosen them as his own people. They were the seed of Abraham whom God had chosen and called. They were not a nation who had chosen to worship this particular god. Rather, this God had chosen them as his particular people. They would not exist at all apart from that divine choice and calling. Two things need to be said immediately.

First, the Israelites were not to imagine that their election by God owed anything to their own numerical greatness or moral superiority. Far from it, they were a tiny nation, and no more righteous than other nations. The roots of election lie exclusively in the love and grace of God and for reasons known only to him (Deuteronomy 7:7–10).

Second, they had been chosen, not primarily for their own benefit but for the sake of the rest of the nations. As has been seen, the call of Abraham is God's response to the parlous state of the world of nations in their rebellion and division. Blessing Abraham and his descendants was God's intended means of bringing blessing to all nations. Election, then, is not primarily a privilege (though it certainly is that), but a responsibility. It means being chosen for a task, being a chosen instrument by which God will fulfil his mission of universal blessing.

'You' said Peter in his letter to the scattered groups of early Christians, 'are a chosen people' (1 Peter 2:9). The church stands in organic continuity with Israel as the elect people of God. But the same vital points apply to the New Testament church as to Old Testament Israel. Such election is entirely by God's grace, not based on anything in us that makes us 'choice-worthy'. And election is fundamentally missional in purpose. We are chosen, not so that we alone might enjoy salvation, but so that we should be the means of God's salvation reaching others – as Peter went on to point out in subsequent verses. The church exists in the world as the community that God has chosen and called in order to serve God's mission to bring the nations from the situation described in Genesis 4–11 to that portrayed in Revelation 7.

REDEMPTION

Israel knew themselves to be a people whom God had redeemed. They looked back to the great historical deliverance of their ancestors from slavery in Egypt and saw it as the proof of the love, justice, power and incomparable greatness of their God. The language of exodus (redemption, deliverance, mighty acts of justice) filled the worship of Israel, motivated their law and ethics, and inspired hope at both national and personal levels for God's future deliverance. The memory of exodus was kept alive in the annual Passover celebration. Israel was a people who knew their history. And through their history they knew their God.

The New Testament explicitly sees the cross of Christ through the lens of the exodus (Luke 9:30–31). For on the cross God achieved the redemption of the world, the defeat of the forces of evil, and the liberation of his people. The Christian church therefore looks back to Calvary as much as Israel did to the exodus. For Christ, the Passover lamb, has been sacrificed for believers (1 Corinthians 5:7). Christians too are people of memory and hope, both of which are focused in their central feast, the eucharist or Lord's Supper. So the church stands in organic continuity with Old Testament Israel as the people whom God has redeemed.

COVENANT

Another dominant concept in Israel's theology was their covenant relationship with God. This too goes back to Abraham. Covenant involves a promise or commitment on the part of God, and a required response on the part of the one with whom the covenant is made. God promised Abraham to bless him, make him a great nation, and to bless all nations through his descendants. Abraham's response was faith and obedience. God extended this covenant to the whole

> 'You cannot have God as your Father unless you have the Church as your Mother.'
> Cyprian of Carthage

nation of Israel at Mount Sinai after the exodus. In the same context, God makes known his personal name, Yahweh (see page 57). This name was forever associated in Israel's mind with the exodus (in which Yahweh proved his redemptive power), and Sinai (at which Yahweh revealed his character, covenant and law to Israel). So Israel understood themselves to be uniquely the community of Yahweh God. He was committed to them in saving grace, historical protection and blessing, and long-term purpose for the world. They were to be committed to him in sole loyalty and ethical obedience.

Here again there is organic continuity between the Testaments. For the church is also the covenant community, the people of the new covenant, foretold in the Old Testament and inaugurated by Christ through his death and resurrection. So the church is a community in committed relationship with God. He is committed to those who are united to Christ through faith in his blood, and they are committed to him in exclusive worship and ethical obedience.

WORSHIP

Jesus, it has been said, came to a people who knew how to pray. The people of Israel were committed to worship the one living God, and the rich heritage of that is to be found, of course, in the book of Psalms. The language of adoration, praise, thanksgiving, appeal, lament and protest was well developed in the worshipping life of Israel. So much so that Deuteronomy could ask what other nation had their gods near them the way the Lord was close to Israel when they prayed to him (Deuteronomy 4:7).

Naturally, therefore, the Christian church that sprang from the womb of Old Testament Israel began as a worshipping community. Indeed this is one of the commonest postures of the church in the book of Acts – gathered for worship, prayer, and scriptural teaching, just as the Jews did. And it is presupposed in all Paul's letters that the churches to which he wrote were fundamentally communities that knew how to worship God, even if their enthusiasm to do so could itself present problems. As we shall see, worshipping God is of the very essence of the church, and will be so eternally.

STRUGGLE

Israel had high ideals, drawn from their covenant relationship with God, but there was nothing idealistic about their historical existence. It is vital to remember that all the truths mentioned above were lived out in the struggle of being an all-too-human society in the midst of the world of nations just as fallen and sinful as Israel itself. So the Old Testament honestly and painfully records Israel's terrible failures alongside all the remarkable affirmations of their faith and aspirations. They sinned and they suffered. They failed internally and they were attacked externally. Their history is a long catalogue of struggle between those who brought the word of God to them and those who were determined to resist the will and ways of their God.

And in all of this too we see the church as in a mirror. The following paragraphs survey many aspects of the Bible's teaching about what the church is and is meant to be. But we must not lose sight of the fact that, although the church is ultimately God's own creation, draws its identity and mission from God, and will accomplish God's purpose, the church is also a community of sinners – forgiven sinners, to be sure, but fallen sinners still.

In all these ways, then, and many more, the church stands in organic continuity with Old Testament Israel. Of course there are differences, and the New Testament itself makes it clear that God deals with his people in different ways at different times, even as his promises develop and expand over the centuries until they find their climactic fulfilment in Christ. However, the unity of God's people in the Bible is a far more important theological truth than the different periods of their historical existence. Throughout the whole Bible, the people of God are those who are chosen and called by God to serve his purpose of blessing the nations. They are those who have experienced the redeeming grace and power of God in history, ultimately accomplished through Christ on the cross. They are those who stand in committed covenant relationship with God, enjoying the security of his promise and responding in exclusive loyalty and ethical obedience. They are those who are set apart by him and for him to be, and to live as, a distinct and holy community within the surrounding world. They are those who live to worship the living God eternally, and yet also live within all the ambiguities of historical life on this sinful planet and are as yet far from perfect. In all these things, the church stands in continuity with Old Testament Israel for, as Paul puts it, all believers are sharers in the same promise, the same inheritance and the same good news (Ephesians 3:6). In Christ Jesus, they belong to the same olive tree (Romans 11:17–24; see page 224).

The Church in the New Testament

In what new ways is the church described in the New Testament? Most obviously, the person of Jesus Christ becomes the central and defining presence, to which all descriptions of his followers relate. It is worth noting how the New Testament sees Jesus as the fulfilment of the promise of God in the Old Testament, and therefore sees

The coming of the Holy Spirit in *Pentecost* by El Greco.

the followers of Jesus as those who live in the light of that fulfilment. From that foundational understanding (that Jesus and the church fulfil the Old Testament Scriptures), follows naturally several other terms that the New Testament uses for those who formed the earliest Christian church.

THE TIME IS FULFILLED

In the earliest recorded preaching of Jesus (Mark 1:15), we hear the note of fulfilment that dominates the gospels. Throughout the Old Testament period and beyond, the people of Israel grew in expectation that their God would bring about a new state of affairs in human history. From the promises God had made in his covenants with them (especially the covenant with Abraham, and with David, and the prophesied new covenant in the future), and from the words of prophets and Psalmists, they looked forward to a future in which several things would take place. These scripturally founded expectations included the following:

1. The God of Israel, who was acknowledged as king within Israel, would establish his reign in a much wider sense in the world.

2. Israel, from being estranged from God and under the oppression of their enemies, would be restored through repentance and forgiveness. They would be delivered, while their enemies would be overthrown.

3. These things would take place through a coming one who is variously described as God's Servant, God's anointed one, the coming king, and so on. But the mission of this coming one would be wider than just bringing Israel back to their God. The sequel to the restoring of Israel would be the ingathering of the nations, in fulfilment of God's promise to Abraham that all the nations would find blessing through his descendants.

4. Beyond that, the whole of creation would ultimately be redeemed in a new age of justice and peace under the reign of God and the outpouring of his Spirit.

This, said the New Testament writers, is what was inaugurated in the life, death and resurrection of Jesus. As Messiah (God's anointed one), Jesus embodied Israel in his own person – taking their destiny and fulfilling their mission. So in his life and teaching he inaugurated the kingdom of God, demonstrating the power of God's reign in word and deed. In his death he took upon himself the judgment of God against sin, not just on behalf of his own people Israel but for the whole world. In his resurrection, God fulfilled his promise to redeem Israel. As Paul put it, 'what God promised our fathers he has fulfilled for us, their children, by raising up Jesus' (Acts 13:32). Before his ascension, he commissioned his followers to carry forward the Abrahamic mission of Israel, now focused on the name of Christ himself, to bring the blessings of repentance and forgiveness to all nations (Luke 24:46–47). And to empower them for this, the risen Christ sent the Holy Spirit, whose outpouring had been prophesied as a sign of God's new age of salvation and blessing (Isaiah 32:15–20; Joel 2:28–32).

No wonder then that the day of Pentecost can be seen as the birthday of the church in this new sense. For it was the outpouring of the Spirit of God on that day that demonstrated that the new era of fulfilment had begun. The crucifixion, resurrection and ascension of Jesus of Nazareth had accomplished what God had promised. Those who were responding in repentance and faith could now belong to the restored Israel in Christ, whether they were Jews like his first followers, or Gentiles from the nations who were also now invited to belong to this new community. This is why the emphasis in the early preaching in the book of Acts is so strongly on the note of fulfilment. God has now acted decisively to inaugurate his kingdom through Jesus, whom he has made Lord and Christ. There is, of course, a surprise in that the old age continues and we still live within this world and its history. The New Testament sees an 'overlap' between this age (our old world and its history) and the age to come (the new order of God's rule of peace, justice and salvation). There is an 'already' and a 'not yet' about the kingdom of God. But the key thing is that the decisive moment has happened in Christ. Like seed sown in the soil, or yeast added to the dough, the kingdom of God is already present and at work in the world. We are already in 'the end times'. The church, then, is the community that must live in the present in the light of both the past (what God has accomplished in Christ), and the future (what Christians look forward to when he returns).

As the community of those who have responded to God's action in Jesus Christ, then, the church in the earliest records of the New Testament is described by several simple terms. These are terms that were used even before the term 'Christian' was invented, and they remain perennially true. In a sense, these terms are the most basic descriptions of the church, in that they describe the people who belong to it. They are not metaphors or theological concepts or institutional titles. They simply tell us what it means to be a Christian (even though that was not the first term used). At first they were just *disciples* – followers of Jesus. Then they were also called *witnesses* to him, and *believers* in him. Eventually, with such an emphasis on Christ, they attract the nickname, 'Christ-folk' – *'Christianoi'* and, ironically, it is the nickname given by outsiders that has gone down in history.

DISCIPLES
The nucleus of the Christian church in the New Testament was the group of disciples of Jesus, who are present in

> 'The Church exists for nothing else but to draw men into Christ, to make them little Christs. If they are not doing that, all the cathedrals, clergy, missions, sermons, even the Bible itself, are simply a waste of time. God became Man for no other purpose.'
> C.S. Lewis

the gospels almost everywhere that Jesus is. 'Disciples', means learners – those who are the followers and adherents of a teacher or master. Jewish rabbis had their disciples, and Jesus was no exception. But there were significant differences. The rabbis taught the Scriptures and all their authority rested there. Jesus certainly also taught the Scriptures, but he spoke on his own authority and called for loyalty to himself. The disciples of the rabbis intended one day to be rabbis themselves, 'graduating', as it were, from the school of their master. For Christians, there is no 'graduation' from the school of Jesus; instead, there is a call to lifelong discipleship.

The gospels reveal that there were three main aspects to being disciples of Jesus, all of which continue to be marks of belonging to his church:

1. Disciples are those whom Jesus has called to himself, to be with him. This is not just a matter of following the teaching of a dead or absent leader. To be a disciple is to be in a constant relationship with Jesus; or rather, it is to experience the truth of the last promise he made to his disciples, 'I am with you always' (Matthew 28:20).

2. Disciples are those who obey Jesus. It is a matter of personal loyalty, in which Christians take all Jesus said with great seriousness, and submit to his authority. Jews spoke of submitting to the yoke of the law. Jesus called his disciples to 'take my yoke upon you and learn of me' (Matthew 11:29). That means submission of mind, heart and will to Jesus Christ.

3. Disciples are commissioned and sent out by Jesus, in his name (which means, with his authority), to make disciples of the nations. That is, discipleship is a self-replicating mission.

In the gospels, Jesus had a special group of twelve close disciples, eleven of whom became known as *apostles*. These (and a few others mentioned in the New Testament) had a unique authority in bearing witness to Christ (because they had known him and witnessed his resurrection) and establishing and guiding the early churches (see page 235). But the gospels also speak of a wider group of disciples, ordinary followers of Jesus. And although the word 'disciple' itself is not greatly used in the New Testament after the gospels, it is clear that the church is always intended to be a community of disciples, the followers of Jesus who live with his presence, submit to his teaching, and carry forward his mission.

WITNESSES

'You will be my witnesses,' said Jesus to his disciples, after his resurrection and before his ascension (Luke 24:48; Acts 1:8). Almost certainly Jesus was echoing the same words that God had spoken to Israel in Isaiah (43:10–12). Israel was supposed to be the people who bore witness among the surrounding nations to the reality of their God, Yahweh. Other nations might call their witnesses for their own gods, if they could, but Yahweh entrusts his own case to his people. They must declare what they know from their history about the God who had called and redeemed them. The nations would come to know who is really God from the testimony of those to whom he has entrusted the task of witnessing to their own historical experience of him.

Similarly, Jesus is entrusting the truth about himself to those who had witnessed him. Originally, of course, the words were spoken to the first apostles, who had indeed witnessed the life, teaching, death and resurrection of Jesus. Peter claims as much explicitly when challenged about

A twelfth-century carving of Jesus calling the first disciples.

his healing and preaching (Acts 3:15). But by extension, all Christians are called to bear witness to what they have experienced of the saving love of God in Christ. The church is the guardian of that apostolic witness. Sometimes the cost of bearing that witness is high, as the earliest Christians found, and countless others down the centuries have also proved. The word 'martyr' originally meant simply 'witness'. But since that witness so often ended in death at the hands of those who rejected the word of witness, it acquired the added meaning of one who gives his or her life rather than compromise their testimony.

BELIEVERS

The next common description of the earliest Christians (before they were so named) in the New Testament book of Acts is 'believers'. This too goes back to the gospels, of course, because Jesus so frequently called for faith, along with repentance. Faith is the key to entering the kingdom of

God, and to receiving its blessings, including forgiveness, healing, and eternal life. Faith too, like discipleship and witness, is entirely directed to the person of Jesus himself. It is not just a matter of believing certain propositions, though it does include believing the claims of Christ. Rather it means an act of personal trust in God, focused on Jesus as the one who has fulfilled God's promises and who died and rose again for the salvation of humankind.

In these early terms, then, which were eventually subsumed under, but not replaced by, the generic name, 'Christians', we find some of the distinctive features of what the church is meant to be. It is first and foremost a community of the disciples of Jesus, seeking to experience his presence, obey his teaching, and fulfil his mission. It is necessarily a community of witnesses, often called to pay the cost of bearing witness, for the kingship of God and the message of the cross bring an unwelcome challenge to a hostile world. And it is a community of believers, who follow Abraham in being first of all justified by faith and then living by faith.

Images of the Church

The church is much more than just a collection of like-minded people, an aggregate of individuals who claim to be disciples of, witnesses to, and believers in Jesus Christ. The church *as a whole* is a significant entity. It is a historical reality in the world, with its spiritual roots going right back to Abraham. The Bible provides many metaphors, or pictures, to convey different aspects of this reality. Most of them are found in the Old Testament as ways of describing Israel and are then extended in the New Testament to those who are believers in Christ. One metaphor, however, the concept of the church as a body, or as the body of Christ, seems unique to

Shabbat being celebrated during Passover (*Pesach*), two of the most important Jewish festivals.

the New Testament. Some of the more important biblical metaphors for the church are the following.

A HOUSEHOLD OR FAMILY

Old Testament Israel was a kinship-structured society, divided into tribes, clans and households. The basic unit in this arrangement was the 'father's house' or *beth-ab*. This was the extended family of three or even four generations, including married sons and their children, household servants, agricultural workers and even resident foreigners practising their trade. This robust organism not only functioned as the basic unit of Israel's social, educational, economic, judicial, religious and even military life; it also provided the individual Israelite with some vital support. The household was the place in which the individual found personal *identity* and *inclusion* (personal names always included the father's house, as well as clan and tribal names). It was the place of *security*, since the household had its inherited portion of the land. And it

was the place of spiritual *nurture and teaching* in the law of God. Already in Old Testament times, the whole nation of Israel could be metaphorically described as a household. 'House of Israel' *(beth-yisrael)*, is a common term for the whole nation. Sometimes 'House of Yahweh' could be used as well, picturing the whole people as a family belonging to God.

With this metaphor already well established for Israel in the Old Testament, it is not surprising that the early Christians adopted similar language to speak of the church community. Paul calls it 'the household of God' (1 Timothy 3:15). 'We are his house,' says the writer to the Hebrews (3:6). Applying this metaphor was undoubtedly made even easier by the fact that the first Christians met in homes, and the sense of being an extended family must have been strong. The Greek word *oikos* was used for the household in as broad a sense as the Old Testament *bayith*. As in the Old Testament, the church as a household or family was the place of

identity (in Christ), *inclusion* (in the fellowship), *security* (in an eternal inheritance), *nurture and teaching* (in the Scriptures and teaching of the apostles). For those who had been severed from their natural family connections because of loyalty to Christ, the church as a new family in all these senses was of great importance, and still is.

Thinking of church as family has other implications, of course. With God as their Father, all believers are brothers and sisters (Greek *adelphoi* includes both genders), which is how the New Testament writers often address them, and how they ought to behave towards one another. Christians are also all children of God, with Jesus himself the 'firstborn among many brothers' (Romans 8:29). They all belong to 'the same family. So Jesus is not ashamed to call them brothers' (Hebrews 2:11).

A PEOPLE

Old Testament Israel was a nation *(goy)* among other nations. But they also referred to themselves as a people *('am)*, which is flavoured more by community than by ethnicity. In fact, although the core of Israel was of course the ethnically related community descended from the twelve tribes – the original sons of Jacob (Israel) – the reality was that it was a very mixed society. Many other groups came out of Egypt with the Israelites at the exodus (Exodus 12:38). Many Canaanites survived and blended in with the Israelites after their settlement (Joshua 9). Aliens were to be welcomed and given basic rights in Israel's social legislation (Leviticus 19:33–34). What held Israel together was not so much the one ethnicity as *covenant loyalty* to the one God – Yahweh. So they were above all 'the people of Yahweh'. Furthermore, that was a title that was open to expansion. The Old Testament could envisage

'The church must be a mother to all who are weary and heavy laden, to all who have strayed and gone wrong — even to those who have forsaken their mother... and fallen victim to strange ideas. And therefore its task is not to look to the great... but rather to visit the prisoners and preach the gospel to those who cannot help the church because they have no privileges to bestow.'

Helmuth Thielicke

people of other nations coming to be included in the people of Yahweh (Isaiah 19:24–25; Psalm 87; Zechariah 2:11), and that is exactly what the New Testament says has happened through the mission of the church.

So the church is a people, or rather it is *the* people of the biblical God, through faith in Christ. But it is also and essentially a multinational people, in which membership is open to all, Jew and Gentile, male and female, slave and free (Galatians 3:28). So the language that had first applied to Israel is now extended to people of all nations. 'You,' says Peter, 'are a people belonging to God… once you were not a people, but now you are the people of God' (1 Peter 2:9–10). As a worldwide community of peoples, the church fulfils the promise of God to Abraham and anticipates the ultimate gathering of God's people in the new creation (Revelation 7:9, 21:3).

A BRIDE

We have already spoken of the covenant relationship between God and Israel in the Old Testament. The language of *love* was a significant

Calling the church 'the bride of Christ' highlights God's love for this community.

part of that relationship – in both directions. God's love for his people was the fountain of all he had done for them. 'It was because the Lord loved you and kept the oath he swore to your forefathers that he brought

you out with a mighty hand and redeemed you from the land of slavery' (Deuteronomy 7:8). And the first and greatest commandment in the law, as Jesus called it, was 'You shall love the Lord your God with all your heart, and with all your soul and with all your might' (Deuteronomy 6:5). From there it is a short step to considering the relationship between Yahweh and his people in terms of the marriage covenant. The prophet Hosea seems to have been the first to make that comparison. However, he uses the metaphor negatively to accuse Israel of being an unfaithful bride (Hosea 2; Jeremiah 2:1–2; Ezekiel 16). Nevertheless, it is clear that what God wants is a people who are united to him in mutual loving devotion as husband and wife ideally should be.

In the New Testament the church is portrayed as the bride of Christ. On the one hand, the metaphor highlights Christ's love for the church, and especially his self-giving, sacrificial care for his bride. On the other hand, it speaks of the beauty and adornment of the bride, who will one day be perfect and without blemish for her divine husband (Ephesians 5:25–27; Revelation 21:2). In both directions, the picture is one of love, commitment, and beauty. And since a wedding is also an occasion of great joy, there is a dimension of celebration in this picture too. The destiny of the church is the great wedding feast of the Lamb (Revelation 19:9).

A PRIESTHOOD

'You will be for me a priestly kingdom,' said God to Israel at Mount Sinai (Exodus 19:6). The metaphor draws its point from the role that priests played within Israel itself. Priests stood in the middle between God and the rest of the people. They operated as mediators in both directions. On the one hand they taught the law of God to the people. On the other hand they brought the people's sacrifices to God. Through the priests, God came to the people and through the priests, the people came to God. And it was also the job of the priests to bless the people in the name of Yahweh (Numbers 6:22–27). Then, by analogy, God tells Israel that they will stand in a similar position between him and the rest of the nations of the earth. Through Israel, God will become known to the nations (Isaiah 42:1–7; 49:1–6). And through Israel God will ultimately draw the nations to himself (Isaiah 2:1–5; 60:1–3; Jeremiah 3:17). And, of course, Israel was to be a blessing on the earth – another priestly function.

'You,' said Peter to the Christian assemblies of Asia Minor (modern Turkey), 'are a… royal priesthood' (1 Peter 2:9–12). That priestly identity of Old Testament Israel is now inherited by those who are in Christ. So, as God's priesthood, the church consists of those who are to declare the praises of God and what he has done. And as a holy priesthood, Christians are to live in such a way that the nations are drawn to praise God. Priesthood is a missional concept, for it puts the church between God and the world with the task of bringing the two together in Christ – making God known to the nations, and calling the nations to repentance and faith in God and to the sacrifice of the cross. This double direction of movement seems to have been in Paul's mind when he spoke of his own missionary work as a 'priestly duty' in Romans 15:16.

A TEMPLE
The actual priests in Old Testament Israel, of course, served in the Temple in Jerusalem. The Temple, built by Solomon, was the successor to the tabernacle, or large tent and surrounding courtyard, that had served Israel during their years in the wilderness. The tabernacle is described in Exodus 36–40, while the Temple is described in 1 Kings 6–7. The Temple became one of the central pillars of Israel's faith and identity. It had a primary and a secondary significance.

First of all, the Temple (like the tabernacle before it) was regarded as the place of God's dwelling. Israel knew, of course, that the creator of the universe did not actually live in any construction made by human hands. Even heaven could not contain God (1 Kings 8:27). Nor did he have any need for such an earthly house (2 Samuel 7:1–7). But nevertheless, this Temple was the place that God had chosen to make his name dwell (1 Kings 8:29), and where his glory would be tangibly felt. In this respect (as the symbolic place of God's presence among his people), the Temple was the focal point for a significant element in God's covenant promise to his people – namely that he would live among them, in intimate, protective, blessing.

> 'The birth and rapid rise of the Christian church therefore remain an unsolved enigma for any historian who refuses to take seriously the only explanation offered by the church itself.'
>
> C.F.D. Moule

I will keep my covenant with you… I will put my dwelling-place among you, and I will not abhor you. I will walk among you and be your God, and you will be my people (Leviticus 26:9–12).

Secondly, the Temple was a place where Israelites would come to meet with God. The original tabernacle had also been called a 'tent of meeting'. Again, they knew that the living God was everywhere present and that they could call on him anywhere at any time. Nevertheless, the Temple provided a 'direction' for their prayer (1 Kings 8), and pilgrimage to the Temple in Jerusalem became a significant and joyful undertaking (though it never seems to have become an obligatory religious ritual). Psalms 120–134 are songs for such pilgrimage, and they express the joy (in the midst of struggles too), of knowing, meeting, trusting, and worshipping God in Zion – the place where the Temple stood and where God's people celebrated his presence. But those who came to worship God in this way had to come worthily. So other Psalms lay out moral criteria for acceptable worship – summarized as 'clean hands and a pure heart' (Psalms 15 and 24), and the prophets hammered home the message that mere religious rituals in the Temple made no impression on God if there was no corresponding commitment to personal and social justice, compassion and integrity (Isaiah 1:10–17; Jeremiah 7:1–15).

At the time of the first writings of the New Testament, the Temple in Jerusalem was still standing. It was destroyed in AD 70 by the Romans, but in the lifetime of Christ and the apostles, it was still there. However, as was pointed out above, Jesus himself and his followers believed that in him, as the Lord's anointed Messiah and king, God had fulfilled his purpose for Israel. This had major implications for the physical Temple. Jesus himself took over its role and significance, as the person (no longer the place) in whom God's presence is among his people (Immanuel), and as the person through whom people must now come to God in worship (John 4:2–26). So, the writer to the Hebrews points out that by coming to Christ, Christians have already come to Mount Zion (that is, to the Temple), and in him they have an altar, the perfect sacrifice, and God's great high priest (Hebrews 12:22).

However, Paul goes further and sees the church itself as the Temple of God. Not in the sense of a physical building (Christians did not start building 'churches' in that sense for a long time after the New Testament period. Using the word 'temple' to describe a building where Christians meet is not found at all in the New Testament.)

Rather, the church is the community in which God dwells by his Spirit, and to which people gather to meet with God – the double function of the Old Testament Temple.

Actually, Paul uses the Temple imagery at three distinct levels: the individual Christian, the local church, and the whole church, but all with the basic idea of a dwelling place for God.

1. In 1 Corinthians 6:19, Paul warns Christians that they cannot use their bodies in any way they like, especially not for sexual immorality. This is because, since the Holy Spirit lives in the Christian believer, 'your body is a temple of the Holy Spirit.' This is the only individual application of the concept.

2. In 1 Corinthians 3:1–17, Paul speaks in a very similar way, but extends the picture to include all the Christians at Corinth as, collectively, God's Temple. The 'you' in these verses is plural. 'God's temple is sacred and you [plural] are that temple.' Similarly, in 2 Corinthians 6:16, Paul warns the Corinthians that they must not take part in things that are connected with pagan temples for there can be no agreement between such idolatrous temples and the true temple of God – which is what the church is. 'For we are the temple of the living God.' To reinforce his point, Paul quotes from the Old Testament text Leviticus 26:12, referred to above, in which God promises to dwell with his people in covenant communion – provided they keep themselves clean before him.

3. In Ephesians 2:21–22 Paul is addressing Gentile believers. He has been explaining how they have now been united with believing Jews into one single community through the death of Christ. He uses Temple imagery to describe how the 'dividing wall' has been torn down (Ephesians

2:14; which is probably a reference to the partition in the Temple courts that kept the Gentiles out of the holier courts of the compound). But then he uses it again to describe how all Christians, Jews and Gentiles, are being built together into a Temple for God to dwell in by his Spirit. The reference is probably to the whole church, not just the Ephesian assemblies. Indeed some scholars think that 'the whole building' (Ephesians 2:21) should be translated 'all the churches' – which are joined together as 'a holy Temple in the Lord'.

It is significant that the New Testament only ever speaks of the church as a single temple, even though there were many individual believers and many local assemblies. This may again be due to the strong Old Testament background to the idea. The Greeks and Romans had many temples to many gods. Israel, in stark contrast, had only one Temple to only one God. Likewise, the Temple image as applied to the church implies that there is only one church – the people of the one living God, who has only one dwelling place, through his one Spirit. The big difference in the New Testament is that, whereas the Temple in the Old Testament was for Israelites, God had promised that it would be 'a house of prayer for all nations' (Isaiah 56:7). Indeed Solomon had prayed for it to be a place of blessing for foreigners when it was first dedicated (1 Kings 8:41–43) and, through Christ and the gospel, that became a reality. The Temple of God is now truly the multi-national community of believers from all nations.

A VINE AND AN OLIVE TREE
Two pictures of the people of God are drawn from horticulture. Both in the Old and New Testaments, they are compared to a vine and an olive tree. Jesus uses the first and Paul the second.

In John 15, Jesus says he is the true vine. Doubtless he is referring to the fact that in the Old Testament, Israel is likened to a vine that the Lord God had planted in his own land (Psalm 80). Unfortunately, as several prophets pointed out, God's expectations from his vine were

The apostle Paul likened the people of Israel to an olive tree onto which Gentile believers were being grafted.

Jesus' gospel extends God's covenant with the people of Israel to all nations.

rudely disappointed. Isaiah pictures God looking for a harvest of good grapes from his people to reward his loving investment in them, but instead of justice, he finds bloodshed, and instead of righteousness, cries of the oppressed (Isaiah 5:1–7). Ezekiel even more tartly points out that the wood of a vine is useless for anything when it is living; how much less when it is burnt in the bonfire – which is the fate of Israel under God's judgment (Ezekiel 15).

Jesus similarly is concerned about the fruitfulness of his followers. So he not only describes them as branches in the vine, which is himself, but also warns that failure to bear fruit (which is a way of alluding to the practical response of obedient discipleship) will lead first to pruning and potentially to destruction. Abiding in Christ is the only way to fruitfulness as God's people.

In Romans 11:13–36, Paul compares Israel to an olive tree. In the Old Testament that picture is used simply as a metaphor for beauty along with other trees (see, for example, Jeremiah 11:16; Hosea 14:6). Paul, however, builds a whole theology around the horticultural practice of stripping some branches off a tree and grafting in others – a practice which is intended to rejuvenate the original tree and increase its fruit-bearing. Paul sees an analogy to the way Gentiles are being grafted into the original covenant people of God, Israel, while some of those original people were being cut off because they failed to respond to what God had now done in Jesus Christ. His point is addressed particularly to Gentile believers, warning them not to boast of their new status. Only faith in Christ is the qualification for membership in the olive tree of God's people – whether Jew or Gentile – but it is still the same, original olive tree.

It is important to note that God's response to the failure of many Jews to believe in Jesus was not to chop down the olive tree and plant a completely new one. Some branches might be lopped off, and other branches wonderfully grafted in, but the roots and the trunk remain. Paul thus confirms the continuity between Old Testament Israel and the church, and the unity of believing Jews and Gentiles in the one new people of God. There is only one olive tree – only one covenant people of God throughout both Testaments and all of history. And (in a miraculous expectation, not paralleled in the world of horticulture), there also remains the opportunity for branches that have been cut off to be grafted in again, if they turn in repentance and faith to God through Christ.

A FLOCK

Another picture of the church that is found in both Testaments is also drawn from the world of agriculture – a flock of sheep. It is, perhaps, a rather passive and not very flattering image, but it is used in two significant ways, depending on who is pictured as the shepherd or shepherds.

1. God as Shepherd.

'We are his people, the sheep of his pasture', sang the Israelites (Psalm 100:3). The main point of this metaphor was to highlight God's providential and tender care for his people, as a shepherd cares for his flock. Individuals could take comfort from this (Psalm 23), but the whole nation could envisage itself being led by their divine Shepherd (Isaiah 40:11).

2. Leaders as shepherds.

Across the ancient world of Israel's surrounding nations, it was common to speak of kings as shepherds of their people. Care, provision, guidance and protection was what was expected of them – in theory at least. In reality, in Israel, the complaint was that their 'shepherds' more often exploited the sheep than cared for them. So Ezekiel vigorously condemns such shepherds (meaning the kings of Israel), and says that God himself will take on again the job of shepherding his own flock (Ezekiel 34).

It was against this background that Jesus claimed to be the good, or model, shepherd in John 10. This is more than a promise of tender care in the mode of Psalm 23. It is a bold claim to be the true king of Israel, indeed to be the divine king himself, as promised by Ezekiel. Not surprisingly, it led to a violent reaction (John 10). But in the process, Jesus portrays his followers (that is, the embryonic church) as his own sheep whom he knows and who know him – and points forward to the inclusion of others, but within a single flock under a single shepherd (John 10:16 – echoing Ezekiel 37:22–24).

As a natural extension, those who are called to leadership within the church are also portrayed as shepherds, or, as Peter puts it, as under-shepherds of the Chief Shepherd, who is Jesus. Unlike the kings of Israel in Ezekiel 34, Christian leaders are to work with love, without greed, with servant hearts, and as good examples to the rest of the flock (1 Peter 5:1–4). Paul adds the additional duty of defending the flock from ravaging wolves – his matching metaphor for false teachers who seek to devour the sheep. And he reminds leaders that the church never belongs to them, but to Christ alone, who died for it.

Keep watch over yourselves and all the flock of which the Holy Spirit has made you overseers. Be shepherds of the church of God, which he bought with his own blood (Acts 20:28).

A BODY

Finally we come to the one major picture of the church that is unique to the New Testament and, indeed, unique to Paul – that is, the church as a body, or specifically as the body of Christ.

Before summarizing the primary ways in which Paul uses this language, it is worth establishing what he does not mean. Paul uses the body language both as a simile (the church is *like* a body – mainly in 1 Corinthians and Romans), and as a metaphor (the church *is* a body and Christ is its head – mainly in Colossians and Ephesians). He does not use the term literally. That is, it is a misunderstanding to think that the church is an extension of the incarnation, in the sense that the church has now replaced the physical body of Jesus of Nazareth. This is ruled out by the way Paul distinguishes between Christ as the head and the church as his body, and also by the fact that while Jesus was sinless, the church is still very much composed of failing and sinning people in this world. In addition, it is mistaken to think of the church as simply identical with the risen body of Christ. Paul has a distinct theology of the resurrection of Jesus, and certainly affirms that Christians are risen in and with him. But he distinguishes Christ from believers, in that they still await their resurrection bodies (Romans 8:23; 2 Corinthians 5:1–5), in which they shall then be *like* his resurrection body (Philippians 3:21), not *identical* with it – now or then.

Four key points emerge from Paul's rich development of this picture of the church.

1. Unity and diversity of members.
Paul's first use of the body imagery is simply as very effective simile. In 1 Corinthians 12:12–31, he likens the believers within the church to the different members of the human body. There are many physical parts of a body, but they all cohere within the one body; they all assist one another; they all experience joy or pain together; and they all contribute to the healthy functioning of the body as a single organism. His main point in this context is that God has arranged things in this way for the good of the whole (that is, the whole human body, and the church taken as a whole). So no single part should think that it is so important that it has no need of any other part of the body; and no single part should consider itself less important than some other more prominent part.

Paul's point in relation to the church is that all the spiritual gifts God has distributed among different members of the church are actually given for the benefit of the whole. So, in Romans 12:4–8, using the same comparison, he urges those with different gifts to use them wholeheartedly and with humility. There is diversity within the church, but it exists within the fundamental unity that we all belong by baptism to the one Christ and share the one Spirit. The church, then, like the human body is an organic unity with functional diversity.

2. Christ as the head.
The main emphasis in the preceding section was on the 'horizontal' relationship between the different members of the one body. But in Colossians and Ephesians, Paul develops the picture in a more 'vertical' direction by speaking of Christ as the head, in such a way that the church relates to Christ as the rest of the human body is related to the head. There seem to be three elements to this picture.

First, in both letters Paul puts this description of Christ as the head of his body, the church, in the same context as Christ's sovereignty over the whole

Christian ethics

Does Christianity have a distinctive ethic? And if so, how is this shaped and nourished by Christian beliefs? Many writers, sympathetic to Enlightenment rationalism, argued that there was a universal morality which Christianity reflected. It was not necessary to know anything about Christian theology to make ethical judgments. The Christian, Buddhist, Hindu, Muslim, humanist and atheist were all, it was argued, committed to much the same set of moral principles (with ultimately unimportant local variations).

This approach is now regarded as discredited. In the first place, the idea of some 'universal morality' is now accepted as illusionary. Morality depends on a vision of the 'good life' – and what is 'good' is shaped by deeply held beliefs about the meaning of life. The Christian faith offers its own distinctive vision of the place and purpose of humanity, which is expressed in its beliefs.

A good example of the way in which belief shapes Christian ethics concerns the identity of Jesus Christ. Paul asks his readers to 'be imitators of God' (Ephesians 5:1). But in order to be 'imitators of God', believers need to know what God is like. The doctrine of the incarnation affirms that Jesus Christ's words and actions show what God is like. Christians are urged to 'love one another' (1 John 4:7–11). But what does this word 'love' mean? The doctrine of the incarnation allows us to flesh out what we mean by the 'love of God'. Throughout his ministry, we notice Jesus Christ accepting individuals, being prepared to associate with those who were regarded as socially acceptable as much as those who were regarded as social outcasts. The good news of the kingdom was for all, without distinction. That same pattern of divine acceptance should be ours as well. To recognize that Jesus Christ is God incarnate is to recognize that he maps out patterns of behaviour that ought to be characteristic of Christians. Yet no one is saved by imitating Christ; it is by being saved that believers are moved to be conformed to his likeness, as they seek to be imitators of God through him.

So what are the fundamentals of Christian ethics?

1. *The sanctity of life.* Christians believe that life is a gift of God, and that the taking of life – whether voluntary (as in suicide) or involuntary (as in murder) – is unacceptable. The doctrine of creation lays the foundation for this important idea.

2. *Caring for the poor and destitute.* Christians have long recognized that the gospel calls them to social action. Both through his example and teaching, Jesus reached out and ministered to the poor, outcast and marginalized, and calls on his church to do the same. Christians are asked to see others as they are in Christ, not as the world values them.

3. *The danger of wealth and possessions.* Although Christianity does not demand poverty on the part of its followers, it recognizes that wealth and possessions can become a barrier to a right relationship with God. It is fatally easy to allow these to become the grounds of our security. Instead, Christians should see these as things that have been entrusted to them, to use in God's service.

Christianity and Social Justice

From the outset, Christians have been deeply concerned about issues of social justice. Throughout his ministry, Jesus reached out to the marginalized, oppressed and needy, with a particular concern for the poor. In his sermon preached in the synagogue at Nazareth, which inaugurated his ministry, Jesus declared that he had been sent to 'preach the gospel to the poor' (Luke 4:18). The book of Acts records how the early Christians shared their goods, in order to promote fellowship and mission, and relieve poverty and need within the church. The letter of James offers much practical advice and wisdom to Christians, including exhortations not to privilege the wealthy and powerful, and to care for the poor and lowly.

The same concerns can be seen throughout Christian history. The founding of the monasteries was of major importance to the Christian vision of social justice. However, the late eighteenth and early nineteenth centuries are often singled out as periods when this concern for social justice was of particular significance. William Wilberforce (1759–1833) was a leader of the anti-slavery movement. His 1789 speech to parliament, arguing for the abolition of slavery on Christian humanitarian grounds, eventually led to the ending of the slave trade in 1807, despite the delaying tactics of its opponents.

A new series of social evils, however, was caused by the Industrial Revolution in England. The need to operate machinery and produce goods as cheaply as possible led to the rise of factories with squalid, degrading working environments. The Christian social reformer Lord Shaftesbury (1801–85) worked to bring about better working conditions for children, and sought to eliminate inhuman working conditions in factories.

The Salvation Army, established in London's East End in 1865, combined an active evangelistic ministry to working class people, and a social programme to ensure that they were properly cared for. Its founder, William Booth, was foremost in campaigns to support the needs of the urban poor, and was instrumental in bringing about much-needed social reforms. A similar pattern of social engagement can be seen in American revivalist movements of the late nineteenth century, which often combined a call for personal repentance and renewal with a commitment to fight social evils.

Probably the most significant Christian movement to engage with issues of social justice at this time was the 'social gospel movement' in North America. One of its most significant leaders was Walter Rauschenbusch (1861–1918), a Baptist pastor. Convinced of the need to get involved in community work, in 1886 Rauschenbusch took up a pastorate at the Second German Baptist Church in New York, located in a poor and dangerous neighbourhood known as 'Hell's Kitchen'. Here, he worked to develop church social action, while at the same time trying to 'infuse the religious spirit' into the secular reform movements also active at this time.

Social justice remains high on the agenda for Christians in the developing world, where injustice remains a significant issue. Some of these injustices linger from colonial times; others arise from the impact of trade agreements, which often cause economic problems in the developing world – for example, encouraging migration from the countryside to cities has led to a surge in the ranks of the urban poor. In recent years, Pentecostalism has played an especially important role in ministering within these deprived areas.

of creation (Colossians 1:15–18; Ephesians 1:19–22). The implication is that Christ exercises lordship and control over the church, as the head is the 'control tower' of the body. This, however, as Paul stresses elsewhere, is a headship that is exercised in tender love and servanthood, with self-sacrificial, self-giving care (Ephesians 5:23–30).

Second, in Ephesians 1:23, Paul speaks of Christ 'filling the church' (just as he fills the whole of creation). In the context of body language, this may mean something like the human consciousness, in which the whole body is within the conscious awareness of the head – as if the mind fills the body with its presence and direction. Likewise, Christ is everywhere present and active within his church.

Third, just as a body grows as a living organism under the direction of the head, so Paul describes the church as growing up, both 'from' and 'into' Christ (Colossians 2:19; Ephesians 4:12–14). So the body metaphor is useful for Paul's passion for maturity among his churches. As a body cannot grow if it is severed from its head, neither can the church grow if it does not remain vitally connected to Christ.

3. Reconciliation of Jew and Gentile.

We have seen that the body provided Paul with a picture of unity in the midst of diversity. The most fundamental division in his world was that between Jews and Gentiles. And it was of the very essence of Paul's understanding of the gospel and of the church that God had dissolved that barrier through the death of Jesus the Messiah. So, in Ephesians 2:14–18 he describes how God has brought both together, first by removing the cause of the conflict, then by uniting the two in a single new humanity, and third by presenting them both together to God. In this third stage he uses the body language again, saying, that Christ's intention was 'in this one body to reconcile both of them to God through the cross, by which he put to death their hostility' (Ephesians 2:16). 'This one body' here clearly means the church of believing and reconciled Jews and Gentiles in Christ. So crucial was this conviction to Paul that he probably coined a new Greek word to describe it in Ephesians 3:6, where he says that Gentiles constitute a 'co-body' (*syssoma*) with Israel, as well as co-heirs and co-sharers in the promise in Christ Jesus. The church in *this* sense is a new and unprecedented reality in history – nothing less than a new humanity.

4. Appropriate behaviour.

We saw above that the least that members of a body can do is cooperate. There is no place among the members of the same body for either a superiority complex (rejecting others as less important than oneself), or an inferiority complex (rejecting oneself as of no importance in comparison with others). This is the message of 1 Corinthians 12:14–26. However, Paul takes the metaphor further into the realms of positive Christian behaviour within the church. Ephesians 4 is a rich chapter about how Christians should behave in the light of all that God has done and all that they are in Christ. Twice Paul applies the body metaphor to reinforce his exhortation. In verses 15–16, Christians should speak the truth in love with one another, because they are to be growing up in love as a whole body under Christ. And in verse 25 he urges Christians to truthfulness, and doubtless the rest of the instructions that follow, on the basis that 'we are all members of one body'. Church unity, then, is not just an ecumenical or institutional dream. It is a fundamental basis for Christian ethics.

This completes our survey of major biblical pictures for the church as the

> 'He who begins by loving Christianity better than truth will proceed by loving his own sect or church better than Christianity, and end in loving himself better than all.'
>
> Samuel Taylor Coleridge

people of God. None should be set up as dominant, at the expense of the others, and none should be neglected. Also, we should not imagine that these are pictures only of some idealized or mystical church. These are ways in which the Old Testament spoke about historical Israel, and the New Testament speaks about the actual assemblies of Christian believers in the early church. Both Israel and the church were filled with very ordinary people with many faults and failures. By means of these metaphors and images, however, God reminded them of the real identity that they had, and emphasized different aspects of their relationship with Christ and with each other.

Identity Marks of the Church

As the church continued to define itself in relation to the surrounding world of the early centuries, believers formulated their core beliefs in the form of short statements known as creeds. In the Nicene Creed (see page 24), Christians summarize and affirm their conviction about the church as follows: 'I believe in one, holy, catholic and apostolic church.' Each of these words is an essential identity mark of what Christians believe about the church. The creeds reflect truths that are contained in the biblical pictures that have been examined above, but condense them into this short list of terms.

ONE
This is not, perhaps, the first thing that an outsider might observe about the Christian church. There seem to be many different 'brands' of Christianity. There are major distinct traditions, such as Roman Catholic, Orthodox, Protestant. Within these there are many more subdivisions and denominations (literally thousands of them). And even within the same denominations, there are different national branches, different cultural

expressions, different preferences in worship, liturgy, and so on. And for all the attempts that have been made to bring greater unity among some of these great traditions, new denominations and groupings are springing up every few days, as the church continues to expand throughout the world. *One* church? The conviction that, in spite of all its diversity, and indeed in the midst of much sinful disunity, the church is essentially one rests on several foundations.

1. The church is one in relation to Christ.
What unifies the church is not any one of the external aspects of its life, such as its leaders (not even a single leader as in the case of the Roman Catholic Church's pope), or its structure, or its great statements. In essence, the church is constituted by those who belong to Christ. This is an objective fact, not dependent on how we feel about it, or about each other. People who have the same biological father and mother are siblings in objective fact – whether they like it or not, or like each other or not, or even know each other, and no matter how they treat each other. Likewise, all who are children of God the Father through being born again by his Spirit, belong to Christ, who is their brother, and are brothers and sisters within the one family of God.

2. The church is one in relation to the one living God.
The one God is creating a single new humanity, which is what the church even in all its ethnic diversity will ultimately be (as seen in Revelation 7). So monotheism is also the foundation of the oneness of God's people. Likewise, the unity within the Trinity is the model for the unity of the church. Jesus prays that the church may be one, as he and the Father are one (John 17:11, 21–23). This is not just a

forlorn wish. It affirms a truth about God and a matching truth about the church.

3. The church is one in history.

As we have seen, there is an organic unity of God's people ever since the call of Abraham, and all its historical divisions, while sad and often sinful, cannot finally destroy God's purpose for that one people. An early example of God's promise in this regard may be read in Ezekiel 37:15–28.

4. The church is one in the pictures the Bible uses to describe it.

This is clear from our survey above. Even when the pictures include plurality within themselves (for example, a family has many members, a vine many branches, a flock many sheep, a body many parts, and so on), all of them are exclusively singular in the way they are used in the Bible to describe the church. There is only one family and people of God; only one bride of Christ; only one vine; only one priesthood and temple; only one flock; only one body – the body of Christ.

HOLY

'You shall be holy, for I the Lord your God am holy,' said God to Israel (Leviticus 19:2). Essentially, this meant that Israel was to be a distinctive community among the nations. Holiness did not mean merely that they were to be specially religious. It meant being different by reflecting the very different kind of God that Yahweh revealed himself to be. There were in fact two aspects to Israel's holiness, both of which are relevant for the church.

On the one hand holiness was a *given* – a fact of their existence. That is to say, God had set apart Israel for himself. It was his initiative and choice. 'I am the Lord your God who sanctifies you' – that is, makes you

holy, separate, from the nations (Leviticus 20:26; 22:31–33).

On the other hand, holiness was a *task*. That is, Israel was to live out in daily life the practical implications of their status as God's holy people. 'Be what you are,' was the message. In Old Testament Israel, this practical task of holiness had two dimensions. It had a symbolic dimension, in which they gave expression to their distinctiveness from the nations through a complex system of regulations about clean and unclean animals, foods and other daily eventualities. It also had an ethical dimension, for being holy meant living lives of integrity, justice and compassion in every area – including personal, family, social, economic and national life (see especially Leviticus 19).

The church too is called to be holy. The same language is applied to Christians, for example in 1 Peter 2:9–10. And the same two aspects apply to the church. Holiness for the church is both a given status and a moral and practical challenge.

On the one hand, Christians are those whom God has already sanctified – that is, set apart for himself as his own distinct people in Christ. That is why all Christians are called 'saints' in the New Testament. Saints, in New Testament terms, are not a special category of super-religious Christians. The word *hagioi* just means 'holy ones', and includes all those whom God has called to be his own. It does not mean they have already achieved some super-human stage of moral perfection.

On the other hand, Christians are called to live holy lives. This includes both negatively abstinence from the sin and impurity of the world, and positively living characterized by love, honesty, truth, compassion, goodness and all the other fruit of the sanctifying Holy Spirit. Once again we find a high degree of continuity between the moral dimension of what the church ought to

'It is not possible to have Christ apart from the church. We try. We would very much like to have Christ apart from the contradictions and distractions of the other persons who believe in him, or say they do.'

Eugene Peterson

be and the quality of life that God required of Israel (and a sad and correspondingly high degree of divine disappointment in failing to find what he is looking for in either).

CATHOLIC

The use of this word in the creeds was established long before its particular use in connection with the branch of the church known as Roman Catholic. It is unfortunate that many people use the single word 'Catholic' when they mean *Roman* Catholic, since the word originally applied to the whole church throughout the world, and still should. The Greek word *katholikos* means 'universal' or (more literally) 'as a whole'. We may think of it in at least four ways.

1. The church is universal in its membership.

It was of the very essence of the gospel preached by Paul that there were no barriers to membership of the church. The church was not just for people of one nation, or a single ethnicity. Just as there is no difference between different nationalities in their sinfulness (for sin is common to all human beings), so there is no difference in salvation. For the only way that sin can be dealt with is through the cross of Christ (and that is available to all human beings). The only conditions, therefore, are repentance from sin and faith in Christ. On those grounds, membership of the church is truly universal – open to all. Anyone can repent, anyone can believe in Christ, anyone can belong to the church. No other criteria apply.

2. The church is universal in extent.

Although the New Testament understanding of the extent of the civilized world is more limited than our modern understanding of the globe, the church was still 'worldwide' in their terms. Whether you were a

Christian in Antioch, Jerusalem or Rome made no difference. It was the same church of Christ to which you belonged. As history progressed and the church spread, this remained true, even though the grievous historical and geographical divisions of the church have spoiled most people's appreciation of it. A Christian in Indonesia (no matter what their denomination) is part of the same 'catholic' church of Christ as a Christian in Peru.

It is particularly important to remember this truth about the church (that it is 'catholic' – that is, global in extent), when people tend to think of Christianity as 'the western religion' – whether they mean European, or American (or both). Certainly in the history of the church, some parts of the world have had a greater dominance. In early centuries in India, people thought of Christianity as 'the Syrian religion' – because that was the heartland of the faith that came to them. In the same early centuries in Europe, Christianity was dominated by North Africa, especially Tunisia and Egypt. But the Christian faith belongs to no single race or region, or rather, it belongs to all. And today, the church is truly global – not just in theological affirmation, but in geographical reality. The great majority (at least seventy per cent) of the world's Christians are not western at all, but live in the continents of the south and east – Africa, Latin America and Asia.

3. The church is universal throughout time.

We have observed from the start that the church, as the people of God, stands in organic continuity with Old Testament Israel. God's plans include all those, throughout time, who have responded to him with faith (Hebrews 11:40). So believers of all ages are part of the 'catholic' church. Even in the Old Testament there was an intuition that a

Augustine and the Donatist controversy

Under the Roman emperor Diocletian (284–313), the Christian church was subject to various degrees of persecution. Under an edict of February 303, Christian books were ordered to be burned and churches demolished. One of the Christian leaders who collaborated with the authorities, and handed over his books to be burned, was Felix of Aptunga, who later consecrated Caecilian as bishop of the great North African city of Carthage in 311.

Many local Christians were outraged that such a person should have been allowed to be involved in this consecration, and declared that they could not accept the authority of Caecilian as a result. The new bishop's authority was compromised, it was argued, because the bishop who had consecrated him had lapsed under the pressure of persecution. As a result, the hierarchy of the Roman Catholic Church was deemed to be tainted. The church ought to be pure, and should not be permitted to include such people. By the time Augustine – destined to be a central figure in the controversy – returned to North Africa from Rome in 388, a breakaway faction – the Donatists, who based themselves on the teachings of Donatus – had established itself as the leading Christian body in the region, with especially strong support from the local African population.

Augustine responded by putting forward a theory of the church which he believed was more firmly grounded in the New Testament than the Donatist teaching. In particular, Augustine emphasized the sinfulness of Christians. The church is not meant to be a 'pure body', a society of saints, but a 'mixed body' of saints and sinners. Augustine finds this image in the biblical parable of the wheat and the tares (Matthew 13: 24–31). The parable tells of a farmer who sowed seed, and discovered that the resulting crop included both wheat and tares – grain and weeds. What could be done about it? To attempt to separate the wheat and the weeds while both were still growing would be to court disaster, probably involving damaging the wheat while trying to get rid of the weeds. But at the harvest, all the plants – wheat and tares – are cut down and sorted out without any danger of damaging the wheat. The separation of the good and the evil thus takes place at the end of time, not in history. For Augustine, this parable refers to the church in the world. It must expect to find itself including both saints and sinners. To attempt a separation in this world is premature and improper. That separation will take place in God's own time, at the end of history. No human can make that judgment or separation in God's place.

So in what sense is the church holy? For Augustine, the holiness in question is not that of its members, but of Christ. Church members are contaminated with original sin. The church will only be perfected and its holiness finally realized at the last judgment.

Augustine of Hippo (modern Algeria), who opposed the Donatists' unorthodox beliefs.

single lifetime was not the limit of God's saving power. His covenant with his people was 'from generation to generation'. So, one Psalmist could combine those already dead with those as yet unborn in his great vista of faith and praise (Psalm 22:29–30). With the same faith, Paul could reassure the believers in the young church of Thessalonica that those of their family and friends who were Christians, but had recently died, still belonged to Christ and would not miss out on all that he planned for the church (1 Thessalonians 4:13–18). Christ explicitly promised that death and Hades (that is, the grave) could not prevail against the church he is building.

Another phrase from the creeds expresses this dimension of the catholicity of the church – 'I believe in the *communion of saints*.' All God's saints (in the sense defined above) from all generations are united in communion with him and one another. Death separates us neither from God nor from one another in Christ (Romans 8:38–39).

The distinction between those who belong to the church now living throughout the earth, and those who belong to the church but are now dead, is sometimes expressed in the terms '*church militant*' (to describe the former), and '*church triumphant*' (to describe the latter). The first reminds us that here on earth the church is involved in a constant battle against sin and evil (it is not meant to imply that Christians are literally to engage in fighting and militancy to spread their faith). The second reminds us that Jesus has won the victory over evil, and those who have died now share in that victory as they wait for the final establishing of his reign over all creation. The 'catholic' church comprises all believers in Christ – the living and the dead, the universal people of God throughout all of history.

4. The church is universal in the eyes of God.

'The Lord knows those who are his,' said Paul (2 Timothy 2:19), with the implication that we may not always be so sure. Ultimately, only God knows the full extent of the church, and the full number and personal identity of all who truly belong to it. For this reason, a distinction is sometimes made between the visible church and the invisible church. We need to use these terms with care, and not set one in opposition to the other. The phrase 'visible church' recognizes that, from a human standpoint, the church includes hundreds and thousands of institutions, organizations, individuals and groups, structures and processes, and is intertwined in all kinds of ways with the legal, social, cultural and even political and economic aspects of wider society in hugely different cultural contexts. Not all of those involved in this vast human reality called 'the church' have been, are now, or will be in the future, true disciples of the Lord Jesus Christ. The church is a great mixed company. Jesus warned that not everyone who called him Lord would belong to the kingdom of God, and that many who would use his name would not even belong to him in any way he would own (Matthew 7:21–23). The phrase, 'invisible church' recognizes two things. On the one hand, it reminds Christians that ultimately it is not those who are seen 'in church' who necessarily belong to it, but those who are seen and known by God. On the other hand, it acknowledges that there are those around the world who have trusted in Jesus secretly, for whom there is no possibility of belonging to an institutional church. Such people may be invisible to other believers, but they are certainly known by God and included among his church.

So both words are describing an

aspect of the truth. Both are describing reality. No one should think that 'invisible' means 'only imaginary'. Nor should they disparage or dismiss the 'visible church', as if only the 'invisible church' were 'the real thing'.

Having considered these dimensions of what it means to speak of the 'catholic church', we must remember that the predominant emphasis in the New Testament itself is on the local church – that is the assembly of believers in any given place, which in New Testament times mostly met in homes. The commonest word for the church in the New Testament is *ekklesia*. This was a common secular word at the time for an assembly of people, particularly the political body in Greek cities, in their remarkable democratic system, to which all citizens belonged, which they were expected to attend, and in which they were eligible to speak and vote on matters brought before them.

An *ekklesia* was simply an assembly of people formally gathered for a specific common purpose. So when applied by Paul and others to groups of Christians, it is not a metaphor for the church (such as 'body' or 'temple' are), but a simple description of the assemblies in which Christians would meet (see 1 Thessalonians 1:1; Romans 16:5). There could be several such local assemblies in the same city or region, in which case the word could be plural (1 Thessalonians 2:14; Galatians 1:2). And at times Paul can speak in general terms of 'all the churches' (assemblies), 'of the Gentiles' (Romans 16:4), or 'of Christ' (Romans 16:16), or 'of God' (2 Thessalonians 1:4).

Although *ekklesia* (from which, of course, we get English words like 'ecclesiastical' and 'ecclesiology') has come to be translated as 'church', for Paul it retained its primary meaning as 'an assembly' – the local gathering of

Christians for worship and teaching. These were the groups which Paul established in his missionary travels, and to which he wrote most of his letters. From this fact, some have argued that the local church is the only real manifestation of the church, and that the New Testament does not envisage 'the church' in the collective or universal sense outlined above, still less in the sense of denominations or national churches that have developed in later history.

However, it is mistaken to base one's whole doctrine of the church solely on the use of the single word *ekklesia* in the New Testament, since the other metaphors, as we have seen, refer to the church as a collective whole. Furthermore, the word is sometimes used in the singular with a collective sense for the church (meaning all the local assemblies) in a region (Acts 9:31), or universally (1 Corinthians 12:28; Ephesians 5:25; Colossians 1:18).

APOSTOLIC
Of the four terms in the creed, this is the one that most closely links the church to the New Testament, for that, of course, is where we find the apostles themselves. To speak of the apostolic identity of the church draws attention to at least three things.

1. The church was founded by the apostles.
Paul says that the church is built upon the foundation of the apostles and prophets (Ephesians 2:20). Almost certainly 'prophets' refers to the Old Testament prophets of Israel, and Paul is affirming the continuity of God's people throughout the Bible. In the New Testament the word 'apostle' is used sometimes a little loosely to include those associated with church planting and itinerant missionary work. But strictly speaking it applies to those who were commissioned by Jesus to be

> 'Going to church doesn't make you a Christian any more than going to a garage makes you into an automobile.'
>
> Billy Sunday

his authorized witnesses. Initially this meant the twelve close disciples, who had been with him throughout his ministry and heard his teaching. When Judas excluded himself by his betrayal, his place was taken by Matthias, who, like the other eleven, had also witnessed Jesus' resurrection (Acts 1:21–26). Saul of Tarsus was given a unique individual encounter with the risen Jesus, and a personal commissioning that led to his ministry as the apostle Paul. His conflicts with various false apostles led him to defend and define his apostleship (most clearly in 2 Corinthians), from which it is clear that witness to the resurrection of Jesus and teaching authority (along with authenticating signs) were the vital marks of the New Testament apostles.

The New Testament apostles were unique in their experience and office. They bore accredited testimony to the life, death and resurrection of Jesus of Nazareth, because they were witnesses. Since Jesus was the climax and completion of God's revelation and redemption, their witness was both essential and final. The apostles had no successors in that role, since no others could ever again witness the historic earthly life of Christ as they had. The writings of the early church fathers show that a clear distinction was made between the New Testament apostles who knew Jesus (plus Paul), and all those who followed them as leaders in the churches. This is the reason for the closure of the canon of Scripture. The Scriptures bear witness to Christ – both through the Scriptures of the Old Testament that prepared the way for him, and in the documents of the New Testament that record his life, death and resurrection, and interpret the significance of these events. Once that testimony was complete, by those to whom Jesus entrusted the task, there is no more biblical revelation, just as there are no more apostles equivalent

to those appointed by Jesus. The Holy Spirit, of course, continues to illuminate the Scriptures and to teach ever more clearly and in new contexts the truth contained in them. But in Christ, God has said all he needs to say, and has done all he needs to do, for humankind to know the truth and to be saved.

So although some Christian denominations and networks do speak of their leaders as 'apostles', such persons can never have, and should not claim or be given, a status or authority in the church equivalent to the New Testament apostles, on whose witness and teaching the church itself is founded.

2. The church is to be faithful to the teaching of the apostles.

Jesus promised his apostles in advance that the Holy Spirit would lead them into all truth, and teach them much more than he had been able to teach them in his earthly life (John 16:12–15). In other words, these men were given their authority to teach the church directly from Jesus, and consciously did it with the help of the Holy Spirit (1 Corinthians 2:12–13). So Paul did not hesitate to exercise this authority. He could distinguish clearly between sayings of Jesus that relate to any issue, on the one hand, and the advice or instruction that he gave in his own right, on the other. But in either case, those to whom he was writing were expected to accept the authority of his words. Later, when Paul was conscious that his own life and ministry were approaching their end, he was careful to insist that the teaching he had entrusted to his younger partners, such as Timothy and Titus, should be carefully passed on to others in a continuous chain of teaching (2 Timothy 2:2).

For Paul, himself, of course (as for Jesus), the Scriptures of the Old Testament constituted the authoritative

'Evangelism is just one beggar telling another where to find bread.'

D.T. Niles

word of God, and he reminded Timothy of this in the same letter in which he insisted that his own teaching be passed on (2 Timothy 3:15–16). Already within the New Testament period the teaching and writings of the apostles were being placed on the same level of authority as 'the other Scriptures' (2 Peter 3:16).

So then, to speak of the church as being 'apostolic' means that it is subject to the doctrinal authority of the New Testament apostles, that is to say, to the Bible itself. For the apostles endorsed the authority of the Old Testament, and either wrote the documents that are now included in the New Testament, or were closely associated with those who did. And in submitting to the authority of the Bible, the church submits to the authority of Christ.

3. The church is to follow the mission of the apostles.

Another sense of the word 'apostolic' relates to the root meaning of the word itself. It comes from the Greek word, *apostello*, to send out with a purpose, or message to deliver, or on a mission. In the gospels, the word is first used when Jesus chose the twelve and specifically called them apostles, 'that they might be with him and that he might send them out to preach and to have authority to drive out demons' (Mark 3:14–15). Then at the end of the gospels and the beginning of Acts, Jesus commissioned these apostles to fulfil the mission of making disciples of the nations (Matthew 28:16–19), of being witnesses to him and preaching repentance and forgiveness in Christ's name to all nations (Luke 24:45–48).

So in some traditions, the word 'apostolate' is used to describe the missionary work of the church. Certainly, the New Testament makes it clear that it is God's intention that the message of Christ in all its fullness should go to the ends of the earth. That was why Christ chose and sent out his apostles, and that mission is

Baptism symbolizes cleansing from sin, being given the Holy Spirit and being welcomed into the church.

> 'When we preach on hell, we might at least do it with tears in our eyes.'
>
> D.L. Moody

Should the Church Baptize Children?

Matthew's Gospel records Jesus Christ as commanding his disciples to go and make disciples, and baptize them (Matthew 28.17–20). But what about children? Does this command extend only to adults, or does it include infants? The New Testament includes no specific references to the baptism of infants. However, neither does it explicitly forbid the practice, and there are also a number of passages which could be interpreted as condoning it – for example, references to the baptizing of entire households, which would probably have included infants (Acts 16:15, 33; 1 Corinthians 1:16). Paul treats baptism as a spiritual counterpart to circumcision (Colossians 2:11–12), suggesting that the parallel may extend to its application to infants.

Most mainstream Christian churches accept that the baptism of infants is a valid practice, with its roots in the apostolic period. Martin Luther and John Calvin, though severely critical of the Roman Catholic Church over many points of doctrine and practice, held that infant baptism was an authentic biblical practice. The reasons given for infant baptism vary. Augustine of Hippo argued that, since Christ is the saviour of all people, all people require salvation. As baptism is both recognition of the need for human salvation and of God's gracious willingness to provide it, all should be baptized. After all, he argued, little children were as much in need of salvation as adults.

Another line of defence of the baptism of infants lies in the Old Testament, which stipulated that male infants born within the bounds of Israel should have an outward sign of their membership of the people of God. The outward sign in question was circumcision – that is, the removal of the foreskin. Infant baptism was thus to be seen as analogous to circumcision – a sign of belonging to a covenant community. Writers such as Huldreich Zwingli (1484–1531) argued that the more inclusive and gentle character of Christianity was publicly affirmed by baptism of both male and female infants; Judaism, in contrast recognized only the marking of male infants. The more gentle character of the gospel was publicly demonstrated by the absence of pain or the shedding of blood in the sacrament. Christ suffered – in being circumcised himself in addition to his death on the cross – in order that his people need not suffer in this manner.

But not all are persuaded of the case for infant baptism. Many Baptist writers reject the traditional practice of baptizing infants. Baptism was to be administered only when an individual showed signs of grace, repentance, or faith. The practice of baptizing infants is held to be without biblical foundation. It may have become the norm in the post-apostolic period, but not in the period of the New Testament itself. It is also argued that the practice of infant baptism leads to the potentially confusing idea that individuals are Christians as a result of their baptism, thus weakening the link between baptism and Christian discipleship.

certainly passed on to succeeding generations. So although the church no longer has apostles with equivalent status and authority as the New Testament apostles, in relation to its doctrinal foundations, the church certainly does inherit the apostolic task of mission, for that task was always intended to be self-replicating. When Jesus said, 'teaching them to observe all that I have commanded you', this must have included this final command itself.

The church, then, is apostolic because it was founded by those original and unique apostles appointed by Jesus, but it is only truly apostolic when it remains faithful to the apostolic teaching and continues to engage in the apostolic mission.

How, then, can we discern the presence of the true church of God, when we know that the visible church is inevitably mixed? All members of any church on earth are still sinners, as Paul's letters to all 'the saints' in the churches of the New Testament show. What marks should we look for? Various answers have been proposed to this question over the years, and at least the following should be in evidence. A true church will be one where:

1. There is Trinitarian faith in God the Father, Son and Holy Spirit, with explicit acknowledgment and worship of Jesus of Nazareth as Lord and Christ.

2. The Bible is preached as the word of God (in both Testaments), in such a way that the gospel of grace is understood and Christian discipleship nurtured.

3. The two gospel sacraments of baptism and the Lord's Supper (see pages 239–246), are being administered regularly.

4. The mission of God is being carried forward in all its dimensions, evangelism, practical loving care and action in society, seeking the justice of God's kingdom, making disciples among the nations.

Identity Actions of the Church

All human communities have symbols and rituals by which they express their sense of identity and unity. These can be simple and informal (like the colours, scarves and chants of the supporters of a football team), or they can be very complex and formal (like national or military ceremonial occasions). But the essential element is the same: by doing these things (which are visible or tangible), we signify that we belong to this particular group, affirm our unity with all who share the symbols, and sustain our existence over time from one generation to another by continued adherence to these honoured symbols or traditions.

Over the centuries, Christians have spread all over the world and developed many local cultural expressions of their identity. However, two particular actions go right back to the New Testament itself and are universally accepted by Christians as essential actions through which the identity and unity of the church are given visible and tangible expression: these are the sacraments of baptism and the Lord's Supper.

The word 'sacrament' is not specifically found in the Bible, but it has been used to describe a feature of biblical faith in both Testaments. Because God is the creator of all that exists, both in the spiritual and physical realm, the Bible sees no radical separation, or duality, between these realms. The physical creation is the good work of God, declares his presence and glory, and can be the means through which he acts in blessing or judgment. We ourselves are part of that physical creation, and God

'Evangelism is the spontaneous overflow of a glad and free heart in Jesus Christ.'

Robert Munger

relates to us fully in the physical realm. The incarnation of God in the humanity of Jesus, and the bodily resurrection of Jesus, therefore, are central affirmations of the goodness of the physical creation. One definition of 'sacrament' is that it is 'an outward and visible sign of an inward and spiritual grace'.

In both Testaments, then, God employs the physical objects or actions as ways of expressing major truths about what God has done for his people, or how they should live out their faith, responding with grateful memory, practical obedience and tenacious faith and hope. In the Old Testament, Israelites circumcised infant boys – a ritual in the flesh that expressed membership of the covenant community and commitment to obedience. They celebrated the Passover, with the physical symbols of a meal and various ritual actions, to remind them annually of the great deliverance of their ancestors from Egypt at the exodus. In the New Testament, the two sacraments that give visible and tangible expression to Christian faith (baptism and the Lord's Supper) make use of the most basic and common 'stuff' that is part of everyday life – water, bread and wine – and consecrate them as signs (or pointers) of the great truths of the gospel. They are more than just 'symbols'. They 'send a message', giving visible expression to the underlying story that lies at the heart of the Christian faith.

BAPTISM

The essential element in baptism is water. Ritual washing has been a part of many religious traditions, and at the time of Jesus the Jews already used a form of baptism in water as part of the rituals involved in a Gentile converting to Jewish faith. John baptized people with water (hence acquiring the popular description in Christian tradition – John the Baptist), as a sign of their repentance and preparation for the coming of the Lord's Messiah. Jesus, by being baptized by John, was not confessing personal sin, but identifying himself with those within Israel who were preparing for the Lord's coming.

In his final commission to the apostles before his ascension, Jesus told them to 'make disciples of all nations, baptizing them in the name of the Father and of the Son and of the Holy Spirit' (Matthew 28:19). Literally the phrase is 'into the name of'. That is, baptism brings a person into intimate relationship with God as he is fully revealed in all three persons of the Trinity. The baptized person now fully belongs to the one in whose name he or she is baptized. So, no matter what additional forms, liturgies and rituals surround the occasion of baptism, the two essential elements of baptism are that it must include the use of water, and it must be done in the name of the Trinity. Water is essential for it to be the sacrament of baptism. The names of all three persons of the Trinity are essential for it to be Christian baptism. In the New Testament, baptism is sometimes 'in [or into] the name of Jesus Christ' (see Acts 2:38; Galatians 3:27). But such a formula still implies the whole Trinity, inasmuch as Jesus was the Son of the Father and the sender of the Spirit.

The mode of baptism and the amount of water involved, has caused much controversy and practices differ. Complete immersion (going under water) seems to fit New Testament language about burial and resurrection. However, effusion (pouring of water over a person) can equally speak of the outpouring of the Holy Spirit. And sprinkling with water matches Old Testament sacrificial rites involving blood, which are later fulfilled in the blood of Christ. As long as water is

'Anyone who is not burning will not be able to set anyone else on fire.'
Peter of Rheims

clearly used, any method can be valid. And in the vast multi-cultural spread of the church, baptism is carried on in many different ways – from ornate fonts and baptistries in church buildings, to simple ceremonies in rivers and lakes, swimming pools, and even the sea.

Christian baptism has several layers of significance.

Cleansing from sin.

The most obvious significance of a rite involving water is that it speaks of washing. Sin makes people dirty and defiled in the sight of God, so that they stand in need of cleansing. Baptism is a symbolic bath (Acts 22:16). However, Christians do not believe that water in itself washes away sin. Baptism is a sign. It directs our attention to what God does in washing away the believer's sins by his grace. 'He saved us, not because of righteous things we had done, but because of his mercy. He saved us through the washing of rebirth and renewal by the Holy Spirit' (Titus 3:5). Cleansing from sin was powerfully symbolized in what seems to have been the early practice of the church: the person to be baptized put off old and dirty clothes, before going down into the water of baptism; then, after the act of baptism, they were clothed in new clean clothes. This symbolism is almost certainly reflected in several places in the New Testament where 'putting off' and 'putting on' are used as metaphors for a Christian's old and new life respectively (Colossians 3:9–12; Ephesians 4:22–24).

Union with Christ in his death and resurrection.

If water by itself cannot wash away sin, what can? Christians see such power only in the cross, where Jesus died in our place, bearing our sins. Baptism, by identifying the believer with Jesus, unites them to that death on our behalf. Going through the water of baptism is a symbolic death, burial and resurrection, in union with Christ. 'Don't you know that all of us who were baptized into Christ Jesus were baptized into his death? We were therefore buried with him through baptism into death in order that, just as Christ was raised from the dead through the glory of the Father, we too may live a new life' (Romans 6:3–4; compare Colossians 2:12). Once again we note that the sacrament points primarily to what God's grace has done for us (the death of Jesus for our sin), but also points toward the appropriate response on our part, which is not only faith (which is what unites believers to Christ and accepts for ourselves what he has done for them), but also a new, transformed life (see below).

The gift of the Holy Spirit.

Just as the Holy Spirit came upon Jesus at his baptism to anoint him for his ministry as Messiah, so baptism in the name of Jesus is associated with the gift of the Spirit to believers elsewhere in the New Testament. John anticipated it (Matthew 3:11). Peter promised it on the day of Pentecost, along with forgiveness of sins, to those who would repent and be baptized (Acts 2:38). Anomalies in Samaria and Ephesus (Acts 8:14–17; 19:1–7) only prove the point: baptism into Christ included baptism in the Spirit (Acts 10:44–48). Indeed, Paul went on to say that, behind the rite of water baptism, it is actually the Spirit who baptizes believers into the body of Christ (1 Corinthians 12:13; cf. Titus 3:5–6).

Membership in the church.

The body of Christ is, as we have seen, a metaphor for the church. So baptism into the body speaks of coming into membership of the church. Baptism is thus the prime rite of initiation by which a person is accepted into Christ's church. Baptism is the new beginning of a new belonging. We have seen that the New Testament strongly affirms that the church stands in organic continuity with the people of God in the Old Testament – Israel descended from Abraham. So Paul, writing to the Gentile converts who were the fruit of his mission, assured them that their baptism into the Messiah (Christ) Jesus also made them part of that ancient people of God, the spiritual seed of Abraham (Galatians 3:26–29). In fact, baptism becomes the spiritual equivalent of circumcision (the Old Testament Jewish rite of initiation) for Christians and speaks in the same way of entering into the spiritual privileges and responsibilities of membership in God's covenant people (Colossians 3:11–12).

Commitment to mission.
If baptism means becoming part of the people of Abraham in Christ, then we recall that God called that people into existence with the mission that all nations would be blessed through them (Genesis 12:1–3). Furthermore, when Christ gave the apostles their commission to go and make disciples of the nations, he explained that it should include 'baptizing them' (Matthew 28:19). Thus, baptism is an integral part of the method of mission, by which the church in all nations grows and spreads. But at the same time, for the individual, baptism into the church means joining a community of mission, the mission of bringing blessing to the nations.

Is Christ Present in the Lord's Supper?

At the Last Supper, Jesus commanded his disciples to remember him through the bread and wine. It is clear that this was done from the earliest of times. The New Testament itself refers to the first Christians obeying Jesus Christ's command to remember him in this way (1 Corinthians 11: 20—27). This act of celebration and remembrance is referred to in different ways by Christian churches, including the Mass, the Holy Communion, the Lord's Supper, and the Eucharist (derived from the Greek word for 'thanksgiving').

An important debate within Christianity concerns whether, and in what manner, Christ may be said to be present at the Lord's Supper. This is often linked with the words spoken by Christ at the last supper. Taking the bread, he told his disciples: 'this is my body' (Matthew 26:26). What does this mean? The majority opinion within global Christianity is that Christ's words can only mean that, in some sense, Christ's body is present in the bread of the Lord's Supper. The doctrine of 'transubstantiation', which was formalized in 1215, holds that the outward appearance of the bread remains unchanged, whereas its inward identity is transformed. In other words, the bread continues to look, taste, smell and feel as if it were bread; at its most fundamental level, however, it has been changed. By a similar argument, the wine is held to have become the blood of Christ. This position is often stated using the Aristotelian ideas of 'substance' (that which gives something its inward identity) and 'accidents' (mere external appearances). On this view, the substance of the bread and wine is changed, but their appearance remains unaltered.

Although this position is especially associated with the Roman Catholic Church, related viewpoints can be found in Eastern Orthodoxy. Martin Luther developed a slightly different idea, often known as 'consubstantiation', which holds that the bread remains bread, but is additionally the body of Christ. Luther illustrated this idea by demonstrating how a piece of iron, when placed in a hot fire, becomes red-

Commitment to ethical discipleship. In the same breath, Jesus added, 'teaching them to observe all that I have commanded you'. Baptism is thus the preliminary to teaching. And teaching is aimed at producing obedient disciples of Christ. As the church developed, teaching of new converts often came before they were baptized, as a way of ensuring that only those who fully understood, and could be tested on, their commitment to Christian discipleship were actually baptized. The danger in this is that baptism can seem like a prize or reward. The New Testament practice seems to have been the other way round. Converts were baptized as soon as possible, once they professed repentance and faith in Christ (e.g.

Acts 2:41; 8:12, 36–38; 9:18; 10:47–48; 16:14–15, 31–33). From that point on, Paul would assume that they now ought to live as baptized believers, and so he built much of his detailed ethical teaching on that foundation. Baptism is the beginning, not only of a new belonging, but also of a new behaving.

Paul wrote his most extensive explanation of baptism precisely in order to challenge believers to live out the implications in lives that are to be dead to sin and alive to God and his righteousness (Romans 6). God's grace, received in baptism, is not to be the excuse for continued sinning, but rather the opposite. Grace leads to the response of grateful holiness in a life offered to God. In even greater detail,

hot. Although remaining iron, it has heat added to it. In the same way, the bread of the Lord's Supper remains bread, but additionally contains or conveys the body of Christ.

Not all Christians take this position. Some, following John Calvin, argue that the bread is an 'efficacious sign'. In other words, although the bread is not the body of Christ, it represents this in such a way that what is signified is effectively conveyed. Others follow the Swiss reformer Huldreich Zwingli, who argued that the bread symbolized Christ's body. The bread and the wine of the Lord's Supper are there to help believers recall the events of Calvary, and to encourage them to recommit themselves to the church, to God, and to each other. Zwingli's approach is sometimes known as 'memorialism'. It holds that there is no objective change in either the bread or the wine. Any change that takes place is subjective, taking place in the mind of the beholder, who now 'sees' the bread as a sign of Christ's body, and a reminder of his sacrifice upon the cross.

Opinion is divided about what happens to the elements during the Lord's Supper.

Although the Lord's Supper is celebrated in different ways throughout the Christian church, the two elements of bread and wine are always present.

the ethical teaching of Colossians and Ephesians is based on the foundation of baptism (note how Colossians 2:12 heads the section that runs through to 4:6; and how Ephesians 4:5 stands in the preface to the rest of the practical teaching of the letter).

THE LORD'S SUPPER

Eating and drinking are among the most basic actions that human beings do. And having meals together is one of the most fundamental social actions in which we engage. Many religions and cultures use food, drink and communal meals in ritual and symbolic ways. In the Old Testament, some of the sacrifices were accompanied by meals shared among the worshippers (see 1 Samuel 1), and the major annual festivals were to be joyful times of eating and drinking together (Deuteronomy 16; compare Nehemiah 8:10–12).

The most important meal in Old Testament Israel was the annual

Passover, which celebrated how God had delivered Israel out of slavery in Egypt (Exodus 12). It was in the context of the Passover, just before his crucifixion, that Jesus and his disciples had what came to be known as their 'last supper' together. During or after that meal, Jesus used bread and wine as a way of portraying his coming death, of explaining its significance, and ensuring it would be remembered (Matthew 26:17–30; Mark 14:12–26; Luke 22:7–20). By doing this in the context of Passover, Jesus linked his own death to the central story of Old Testament Israel – the exodus. This is further evidence for the organic link between Old Testament Israel and the Christian church (see 1 Corinthians 5:7).

Like baptism, the Lord's Supper has come to be celebrated throughout the Christian church in many different ways and to be known by different common names, including the Holy Communion, the Eucharist, and the

Mass. Some Christian communities have developed elaborate liturgical rituals over many centuries, sometimes accompanied by beautiful music and ornate spectacle. Many others prefer to celebrate it as a very simple act of worship with minimal formality. But whether elaborate or simple, there are always two elements – bread and wine. And there are three aspects – looking back, looking forward and looking around.

Two elements: bread and wine.
The actions and words of Jesus at the Last Supper, upon which the ongoing sacrament of the Lord's Supper are based, focused on two basic elements in all Jewish meals at the time: the breaking of bread with thanksgiving to God, and the pouring out and sharing of wine. Paul's account in 1 Corinthians 11:23–26 reflects very early Christian tradition, probably even earlier than the written gospels. There are slight variations in the words in the different accounts, probably reflecting the fact that Jesus was not simply reciting a liturgy, but probably paused to explain what he was saying. Combining the different accounts we find the following:

Breaking the bread, Jesus said, 'This is my body, which is given for you.'

The words link the broken bread to the death of Jesus, in a way that shows it was voluntary (he gave himself in this way), and vicarious (it was 'for you').

Taking the cup of wine, Jesus said, 'This cup is the new covenant in my blood, which is shed for you and for many for the forgiveness of sins.'

These words link his shed blood to the sacrificial blood of the old covenant, showing that the death of Jesus was a sacrifice through which sins would be forgiven. This was an essential aspect of the new covenant as prophesied in Jeremiah 31:31–34.

There can be no doubt that Jesus meant, and his disciples understood, his words symbolically and not literally. The literal, physical body of Jesus was there in the room, serving them. The symbolism was clear: the body and blood of Jesus would be given in sacrificial death. The focus was on the cross, not on the elements themselves.

With both the bread and the wine, Jesus added, 'Do this [that is, break bread and share wine], in remembrance of me.' In the context of the Passover meal that Jesus and his disciples had shared, this meant more than simply 'a reminder'. When Jews celebrate Passover every year, it is done, 'as if we were there'. That is, it re-enacts the original redemptive action of God in such a way that every new generation of Israelites benefits from it, as if they had been present. Similarly, when Christians eat and drink the bread and wine, it is to remember the cross of Christ, 'as if they were there'. That is, they appropriate for themselves the blessings Christ refers to when he said 'given *for you*… shed *for you*'. It is a visible proclamation of the essential gospel – Christ died for all.

In conclusion Jesus added (according to Paul), that by doing these things, believers would 'proclaim the Lord's death *until he comes*', and (according to the gospels), that Jesus would one day feast again with his disciples in the *kingdom of God* (Matthew 26:29; Luke 22:16, 18). So the Lord's Supper is not just a memorial of the past, but an anticipation of the heavenly banquet, as life with God in the new creation is sometimes portrayed (Isaiah 25:6–9; Matthew 8:11).

Three aspects: backwards, forwards, and around.
From these actions and words, and the

What is Christian Ministry?

The basic idea underlying all Christian ministry is that of service. The two Greek terms used to refer to Christian leaders in the New Testament are *doulos* and *diakonos* – words that are best translated as 'slave' (or perhaps 'servant') and 'waiter'. Both avoid any suggestion that Christian leaders have a superior status to other believers. The New Testament makes it clear that ministry is a service which is commanded by Christ, and which is laid upon every Christian believer as a task.

The New Testament never uses the term 'priest' to refer to any kind of Christian ministry or to anyone who holds office in the church. It is important to note that Jesus does not draw his images of service from the priestly ministry of the Old Testament, but from the secular world around him. The New Testament uses the concept of 'priesthood' in two contexts only:

1. To refer to the unique and once-for-all ministry of Jesus Christ.

2. To refer to the royal and prophetic priesthood of all believers as the people of God. It is thus Christ and the people of God who can be described as 'priestly'; no one individual or group can be singled out in this way.

The theme of service is thus of central importance to the Christian understanding of leadership. We find this kind of ethos clearly set out in both the words and deeds of Jesus himself, especially towards the end of his ministry, as he began to prepare for his final period in Jerusalem (Matthew 20:25–27):

Jesus called them to him and said, 'You know that the rulers of the Gentiles lord it over them, and their great men exercise authority over them. It shall not be so among you; but whoever would be great among you must be your servant, and whoever would be first among you must be your slave; even as the Son of man came not to be served but to serve, and to give his life as a ransom for many.'

A *diakonos* is someone who waits at table, who renders service at a meal. Many Christian ecclesiastical traditions suggest that their ministers should wear stoles when ministering, as a reminder of the towels that would be carried by those who waited at table in ancient Rome. However, it is important to note that the New Testament also seems to suppose a distinction between a general ministry of service, in which every Christian tries to be of whatever use he or she can to others, and a more specific or public form of ministry.

Luther's doctrine of the 'priesthood of all believers' is of importance here. For Luther, every Christian was a priest as a result of his or her baptism. There was no fundamental difference in status between the ministers of the gospel, by whatever name they might choose to be known, and the ordinary believer. Hence, believers as a whole take part in the 'royal priesthood' (1 Peter 2:9) of the people of God. There is no 'priestly elite' set above ordinary believers, but a shared corporate ministry and service, in which every part of the body of Christ is called to serve each other.

further teaching of Paul, Christians may be said to look in three directions when they celebrate the Lord's Supper.

First, they look *back* to the death of Jesus. They do so certainly in order to remember it. But much more, they do so in order to renew their participation in the blessings it has achieved, especially the forgiveness of sin. As with baptism, the sacrament of the Lord's Supper speaks primarily of what God has done for Christians, in the self-giving sacrifice of the Son of God on our behalf. In sacramentally eating his flesh and drinking his blood, Christians not only feed on him spiritually and are united to him in his life-giving power (cf. John 6:53–58), they also gratefully receive the grace and forgiveness that his death has made possible. The expression 'drink the blood of' was a Hebrew idiom that could mean to benefit from someone's death (see 1 Chronicles 11:17–19). So, in metaphorically drinking the blood of Christ, Christians declare that they benefit from his death on their behalf – for that is the only grounds on which they can receive forgiveness and eternal life. Christians also look backwards in the sense that the death of Christ on the cross was a once and for all historical event that can never be repeated and never needs to be. So although the Lord's Supper is a symbolic re-enactment of his death, in broken bread and outpoured wine, it is not a repetition or a continuation of his sacrifice, or a sacrifice in its own right. The focus is entirely on what Jesus did for Christians, not on anything they do for themselves.

Secondly, they look *forward* to the return of Christ and the heavenly banquet. Though there is a solemn dimension to sharing in the Lord's Supper, as a recollection of Calvary, it is also an occasion of great joy and hope. This is captured in the triplet found in some Holy Communion liturgies: 'Christ has died. Christ is risen. Christ will come again.' So this simple meal is a symbolic anticipation of the joy that will accompany his return and the establishing of his kingdom (see Revelation 19:9).

Thirdly, they look *around*, for the Lord's Supper is a shared action in which Christians declare their communion, not only with the Lord (vertically), but also with one another (horizontally). So it becomes a primary focal point of Christian love and unity. We saw that Paul's major teaching on baptism was given in order to show Christians the ethical response that it required. Similarly, his account of the Lord's Supper in 1 Corinthians 11 is given in the context of warning the church at Corinth about the evil of factions in the church – especially those caused by social divisions. It seems that a wealthier elite within the church were conducting the Lord's Supper like a grand social occasion in which they could flaunt their rich food and drink, while poorer believers were being humiliated. Paul condemns such behaviour as incompatible with the Lord's table. In the previous chapter he warned the Corinthians against participating in idolatrous practices, since they also are incompatible with participating in the body and blood of Christ, illustrating his point from the sins and rebellions of Israel in the Old Testament. Clearly, the sacrament must be taken seriously, for what it affirms and what it excludes. So Paul makes it the occasion for careful personal moral self-examination (1 Corinthians 11:27–32).

THE SACRAMENTS AND CHRISTIAN LIVING

We have seen that both baptism and the Lord's Supper are connected in the New Testament with living lives that make appropriate ethical responses to what the sacraments proclaim. In fact, since the two sacraments point to the whole gospel of God's grace and the means of

> 'The church must be prophetic – or it will be pathetic.'
>
> Cecil Murray

salvation, they also provide the shape of Christian ethics. Several key elements of New Testament ethical teaching can be linked to the message of the sacraments.

Grace comes before ethics.

The sacraments both point to what God has done for Christians, not what we can do for God. For this reason humility is a key characteristic of Christian behaviour. The biblical ethic is not a means of impressing God or earning his favour or salvation. Rather it is a practical response of humble and grateful obedience to God's saving grace.

Grace is received by faith.

Both sacraments call Christians to put their trust in God and what he has done for us through Christ. Practical Christian living is therefore also living by faith. Christian behaviour is not governed primarily by instincts, or prudence, or what just seems to work best, but by a trusting obedience to God and his word.

Christians respond to God by imitation.

They are called to love as he loved; to forgive one another as he forgave; to give themselves for one another as Christ gave himself; to refuse violence

Women in Ministry

There are excellent reasons for supposing that women were deeply involved in various kinds of ministry within the church during the first two centuries. The New Testament itself gives a remarkably high profile to the pastoral and evangelistic ministry of women. However, with the conversion of the Roman emperor Constantine, it seems that things began to change. Classical Roman models, which militated against women being involved in public life, whatever positions of importance they may have held in private, began to exercise influence within the church, which appears to have been concerned to gain increasing cultural acceptability at this critical moment in its history. It appears to have given in to cultural pressures which were opposed to women having positions of public responsibility and authority. The post-Constantinian ethos appears to have become accepted as normal thereafter, and continues to have a major impact today.

In the Middle Ages, women had a distinct and significant role in Christian life and thought. The rise of the monastic movement as a reaction against the worldliness of the church inevitably led to the rise of the convent, as well as of the monastery. Religious houses were established for the exclusive use of women. Within these convents, women had positions of authority and pastoral care. The convents of Europe served as environments in which women could discover and affirm their distinctiveness, without feeling that they were oppressed or overshadowed by men. The contribution of women to the spiritual life of the church was considerable. For example, in sixteenth-century Spain, Teresa of Avila was instrumental in a major programme of reform and spiritual renewal within the church.

More importantly, the convent provided an environment in which women could undertake positions of spiritual responsibility and leadership. Women ministered to women, pastorally and spiritually. The convent provided an environment in which women were able to discover and put into practice their gifts for ministry and leadership – gifts which really existed, but which could not be exercised in either the church or medieval society, because of the strongly patriarchal social conditions of the time.

and revenge, as Christ did. The things they celebrate in the sacraments should be the things that shape their daily lives.

Living as a Christian is a radical contrast from the old life of the world. Baptism points to a radical break – dying to the old and putting on the new. Practical life should show the difference. This is the full meaning of repentance – turning away from sin and evil in radical renunciation, and turning towards Christ and all that he calls his followers to. The words found in some baptismal liturgies express this: 'I renounce evil; I repent of my sin; I turn to Christ.'

The Christian life is one of discipleship
Baptism commits us to learning and obeying the teaching of Jesus. So the practical teaching of the gospels forms an essential part of Christian ethics. At the heart of that teaching lie what Jesus called the two greatest commandments – both drawn from the Old Testament – to love the Lord our God and to love our neighbour as ourselves.

Christian ethics are community ethics, not merely a personal moral code.
Of course individual choices matter, but the Lord's Supper points to the centrality of fellowship and

The rise of the Reformation led to the pastoral and leadership roles which had been exercised inside the convents being transferred to domestic situations, with women assuming major responsibilities for both the organization and the pastoral care of the extended households of that period. The household was a major social institution at the time, and being placed in charge of it was equivalent to being given managerial, pastoral and leadership roles.

The church today continues to engage with the role of women in ministry, attempting to balance the gospel declaration that there is in Christ no male or female (Galatians 3:28) with local traditions and expectations. Christian churches draw different conclusions as to the admission of women to the ordained ministry. An increasing number of churches have decided that there is no biblical or theological reason against ordaining women, and many of them have subsequently proceeded to do so. Yet many churches hold that the tradition of the church in this regard must not be changed, and they limit the ministerial roles of women accordingly.

An increasing number of churches are deciding there are no biblical or theological barriers against women's equality within the hierarchy of the church.

communion. Those who share the same table with the Lord must also share love, compassion, unity, mutual support, truthfulness and forbearance, with each other.

Christian ethics are also future orientated.
Christians are to behave now in the light of what is to come, 'as children of the light'.

Should Christians Fight in Wars?

There is little doubt that the early church was pacifist, and saw this as being the natural interpretation of the teaching of Jesus. Had not Jesus taught that retaliation was inappropriate? If anyone slapped us on the right cheek, we were to turn the other one, so that it might also be slapped (Matthew 5:39). The Roman theologian Tertullian, writing in the second century, held that serving in the army was incompatible with the Christian faith. Similar attitudes can be found in later Christian

Christian faith often offers great support to those engaged in battle, but the issue of whether war is in conflict with Christian doctrine remains one that is widely debated.

history. The radical Reformers of the sixteenth century – often known as the 'Anabaptists' – held that Christ forbade his followers to bear arms, serve in armies, fight in wars, or use any form of force or violence in society as a whole. The ethos of non-violent resistance, which became particularly significant in the twentieth century, can be traced back to the New Testament.

However, the New Testament context needs to be noted here. Christians are assumed to be on the margins of society. They are not people of power. During the first three centuries, this remained the case. Christians were treated with contempt or bemusement by the Roman authorities, and occasionally subjected to persecution. However, the situation changed radically under Constantine, the first Christian

Christian ethics are shaped by mission. The church that is to be a blessing to the nations must also live differently from the standards of the nations. The call to holiness is a call to distinctiveness. Mission includes making disciples of all nations, by baptizing and teaching. So well-taught obedient discipleship is both the product of mission, and the means of mission.

emperor of Rome. Christianity now found itself in power, having to confront issues that had not even been issues in previous generations. Christians increasingly developed positive attitudes and working relationships with the Roman state, leading to involvement in state-sanctioned executions and wars. If the state was now Christian, should Christians fight its wars?

This approach indirectly led to the crusades of the Middle Ages, in which violence against Jews and Muslims was sanctioned on the basis of a 'just war' ethic. This argued that it was legitimate to fight wars in pursuit of just causes – such as

the establishment of peace, or the protection of religious sites or peoples. The 'just war' tradition has remained important in Christian ethical thought ever since, and remains influential in North America. In general, the closer the involvement of the church with the state, the more likely Christians are to defend wars, and to become involved with them. The idea has also become secularized – as, for example, in the case of the First World War, often portrayed as 'making the world safe for democracy' or 'the war to end all wars.' The debate over precisely what constitutes 'last resort', 'just war' and 'just intention' continues within the churches today.

Yet pacificism has also played a significant role in Christian thinking, especially in response to what are seen as the excesses of war. Many Christians believe that the use of violence is a sin against God, in that it violates and damages the height of creation – humanity. The Second Vatican Council (1962–65) ruled that pacifism was a legitimate position for Christians in the face of war. Many Christian denominations have followed suit. Martin Luther King's campaign of non-violence in support of civil rights issues is widely seen as one of the most successful and important examples of such an approach.

'The church's foundation is unshakeable and firm against the assaults of the raging sea. Although the elements of the world crash against it and batter it, the church offers the safest harbour of salvation for all in distress.'

Ambrose of Milan

Service in the Church

'I am among you as one who serves,' said Jesus (Luke 22:27). The servanthood of Jesus is the model for life within the Christian church. Jesus said this in the context of a dispute about leadership: the disciples were arguing over which of them was the greatest. Jesus turned their perceptions upside down and defined leadership within the church in terms of servanthood.

A common term for Christian activity is 'ministry'. It comes from the Latin word for servant. In the New Testament, the equivalent words are *diakonos*, *diakonia*, meaning servant, service. They are words of very broad

What Were the Origins of Monasteries?

Monasteries have long played an important role in Christian mission. The origins of the monastic movement are generally thought to lie in remote hilly areas of Egypt and parts of eastern Syria. During the third century significant numbers of Christians began to make their homes in these regions, in order to get away from major population centres, with their many distractions. For, example, Anthony of Egypt, left his parents' home in 273 to seek out a life of discipline and solitude in the desert. Only by getting away from the corruption of the city could people devote themselves to developing their spiritual lives.

The theme of withdrawal from a sinful and distracting world became of central importance to these monastic communities. While some lone figures insisted on the need for individual isolation, the concept of a communal life in isolation from the world gained the upper hand. One important early monastery was founded by Pachomius during the years 320–25. This monastery developed an ethos which would become normal practice in later monasticism. Members of the community agreed to submit themselves to a common life which was regulated by a Rule, under the direction of a superior. The physical structure of the monastery was significant: the complex was surrounded by a wall, highlighting the idea of separation and withdrawal from the world. The members of such monastic communities shared a corporate life, characterized by common clothing, meals, furnishing of cells (as the monks' rooms were known) and manual labour for the good of the community.

The monastic ideal had a deep attraction for many people. By the fourth century, monasteries had been established in many locations in the Christian East, especially in the regions of Syria and Asia Minor (modern Turkey). It was not long before the movement was taken up in the western church. By the fifth century, monastic communities had come into existence in Italy (especially along the western coastline), Spain and Gaul. Augustine of Hippo, one of the leading figures of the western church at this time, established two monasteries in North Africa at some point during the period 400–25. For Augustine, the common life was essential to the realization of the Christian ideal of love. He supplemented this emphasis on community life with an appreciation of the importance of intellectual activity and spiritual study.

During the sixth century, the number of monasteries in the region grew considerably. It was during this period that one of the most comprehensive monastic Rules – the 'Rule of Benedict' – came into being. Benedict of Nursia (died about 550)

application, not confined to what we would now call 'ordained' or 'pastoral ministry'. The theme of service in the church can be considered from two angles. On the one hand, all believers have a share in the gifts of the Holy Spirit which equip them for a wide variety of ministries. On the other hand, some persons in the church are entrusted with specific tasks and responsibilities for which certain titles are used.

GIFTS AND MINISTRIES

We saw above that one of Paul's favourite pictures of the church is the body, and the major point he makes from this metaphor is that every part

established his monastery at Monte Cassino at some point around 525. The Benedictine community followed a Rule which was dominated by the notion of the unconditional following of Christ, sustained by regular corporate and private prayer, and the reading of Scripture. The later great monasteries of Europe maintained many features of the earlier monastic movement. They acted as centres of mission, learning and devotion during this period, and were associated with the great revival of both church and society in western Europe during the Middle Ages, and continue to play these roles in today's world.

Communities such as the Dionysiou Monastery on Mount Athos enable individuals to focus on their spiritual lives away from worldly distractions.

of the body has its own unique and indispensable function. In the same way, every member of the church is called to serve the whole in different ways, according to the calling and gifting of the Holy Spirit. In the preface to his extended treatment of this theme he says, 'There are different kinds of gifts, but the same Spirit. There are different kinds of service, but the same Lord' (1 Corinthians 12:5). In several places Paul gives lists of the kinds of gifts that the Spirit gives to Christians (Romans 12:6–8; 1 Corinthians 12:7–11; Ephesians 4:7–13). In all of these, there is a strong emphasis that the purpose of these gifts is for the common good of the whole church, so that its members can serve one another and the Lord by exercising them. They are given 'to prepare God's people for works of service, so that the body of Christ may be built up' (Ephesians 4:12). Peter makes the same point, 'Each one should use whatever gift he has received to serve others, faithfully administering God's grace in its various forms' (1 Peter 4:10).

Three basic points are to be emphasized about spiritual gifts, then. They are gifts of God's grace, through his Spirit, in which he takes the initiative in distributing them. They are given to all believers throughout the church, not to a special elite. They are given for the benefit of all, by enabling church members to serve one another in many different ways.

Billy Graham and Christian Mission

One of the most remarkable features of the mission of the church in the twentieth century has been the rise of individual evangelistic ministries. Although many such individuals deserve to be noted, by far the most famous is Billy Graham. Graham was born in North Carolina in 1918, and was converted in 1934 through the preaching of revivalist Mordecai Fowler Ham. He attended Wheaton College, near Chicago, from

Billy Graham's evangelistic ministry was one with global impact.

1940 to 1943, and served for some years as a Baptist pastor in another Chicago suburb, Western Springs. Graham began to lead evangelistic rallies across the United States. These did not attract national attention until the Los Angeles crusade of 1949, when several national newspapers began to lionize him.

Although Graham was initially associated with the fundamentalist wing of American Protestantism, he gradually found himself alienated by its rigidity in relation to his burgeoning evangelistic ministry. For Graham, fundamentalism had become a barrier to the preaching of the gospel. Where an older generation saw defending the gospel from secular culture as being of supreme importance, Graham saw its proclamation to that culture as being critical. Graham went on to lead major evangelistic rallies in most major American cities during the 1950s and 1960s, as well as extending his ministry to England, Australia, and South America.

Billy Graham developed a distinctive style of evangelistic rally for which he will

OFFICES

We have seen the many ways in which the Bible speaks of the church as a spiritual reality in relation to God. But the church is also a human institution. And like all large human institutions, it necessarily requires organization, order, structure and leadership. Even in its earliest years in the New Testament, this became apparent quite quickly. Over the centuries that followed, organizational patterns within the Christian church around the world have developed with great variety. A confusing number of different terms and titles are used for those who hold office within the church at many levels (terms such as elder, deacon, priest, bishop, minister, pastor, vicar, canon, cardinal, and so on). And different denominations have different convictions about how they believe the church should best be structured and governed. In fact, some of the historic denominations arose precisely out of disputes about forms of leadership and authority within the church. Our purpose here, however, is not to survey all the variety of historical leadership patterns in the church, but to summarize essential Christian belief on the subject. And for that, as for all core beliefs, it is necessary to turn to the Bible.

Recognized roles.
Although Old Testament Israel eventually had a king to govern the whole nation, at local level power was diffused among elders in each community. These were the heads of families, who had a major role in

always be remembered. A typical format consisted of singing by a volunteer choir, followed by a testimony by some well-known person local to the area in which the rally was being held. An offering would be taken in support of the Billy Graham Evangelistic Association, and some solo items sung, often by Graham's long-term associate, George Beverly Shea. This led into the climax of the evening: the sermon, followed by an 'altar call', in which individuals were invited to come forward, either to renew their commitment or begin the life of faith.

As the rallies became more sophisticated, increased attention was paid to following up those who came forward, ensuring that they were put in touch with local churches and offered helpful literature. Graham's organization also realized the importance of the media, and made effective use of journalism, radio and television to disseminate Graham's message, and support his followers. Graham represents a style of mission which managed to capture the public imagination and make effective use of technology, while at the same time offering an intensely personal style of preaching, firmly grounded in the New Testament.

Graham's worldwide evangelistic ministry brought him into contact with more people than any evangelist in the past. It is estimated that the Global World Mission television broadcast of April 1996 was seen by 2.5 billion people. The worldwide appeal of Graham's message can be seen both as an endorsement of the universal relevance of the Christian gospel, as well as a sign of the convergence of global cultures in the late twentieth century, often referred to as 'globalization'.

judicial matters (settling disputes), in teaching their families the law of God; and in making significant community decisions. This Israelite system of plural elders in each local community (usually a village or town), provided a model for the early Christian believers. As assemblies of believers began to multiply, people were appointed for different tasks, and given popular recognition for the office with which they were entrusted. There seem to have been two main forms of officially recognized responsibility in the New Testament churches.

Firstly, there were *elders*. From the earliest days of his missionary travels, Paul appointed elders in the churches he planted (Acts 14:23). It seems they were always plural – that is a group of elders in every church. Their appointment included laying on of hands, and acceptance by the local congregation. The word *presbyteroi*, suggests they were senior people, and later instructions required that they should be mature and respected. Another term for the same group was *episkopoi*, which means, overseers. This is the word from which we get 'episcopal' and 'bishop'. However, although some major church traditions have distinguished bishops and presbyters as two distinct levels of leadership, it is clear that the two words are used interchangeably in the New Testament (see Acts 20:17, 28; Titus 1:5–7). The first describes the quality of person (senior), the latter describes the nature of their task (to watch over the people in their church).

Secondly there were *deacons (diakonoi)*. The word means simply 'servants', and as was seen above, applies in a general sense to all forms of Christian service. However, as early as Acts 6 some people can be seen to be chosen and entrusted with specific practical functions within the growing

> 'Where we see the Word of God purely preached and heard, there a church of God exists, even if it swarms with errors.'
>
> John Calvin

churches – in that particular case, to organize daily food distribution for the needy. It is worth noting that, although the apostles set this group up in order to be able to give themselves fully to the 'ministry' of the Word (their particular primary calling), they also describe this practical responsibility as 'ministry', and require that those appointed must be filled with the Holy Spirit. The people chose them and the apostles laid hands on them – a combination of appointment 'from below and from above'.

Responsibilities.
The responsibilities of elders in the New Testament churches were two-fold: leadership and teaching (1 Timothy 5:17). Leadership was to be exercised, however, in the manner of Christ himself, with the pastoral care and gentleness of a shepherd with his sheep, and with unselfishness, accountability and exemplary behaviour (1 Peter 5:1–5; Hebrews 13:17). Teaching is the major practical duty of elders. Those appointed to the role of elder are to be 'apt to teach' (1 Timothy 3:2). That is why they need to be mature people, with a good grasp of sound biblical teaching themselves (Titus 1:9). In Ephesians 4:11, although the word 'elder' is not used, it would most naturally be the elders who would exercise the dual role that Paul refers to as 'pastors and teachers'.

The responsibilities of deacons seem to have been whatever else needed to be done in the church of a practical nature – perhaps especially anything connected with finance and administration, since they had to be trustworthy and not greedy. If Acts 6 sets a precedent, then deacons were probably involved in the church's compassionate care of the poor and needy (for example, 1 Timothy 5:3–10).

Qualifications.

Paul twice gave teaching on the kind of people who should be appointed as elders and deacons (1Timothy 3:1–13; Titus 1:5–9; cf. Acts 20:28–35; 1 Peter 5:1–5). By far the most emphasized in his list of requirements are those that describe moral and spiritual qualities of Christian character, rather than academic or technical skills. Those who are appointed to lead the people of Christ must themselves be Christlike in their personal, social and family lives.

Two levels, or three?

Some Christian traditions believe they should adhere only to the twofold pattern of leadership described above: elders (or overseers), and deacons. Others (for example, Anglicans and Roman Catholics) have developed a threefold pattern: bishop, presbyter/priest and deacon. As we have seen, the New Testament does not distinguish episkopoi (bishops) from presbyteroi (elders), but regards them as different ways of describing the same group of people in church leadership. However, there is New Testament precedent for some people having a wider, regional level of leadership. Timothy and Titus, who had both been colleagues of Paul in his church-planting ministry, were entrusted by Paul with the responsibility of appointing elders in the churches – in Timothy's case in the large metropolis of Ephesus, where there would have been several assemblies, many believers, and groups of elders; and in Titus's case, on the whole island of Crete. So although these men are never called 'bishop' in a technical sense, they did exercise a regional oversight among a geographical group of churches, which was how the office of bishop later developed. And it is clear from what Paul writes to Timothy and Titus that the major responsibility of those who exercise this wider level of oversight is, on the one hand, to preserve the sound biblical teaching of the apostles by proclaiming it in evangelism and by defending it against attack and false teaching, and on the other hand, to ensure (through teaching and personal example) that those who claim membership in the churches under their care actually live out the demands of that commitment in transformed lives that are a witness to the world.

Clergy or laity?

This distinction is quite foreign to the New Testament church. Clergy comes from a word that means an elite officer class, whereas laity comes from the word that simply means 'the people'. It is a regrettable distinction that owes more to worldly patterns of authority and leadership than to anything Christ taught. In fact he taught the opposite (Luke 22:25–27). All believers (including elders, pastors, etc) belong to the laos, the people of God. All Christians (not just elders and pastors) have a ministry in which they exercise gifts of the Spirit for the good of others. Some Christians are called and appointed to particular functions within the church – especially to the task of teaching the Scriptures and sound doctrine. But none is superior or 'closer to God' than any other. The whole body of Christ is intended to grow to maturity together. The task of those entrusted with leadership is to facilitate this common growth in all its dimensions.

One of the most regrettable misunderstandings that many ordinary Christians have, because of a socially and culturally ingrained distinction between clergy and laity, is that they come to church on Sunday in order to support the pastor in his ministry. In fact precisely the reverse is more in line with the New Testament. Pastors come

> 'The nearer the Church, the further from God.'
>
> Launcelot Andrewes

> 'The church has nothing to do but save souls; therefore spend and be spent in this work. It is not your business to speak so many times, but to save souls as you can; to bring as many sinners as you possibly can to repentance.'
>
> John Wesley

> 'The church exists by mission, as fire exists by burning.'
>
> Emil Brunner

to church on Sunday in order to support the believers in their ministry, though their teaching, leadership and example.

Serving the World: the Church's Mission

We have seen that the church as the people of God has its biblical origin with the call of Abraham, which was because he wanted to bless all nations (Genesis 12:1–3). So the church's very existence flows from the universal purpose of God. In trying to describe the mission of the church, it is actually important not to begin with the church, but with God. If we begin with the church itself, it is easy to get absorbed in all its institutional and internal dimensions. Mission, or missions, then become listed among the many things that Christians are supposed to do, and often somewhere towards the end of the list as well. Furthermore, it becomes harder to define, because 'mission' itself is not particularly a biblical word. It comes from the Latin word for 'sending', and so is often linked to the fact that Jesus sent his disciples, as he put it, into the world, just as the Father sent him into the world. But this tends to link the word mission in people's minds with the image of the 'missionary' – one who is sent across geographical boundaries to other nations and cultures to preach the gospel. Certainly, the New Testament shows that there were such people in the early church, but by no means all Christians were expected to undertake being 'missionaries' in that specific sense. Mission is not just about missionaries, though missionaries have always been, and still are, an essential part of the church's mission.

However, if we start with God, we perceive a prior sense of the word 'mission' – namely as a purpose, or goal to be achieved. And the whole Bible shows God with a mission in that sense. God's ultimate goal is the redemption of his whole creation from the ravaging effects of sin and evil. God's mission is to restore creation and all nations of humanity to the blessing that is such a dominant note in the creation narrative. And for that mission, God called into existence this people – the seed of Abraham. Mission, then, is not just 'one of the things the church does', it is the reason the church exists. It is not so much the case that God has a mission for the church in the world, as that God has a church for his mission in the world. Our mission flows from God's mission. Christian mission means the committed and obedient participation of the church in the mission of God to bring about the blessing of the nations and redemption of creation.

When we see mission in these broad terms, it opens our thinking to all that God's love and grace seeks for human life, in our present world and ultimately within the new creation. The whole Bible bears on the shape of the church's mission, because it reveals the whole mission of God. As has been seen, the church as the community of God's people stands in continuity with Old Testament Israel, called into existence through Abraham to be a light to the nations, shaped and taught through the law and the prophets to be a community of holiness, compassion and justice. From the New Testament we see that the church, redeemed through the cross and resurrection of Jesus Christ, exists to worship and glorify God for all eternity, and to participate in the mission of God within history. Christians have been provided with the model for mission by Christ's incarnation and self-giving life, and the essential message of mission, which is the cross of Christ and all that it has accomplished for humanity and creation. Furthermore, the church has been commissioned by Christ and empowered by the Holy Spirit to bear witness to Jesus as Lord and Saviour, to confront evil in his name, to be an agent of blessing and healing, and the bearer of the good news of salvation to the nations and the whole creation.

This holistic mission involves every aspect of life. The church itself must live as the community of reconciled sinners in sacrificial Christian love and humility. On the basis of that life, it must proclaim the message on which it is based, making known to all nations the gospel of God's grace through forgiveness in Christ, calling people to repentance, faith, and discipleship. But as well as this evangelistic verbal witness, Christians are also called, like the first disciples, to demonstrate the values and the power of the kingdom of God, facing the reality of suffering and proving Christ's triumph over evil. And as we do so, we can never forget that Jesus endorsed the Old Testament's teaching of practical social love and justice, for it is also part of our mission to love our neighbours as ourselves through compassionate service of the needy, the pursuit of social justice and peace, and the care of God's creation.

When we understand Christian mission from the angle of God's own mission, springing from his heart of love for his whole world, his hatred of all forms of evil, oppression and sin, and his compassion for every form of human brokenness, suffering and need, then we will avoid dividing what God has joined together. There is no need to separate spiritual and physical, evangelistic and social, for God's mission clearly includes all of these. Of course, every individual Christian cannot do every kind of mission. But that is exactly why God has called a whole people into existence. God's mission requires all God's people and all God's gifting and calling, distributed among his people for every kind of service, in the church and in the world.

6 The Christian Hope

ALISTER MCGRATH

The New Testament is shot through with the theme of hope – not a vague, feeble aspiration that things will improve, but a sure, firm and confident expectation of being with the risen Christ in heaven. The resurrection of Christ makes possible a new beginning, overturning the cycle of sin and death which has enmeshed and ensnared humanity since the fall. We have been given a 'new birth into a living hope through the resurrection of Jesus Christ from the dead' (1 Peter 1:3). The resurrection of Jesus Christ from the dead does more than establish the identity of Jesus as the Son of God; it creates a new and life-changing hope for those who put their trust in him.

The Birth of a New Hope

Something new has taken place in the life, death and resurrection of Jesus. This belief saturates the New Testament. A new age has dawned, and with it, a new hope. This theme can be seen both in the preaching of Jesus in the gospels, and the proclamation of Christ in the remainder of the New Testament.

The dominant theme in the preaching of Jesus is the coming of the 'kingdom of God'. This phrase is rare in contemporary Jewish writings, and is widely regarded as one of the most distinctive aspects of the preaching of Jesus. This term, or closely related ideas, occurs about seventy times in the gospels. The use of the word 'kingdom' in this context is potentially misleading. Although this English word has been used regularly since the sixteenth century to translate the Greek term *basileia*, the term 'kingship' is more appropriate. The term 'kingdom' suggests a definite geographical region which is being ruled, whereas the Greek term refers primarily to the act of ruling itself. The term 'the kingly rule of God' has often been used to make this point clear.

Although many nineteenth-century liberal writers interpreted the kingdom of God in terms of the development of the moral values of society, it is clear that, as used by Jesus, the term has both present and future associations. The kingdom is something which is 'drawing near' (Mark 1:15), yet which still belongs in its fullness to the future. The Lord's Prayer, which remains of central importance to individual and corporate Christian prayer and worship, refers to the future coming of the kingdom (Matthew 6:10). Jesus speaks of this in terms of the resurrection of the dead (Mark 12:26), including the rewarding of the righteous, and the punishment of the wicked.

At the Last Supper, Jesus spoke to his disciples of a future occasion when they would drink wine in the kingdom of God (Mark 14:25). New Testament scholars generally agree that there is a tension between the 'now' and the 'not yet' in relation to the kingdom of God, similar to that envisaged by the parable of the growing mustard seed (Mark 4:30–32). Something has begun which will reach its culmination in the future. The kingdom of God is thus not something that is postponed to the future. It is something that is experienced in part now, preparing the way for its complete realization in the future.

In the preaching of Jesus, there is a clear link between the coming of the kingdom of God and the resurrection of the dead. In his controversy with the Sadducees (Matthew 22:23–33; Mark 12:18–27; Luke 20:27–38), Jesus draws a clear distinction between the 'people of this age' and 'those who are considered worthy of taking part in that age and in the resurrection from the dead' (Luke 20:34–35). Jesus' teaching about future rewards and judgments is also closely linked with the theme of resurrection. Some will rise from the dead to be rewarded, and others to be judged.

These themes are developed further in the letters of Paul. Four general principles can be identified as underlying his understanding of the new situation brought about by the coming of Christ.

1. The presence of a 'new age.' At several points, Paul emphasizes that the coming of Christ inaugurates a new era or 'age' (Greek: *aionos*). The old era has passed away, and the new has been born. Paul characterizes the 'old age' as 'evil' (Galatians 1:4; Ephesians 5:16), and refers to those who inhabit it as a 'crooked and perverse generation' (Philippians 2:15). It is clear that Paul intends this to be understood to refer to those who live according to the standards of this passing age, rather than adopting the beliefs and values of the new age inaugurated by Christ. The question is whether people align themselves with the present age, or with the new age that has now begun.

Although this new age – which Paul designates a 'new creation' (2 Corinthians 5:17) – has yet to be fulfilled, its presence can already be experienced. For this reason, Paul can refer to the 'end of the ages' in Christ (1 Corinthians 10:11). In this letter, Paul opposes a teaching which holds that each and every aspect of the age to come has been fulfilled in the present. It seems that Paul's opponents at Corinth were teaching that the final age was now present, and all the benefits of eternity were to be had in the here and now. For Paul, there is an element of postponement: the ultimate transformation of the world is yet to come, but may be confidently awaited. The Christian believer is thus caught up in the tension between the 'now' and the 'not yet'.

2. The resurrection of Jesus is seen by Paul as affirming that this new age really has been inaugurated. Although this does not exhaust the meaning of Christ's resurrection (which has significant implications for our understanding of the identity of Christ), Paul clearly sees Christ's resurrection as an event which enables believers to live in the knowledge that death – a dominant feature of the present age – has been overcome. Yet the new age has not merely begun; it is something in which believers may share. Paul's use of the 'first fruits' imagery (1 Corinthians 15:20, 23) is intended to emphasize that Christ is both the guarantee of the resurrection of the believer, and the model of what this resurrection will be like. Christ rose from the dead as the 'first fruits' of the resurrection, inaugurating the great harvest that will follow. Christ is the first representative of the whole resurrection harvest that will take place when he returns. What happened to Christ will one day happen to believers, who share in both Christ's glory and resurrection.

3. Paul looks forward to the future coming of Jesus Christ in judgment at the end of time, confirming the new

> 'We must accept finite disappointment, but never lose infinite hope.'
>
> Martin Luther King

life of believers and their triumph over sin and death. A number of images are used to refer to this, including 'the day of the Lord.' At one point (1 Corinthians 16:22), Paul uses an Aramaic term, *maranatha* (literally, 'Come, our Lord!') as an expression of the Christian hope. The Greek term *parousia* (meaning 'appearing') is often used to refer to the future coming of Christ (see 1 Corinthians 15:23; 2 Thessalonians 2:1, 8–9). For Paul, there is an intimate connection between the final coming of Christ and the execution of the final judgment.

4. A major theme of Paul's thought is the importance of the coming of the Holy Spirit. Paul, building on a long-standing aspect of Jewish expectations, sees the gift of the Spirit as a confirmation that the new age has dawned in Christ. One of the most significant aspects of Paul's thought at this point is his interpretation of the gift of the Spirit to believers as an *arrabon* (2 Corinthians 1:22; 5:5). This unusual word has the basic sense of a 'guarantee' or 'pledge', affirming that the believer may rest assured of ultimate salvation on account of the present possession of the Spirit.

THE CHRISTIAN HOPE

> 'Has this world been so kind to you that you should leave with regret? There are better things ahead than any we leave behind.'
>
> C.S. Lewis

The Crisis of Hope in Modern Western Culture

One of the most striking features of western literature, film and art of the twentieth century is a recurring, profound sense of pessimism about the human condition. It is as if humanity is spiritually dislocated, cut off from its true destiny. We are condemned merely to exist, rather than to live life to its full. A work of art that is widely held to reflect this deepening unease is *The Scream* (1893), by the Norwegian artist Edvard Munch. His bleak and pessimistic outlook on life is reflected in many of his works of this period, including *The Sick Child* (1886), *Vampire* (1893–94) and *Ashes* (1894). *The Scream* is often interpreted as a heartfelt cry of utter despair at the meaninglessness of life and the hopelessness of the human situation. All that we can do is protest; we cannot change anything.

In part, this deepening sense of despair reflects the rise of mechanization, often seen as dehumanizing. Although this theme can be found in many writers of the Victorian era, it is perhaps best seen in Charlie Chaplin's film *Modern Times* (1936). The film vividly depicts human alienation in the face of a mechanized universe. It is especially noteworthy for its use of sound. The screeches, groans, and grinding noises of the factory machines are given prominence over human sounds. Furthermore, no natural human voices are heard throughout the film. We hear spoken voices only when they come from mechanical devices, such as the videophones used by the factory president, the phonograph salesman, and a radio in the prison warden's office. The moral is simple: technology leads to dehumanization. In one scene, Chaplin's 'Little Tramp' gets caught up in the factory machinery, with hilarious results. But the point being made is that humanity is trapped by the machines that it has created, and that this is far from being a laughing matter.

Twentieth-century literature also reflects a pessimistic sense of frustration, disconnection and pessimism about the future. Some of the most powerful expressions of anxiety date from periods of economic and political crisis, such as the 1920s (the time of the Great Depression) and the late 1930s (the rise of political totalitarianism). An excellent example of a novel to reflect absence of hope is *The Trial* (1925), by Franz Kafka, a member of the German-speaking Jewish community of early twentieth-century Prague. *The Trial* centres around the main protagonist, Joseph K. who awakes on the morning of his thirtieth birthday to find two strangers

Although salvation remains something which will be consummated in the future, the believer may have present assurance of this future event through the indwelling of the Spirit.

It will be clear from what has just been said that the interplay of 'now' and 'not yet' is of major importance to the Christian understanding of hope. So how does this relation between the 'now' and the 'not yet' work out in practice? To explore this a little further, we may briefly examine some of Paul's central teachings concerning the impact of the death and

resurrection of Christ on believers – justification and salvation. Justification refers to the past and the future (Romans 2:13; 8:33; Galatians 5:4–5). As used in the New Testament, the term embraces both the beginning of the Christian life and its final consummation. Something already has happened; yet something more *will* happen. Justification is a complex and all-embracing notion, which anticipates the verdict of the final judgment (Romans 8:30–4), declaring in advance the verdict of final deliverance. The believer's present justified Christian existence is thus an anticipation of and

Modern secularism has given rise to the belief that we are all just cogs in a machine with no hope of change or salvation.

in his room, come to inform him that he has been arrested. He does not know why; he does not know when he will be judged; he does not know the evidence against him; and has no idea what court he will be brought before. He enters a nightmare world that is all too real, where he finds himself confronted and overwhelmed by the truth of his life, which he had managed so far to avoid. In an abortive effort to maintain his sanity, he indulges in furtive and hasty sexual liaisons, before succumbing to self-doubt and fatalism. The novel vividly depicts the deep uncertainties of human nature – its constant self-doubt and appeal to outside opinion for reassurance. Hope, it seems, is futile. We are condemned to live in a world which we can neither understand nor master.

The Christian hope rests securely on God's reliability, as believers trust both what he has done and what he will do.

an advance participation in their deliverance from the wrath to come, and an assurance in the present of the final verdict of acquittal (Romans 5:9–10).

Similarly, the related idea of sanctification can also refer to a past event (1 Corinthians 6:11) or a future event (1 Thessalonians 5:23). Salvation is an exceptionally complex idea, embracing not simply a future event, but something which has happened in the past (Romans 8:24; 1 Corinthians 15:2) or which is taking place now (1 Corinthians 1:18). The Christian understanding of salvation thus presupposes that something *has* happened, that something *is now happening*, and that something further *will still happen* to believers. This complex idea is well expressed in the famous story of the Salvation Army captain, who was asked whether he was saved. After a pause, he replied as follows. 'I *have been saved* from the penalty of sin. I *am being saved* from the power of sin. And I *will be saved*

from the presence of sin.' It is a neat summary of the core elements of the Christian hope, and helps us understand how we can both understand and sustain that hope in the present.

The Christian hope is thus poised between past and future. The journey of faith is sustained by memory on the one hand, and anticipation on the other. We can see this clearly in the case of Israel wandering in the wilderness of Sinai, following the exodus from Egypt. On the one hand, the people looked back to their deliverance from Egypt, and remembered the faithfulness of the God who had called Israel into being. They looked ahead with an eager hope to the final entry into the land which flowed with milk and honey. As they struggled through the wilderness, these were anchors which secured faith in times of doubt.

In the case of Christians, we look back to the once-for-all deliverance from sin that Christ achieved through his cross and resurrection, and also look forward to finally being with the risen Christ in heaven, when suffering, pain, sin and death are things of the past. The old order will finally have been abolished. In the meantime, however, we must live out our lives on earth – but we can do so in hope, trusting in both what God has done, and what he will do.

Christians thus live 'between the times', experiencing an interplay of past and future. It is like the trapeze artist, who lets go of the security of one bar, and soars through the air, poised to catch the next support. Each of the trapeze bars offers security; yet for a moment, the artist is not supported by anything. She is suspended between her securities, caught in an act of faith. The Christian life on earth is like those mid-air moments – moments of uncertainty and risk, which are only finally resolved when we take hold of what lies ahead of us, and grasp it securely and irreversibly. The Christian hope rests securely on the total reliability of God, and his complete faithfulness to his promises.

It will thus be clear that the idea that a new age has dawned is integral to the gospel hope. But we need to explore how this is related to the resurrection of Christ in more detail.

The Resurrection of Christ

It is no exaggeration to say that the resurrection of Christ is woven into just about every book of the New Testament, whether verbally or conceptually. It is the central event which shaped the form of the Christian faith, and which determined the content of the Christian proclamation of the good news. Christ's resurrection can be seen as anticipated in his ministry. The raising of Jairus' daughter (Mark 5:21–24, 35–43), of the son of a widow of Nain (Luke 7:11–17) and of Lazarus (John 11:1–44) can each be seen as anticipating the raising of Christ by God himself.

To ensure that the raising of Christ is distinguished from these healings, they are often referred to as 'resuscitations' rather than as 'resurrections'. Each of those who was resuscitated would eventually die; in the case of Christ, he was raised to life, never to die again. The gospel writers see these miracles as confirmation of Christ's authority over death itself, and anticipation of Christ's own resurrection. The fact that death had no authority over Christ is demonstrated both by these three miracles, as well as by his own resurrection.

The idea of a resurrection in human history, at a specific moment, and at a specific place, is actually very strange. Far from fitting into popular Jewish expectations of the resurrection of the dead, what happened to Jesus actually contradicted it. The sheer novelty of the Christian position at the time has been obscured by two thousand years' experience of the Christian understanding of the resurrection. At the time, however, it was highly unorthodox and radical.

Most Jews at this time seem to have believed in the resurrection of the dead. Yet the prevailing general belief concerned the future resurrection of the dead, at the end of time itself. Nobody believed in a resurrection before the end of history. The Pharisees may be regarded as typical in this respect: they believed in a future resurrection, and held that men and women would be rewarded or punished after death, according to their actions. The Sadducees, however, insisted that there was no resurrection of any kind: No future existence awaited men and women after death. (Paul was able to exploit the differences between the Pharisees and Sadducees on this point: see Acts 26:6–8).

'Nothing is far, to God: and I have no need to be afraid that at the end of the world he will not know where the place is, when the time comes to raise me up.'

Monica, mother of Augustine of Hippo

The Christian claim of the resurrection of Christ in history – rather than at the end of history – thus does not fit any known Jewish pattern at all. The resurrection of Jesus is not declared to be a future event, but something which had already happened in their own world, in front of witnesses. What the Jews thought could only happen at the end of the world was recognized by some to have happened in human history, before the end of time, and to have been seen and witnessed by many. There was something quite distinct and unusual about the Christian claim that Jesus had been raised from the dead, which made it rather difficult to account for.

To put this question pointedly: Why should the first Christians have believed something which was so strange by the standards of their time, unless something had happened which forced

Did Jesus Really Rise From the Dead?

A physical resurrection would indeed be unique in human history. But this is what the New Testament writers (especially in using the word *anastasis*) are claiming for Jesus – a physical occurrence in the real world, not some fantasy or wishful thinking.

In fact, the resurrection of Jesus may be viewed as 'one of the best attested facts of ancient history'. Consider these three factors that make no sense if Jesus was not raised:

1. Early Christian statements about Jesus. The New Testament writers speak of Jesus, not as dead, but as alive: 'he cannot die again' (Romans 6:9); 'he always lives' (Hebrews 7:25). Moreover, they give him a range of titles – such as 'Lord', 'Son of God' and 'eternal High Priest' – which are totally inappropriate if applied to a recently crucified 'criminal'. Even the idea that Jesus is 'Messiah' ('Christ') would be nonsense, in that Jesus had evidently not fulfilled some aspects of the Messianic expectations of the time (for example, overthrowing the Romans). The apostles could never make this claim unless some irrefutable event forced them to see he was the true Messiah.

2. Early Christian behaviour. Jesus' followers were suddenly transformed – from cowards and doubters (like Peter and Thomas) into bold missionaries. Many would be martyred for their faith.

3. The appearances of the risen Jesus. Jesus is described as meeting his disciples after his death for forty days: 'he gave many convincing proofs that he was alive' (Acts 1:3). These appearances were varied in nature – quite unlike hallucinations – sometimes to individuals but also to groups (on one occasions to over 500 people: 1 Corinthians 15:6).

A historian must reckon with this information and offer a satisfactory explanation. The New Testament solution, even if theologically surprising, is historically the simplest.

The same is true when the historian looks more closely at the stories about the first Easter Day, for either the tomb was empty or it was not. If it was not (with Jesus' body still there), then the disciples were either mistaken (going to the wrong them to this conclusion – something unexpected and shattering, which called their existing ideas into question? The simplest answer is that they were confronted with the resurrection of Jesus, and had to rethink their entire conceptual world as a result. For Paul, the resurrection was a public event, open to challenge and verification by the five hundred or so who had witnessed it (1 Corinthians 15:3–8).

So what was the result of this reflection on the resurrection? One outcome was a realization of the unique status of Jesus himself. Paul opens his letter to the Christians at Rome by making a crucially important statement concerning Jesus Christ. Jesus 'was descended from David at the human level, and was designated as the Son of God… by his resurrection from the dead' (Romans 1:3–4). This brief statement picks out two reasons why Jesus is to be regarded as the Son

tomb?) or blatantly deceitful (claiming Jesus was physically raised, when clearly he was not). Either way, their claim could have been refuted instantaneously by anyone in Jerusalem.

Alternatively, if the tomb was indeed empty (and the earliest critics of the resurrection readily concede this point, see Matthew 28:13), then we have to assume either that someone stole the body (but who and why? And why was it not later produced?); or that Jesus himself left the tomb by himself. If so, there are only two further options. Either Jesus had not truly died, but only swooned (but on the Friday both friends and foes knew he was truly dead; and, anyway, would lying on a cold slab for two days really be likely to revive him?). Or else he was truly raised from death by an act of the Living God.

The lines of historical enquiry converge on this obstinate truth – that Jesus broke through death. The daily experience of Christians ever since only confirms this – as people encounter Jesus today as a knowable person: 'I am the Living One', he says, 'I was dead, and behold I am alive!' (Revelation 1:18).

Christ's resurrection confirmed his unique claims and that he had accomplished what he had promised.

of God. First, on the physical level, he was a descendant of David, the great king of Israel to whom God had promised a future successor as king. A similar point is made by Matthew, as he opens his Gospel (Matthew 1:1). Second, Jesus' resurrection established his identity as the Son of God. We see here an appeal to the resurrection as clinching the argument as to the true identity of Jesus.

But there is another meaning to the resurrection – that those who believe in him will one day share that same destiny. As Paul remarks, since believers have been adopted as children of God, they share the same inheritance rights as the natural child. Christians are thus 'heirs of God' and 'co-heirs with Christ' (Romans 8:17), in that they share in the same inheritance rights as him. This means that, just as Christ suffered and was glorified, so believers may expect to do the same. All that Christ has inherited from God will one day be theirs as well. For Paul, this insight is of considerable importance in understanding why believers undergo suffering. Christ suffered before he was glorified; believers must expect to do the same. Just as suffering for the sake of the gospel is real, so is the hope of future glory, as believers will share in all that Christ has won by his obedience. Their situation has been transformed.

Paul develops the centrality of the resurrection of Christ to the Christian faith in a number of ways. In the first place, if Christ was not raised from the dead, then faith is pointless (1 Corinthians 15:13–14). If there was no resurrection, then the crucifixion of Christ failed to achieve anything for humanity, and we remain in our sins. If Christianity is simply about this physical life, in which we die to never exist again, then it makes little difference what we do, how we live, or what we believe. If the hope that Christ offers applies only to this present life, then Christians are to be pitied more than anyone (1 Corinthians 15:19). If there is no future for Christians after death, then they might as well concentrate on having a good time while they can (1 Corinthians 15:32). Paul is adamant: the Christian faith has a transcendent goal and a transformative power – and both are grounded in and dependent upon the resurrection of Christ.

This dawn of hope is evident among the disciples themselves at the time of Christ's resurrection. It is impossible to read the gospel accounts of the transformation of the outlook of the disciples and fail to realize that something dramatic has taken place. It is clear from the gospel accounts of Jesus' betrayal that the disciples were devastated by his arrest and execution. The fact that Peter was moved to deny Jesus at this point is particularly significant (Mark 14:66–72). The gospels do not record the presence of any of the leading disciples at Calvary.

Mark notes the presence of three women in particular at the scene (Mark 15:40–41), but his attention appears to be mainly directed towards the reaction of the Roman centurion to Jesus' death (Mark 15:39). He also fails to note the presence of the disciples at Christ's burial (Mark 15:42–7), and appears to go to some lengths to emphasize that the only witnesses to Jesus' death and burial (Mary Magdalene and Mary the mother of James) were also those who first discovered the empty tomb (Mark 15:40, 47; 16:1–8). John's Gospel notes that the disciples met secretly indoors in the aftermath of the crucifixion, 'for fear of the Jews' (John 20:19).

It is obvious from the gospel accounts of the crucifixion of Jesus that the first disciples thought that this was the end of everything. The man for whom they had given up everything to

> 'I am ready to meet my Maker. Whether my Maker is prepared for the great ordeal of meeting me is another matter.'
>
> Winston Churchill

> 'Death – the last sleep? No – the final awakening.'
>
> Sir Walter Scott

follow was executed. We can feel a profound sense of sadness as we read those gospel accounts. The disciples slink away, demoralized and dispirited. They give every impression of being hopeless and helpless, like sheep without a shepherd. And then suddenly all this changes. This band of sad, demoralized cowards is transformed into a joyful group of potential martyrs, for whom death no longer holds any terror. Like Paul in Athens, they proclaimed Jesus and the resurrection as the essence of the Christian gospel. A new hope had been born.

We know that two sacraments or rites became normative within the church in a remarkably short period, both being witnessed to in the New Testament itself. These are baptism and the rite now known variously as the 'Lord's Supper', 'breaking of bread', 'Communion', or 'Eucharist'. Both reflect a strong belief in the resurrection. Paul states that baptism calls to mind the death and resurrection of Jesus (Romans 6:4–5). It is interesting that the early church baptized its converts on Easter Day, to bring home fully the significance of the resurrection to the sacrament.

Equally, a strong belief in the resurrection has always led to the Lord's Supper being seen as a celebration of the living presence of Christ in his church, rather than a veneration of a dead teacher. Baptism and the Lord's Supper alike are essentially celebrations of Christ's Easter victory, rather than solemn memorials of the debacle of Good Friday. The belief that the Jesus who was crucified is now alive and present within his church has exercised an enormous influence over Christian worship down the ages, going back to the earliest of times.

The New Testament affirms that the death and resurrection of Christ represent a decisive act of divine deliverance, by which humanity has been liberated from the tyranny of sin and death. Paul draws on images of conflict taken from the battlefield, the amphitheatre and the athletic stadium to bring out the full significance of this theme of victory. 'Thanks be to God who gives us the victory through our Lord Jesus Christ' (1 Corinthians 15:57). For the writers of the New Testament, the forces of evil are as real as the forces of good. Despite the fact that they have little to say to explain its origins, they never attempt to explain it away. For Paul, God 'disarmed the principalities and powers, and made a public example of them, triumphing over them in him [Christ]' (Colossians 2:15). A new age has dawned – an age of hope. Socrates may have shown humankind how to die with dignity; Jesus Christ shows his followers how to die in hope.

The Resurrection Hope of Believers

The resurrection is of importance in part because it proclaims the unique divinity of Christ. Yet it is also of importance to the future of believers. A fundamental theme of the Christian gospel is that those who believe in Christ will share in his resurrection. While the resurrection of Christ discloses his divine identity, it also discloses the future destiny of believers with Christ. The resurrection transformed the lives of individuals. John 20:11–18 is an account of how the resurrection was recognized to be good news by Mary Magdalene, who is presented to us as a grieving and distraught individual, convinced that she has lost her Lord for ever: 'They have taken away my Lord, and I do not know where they have laid him' (John 20:13). This is followed by what is often regarded as one of the more tender moments of the New Testament, when Mary suddenly realizes who it is who is addressing her. The moment of

'In heaven after ages of ages of growing glory, we shall have to say, as each new wave of the shoreless, sunlit sea bears us onward, "It doth not yet appear what we shall be."'

Alexander Maclaren

'Christ made love the stairway that would enable all Christians to climb up to heaven. So hold fast to love in all sincerity.'

Fulgentius of Ruspe

recognition and the simultaneous dawning of hope and joy are a powerful testimony to the personal relevance of the gospel of the resurrection in this case.

In the case of Peter, we encounter a betrayer, a failed apostle who denied Christ when he was convinced he would have given his life for the privilege of confessing his name. Peter was called to be an apostle by the lakeside (Luke 5:1–11). The scene of his failure was the 'charcoal fire' in the courtyard of the high priest (John 18:18). With great skill, John draws our attention to the fact that the final encounter between Peter and the disciples and the risen Lord incorporates both these elements (John 21:1–19), in a new commissioning of Peter and the disciples by the risen Christ. The symbols of calling and failure are there, reminding them of the past; the risen Christ is also there, the symbol of hope, forgiveness and a new beginning, summed up in the new commissioning of the disciples. Peter

Noli Me Tangere by Correggio depicts the transformational moment when Mary Magdalene meets the resurrected Christ.

Christian Attitudes towards Work

How does a heavenly calling affect Christian attitudes to everyday life? An excellent way of exploring this is to consider Christian attitudes towards work. Those of the first Christians were often quite negative. The social patricians of ancient Rome regarded work as below their status, and similar attitudes seem to have developed within early Christianity, with somewhat negative and dismissive attitudes emerging towards manual labour. The early monastic tradition appears to have inherited this attitude, at least to some extent, with the result that work often came to be seen as a debasing and demeaning activity, best left to one's social – and spiritual – inferiors. Such attitudes probably reached their height of influence during the Middle Ages. Many religious orders required monks to work, not simply as a productive activity, but as a means of maintaining personal humility. To work was seen as encouraging humility. Work was demeaning and degrading, the sort of thing which no respectable person would consider doing. By working, the monk undertook something painful and humiliating as a way of purging his soul.

The sixteenth-century Reformation gave rise to a radical re-evaluation of this way of thinking. For Martin Luther, Christians were called to be priests to the world, purifying and sanctifying its everyday life from within. Luther even extolled the religious value of housework, declaring that although 'it had no obvious appearance of holiness, yet these very household chores are more to be valued than all the works of monks and nuns'.

Underlying this new attitude to work is the notion of the 'calling'. In the Middle Ages, one was 'called' out of the world and into a monastery. For Luther, God calls his people, not just to faith, but also to express that faith in quite definite areas of life in the everyday world. One is called, in the first place, to be a Christian, and in the second, to live out that faith in a quite definite sphere of activity within the world. Whereas monastic spirituality regarded vocation as a calling out of the world into the seclusion and isolation of the monastery, Luther and Calvin regard vocation as a calling into the everyday world. Work was thus to be seen as an activity by which Christians could deepen their faith, leading it on to new qualities of commitment to God. The Christian calling was a call to commitment to and action within the world. Activity within the world, simultaneously motivated, informed and sanctioned by Christian faith, was the supreme means by which the believer could demonstrate his or her commitment and thankfulness to God. To do anything for God, and to do it well, was the fundamental hallmark of authentic Christian faith. Although this attitude was vulnerable to secularization in the modern western world – with work being seen as an end in itself – its original roots are still evident in the word 'vocation', which continues to express the idea of 'being called' to work in a specific way.

It will thus be clear that the hope of heaven is no disincentive to action on earth. If anything, the believer's heavenly calling offers a new motivation to work in the world – to serve God and others.

will not fail to confess Christ again. In an aside, we are reminded of the price he finally paid for that confession (John 21:19).

The theme of the resurrection of believers is of especial importance in the Pauline letters. Paul declares that the resurrection is a *mysterion* (1 Corinthians 15:51). This Greek word, which is normally translated as 'mystery', needs to be explained. It does not mean a 'logical puzzle', as the English word suggests. Rather, it means something that is so deep, so complex, that we can never hope to give a full description of it. Paul's own account of the resurrection is rich in analogies and metaphors, demonstrating the difficulty of communicating the idea of resurrection. It involves the total future transformation of the believer, which changes the way in which we think and act in the present. The resurrection is not to be understood as the future survival of a disembodied soul or spirit, but as the resurrection of the body, which guarantees continuity between our present existence and our future hope.

Paul's explanations of the significance of the resurrection to believers weave together a number of themes. In each case, the same basic pattern emerges: because believers are 'in Christ' through faith, they will share in the qualities of his resurrection.

1. The resurrection transforms believers completely to be like the risen Christ. This theme is especially important in the letter to the Philippians, in which Paul speaks of believers 'taking on the same form' *(symmorphizo)* of their risen Lord (Philippians 3:10, 20–21). At his coming in glory, Christ will utterly transform their lowly bodies. In a moment, or the 'twinking of an eye', they shall be changed (1 Corinthians 15:51–52).

2. Resurrection is about the glorification of the believer. To be a Christian is to share in the great hope of attaining the glory of Christ (1 Thessalonians 2:12–14). The 'mortal bodies' and 'mortal flesh' of believers will be transformed, and glorified (Romans 8:11–17; 2 Corinthians 4:10–18).

3. The resurrection bestows immortality and incorruptibility. Paul declares that the resurrection removes Christians altogether from the present age of suffering, decay and death (1 Corinthians 15:42–44). What was born corruptible will become incorruptible. The mortal nature of believers will be radically changed, so that they take on immortality (1 Corinthians 15:53–54).

The resurrection is thus good news for believers today. It brings them hope, by assuring Christians that they shall share in the resurrection of Jesus, and be with him forever. Nothing, not even death, can break the bonds which unite them to him. To become a Christian is to begin a relationship with Jesus Christ as your living Lord and Saviour which is not ended by death, but is rather brought to its consummation. Christians need not bid farewell to Jesus when they die; they can rest assured that they will be raised with him forever. The resurrection also reminds believers that there are no doors which are closed to the healing presence of Jesus. Suffering and death have been conquered by him.

The Resurrection and Human Hope

The theme of hope is of central importance in human history. Despair drives peoples and societies into all kinds of disasters. A faith which offers the world no hope is irrelevant; a faith which offers the world a false hope is fraudulent. One of the greatest wonders of the gospel is that it offers

'The doctrine of the kingdom of Heaven, which was the main teaching of Jesus, is certainly one of the most revolutionary doctrines that ever stirred and changed human thought.'

H.G. Wells

273

the world a real hope, grounded in the bedrock of history, and guaranteed by the presence and power of the risen Lord Jesus. Jesus chose to suffer and die, so that those who put their trust in him might suffer and die in hope.

In John's Gospel, the cross is also interpreted as a symbol of victory – victory over darkness, death and the world (John 12:31–33 is particularly important here). Thus the final words of Jesus from the cross – 'It is finished' (John 19:30) – should not be seen as a cry of hopeless defeat, meaning 'It is all over'. Rather, those words should be seen as a shout of triumph and exultation: 'It is accomplished!' What needed to be done was done, and was done well.

These ideas were subsequently developed by Christian writers and theologians. A highly influential way of exploring the New Testament's emphasis upon victory over sin and death through Christ may be found in a famous eleventh-century Easter hymn by Fulbert, bishop of Chartres:

For Judah's Lion bursts his chains
Crushing the serpent's head;
And cries aloud through death's domain,
To wake the imprisoned dead.

This highly imaginative hymn takes up the image of Jesus Christ as the conquering lion of the tribe of Judah, developed in the book of Revelation (Revelation 5:5), who fulfils the great promise of redemption made to Adam, by which he will trample the serpent under his feet (Genesis 3:15). The tyranny of death over sinful humanity is broken by Christ's death and resurrection. It is interesting to note that Christ uses death to defeat death, a point often made by preachers during this period. Listeners were often reminded of the story of David and Goliath: just as David killed Goliath with the giant's own sword, so

Christ defeated death with its own weapons.

The idea of Christ 'wakening the imprisoned dead' reflects the belief that Christ's death and resurrection were important, not only for those alive at the time and in years to come, but for those who had come before. The basic idea is that Christ's victory over death is retrospective as well as prospective, and is thus good news for those who have already died. These are understood to be prisoners held captive by death, and

through the defeat of death by Christ, they are delivered from their bondage and made free.

Perhaps the portrayal of this powerful image most familiar to modern readers is to be found in C.S. Lewis's *The Lion, The Witch and the Wardrobe*. The book tells the story of Narnia, a land which is discovered accidentally by four children rummaging around in an old wardrobe. In this work, we encounter the White Witch, who keeps the land of Narnia locked in the cold, icy grip of winter. As we read on, we realize that she rules Narnia not as a matter of right, but by stealth. The true ruler of the land is absent; in his absence, the witch subjects the land to oppression. In the midst of this frozen and

The Lion, The Witch and the Wardrobe by C.S. Lewis portrays the victory of good over evil and death.

oppressive land stands the witch's castle, within which many of the inhabitants of Narnia have been imprisoned as stone statues. Lewis graphically describes how Aslan – representing the lion of Judah, who has burst his chains – breaks into the castle, breathes upon the statues, and restores them to life, before leading the liberated army through the shattered gates of the once-great fortress to freedom. Hell has been harrowed. It has been despoiled, and its inhabitants liberated from its dreary shades.

Yet surely there is a difficulty here? If the power of sin, death and evil have been broken, how can we make sense of the fact that they still continue to plague humanity? Human history and Christian experiences of a constant struggle against sin and evil, even in the lives of believers. There is a danger that talking glibly about 'the victory of faith' will seem like empty words. It may even seem to be an attempt to cover up a contradiction between faith and experience. What sort of victory allows our enemies to continue as they were before? So how can we handle this problem?

One of the most helpful ways of dealing with this difficulty is suggested by the Second World War. A group of distinguished writers (such as C.S. Lewis in England and Anders Nygren in Sweden) noticed important parallels between the New Testament theme of the proclamation of victory over sin through the death of Christ, and the liberation of an occupied country from Nazi rule. In order to appreciate the full power of these analogies, we need to try to think ourselves into the mindset of an occupied European country during the Second World War, heavily overlaid with the sinister and menacing idea of an occupying power. Life has to be lived under the shadow of this presence. And part of the poignancy of the situation is its utter

'Weep not, I shall not die; and as I leave the land of the dying I trust to see the blessings of the Lord in the land of the living.'

Edward the Confessor

hopelessness. Nothing can be done about it. No one can defeat the occupying power.

Then comes the electrifying news. There has been a far-off battle. And somehow, it has turned the tide of the war. A new phase has developed, in which the occupying power is in disarray. Its back has been broken. In the course of time, the Nazis will be driven out of every corner of occupied Europe. But they are still present in the occupied country. In one sense, the situation has not changed. But in another, more important, sense, it has

changed totally. The scent of victory and liberation is in the air. The cross and resurrection of Jesus are like distant victories, which break the backbone of evil powers, and usher in a new phase in a long and painful struggle. The struggle will continue for some time (the end of the Second World War in Europe came about a year after the establishment of the bridgeheads in Normandy in June 1944). But an objective change had taken place in the theatre of war – with a resulting subjective change in the hearts and minds of captive people. In one sense, victory has not come; in another, it has. Similarly, the resurrection declares in advance of the event God's total victory over all evil and oppressive forces – such as death, evil and sin. But it is possible to begin to live *now* in the light of that freedom and victory, knowing that their power has been broken, and that the night of their oppression will end.

Parallels have been drawn between the New Testament theme of the victory over sin through Christ's death and the liberation of an occupied country during war.

The Last Things

The section of Christian theology that deals with the theme of the Christian hope is often known as 'eschatology',

Christian Attitudes Towards Possessions

What value are possessions, in the light of the Christian hope? The New Testament challenges the assumption that possessions lead to any form of spiritual privilege, either in the church or in the kingdom of God. If anything, they can be an obstacle to the values of the kingdom. The preaching of Jesus makes it clear that it is the poor who enjoy special consideration in the sight of God. It is, as Jesus pointed out, better to lay up treasure in heaven than on earth (Matthew 6:19–21). The letter of James is severely critical of churches which treat the wealthy preferentially (James 2:1–7). Has not God chosen those who are poor in the eyes of the world to be rich in faith?

So what attitude should Christians adopt towards possessions? Augustine of Hippo argued that the problem was not possessions themselves; the real issue is when possessions come to displace God. They generate anxiety, and can become a false and unreliable source of security. Martin Luther once commented that whatever was our true source of security or our true heart's desire had become our God. In other words, we can allow love of possessions to displace God. In effect, Luther is suggesting that a love of possessions can quickly degenerate into idolatry, in which possessions are worshipped or idolized.

In the New Testament, an excessive longing for possessions – what we might simply call 'greed' – is seen as one of the most serious of sins. The earliest Christians were told not just to avoid greed, but to watch out for it (Luke 12:15), to flee from it (1 Timothy 6:11) or to kill it (Colossians 3:5). Greed is described in most unflattering terms. The love of money is described as 'a root of all kinds of evil' (1 Timothy 6:10), as well as being identified as one of the twelve things which come out of individuals and defile them (Mark 7:20–22).

So how should Christians deal with possessions? In many monastic orders, possessions were seen as an obstacle to spiritual growth. They kept individuals anchored to the economic realities of the present world, instead of encouraging them to focus on heaven. For this reason, most religious orders required their members to take vows of poverty. In this way, they were set free from concerns and anxieties about wealth and status, and enabled to focus on God. A similar attitude emerged during the Reformation in the sixteenth century, where the early Christian practice of having all things in common – witnessed to in the Acts of the Apostles (Acts 2:44–5) – was seen as standard practice for Christian communities.

The American preacher and theologian Jonathan Edwards offers a thoughtful account of how Christians ought to relate to their possessions. In his sermon 'The Christian Pilgrim', Edwards allows Christians to own and enjoy possessions – provided that they do not become a barrier between the believer and God. 'We ought not to take our rest in these things as our portion,' he writes. Rather, 'we ought to possess, enjoy and use them, with no other view but readily to quit them, whenever we are called to it, and to change them willingly and cheerfully for heaven.'

'The road to Hell is paved with good intentions.'
Samuel Johnson

from the Greek phrase *ta eschata*, 'the last things'. These are traditionally understood to be heaven, hell and purgatory, and it will be helpful to explore each of these, before moving on to consider the notion of heaven in more detail.

The word 'heaven' is traditionally used to refer to the hope of dwelling in the presence of God forever. Heaven is a place, though it is beyond our ability to comprehend it in terms of our understanding of space and time. The dominant sense of the word is relational – that is, it is used to designate the state of dwelling with God, without attaching this to any particular understanding of precisely where this dwelling may be located. The Christian vision of heaven is shaped by two controlling images or themes – the New Jerusalem, and the restoration of creation. A radical transformation of all things will bring about a new order, reversing the devastating effects of sin upon humanity and the world. The image of resurrection conveys the ideas of both radical change and continuity – that is to say, that the new order of things, though utterly different from what we currently know and experience, nevertheless demonstrates continuity with the present order. The present age will be *transformed* and *renewed*, just as a seed is transformed utterly in becoming a living plant.

The word 'hell' is traditionally used to refer to permanent separation from God. The New Testament draws a distinction between 'Hades' (the abode of the dead) and 'hell' (a place of punishment). However, this distinction has often been blurred, especially through inadequate translations. There is at present a debate between those Christians who see hell as permanent exclusion from the presence of God, and banishment to a place of eternal conscious punishment, and those who see hell as a place of annihilation. The former is the traditional view, which is familiar from many works of art of the Middle Ages. It is set out with particular clarity in Jonathan Edwards's (1703–1758) famous sermon 'Sinners in the Hands of an Angry God,' preached on 8 July 1741:

It would be dreadful to suffer this fierceness and wrath of Almighty God for one moment; but you must suffer it for all eternity. There will be no end to this exquisite horrible misery... You will know that you must wear out long ages, millions of millions of ages, in wrestling and conflicting with this almighty merciless vengeance.

However, the debate over this matter has raised some important questions. For example, some argued that the existence of hell, understood as a place of eternal punishment, seems to be a contradiction of the Christian assertion of the final victory of God over evil. Others found it difficult to reconcile the idea of a loving God with the notion of the continuing vindictive or retributive punishment of sinners. The main difficulty here was that there seemed to be no point to the suffering of the condemned. While answers may be given to both these objections, there has been a perceptible loss of interest in the idea of hell in both popular and more academic Christian circles, whether Protestant or Roman Catholic.

The idea of 'purgatory' continues to be an important topic of debate between Protestant and Roman Catholic writers. Purgatory is perhaps best understood as an intermediate stage, in which those who have died in a state of grace are given an opportunity to purge themselves of the guilt of their sins before finally entering heaven. The idea does not have explicit scriptural warrant, although a passage in 2 Maccabees

> 'Pride, the first peer and president of hell.'
>
> Daniel Defoe

> 'Hell is full of good meanings and wishings.'
>
> George Herbert

12:39–45 (regarded as apocryphal, and hence as lacking in authority, by Protestant writers) speaks of Judas Maccabeus making 'propitiation for those who had died, in order that they might be released from their sin'. The idea was developed during the patristic period by writers such as Clement of Alexandria (c. 150–215) and Origen (185–254), who taught that those who had died without time to perform works of penance would be 'purified through fire' in the next life.

The idea of purgatory was rejected by the Protestant reformers during the sixteenth century for two reasons. First, it was held to lack any substantial scriptural foundations. Second, it was inconsistent with the doctrine of justification by faith, which declared that an individual

could be put 'right with God' through faith, thus establishing a relationship which obviated the need for purgatory. An individual was placed in a right relationship with God through faith, on account of Jesus Christ. So what purpose did purgatory actually serve? For Protestant critics of the doctrine, it was both redundant and unbiblical.

What Does the Resurrection Body Look Like?

But how are believers to understand this hope of their future resurrection? What will be the relationship of their earthly bodies to their heavenly bodies? The New Testament is very restrained at this point. The image of a seed, used by Paul in 1 Corinthians 15, was taken by many writers to mean that there was some organic connection between the earthly and heavenly body. Gregory of Nyssa is a good example of a writer who reasons like this:

The resurrection is nothing other than the reconstitution of our nature to its pristine state. For we read in Scripture that, in the first act of creation, the earth initially brought forth the green plant; then seed was produced from this plant; and from this seed, when it had been scattered on the earth, the same form of the original growth sprang up. Now the inspired apostle says that this is precisely what also happens at the resurrection. Thus we learn from him not only that human nature is changed into a far nobler state, but also that we are to hope for the return of human nature to its primal condition.

Some early Christian writers thought that it was best to imagine the streets of the New Jerusalem as inhabited by disembodied souls. On this model, the human being consists of two entities –

A group of the damned from an altar panel depicting the Last Judgment.

a physical body, and a spiritual soul. Death leads to the liberation of the soul from its material body. This view was commonplace within the Hellenistic culture of the New Testament period. However, this idea was vigorously opposed by most early Christian theologians. The most significant minority voice in this matter belonged to Origen, a highly creative theologian with a strongly Platonist bent, who held that the resurrection body was purely spiritual. This view was contested by most Christian writers, who insisted that the phrase 'the resurrection of the body' was to be understood as the permanent resurrection of both the body and the soul of the believer.

But what would these resurrected individuals look like? Many early Christian writers argued that the 'citizens of heaven' would be naked, recreating the situation in paradise. This time, however, nakedness would neither give rise to shame nor sexual lust, but would simply be accepted as the natural and innocent state of humanity. Others, however, argued that the inhabitants of the New Jerusalem would be clothed in finery, reflecting their status as citizens of God's chosen city.

It was clear to many writers that the final state of deceased believers was not of material importance to their appearance in heaven. The issue emerged as theologically significant during a persecution of Christians in Lyons, France, around the years 175–77. Aware that Christians believed in the resurrection of the body, their pagan oppressors burned the bodies of the Christian they had just martyred, and threw their ashes in the River Rhône. This, they believed, would prevent the resurrection of these martyrs, in that there was now no body to be raised. Christian theologians responded by arguing that God was able to restore all that the body had lost through this process of destruction.

Methodius of Olympus (died 311) offered an analogy for this process of reconstitution which would prove highly influential in discussing this question. The resurrection could, he argued, be thought of as a kind of 'rearrangement' of the constituent elements of humanity. It is like a statue which is melted down, and reforged from the same material – yet in such a manner that any defects or damage are eliminated.

It is as if some skilled artificer had made a noble image, cast in gold or other material, which was beautifully proportioned in all its features. Then the artificer suddenly notices that the image had been defaced by some envious person, who could not endure its beauty, and so decided to ruin it for the sake of the pointless pleasure of satisfying his jealousy. So the craftsman decides to recast this noble image... Now the melting down of a statue corresponds to the death and dissolution of the human body, and the remoulding of the material to the resurrection after death.

A similar argument is found in the *Four Books of the Sentences*, the masterpiece of the great twelfth-century theologian Peter Lombard (c. 1095–1160). This book, which served as the core textbook for just about every medieval theologian, took the view that the resurrected body was basically a reconstituted humanity, from which all defects had been purged:

Nothing of the substance of the flesh from which humanity is created will be lost; rather, the natural substance of the body will be reintegrated by the collection of all the particles that were previously dispersed. The bodies of the saints will thus rise without any defect, shining like the sun, all their deformities having being removed.

A final question that has caused considerable debate among Christian theologians concerns the *age* of those who are resurrected. If someone dies at the age of sixty, will they appear in the streets of the New Jerusalem as an old person? And if someone dies at the age of ten, will they appear as a child? This issue caused the spilling of much debate, especially during the Middle Ages. By the end of the thirteenth century, an emerging consensus can be discerned. As each person reaches their peak of perfection around the age of thirty, they will be resurrected as they would have appeared at that time – even if they never lived to reach that age. Peter Lombard's discussion of the matter is typical of his age: 'A boy who dies immediately after being born will be resurrected in that form which he would have had if he had lived to the age of thirty.' The New Jerusalem will thus be populated by men and women as they would appear at the age of thirty (the age, of course, at which Christ was crucified) – but with every blemish removed.

A further issue concerning the form of the resurrection body became especially important during the twentieth century, when the practice of cremation became increasingly common in Christian nations, partly because of the increasingly prohibitive cost of burial. Was cremation inconsistent with belief in the resurrection? Was our resurrection to eternal life dependent on being buried intact? The question had been debated in earlier periods and theologians of the time had concluded that God would still be able to raise the bodies of those who had been mutilated in this way. Perhaps the most influential more recent answer to this question was offered by the famous American

> 'I look at life as a gift of God. Now that he wants it back I have no right to complain.'
>
> Joyce Carey

evangelist Billy Graham, who wrote thus in a nationally-syndicated newspaper column:

In Corinthians 5, Paul makes the contrast between living in a tent, a temporary home that can be pulled down and put away, and living in a permanent home that will last forever. Our bodies are our temporary tents. Our resurrected bodies will be our permanent homes. They are similar in appearance but different in substance. Cremation is therefore no hindrance to the resurrection.

Graham's point was clear: the Christian hope of resurrection is grounded in the trustworthiness of the divine promises, not the precise circumstances of a person's funeral arrangements.

The New Jerusalem
The image of the New Jerusalem is perhaps the most familiar way of picturing heaven, not least on account of the important role played by the idea in the closing chapters of the book of Revelation, the final work of the Christian Bible. It is a very powerful and rich image, which deserves close attention. A good starting point would be to explore this theme by considering the importance of the city in the Old Testament itself. Many sections of the Old Testament resound with praise of the city of Jerusalem, which is seen both as a tangible image of the presence and providence of God within its sturdy walls, and also as a pointer to the fulfilment of messianic expectations.

The image of the city has several aspects which have come to be linked with the Christian hope. Above all, a city offered security; its gates and walls protected its population against their enemies, whether these took the form of marauding wild animals or invading armies. One of the great prayers of ancient Israel was that there should be no breaches in the walls of the city of Jerusalem (Psalm 144:14). The security of the city's population depended on the integrity of its walls, towers and gates. To dwell within a city was to live in safety, as a member of its community.

For the Old Testament, of course, one city stands above all others in terms of its significance – Jerusalem. For many prophetic writers, Jerusalem was simply '*the* city'. The rise of the prominence of Jerusalem is directly linked to David's decision to establish his throne within this ancient Jebusite city, and to make it the resting place of the ark of the covenant. These deeply symbolic actions led to Jerusalem being viewed as the chosen habitation of God, 'for the glory of the Lord filled the house of the Lord' (1 Kings 8:10–11). The pilgrim who made the long journey to the city could do so in the sure knowledge that God truly dwelt within Jerusalem's sturdy walls (Psalm 9:11; 74:2; 135:21).

The siege of Jerusalem by the Babylonians, culminating in its capture and the destruction of its Temple in 586 BC, was a devastating catastrophe, both for the city itself, and for the hopes and beliefs of its population. Had Jerusalem lost its special status in the sight of God? Was God still a living presence among his people or in his Temple? The prophet Ezekiel had a vision of the 'glory of the Lord' departing from the Jerusalem Temple. Would it ever return? It was against this background of despair that the prophetic vision of the New Jerusalem began to take shape. A new city of God would arise, in which the throne of God would be established, and within which the 'glory of the Lord' would once more dwell. The glory of this renewed Temple would exceed that of the former Temple, destroyed by the Assyrians (Haggai 2:9).

Initially, this prophetic vision of a New Jerusalem was understood to apply to a future earthly city – a reconstructed city of bricks and mortar, which would rise from the ruins of the old city with the return of its people from their exile in Babylon. The Old Testament books of Nehemiah and Ezra document attempts to restore Jerusalem to its former glory and to fulfil the hopes of a renewed presence of the glory of the Lord. Yet with the passing of time, Jewish hopes began to crystallize around the idea of a heavenly Jerusalem – a future city, beyond this world, filled with the 'glory of the Lord', in which God is seated on a throne. This city is filled with eternal light, which draws people from afar to the safety and rest which it offers.

The future hopes of Israel, which had once centred on the earthly city of Jerusalem and its Temple, now underwent a decisive shift in focus. The calamitous history of Jerusalem led many to look to a future heavenly city, which was somehow represented or foreshadowed in its earthly counterpart. This trend, which was already present in the centuries before Christ, received a massive stimulus as a result of the Jewish revolt of AD 66 against the occupying Roman forces in Palestine. The Roman emperor Titus, in ruthlessly putting down this revolt in AD 70, destroyed the Temple in Jerusalem, leaving only small segments of the original edifice standing (such as the western 'wailing wall', still a site for Jewish prayers). With the destruction of the earthly focus of Jewish hopes, it was perhaps inevitable that a heavenly alternative would be found. The New Jerusalem now came to refer to a future hope which lay beyond history, rather than to the hope of rebuilding the original Jebusite city of David.

The book of Revelation develops this idea, seeing the fulfilment of all Christian hopes and expectations as focusing upon the New Jerusalem, the

'Heaven is not to be looked upon only as the reward, but as the natural effect of a religious life.'

Joseph Addison

'Hope is the last thing that dies in man; and though it be exceedingly deceitful, yet it is of this good use to us, that while we are travelling through life it conducts us in an easier and more pleasant way to our journey's end.'

François de la Rochefoucauld

city of God within which the risen Christ reigns triumphant. The book of Revelation develops this powerful image of heaven as a New Jerusalem, set free from sin, pain, death and suffering. When God makes all things new, these things will pass away.

Then I saw a new heaven and a new earth; for the first heaven and the first earth had passed away and the sea was no more. And I saw the holy city, the new Jerusalem, coming down out of heaven from God, prepared as a bride adorned for her husband. And I heard a loud voice from the throne saying,

Church Architecture and the Vision of God

In what way does Christian architecture reflect the hope of heaven? One answer can be found by exploring the design of churches. The New Testament tends to use the word 'church' (*ekklesia* in Greek) to refer to a gathering of people rather than a building. Indeed, the threat of persecution was such that the early church tended to meet in secret, 'borrowing' buildings which were normally used for other purposes in order to avoid drawing attention to their activities. However, once Christianity was able to exist as a legal religion, the design of churches came to be increasingly seen as a way of communicating some central themes of the Christian faith. Church doors were often decorated with slogans, designed to stress the importance of the institution of the church as a means of salvation. The link between the church and salvation was often reinforced visually through the physical location of the baptismal font close to the church door, thereby affirming that entrance to the church – the community of salvation – is linked with the sacrament of baptism.

> 'Suffer with Christ and for Christ, if you desire to reign with Christ.'
>
> Thomas à Kempis

The rise of the Gothic style of architecture is usually traced back to the twelfth century, a period of relative political stability in western Europe which encouraged the rebirth of art and architecture. One of the most distinctive features of this architectural style is its deliberate use of height and light to generate and sustain a sense of the presence of God on earth. The extensive use of buttresses allowed the weight of the building to be borne by outside supports, thus allowing the external walls to have large glass windows, which ensured that the building was saturated with the radiance of the sun. The use of stained glass helped generate an other-worldly brilliance within the church building, while simultaneously showing gospel scenes to worshippers. The use of tall, thin internal columns created an anticipation of the life of heaven, allowing the worshipper to step into another world, to savour its delights, before returning to the dull routines of everyday life.

The classic design of many churches is cross-shaped, with the altar placed at the east end. This was intended to remind congregations of the central place of the cross as the foundation of the Christian faith and Christian church, and to focus their thoughts on the expected return of Christ. In the Roman Catholic tradition, the altar was the central focus of Christian worship, reminding worshippers of the sacrifice of Christ upon the cross, commemorated in the Mass.

At the time of the Reformation, the emphasis shifted decisively from the altar to the pulpit, as increasing weight came to be placed upon preaching as the primary focus of Christian worship. This shift in emphasis can be seen in St Peter's Cathedral, Geneva, which underwent significant

'See, the home of God is among mortals.
He will dwell with them;
they will be his peoples,
and God himself will be with them;
he will wipe every tear from their eyes.

Death will be no more;
mourning and crying and pain will be no more,
for the first things have passed away.'
And the one who was seated on the throne said, 'See, I am making all things new' (Revelation 21:1–5).

architectural modification under the direction of the Protestant Reformer, John Calvin. The altar at the east end of the cathedral was removed. A massive pulpit was erected to its side, symbolizing the Protestant insistence that the church was under the authority of the preaching of the word of God. Similarly, the design of modern Baptist churches often places the pulpit at the centre of things, to stress the centrality of the public reading of the Bible and the sermon.

The interior of Chartres Cathedral. The light and height of Gothic churches were intended to create a sense of the presence of God on earth.

Pilgrim's treacherous route from the City of Destruction to the Celestial City from *The Pilgrim's Progress* by John Bunyan.

The thought of this future security in the New Jerusalem comforts and encourages those who are suffering on earth, as they are reminded of the great hope that is set before them, which nothing can take away.

The book of Revelation contrasts the consolation of heaven with the suffering, tragedy and pain of life on earth. Many scholars hold that the book of Revelation is addressed above all to Christians who are facing victimization or persecution in the Roman empire in the later years of the reign of the emperor Domitian. The theme of the New Jerusalem is here integrated with motifs drawn from the creation account – such as the presence of the 'tree of life' (Revelation 22:2) – suggesting that

heaven can be seen as the restoration of the bliss of Eden, when God dwelt with humanity in harmony. The pain, sorrow and evil of a fallen world have finally passed away, and the creation is restored to its original intention. The Christians of Asia Minor at this time were few in number, and generally of low social status. There is no doubt that they derived much consolation from the anticipation of entering a heavenly city which vastly exceeded any earthly comforts or security they had known. The holy city was paved with gold and decked with jewels and precious stones, dazzling its inhabitants and intensifying the sense of longing to enter through its gates on the part of those still on earth.

The New Jerusalem – like its earthly

counterpart – is portrayed as a walled city. Its security is beyond question. It is perched on the peak of a hill that no invading army could hope to ascend. Its walls are so thick that they could not be breached by any known siege engine, and so high that no human could hope to scale them. Its twelve gates are guarded by angels. Just as return to Eden was once prevented by a guardian angel, so the New Jerusalem is defended against invasion by supernatural forces.

It is important to note that the twelve gates of the New Jerusalem – though guarded by angels – are permanently thrown open. Whereas the classic fortified city of ancient times was designed to exclude outsiders, the architecture of the New Jerusalem seems designed to welcome them within its boundaries. The city is portrayed as perfectly cubical (Revelation 21:16), perhaps signifying that it is a perfection of the square temple which the prophet Ezekiel envisaged for the rebuilt Jerusalem after the return from exile (Ezekiel 43:16, 48:20).

The careful attention paid to imagery suggests that the New Jerusalem is to be seen in terms of the fulfilment of Israel through the restoration of its twelve tribes (Revelation 21:12–14). Most significantly of all, the New Jerusalem does not contain a temple (Revelation 21:22). The cultic hierarchies of the old priestly tradition are swept to one side. All are now priests and there is no need for a temple, because God dwells within the city as a whole. He is now all in all and in a remarkable transformation of images the city has itself become a temple. Where Old Testament prophets had yearned for the rebuilding of the Temple, Revelation declares that it has become redundant. What it foreshadowed had now taken place. With the advent of the reality of God's presence, its

symbol was no longer required. The dwelling place of God is now with the people of God; it can no longer be contained within a physical structure. The New Jerusalem is thus characterized by the pervasive presence of God, and the triumphant and joyful response of those who had long awaited this experience.

This image of heaven resonates strongly with one of the leading themes of Paul's theology – that Christians are to be regarded as 'citizens of heaven' (Philippians 3:19–21). Paul makes a distinction between those who 'set their minds on earthly things' and those whose citizenship is 'in heaven'. Paul himself was a Roman citizen, who knew what privileges this brought – particularly on those occasions when he found himself in conflict with the Roman authorities. For Paul, Christians possessed something greater: the 'citizenship of heaven', which is to be understood as a present possession, not something which is yet to come. While believers have yet to enter into the full possession of what this citizenship entails, they already possess that privilege. Christians have no permanent citizenship in this world, in that their citizenship is in heaven (Philippians 3:20). As the author of the letter to the Hebrews puts it, 'here we have no lasting city, but we are looking for the city that is to come' (Hebrews 13:14).

This theme of the New Jerusalem has been developed by many Christian writers. Probably the most famous is the account provided by John Bunyan (1626–88) in his best-known work, *The Pilgrim's Progress*, the first part of which appeared in 1678, and the second in 1684. The central narrative of the book focuses on its hero Christian, initially bowed down with a burden of sin upon his back, who flees from the City of Destruction and seeks eternal life. At last, after crossing the bridgeless River of Death, Bunyan's hero is received in the Celestial Jerusalem.

'When I get to heaven, I shall see three wonders there. The first wonder will be to see many there whom I did not expect to see; the second wonder will be to miss many people who I did expect to see; and the third and greatest wonder of all will be to find myself there.'

John Newton

Where Was the Garden of Eden?

Where was the famous Garden of Eden? Although much popular writing assumes that 'Eden' is the name of the famous garden itself, it is very clear that the Bible understands 'Eden' to refer to the geographical region in which the garden is located, rather than the name of the garden itself. Other biblical passages refer to the garden in other ways – such as the 'Garden of God' (Ezekiel 28:13) or the 'Garden of the Lord' (Isaiah 51:3). The Greek word *paradeisos* (which means 'an enclosed garden' or 'a walled park') is used to refer to this garden.

But where was this garden located? Perhaps the best clue lies in the names of the four rivers which enfolded Eden, named by Genesis as the Tigris, Euphrates, Pison and Gihon. The first two of these are easily identified as the great rivers of ancient Mesopotamia. The identity of the others remains unclear. The first-century Jewish historian Josephus suggested that they were actually the Nile and Euphrates.

Adam and Eve succumb to temptation in the Garden of Eden in this painting by Jan Brueghel and Peter Paul Rubens.

On the basis of this identification, Eden has been located in as many diverse areas as the fabulous lost city of Atlantis. Some early Christian fathers and late classical authors suggested it could lie in Mongolia, India or even Ethiopia. Others favoured eastern Turkey: the four rivers of paradise could be identified with the Murat River, the Tigris, the Euphrates, and the north fork of the Euphrates, which branches off in this region.

One recent theory argued that Eden was actually located in the Persian Gulf. This theory suggested that the most promising site for Eden was the ancient land of Sumeria, some 200 kilometres north of the present head of the Persian Gulf. On this view, Eden – like the famous city of Atlantis – was lost beneath the waters of the sea. The waters of the Persian Gulf had risen since biblical times, submerging this earthly paradise. If this were so, then the biblical river of Pison could be identified with the Wadi Riniah and Wadi Batin – the modern Saudi names for a dry riverbed in which water no longer flows – and Gihon was the Karun River, which rises in Iran and flows to the southwest where it enters the Persian Gulf.

Yet the debate over the precise geographical location of Eden perhaps misses the real point at issue. The Christian tradition has never seen the geography of paradise as being of primary importance; rather, the important question has to do with the identity and nature of humanity, and supremely its final destiny. To speak of paradise is not to hope for a return to a specific physical place, but to yearn for the restoration of a specific spiritual state. Christians' hope to enter paradise is not about returning to Sumeria – or wherever Eden may turn out to have been located. It is about enjoying the same close fellowship with God that once existed in that famous Garden, and which Christians will one day share in heaven itself.

The story tells of how Christian and his friends travel through the 'wilderness of this world' in search of the heavenly city. The hope of finding and entering this city dominates the narrative. Bunyan draws extensively on the New Jerusalem tradition from the book of Revelation. This can be seen from the tantalizing description of the heavenly Jerusalem offered by the 'Shining Ones' – angelic beings who reassure Christian and his travelling companions concerning the final goal of their quest.

The talk they had with the Shining Ones was about the glory of the place; who told them that the beauty and glory of it was inexpressible. There, said they, is the 'Mount Zion, the heavenly Jerusalem, the innumerable company of angels, and the spirits of just men made perfect' [Hebrews 12:22–24]. You are going now, said they, to the paradise of God, wherein you shall see the tree of life, and eat of the never-fading fruits thereof; and when you come there, you shall have white robes given you, and your walk and talk shall be every day with the King, even all the days of eternity [Revelation 2:7; 3:4; 22:5]. There you shall not see again such things as you saw when you were in the lower region upon the earth, to wit, sorrow, sickness, affliction, and death, 'for the former things are passed away'.

Bunyan's account of the New Jerusalem brings together a number of biblical images, weaving the imagery of Israel's entry into the Promised Land with that of the New Jerusalem. A river separates humanity from the heavenly city, just as the River Jordan was placed between Israel and its Promised Land. It is only by crossing this river that access to the city can be gained. At the end of his story, Bunyan tells how Mr Standfast prepared to cross the river from this life to the next, trusting that the trumpets would sound for him on the other side:

This river has been a terror to many; yea, the thoughts of it also have often frightened me. Now, methinks, I stand easy, my foot is fixed upon that upon which the feet of the priests that bare the ark of the covenant stood, while Israel went over this Jordan [Joshua 3:17]. The waters, indeed, are to the palate bitter; and to the stomach cold; yet the thoughts of what I am going to, and of the conduct that waits for me on the other side, doth lie as a glowing coal at my heart. I see myself now at the end of my journey, my toilsome days are ended. I am going now to see that head that was crowned with thorns, and that face that was spit upon for me.

The Pilgrim's Progress was of immense importance in establishing the journey from the 'city of destruction' to the 'heavenly city' as a framework for making sense of the ambiguities, sorrows and pains of the Christian life. Bunyan's powerful visual images, coupled with a masterly use of narrative, ensured that the imagery of the New Jerusalem would have a profound and permanent effect on popular Christian spirituality.

The Restoration of Creation

A second biblical image which has played a major role in stimulating Christian reflection on the future hope is that of the restoration of creation. God will make all things new – a theme which, as has been seen, is reflected in the biblical idea of the New Jerusalem. The Christian hope involves God making all things new. What God once created will one day be recreated.

This theme is especially clear in the message of the Old Testament prophets. Hosea, writing in the eighth

> 'It is because of faith that we exchange the present for the future.'
>
> Fidelis of Sigmaringen

What is Spirituality?

In recent years, there has been growing interest in the field of Christian spirituality. Although earlier generations of Protestant writers – such as the Puritans – tended to use terms such as 'piety' or 'godliness' to refer to what is now generally designated as 'spirituality', it is now clear that the term 'spirituality' has gained wide acceptance in recent decades as the preferred way of referring to aspects of the devotional practices of a religion, and especially the interior world of experience in the lives of believers. It is often contrasted with a purely academic, objective or detached approach to a faith. Every branch of Christianity – Protestantism, Roman Catholicism, Eastern Orthodoxy and evangelicalism – has seen a surge of interest in the field. Evangelical writers such as Eugene Peterson, Dallas Willard and J.I. Packer have stressed the importance of the relational aspects of faith, and seen spirituality as a way of deepening both an individual believer's relationship with God, and their appreciation of their faith.

But what is spirituality? How is this word to be understood? It draws on the Hebrew word *ruach*, a rich term that is usually translated as 'spirit', but which includes a range of meanings extending beyond this to include such ideas as 'breath' and 'wind'. To talk about 'the spirit' is to discuss what gives life and animation to someone. Spirituality is thus about the life of faith – what drives and motivates it, and what people find helpful in sustaining and developing it. It is about that which animates the life of believers, and urges them on to deepen and perfect what has at present only been begun.

So how is spirituality related to beliefs? In what way does Christian theology stimulate and inform Christian spirituality? Thomas Merton (1915–68), a Trappist monk who had a major influence on modern western spirituality, argued that it is indeed possible to distinguish spirituality and theology – but that they belong together, as two sides of the same coin. 'We must not separate intellectual study of divinely revealed truth and contemplative experience of that truth as if they could never have anything to do with one another,' he explained. Rather, we must see them as belonging together. 'Unless they are united there is no fervour, no life and no spiritual value in theology; no substance, no meaning and no sure orientation in the contemplative life.'

A similar approach is taken by J.I Packer, whose book *Knowing God* is widely regarded as one of the evangelical spiritual classics of the twentieth century. Defining spirituality as 'the life of God in the soul of Man' or 'the study of godliness in its root and in its fruit', Packer points out how the two disciplines complement each other. He would like to see 'theological study done as an aspect and means of our relating to God' and 'spirituality studied within an evaluative theological frame'. Bad theology makes for bad spirituality. 'Neglect the Son, lose your focus on his mediation and blood atonement and heavenly intercession, and you slip back into the legalism that is fallen man's natural religion, the treadmill religion of works.' So beliefs matter here – as they do throughout the Christian life.

century before Christ, looks forward to a future transformation of the human situation, in which human enmity against other humans is ended, along with a restoration of the integrity of the original created order.

I will make for you a covenant on that day with the wild animals, the birds of the air, and the creeping things of the ground; and I will abolish the bow, the sword, and war from the land (Hosea 2:18).

A related theme can be seen in the writings of Joel, in which a series of paradisiacal images are fused with themes taken from the entry of Israel into the Promised Land.

On that day the mountains shall drip sweet wine, the hills shall flow with milk, and all the stream beds of Judah shall flow with water; a fountain shall come forth from the house of the Lord and water the Wadi Shittim (Joel 3:18).

The future state of Israel is thus depicted in terms of a new Eden: its

> 'Paradise is our native country, and we in this world be as exiles and strangers.'
>
> Richard Greenham

Heaven in Christian Art

The Christian idea of heaven makes a powerful appeal to the imagination. 'While reason is the natural organ of truth, imagination is the organ of meaning' (C.S. Lewis). Heaven is perhaps the supreme example of a Christian concept that is mediated directly through images. To speak of 'imagining heaven' does not imply or entail that heaven is a fictional notion. It is simply to recognize the important role of the human capacity to construct and enter into mental pictures of reality. We are able to inhabit the mental images we create, and thence anticipate the delight of finally entering the greater reality to which they correspond. Marco Polo (1254–1324), having returned to Italy from the court of Kublai Khan, was able to convey some of the wonders of China by asking his audience to imagine a world they had never visited, but which he could recreate, if only in part, by his narratives and descriptions. The unknown could be glimpsed by comparisons with the known – through analogies.

Biblical writers pictured heaven in terms of certain types of earthly realities – realities which possessed distinct qualities capable of disclosing the unique nature of heaven itself. Two such images are of critical importance: the city and the garden. Each has been a powerful stimulus to artists, as they have tried to represent the future joys of heaven in terms of imagery already familiar to their audiences.

Especially during the Middle Ages, heaven was depicted as a fortified city, within which individuals could dwell in safety. This was often stressed by portraying the city as surrounded by a deep moat, isolating the city from hostile forces. The rise of the great Renaissance city states – such as Florence – gave a new impetus to this approach. Renaissance cities – like ancient Jerusalem – represented places of civilization, stability and safety. This process can be seen most clearly in the visionary writings of Gerardesca of Pisa (1212–69), which depict heaven as a city surrounded by seven castles and other minor fortresses, enfolded within a vast uninhabited parkland. Gerardesca clearly recognizes a hierarchy within this celestial paradise and, although she insists that all the saints are inhabitants of the New Jerusalem, her vision places saints of the first rank, including the Virgin Mary, in the central city, and lesser saints in its outlying fortresses.

Yet the imagery of the New Jerusalem found itself existing alongside that of mountains will flow with wine, its hills will flow with milk, and the dry riverbeds will be filled with pure clear water – just as Eden was surrounded and watered by its four great rivers. A similar theme is found in Micah 4:4, which offers a vision of a future state in which the vineyard and fig tree serve as symbols of tranquility and fertility.

A related way of thinking about this aspect of the Christian hope is the notion of 'paradise'. It is in the Old Testament that we are first introduced to the idea of 'paradise'. The word itself has been borrowed from other languages of the ancient Near East, including the Old Persian word *paradeida*, which probably designates 'an enclosed garden' or perhaps 'a royal park'. The Greek word *paradeisos* – borrowed from the Persian original – is often used in the writings of historian such as Xenophon (444–359 BC) to refer to the great walled gardens of the royal palaces of Persian kings such as Cyrus. The original 'Garden of Eden' (Genesis 2) is referred to as 'paradise' in Greek translations of the Old Testament; the

a restored Garden of Eden. Many Renaissance painters preferred to portray heaven as a great walled park, lush with rich vegetation and animal life. For example, Lorenzo de Medici wrote: 'Paradise means nothing other than a most pleasant garden, abundant with all pleasing and delightful things – trees, apples, flowers, fresh running water, and the songs of the birds.' Many Renaissance artists portrayed paradise in terms of local landscapes. This is strikingly evident in a famous fresco of Benozzo Gozzoli (about 1420–97), which depicts paradise as a Tuscan landscape. The publication of John Milton's *Paradise Lost* created new interest in this way of thinking about heaven. Many English gentry of the seventeenth and eighteenth centuries fashioned their estates after the opulent image of Eden presented in Milton's *Paradise Lost*. The interest spread to the world of art and some artists of the time combined both images, depicting heaven as a citadel within a great park.

Angels gathering flowers in heaven by Benozzo Gozzoli.

term is also used at several points in the original Hebrew text of the Old Testament.

Paradise was seen, like the Garden of Eden, as a place of fertility and harmony, where humanity dwelt in peace with nature and 'walked with God'. That idyllic state had been lost at the dawn of human history. Part of Israel's hopes and expectations for the future centred around the nostalgic longing for a restoration of this paradisiacal relationship with the environment and God. This development was encouraged by the classical Greek translation of the Old Testament – the Septuagint – which used the phrase 'paradise of delight' (Genesis 2:15), translating the Hebrew

term for 'garden' as 'paradise', and interpreting the term 'Eden' in terms of the related word *adanim* ('pleasure' or 'delight').

The Anticipation of Heaven in the Christian Life

'Spirituality' is a term often used in contemporary Christianity to refer to ways of deepening our appreciation of faith, or internalizing its central ideas. A central theme of Christian spirituality concerns how the hope of heaven affects the life and thought of believers today. They live in the hope of what shall be, and their actions in the here and now are driven by a vision of this hope. It is this point which underlies the importance of worship in Christian spirituality. In one sense, to worship God is to step into the life of heaven and share its worship. This idea seems to underlie Isaiah's experience in the Temple, in which he catches a vision of God in his glory:

In the year that King Uzziah died, I saw the Lord sitting on a throne, high and lofty; and the hem of his robe filled the temple. Seraphs were in attendance above him; each had six wings: with two they covered their faces, and with two they covered their feet, and with two they flew. And one called to another and said:

'Holy, holy, holy is the Lord of hosts; the whole earth is full of his glory.'

The pivots on the thresholds shook at the voices of those who called, and the house filled with smoke. And I said: 'Woe is me! I am lost, for I am a man of unclean lips, and I live among a people of unclean lips; yet my eyes have seen the King, the Lord of hosts!' (Isaiah 6:1–5).

The role of worship in sustaining the hope of heaven is developed with

Glimpsing, but not entering, the heavenly realms is symbolized in Orthodox churches by the separation of the people from the altar.

particular clarity in the writings of theologians of the Eastern Christian tradition, such as John Chrysostom (c. 347–407) and Gregory Palamas (1296–1359). These writers argue that to share in worship is to stand in a holy place (Exodus 3:5) – a place in which humanity, strictly speaking, has no right to be. The idea of liminality – that is, being on the threshold of the sacred, peering into the forbidden heavenly realms – is represented visually in the structure of Orthodox churches, especially the way in which the sanctuary and the altar are set apart from the people on account of a deep sense of the awesomeness of the mystery of God.

According to such writers, whenever the divine liturgy is celebrated on earth, the boundaries between heaven and earth are removed, and earthly worshippers join in the eternal heavenly liturgy chanted by the angels. During these moments of earthly adoration, worshippers have the opportunity of being mystically transported to the threshold of heaven. Being in a holy place and about to participate in holy things, they on the one hand become aware of their finiteness and sinfulness, and on the other gain a refreshing glimpse of the glory of God – precisely the pattern of reflection set out in Isaiah's vision.

However, the importance of sustaining the hope of heaven is common to all Christian traditions, and is by no means limited to Greek or Russian Orthodoxy. The theme of a 'longing for heaven' is found throughout the writings of C.S. Lewis. Lewis's first popular book was *The Pilgrim's Regress*, based loosely on John Bunyan's *The Pilgrim's Progress*. It was not a great publishing success. Nevertheless, it contained brilliant insights into the human longing for heaven. Lewis first describes the general human sense of longing, and then interprets it as a specific longing for heaven. Nothing created or finite is able to satisfy this yearning. It comes from God, and is meant to lead to God.

The experience is one of intense longing... This hunger is better than any other fullness; this poverty better than all other wealth. And thus it comes about, that if the desire is long absent, it may itself be desired, and that new desiring becomes a new instance of the original desire... The human soul was made to enjoy some object that is never fully given – nay, cannot even be imagined as given – in our present mode of subjective and spatio–temporal experience.

Throughout his long writing career, Lewis was deeply aware of the power of the human imagination, and the implications of this power for our understanding of reality. Perhaps one of the most original aspects of Lewis's writing is his persistent and powerful appeal to the religious imagination. Lewis was aware of certain deep human emotions which pointed to a dimension of our existence beyond time and space. There is, Lewis suggested, a deep and intense feeling of longing within human beings, which no earthly object or experience can satisfy. Lewis terms this sense 'joy', and argues that it points to God as its source and goal. Its origins lie *in* heaven, and it is intended to draw us *to* heaven. Lewis develops these ideas with particular clarity in his autobiography, *Surprised by Joy*, which is, in part, an extended meditation on the theme of 'joy' – as Lewis understands that term – in the imaginative life of humanity.

In this important book, Lewis explains to his readers how he stumbled across the idea of nature and human experiences as pointers to the transcendent. 'Now, for the first time, there burst upon me the idea that there

> 'Joy is the serious business of heaven.'
> C.S. Lewis

might be real marvels all about us, that the visible world might only be a curtain to conceal huge realms uncharted by my very simple theology.' While still a boy, playing around in the vast attics of the family home, Lewis was encountering the idea of a realm beyond experience which was nevertheless signalled by that experience.

Lewis is clearly reluctant to speculate on the precise character and appearance of heaven. Although his *Great Divorce* offers some reflections on the nature of heaven, his most suggestive accounts of this theme are found in his science fiction trilogy – *Out of the Silent Planet, Perelandra* and *That Hideous Strength* – published during the period 1938–45, and especially in the *Chronicles of Narnia* (1950–56). Here, we find heaven explored using two controlling metaphors. In *Perelandra*, Lewis asks readers to imagine a world without a fall. Here, there is no fundamental separation between 'heaven' and 'earth'. Paradise has not been lost, so cannot be regained. Heaven can thus be depicted in terms of an innocent and chaste world.

Perhaps more significantly, Lewis develops a second metaphor, grounded in the famous analogy of the cave, found in Plato's dialogue *The Republic*. In *The Silver Chair*, the fourth volume of the Narnia cycle, Lewis develops the idea of an underground kingdom, whose inhabitants have never seen the light of day, or experienced the fresh air and brilliant colours of the natural world. Lewis depicts the re-entry of the two children Jill and Eustace from the subterranean gloom of the Underland to the beauty of the natural world as a helpful way of thinking about passing from earth to heaven. As the children 'took in great depths of the free midnight air', they experience a transformation of their situation. And

for Lewis, this seems to be the most that can responsibly be said about heaven – that it represents the world changed, and made more than real. Lewis put it like this in his sermon 'The Weight of Glory'.

At present, we are on the outside of the world, the wrong side of the door... We cannot mingle with the splendours we see. But all the leaves of the New Testament are rustling with the rumour that it will not always be so. Some day, God willing, we shall get in.

The Journey of Faith to Heaven

One of the most powerful visual images of the Christian life is that of a journey. The New Testament tells us that the early Christians initially referred to themselves as followers of 'the way' (see, for example, Acts 9:2; 24:14). Perhaps the one most important journey described in the Old Testament is the wandering of the people of Israel for forty years prior to entering Canaan. Just as God led them out of captivity in Egypt into the Promised Land, so the Christian life can be seen as a slow process of deliverance from bondage to sin before being led triumphantly into the heavenly city.

At several points in the writings of the apostle Paul, a modification is introduced to the image of a journey. For Paul, the Christian life is like a race – a long and arduous journey, undertaken under pressure, in which the winners receive a crown (see Galatians 2:2; 2 Timothy 4:7). The image is also used in the letter to the Hebrews, which urges its readers to persevere in the race of life by keeping their eyes focused firmly on Jesus (Hebrews 12:1–2). This image stresses the importance of discipline in the Christian life.

The theme of 'journeying to heaven' has a long history of use within the

Christian tradition. We have already seen how Bunyan's *Pilgrim's Progress* describes Christian's journey from the 'City of Destruction' to 'the Heavenly City'. The image of a 'journey to the New Jerusalem' helps remind believers that the goal of the Christian life is to arrive safely in the heavenly homeland. Anything that distracts from this task is to be seen as potentially dangerous. For this reason, many spiritual writers stress the importance of cultivating indifference to the world. In his sermon 'The Christian Pilgrim', Jonathan Edwards stresses the importance of this point:

We ought not to rest in the world and its enjoyments, but should desire heaven... We ought above all things to desire a heavenly happiness; to be with God; and dwell with Jesus Christ. Though surrounded with outward enjoyments... we ought to possess, enjoy and use them, with no other view but readily to quit them, whenever we are called to it, and to change them willingly and cheerfully for heaven.

Edwards is not in any way disparaging the world as God's good creation. His concern here is that Christians might come to value the creation more highly than the creator, and as a result settle for something that is good, but not as good as God. Setting one's thoughts on heaven is seen as an antidote to excessive worldliness, just as caring for the world is seen as an antidote to the other-worldliness which prevents Christians from serving and proclaiming Christ in this world.

Christian writings about this journey to the New Jerusalem have been especially influenced by two great journeys of the Old Testament: the exodus from Egypt and entry into the Promised Land; and the return of the people of Jerusalem from their long exile in Babylon. Each of these images shares some features that makes them ideal as a way of thinking about the journey to heaven. First, each represents an exodus from a place of bondage or imprisonment – Egypt, in the case of the exodus, and Babylon, in the case of the exile. Secondly, each is about a journey that leads to a goal – entering the Promised Land, and returning home to Jerusalem. Third, each stresses that the journey is arduous and difficult, with many dangers and discouragements. Yet the goal is so attractive and worthwhile that we are able to bear these burdens with patience, and long to complete the journey. In what follows, we shall explore each of them in a little more detail.

ENTERING THE PROMISED LAND

Many Christian writers see the deliverance of Israel from her captivity in Egypt and entry into the Promised Land as a superb framework for making sense of the pilgrimage of faith from earth to heaven. The story of the Exodus (the Greek word *exodos* literally means 'exit' or 'way out') is well known. A new ruler arises in Egypt, who regards the descendants of Abraham as a potential threat. The identity of this pharaoh is unknown, although there are good reasons for suggesting that it may have been Rameses II (who ruled during the period 1279–1212 BC). He subjected the Hebrews to a series of oppressive measures, designed to limit their numbers and influence. Finally, Moses led Israel to freedom. After forty years wandering in the wilderness of Sinai, Israel entered the Promised Land of Canaan.

As writers such as Jonathan Edwards pointed out, this pattern is repeated in the Christian life. Christians have been liberated from bondage to sin through Christ and are now wandering through the wilderness of the world, on their way to the

Jonathan Edwards, clergyman and preacher in the American Congregational church, who encouraged Christians to focus on God, not his creation.

Charles Wesley and the Hope of Heaven

Charles Wesley (1707–88) underwent a conversion experience in London in May 1738, a few days before John Wesley's famous Aldersgate experience (see page 18). He wrote that he now found himself 'at peace with God and rejoiced in hope of loving Christ'. He went on to serve as curate at St Mary's, Islington; however, he soon left this to pioneer, with his brother John, the art of field-preaching. For more than twenty years, Charles Wesley was one of the central figures in the great evangelical revival of the eighteenth century, pioneering the use of hymns as a way of effectively communicating Christian beliefs.

Many of these hymns were written on horseback, as he travelled from one congregation to another. Wesley can be seen as a pioneer of the literary genre of the popular English hymn. Most of the 9,000 hymns which he penned have been forgotten; others remain as classics, and are still sung to this day. An enduring favourite is 'Love Divine', written in 1747 and soon established as a classic.

1. Love divine, all loves excelling,
joy of heaven, to earth come down;
fix in us thy humble dwelling;
all thy faithful mercies crown!
Jesus thou art all compassion,
pure, unbounded love thou art;
visit us with thy salvation;
enter every trembling heart.

2. Come, Almighty to deliver,
let us all thy life receive;
suddenly return and never,
nevermore thy temples leave.
Thee we would be always blessing,
serve thee as thy hosts above,
pray and praise thee without ceasing,
glory in thy perfect love.

3. Finish, then, thy new creation;
pure and spotless let us be.
Let us see thy great salvation
perfectly restored in thee;
changed from glory into glory,
till in heaven we take our place,
till we cast our crowns before thee,
lost in wonder, love, and praise.

The final verse of Wesley's hymn is a powerful statement of the Christian hope, and is based in part on the vision of heaven set out in the Revelation of John. In the King James Version of the Bible (1611), which Wesley himself used, this passage reads: 'The four and twenty elders fall down before him that sat on the throne, and worship him that liveth for ever and ever, and cast their crowns before the throne, saying, Thou art worthy, O Lord, to receive glory and honour and power: for thou hast created all things, and for thy pleasure they are and were created' (Revelation 4:10–11). The imagery of this passage is vividly incorporated into the hymn, and serves as the anchor for Wesley's exposition of the final Christian hope of being with God forever in heaven.

Promised Land of heaven. They are sojourners in the world, not permanent inhabitants. They are heaven-bound, on their way to the New Jerusalem. They pass through this world, but are citizens of heaven. That is where the true destiny of believers lies, and where they are headed.

RETURNING TO THE HOMELAND FROM EXILE
For Christians, the hope of heaven is about returning to a place where we belong, where a joyful welcome awaits us. The image of returning from exile has long been used as a means of crystallizing this hope and expectation of return to the homeland. The exile of Jerusalem to Babylon took place in 586 BC. Judah was invaded by Babylonian forces, and its armies routed. This event was interpreted by writers of the time as the execution of the promised judgment of God against a faithless people and king. Even the furnishings of the Temple were dismantled, and taken to Babylon as booty. The exile had begun.

Old Testament writings dating from this period show that the exile was interpreted as, in the first place, a judgment against Judah for its lapse into pagan religious beliefs and practices; and in the second, a period of national repentance and renewal, which will lead to the restoration of a resurgent people of God. Yet alongside reflection on the meaning of the exile, there is a heartfelt expression of the unutterable sense of loss and bereavement felt by the exilic community, as they remembered their homeland. Psalm 137:1–4 is perhaps one of the most powerful expressions of the pain of exile, and the longing for restoration.

By the rivers of Babylon –
there we sat down and there we wept
when we remembered Zion.
On the willows there we hung up our
harps.

For there our captors asked us for
songs,
and our tormentors asked for mirth,
saying, 'Sing us one of the songs of
Zion!'
How could we sing the Lord's song in
a foreign land?

This powerful psalm of lament for the homeland offers an organizing image for the complexities of the Christian life. Christians are to see themselves as cut off from their homeland, and nourishing the hope of return from exile, often under difficult and discouraging circumstances.

A very similar idea is also developed in the New Testament, especially in Paul's letter to the church at the Roman colony of Philippi, originally founded as the city of Krenides by an Athenian exile, Callistratus. After Anthony and Octavian defeated Brutus and Cassius there in 42 BC, the city was refounded as a Roman colony. After the defeat of Anthony's forces at Actium eleven years later, Octavian reconstituted the colony once more. The city thus developed a decidedly Italian atmosphere, owing to both the permanent presence of Italian settlers, and the large numbers of Roman troops regularly passing through the city, on account of its strategic location in Macedonia. The language, imagery and outlooks of a Roman colony would thus be part of the everyday thought-world of Paul's audience within the city. Philippi was conscious of its ties with Rome, including its language (Latin seems to have been more widely spoken than Greek) and laws. Roman institutions served as the model in many areas of its communal life.

Paul uses the image of a 'colony (*politeuma*) of heaven' (Philippians 3:20) to bring out several leading aspects of Christian existence. By speaking of the Christian community

> 'The man of faith may face death as Columbus faced his first voyage from the shores of Spain. What lies beyond the sea he cannot tell; all his special expectation may be mistaken, but his insight into the clear meaning of present facts may persuade him beyond doubt that the sea has another shore.'
>
> Harry Emerson Fosdick

in this way, he naturally encourages his readers to think along certain lines. Those strands of thought would certainly include the following. The Christian church is an outpost of heaven in a foreign land. It speaks the language of that homeland, and is governed by its laws – despite the fact that the world around it speaks a different language, and obeys a different set of laws. Its institutions are based on those of its homeland. And, one day, its citizens will return to that homeland, to take up all the privileges and rights which that citizenship confers. This image thus lends dignity and new depths of meaning to the Christian life, especially the tension between the 'now' and 'not yet', and the bitter-sweet feeling of being outsiders to a culture – being in the world and yet not of that world. Christians know they are exiles in the world; citizens of heaven rather than of any earthly city.

> 'Every glimpse of God is his gift, to lead us to long more for that most blessed, ever-longing, ever-satisfied knowledge of him, which shall be the bliss of eternity.'
>
> E.B. Pusey

The Second Coming of Christ

The idea of a 'second coming of Christ' is fundamental to the theme of the Christian hope. The same Christ who came to earth in humility will return to judge it. The lowly Galilean will return as judge of the world. In the gospels, Jesus spoke of the 'Son of Man' returning on the clouds of heaven. This seems to be a reference to Jesus himself, picking up a theme found in the prophecy of Daniel (Daniel 7:13). The same 'Son of Man' who had nowhere to lay his head will return in glory as the judge of the world. It is worth noting that the New Testament never actually uses the

term 'second coming' to refer to this event. It speaks instead simply of Christ's future 'presence' or 'arrival' (an idea expressed in the Greek term *parousia*. The origins of the phrase 'the second coming' may lie in Hebrews 9:28, which speaks of the hope of Christ appearing a 'second time'.

The hope of the return of Christ is found throughout the New Testament. Nobody knows when it will take place; the 'Day of the Lord' will come unexpectedly, like a thief in the night (1 Thessalonians 5:2; 2 Peter 3:10). However, it will be preceded by signs, including the proclamation of the gospel throughout the world (Matthew 24:14), and the onset of tribulation (2 Timothy 3:1–5). Although some Christian writers have taken considerable trouble to identify precisely when the second coming will take place, the New Testament does not encourage this kind of speculation. Rather, it urges believers to live out their lives in the expectation that this will happen. They are to be watchful and alert (Mark 13:33), so that they are not found sleeping on his return (Mark 13:35–7). Believers are to set their hopes on the grace that will be theirs with the final appearance of Christ (1 Peter 1:13–16).

One of the most interesting aspects of early Christian reflection concerning the afterlife is its interest in the idea of the millennium – the period of one thousand years which, according to the book of Revelation, intervenes between the coming of Christ and the final judgment.

The hope of heaven helps believers cope with darkness and difficulties in their lives, knowing that one day Jesus will return to lighten up their lives forever.

Then I saw thrones, and those seated on them were given authority to judge. I also saw the souls of those who had been beheaded for their testimony to Jesus and for the word of God. They had not worshipped the beast or its image and had not received its mark on their foreheads or their hands. They came to life and reigned with Christ for a thousand years (Revelation 20:4).

During this period of a millennium, Christ reigns over a restored earth, until the redeemed are finally transferred to their permanent resting place in heaven. The third-century writer Tertullian describes this as follows:

We also hold that a kingdom has been promised to us on earth, but before heaven: but in another state than this, as being after the resurrection. This will last for a thousand years, in a city of God's own making, the Jerusalem which has been brought down from heaven which the Apostle also designates as 'our mother from above' [Galatians 4:26].

Early Christian writers found it irresistible to speculate on what this period of one thousand years might be like. During this era, the earth would be restored to its former status of paradise, and humanity would enjoy the privileges of Adam and Eve. There has also been considerable debate within some Christian circles over how best to understand this idea. In recent years, three general positions have emerged: *millennialism* (the return of Christ leads directly to judgment and eternal life for believers); *premillennialism* (the return of Christ leads to a period of one thousand years in which the saints reign on earth, followed by the general resurrection from the dead); and *postmillennialism* (the return of

Christ takes place after a period of Christian growth and expansion).

A final theme of the Christian hope is sometimes referred to as the 'beatific vision' – the promise of seeing God face to face. In the Old Testament, divine favour is indicated by the face of God being turned towards an individual, just as disfavour is signalled by that face being averted. In cultic petitions of this period, worshippers might invoke God not to turn his face away as a means of securing the acceptance of the sacrifices or prayers being offered (Psalm 27:9; 132:10). If the face of God were 'hidden' or 'turned away,' the believer had no hope of finding divine acceptance (Deuteronomy 31:17; Ezekiel 7:22).

Yet the image of the 'face of God' concerns far more than the notion of the divine pleasure and favour; it evokes the possibility of an encounter with the living God. To 'see the face of God' is to have a privileged, intimate relationship with God – seeing God 'as God actually is' (1 John 3:2), rather than having to know God indirectly, through images and shadows. Now we see God 'as through a glass, darkly;' but we shall finally see God face to face (1 Corinthians 13:12). The book of Revelation affirms that this will be the privilege of those in heaven, where the saints will finally 'see God's face' (Revelation 22:4). The Psalmist set out his longing to see God in these words (Psalm 27:4):

One thing I ask of the Lord,
This is what I seek;
That I may dwell in the house of the Lord
All the days of my life,
To gaze upon the beauty of the Lord.

That, in a nutshell, is the Christian hope. Believers are called to set our hearts firmly upon this wonderful hope, and not to allow anything to distract us from it (Colossians 3:1–4). The

Christian vision of the hope of heaven affirms that what the Psalmist longed for all his life will one day be the common privilege of the entire people of God – to gaze upon the face of their Lord and Saviour, as they enter into his house, to dwell there in peace forever.

Perhaps it is appropriate to allow one of the church's greatest preachers and hymnwriters to have the final word on this topic. Horatius Bonar (1808–89) is perhaps best known for his hymns 'Fill thou my life, O Lord my God' and 'I heard the voice of Jesus say'. Bonar knew great suffering in his personal life: five of his children died in quick succession, leaving him and his wife utterly bereft. Yet the hope of glory kept him going. Belief illuminated the darker side of life, allowing him to look beyond his personal tragedy to the glory that awaited him.

We see here how the Christian hope consoles those who walk though the valley of the shadow of death. For Bonar, it is essential to keep our experience of suffering firmly illuminated by the Christian hope. As he put it in one of his sermons:

'If we suffer, we shall also reign with him' (2 Timothy 2:12). Of this we are assured. Oneness in suffering here is the pledge of oneness in glory hereafter. The two things are inseparable. His shame is ours on earth; his glory shall be ours in heaven. Therefore let us 'rejoice, inasmuch as we are partakers of Christ's sufferings; that, when his glory shall be revealed, we may be glad also with exceeding joy' (1 Peter 4:13).

The hope of heaven allows believers to carry on through the vale of suffering, coping with the hardship of exile, yet knowing that its days are numbered. Like Bonar, they know that one day, they shall return home.

We are but as wayfaring men, wandering in the lonely night, who see dimly upon the distant mountain peak the reflection of a sun that never rises here, but which shall never set in the 'new heavens' thereafter. And this is enough. It comforts and cheers us on our dark and rugged way.

Concise Anthology of Christian Thought

Justin Martyr (died c.165)

We confess that we are atheists, as far as gods of this sort [those of Greco-Roman religion] are concerned, but not with respect to the most true God, the Father of righteousness and temperance and the other virtues, who is free from all impurity. But both him, and the Son who came forth from him and taught us these things, and the host of the other good angels who follow and are made like to him, and the prophetic Spirit we worship and adore, knowing them in reason and truth.

Apology

We have been taught that Christ is the first-born of God, and we have declared above that he is the Word [or reason] of whom all mankind partakes. Those who lived reasonably [with the Word] are Christians, even though they have been called atheists. For example: among the Greeks, Socrates, Heraclitus and men like them; among the barbarians [non-Greeks], Abraham... and many others whose actions and names we now decline to recount, because we know it would be tedious.

Apology

In the name of God, the Father and Lord of the universe, and of our Saviour Jesus Christ, and of the Holy Spirit, they then receive the washing with water... there is pronounced in the water over him the name of God the Father and Lord of the universe... and in the name of Jesus Christ, who was crucified under Pontius Pilate, and in the name of the Holy Ghost, who through the prophets foretold all things about Jesus, he who is illuminated is washed.

Apology

Irenaeus (died c.180)

God the Father uncreated, who is uncontained, invisible, one God, creator of the universe; this is the first article of our faith... And the *Word of God*, the Son of God, our Lord Jesus Christ... who, in the fullness of time, in order to gather all things to himself, he became a human being amongst human beings, capable of being seen and touched, to destroy death, bring life, and restore fellowship between God and humanity. And the *Holy Spirit*... who, in the fullness of time, was poured out in a new way on our human nature in order to renew humanity throughout the entire world in the sight of God.

Demonstration of the Apostolic Preaching

All who wish to see the truth can clearly contemplate, in every church, the tradition of the apostles manifested throughout the whole world. We can list those who were by the apostles appointed bishops in the churches and their successors down to our own time. They neither taught nor knew anything like what these heretics rave about. Suppose the apostles had known hidden mysteries which they were in the habit of imparting to 'the perfect' privately and in secret. Surely they would have handed them down especially to those to whom they were also entrusting the churches themselves. For they wanted their successors to be perfect and blameless in everything.

Against Heresies

The church, though scattered throughout the whole world to the ends of the earth, has received from the apostles and their disciples this faith: in one God, the Father almighty, maker of heaven and earth and the sea and all things in them; and in one Christ Jesus, the Son of God, who was made flesh for our salvation; and in the Holy Spirit, who through the prophets proclaimed God's saving dealings with man and the coming, virgin birth, passion, resurrection from the dead and bodily ascension into heaven of our beloved Lord Jesus Christ and his second coming from heaven in the glory of the Father to sum up all things and to raise up all human flesh so that... he should execute just judgment upon all men.

Against Heresies

The heavenly treasures are indeed great: God cannot be measured in the heart, and he is incomprehensible in the mind; he who holds the earth in the hollow of his hand. Who perceives the measure of his right hand? Who knows his finger? Or who understands his hand – that hand which measures immensity; that hand which, by its own measure, spreads out the measure of the heavens, and which holds in its hollow the earth with the abysses; which contains in itself the breadth, and length, and the deep below, and the height above the whole creation; which is seen, which is heard and understood, and which is invisible? And for this reason God is 'above all principality, and power, and dominion, and every name that is named', of all things which have been created and established. He it is who fills the heavens, and views the abysses, who is also present with every one of us.

Against Heresies

Tertullian (c.160–220)

It is clear that all doctrine which agrees with the apostolic churches – those moulds and original sources of the faith – must be considered true, as undoubtedly containing what those churches received from the Apostles, the Apostles from Christ, Christ from God. And all doctrine must be considered false which contradicts the truth of the churches and Apostles of Christ and God.

Prescription Against the Heretics

The Word, therefore, is incarnate; and this must be the point of our inquiry: How the Word became flesh – whether it was by having been transfigured, as it were, in the flesh, or by having really clothed Himself in flesh. Certainly it was to be unchangeable, and incapable of form, as being eternal. But transfiguration is the destruction of that which previously existed. For whatever is transfigured into some other thing ceases to be that which it had been, and begins to be that which it previously was not. God, however, neither ceases to be what He was, nor can He be any other thing than what He is. The Word is God.

Against Praxeas

We see plainly [in Jesus Christ] the twofold state, which is not confounded, but conjoined in One Person-Jesus, God and Man. Concerning Christ, indeed, I defer what I have to say. [I remark here] that the property of each nature is so wholly preserved, that the Spirit on the one hand did all things in Jesus suitable to Itself, such as miracles, and mighty deeds, and wonders; and the Flesh, on the other hand, exhibited the affections which belong to it.

Against Praxeas

All of them are One, by unity of substance; while we still keep the mystery of the distribution which spreads the Unity into a Trinity, placing in their order the three Persons – the Father, the Son, and the Holy Spirit. But they are three, not in state, but in degree; not in substance, but in form; not in power, but in appearance; yet of one substance, and of one state, and of one power, inasmuch as he is one God, from whom these degrees and forms and appearances are understood, under the name of the Father, and of the Son, and of the Holy Spirit.

Against Praxeas

The Son of God was crucified. I am not ashamed, because it is shameful. The Son of God died. It is credible because it is absurd. He was buried and rose again. It is certain because it is impossible.

The Flesh of Christ

Origen (c.185–253)

The teaching of the church has been transmitted in orderly succession from the apostles and remains in the churches to the present day. That alone is to be accepted as true which in no way conflicts with the tradition of the church and the apostles. The holy apostles, when preaching the faith of Christ, took certain points which they believed to be necessary for everyone and delivered them in the clearest way… The kind of doctrines which are clearly delivered in the teaching of the apostles are as follows: first, that there is one God… secondly, that Jesus Christ himself… was born of the Father before all creatures… thirdly, that the Holy Spirit was associated in honour and dignity with the Father and the Son… After these points the apostolic teaching is that the soul… shall after its departure from the world be rewarded according to its desserts… Regarding the devil and his angels and the opposing spiritual powers, the teaching of the church lays down that these beings indeed exist… It is also part of the church's teaching that the world was made and began at a certain time and that it is to be destroyed on account of its wickedness… Then, finally, that the scriptures were written by the Spirit of God and that they have not only an obvious meaning but also another meaning which escapes the notice of most people.

On First Principles

The God and Father, who holds the universe together, is superior to every being that exists… the Son, being less than the Father, is superior to rational creatures alone (for he is second to the Father); the Holy Spirit is still less, and dwells within the saints alone.

On First Principles

God must not be thought to be any kind of body, nor to exist in a body, but to be a simple intellectual existence, without any addition whatsoever, so that he cannot be believed to have in himself a more or a less, but in Unity, or if I may say, Oneness throughout, and the mind and fount from which originates all intellectual existence.

On First Principles

Athanasius (c.295–373)

And so it was that two marvels came to pass at once, that the death of all was accomplished in the Lord's body, and that death and corruption were wholly done away by reason of the Word that was united with it. For there was need of death, and death must needs be suffered on behalf of all, that the debt owing from all might be paid. Whence as I said before, the Word, since it was not possible for Him to die, as He was immortal, took to Himself a body such as could die, that He might offer it as His own in the stead of all, and as suffering, through His union with it, on behalf of all, 'Bring to nought Him that had the power of death, that is the devil; and might deliver them who through fear of death were all their lifetime subject to bondage'.

The Incarnation of the Word

We were the cause of his becoming flesh. For our salvation he loved us so much as to appear and be born in a human body… No one else but the Saviour himself, who in the beginning made everything out of nothing, could bring the corrupted to incorruption; no one else but the Image of the Father could recreate men in God's image; no one else but our Lord Jesus Christ, who is Life itself, could make the mortal immortal; no one else but the Word, who orders everything and is alone the true and only-begotten Son of the Father, could teach men about the Father and destroy idolatry. Since the debt owed by all men had to be paid (for all men had to die), he came among us. After he had demonstrated his deity by his words, he offered his sacrifice on behalf of all and surrendered his temple (body) to death in the place of all men. He did this to free men from the guilt of the first sin and to prove himself more powerful than death, showing his own body incorruptible, as a first-fruit of the resurrection of all… Two miracles happened at once: the death of all men was accomplished in the Lord's body, and death and corruption were destroyed because of the Word who was united with it. By death immortality has reached all and by the Word becoming man the universal providence and its creator and leader, the very Word of God, has been made known. For he became human that we might become divine; he revealed himself in a body that we might understand the unseen Father; he endured men's insults that we might inherit immortality.

The Incarnation of the Word

Were he [the Word] a mere creature he would not have been worshipped nor spoken of [as in the Bible]. But he is in fact the real offspring of the substance of the God who is worshipped, his Son by nature, not a creature. Therefore he is worshipped and believed to be God… The sun's rays belong really to it and yet the sun's substance is not divided or lessened. The sun's substance is whole and its rays are perfect and whole. These rays do not lessen the substance of the light but are a true offspring from it. Likewise we understand that the Son is begotten not from outside the Father but from the Father himself. The Father remains whole while 'the stamp of his substance' [Hebrews 1:3] is eternal and preserves the Father's likeness and unchanging image.

Orations Against the Arians

Athanasian Creed

Whoever wants to be saved must first of all hold the Catholic faith. Unless one keeps this faith whole and inviolate, he will without doubt perish eternally.

Now this is the Catholic faith: that we worship one God in trinity and trinity in unity – neither confusing persons, nor dividing the substance. For the Father's person is one, the Son's another and the Holy Spirit's another. But the deity of Father, Son and Holy Spirit is one. Their glory is equal and their majesty coeternal.

Whatever the Father is, such is the Son and such also the Holy Spirit. The Father is uncreated, the Son uncreated and the Holy Spirit uncreated. The Father is infinite, the Son infinite and the Holy Spirit infinite. The Father is eternal, the Son eternal and the Holy Spirit eternal. Yet there are not three eternals but only one eternal – just as there are not three uncreateds nor three infinites but only one uncreated and only one infinite. Likewise the Father is almighty, the Son almighty and the Holy Spirit almighty – yet there are not three almighties but only one almighty.

Thus the Father is God, the Son is God and the Holy Spirit is God – yet there are not three Gods, but only one God. Thus the Father is Lord, the Son Lord and the Holy Spirit Lord – yet there are not three Lords but only one Lord. For just as Christian truth compels us to acknowledge each person by himself to be God and Lord, so the Catholic religion forbids us to speak of three Gods or Lords.

The Father is neither made nor created nor begotten from anything. The Son is from the Father alone – not made nor created but begotten. The Holy Spirit is from the Father and the Son – not made nor created nor begotten but proceeding. So there is one Father, not three Fathers; one Son, not three Sons; one Holy Spirit, not three Holy Spirits. And in this trinity no one is before or after another; no one is greater or less than another, but all three persons are coeternal and coequal with each other. Thus in all things, as has been said, both trinity in unity and unity in trinity are to be worshipped. This is how to think of the Trinity if you want to be saved.

But for eternal salvation it is also necessary to believe faithfully in the Incarnation of our Lord Jesus Christ. For correct faith is believing and confessing that our Lord Jesus Christ the Son of God, is equally God and man. God he is, begotten from the Father's substance before time; man he is, born from his mother's substance in time. He is both perfect God and perfect man, composed of a rational soul and human flesh. He is equal to the Father, as God; less than the Father, as man.

Although he is both God and man, yet he is not two but one Christ. He is one however, not by the conversion of his deity into flesh, but by the taking up of his humanity into God. He is one indeed, not by confusion of substance, but by unity of person. For just as rational soul and flesh make one man, so also God and man make one Christ.

He suffered for our salvation, descended into hell, rose from the dead, ascended into the heavens and sat at the right hand of the Father. He will come from there to judge the living and the dead. When he comes, all men will rise again with their bodies and will render account for their own deeds. Those who have done good will go to eternal life, those who have done evil to eternal fire.

This is the Catholic faith. Unless one believes it faithfully and firmly, one cannot be saved.

Creed of First Council of Nicea (325)

We believe in God the Father almighty,
maker of all things, visible and
    invisible.
And in one Lord Jesus Christ,
the only-begotten of the Father,
that is, begotten of the substance of
    the Father,
God from God, light from light, true
    God from true God,
begotten not made,
of the same substance as the Father,
through whom all things were made,
    in heaven and earth;
who for us humans and our salvation
    came down, took flesh, and was
    made human,
suffered and rose again on the third
    day,
ascended into heaven,
and will come to judge the living and
    the dead.
And in the Holy Spirit.

Basil of Caesarea (c.329–79)

Substance relates to hypostasis as universal relates to particular. Each of us shares in existence through the common substance and yet is a specific individual because of his own characteristics. So also with God, substance refers to that which is common, like goodness, deity or other attributes, while hypostasis is seen in the special characteristics of fatherhood, sonship or sanctifying power.

Letter 214

Gregory of Nyssa (c.335–395)

Since with men we can distinguish each one's action while they are pursuing the same task, they are rightly called many men. Each of them is separated from the others by his particular environment and way of working. It is not so with God. We do not learn that the Father does anything on his own without the cooperation of the Son. Nor does the Son act on his own without the Holy Spirit. But every act which extends from God to the creation… originates with the Father; proceeds through the Son and is completed by the Holy Spirit… The holy Trinity effects every act not by separate action according to the number of the persons, but so that there is one motion and disposition of the goodwill which proceeds from the Father; through the Son to the Spirit. So we cannot call those who jointly, inseparably and mutually exercise divine and superintending power and activity to us and all creation, three Gods.

That There Are Not Three Gods

Gregory of Nazianus (died 390)

When I speak of God, you must be enlightened at the same time by one flash of light and by three. There are three individualities or hypostases or, if you prefer, persons. (Why argue about names when the words amount to the same meaning?) There is one substance – i.e. deity. For God is divided without division, if I may put it like that, and united in division. The Godhead is one in three and the three are one. The Godhead has its being in the three or, to be more precise, the Godhead is the three… We must neither heretically fuse God together into one [Monarchianism] nor chop him up into inequality [Arianism].

Oration

Anyone who has trusted Christ as a man without a human mind is himself mindless and unworthy of complete salvation. For what [Christ] has not assumed, he has not healed. It is what he has united to his Godhead that is saved. If only half of Adam fell, then it would suffice for Christ to assume and save only half of man. But if it is the whole of human nature that fell, it must be united to the whole nature of [Christ] and thus be saved, wholly.

Letter 101

Augustine of Hippo (354–430)

For the Christian it is enough to believe that the cause of all created things, in heaven and on earth, visible or invisible, is none other than the goodness of the creator, who is the one and true God: that there is no being whatsoever but God Himself or what comes from Him… As even the infidels admit, the omnipotent God, primal Power of the world, being Himself supremely good, could not permit anything evil in His works, were He not so all-powerful and good as to be able to bring good even out of evil.

Enchiridion

Wherefore, Christ Jesus, the Son of God, is both God and man. He is God before all ages; man in our own time. He is God because He is the Word of God, for *the Word was God*. But He is man because in His own Person there were joined to the Word a rational soul and a body. Therefore, so far as He is God, He and the Father are one; but so far as He is a man, the Father is greater than He. Since He was the only Son of God, not by grace but by nature, in order that He should be full of grace He became likewise the Son of Man; and did not make Him two sons of God, but one Son of God: God without beginning, man with a definite beginning – our Lord Jesus Christ.

Enchiridion

Thus the true Mediator, who 'took the form of a servant' and was thus made 'the mediator between God and humanity, the person Christ Jesus' (1 Timothy 2:5), receives the sacrifice in the 'form of God' (Philippians 2:7, 8), in union with the Father, with whom he is one God. And yet, in the 'form of a servant', he determined to be himself that sacrifice, rather than to receive it, in order to prevent anyone from thinking that such a sacrifice should be offered to any creature. Thus he is both the priest, who made the offering himself, and the oblation.

de civitate Dei

This grace, which perfects strength in weakness, brings everyone who is predestined and called by God to supreme perfection and glory. This grace not only shows us what we ought to do, it makes us do it. It not only makes us believe what we ought to love, it makes us love it.

On the Grace of Christ

Cyril of Alexandria (d. c.444)

We do not say that the nature of the Word was changed and became flesh, nor that it was converted into a whole man, consisting of body and soul. But this we say: that the Word, in a way beyond words or understanding, hypostatically united to himself flesh animated by a rational soul and became man… So then, he who had an existence before all ages and was born of the Father, is said to have been born after the flesh, from a woman. It is not that his divine nature took its beginning from the holy virgin… but because for us and for our salvation he hypostatically united to himself a human body and came forth from a woman, he is said to be born after the flesh… We must not divide the one Lord Jesus Christ into two sons [Son of God and Son of Man]. Nor is it sufficient for sound doctrine merely to hold a union of [two] persons, as do some [Nestorius]. For scripture says not that the Word united himself to the person of a man, but that he was made flesh. That means nothing else than that he partook of flesh and blood like us. He made our body his own, not ceasing to be God.

Letter 4

If anyone will not confess that the Lord's flesh is life-giving and that it is the own flesh of the Word of God the Father – but pretends that it belongs to some other person who is united with him only in honour and in whom the deity dwells – if anyone will not confess that his flesh gives life, because it is the flesh of the Word who gives life to all, let him be anathema.

Anathema

If anyone using the expression 'in two natures'… shall make use of the number [two] to divide the natures or to make of them persons properly so called, let him be anathema.

Anathema

If anyone uses the expression 'out of two natures'… or the expression 'the one incarnate nature of God the Word' and shall not understand these expressions as the holy fathers have taught… but shall try to introduce one nature or substance of the Godhead and manhood of Christ, let him be anathema. For in teaching that the only-begotten Word was united hypostatically [to humanity] we do not mean to say that there was a mutual confusion of natures.

Anathema

If anyone does not confess that our Lord Jesus Christ who was crucified in the flesh is true God and the Lord of Glory and one of the Holy Trinity, let him be anathema.

Anathema

Maximus the Confessor (580–662)

Christ was God by nature and made use of a will which was naturally divine and paternal, for he had but one will with his Father. He was also man by nature and made use of a naturally human will, which was in no way opposed to the Father's will.

Theological and Polemical Works: Short Note

We know God not in his essence but by the magnificence of his creation and the action of his providence, which present to us, as in a mirror, the reflection of his goodness, his wisdom and his infinite powers.

Centuries on Charity

God, and so also the divine, is comprehensible from a certain point of view, incomprehensible from others. Comprehensible in the contemplation of his attributes, incomprehensible in the contemplation of his essence.

Centuries on Charity

Symeon the New Theologian (949–1022)

But your nature is your essence, and your essence your nature. So uniting with your body, I share in your nature, and I truly take as mine what is yours, uniting with your divinity… Glory be to your kindness and to the plan, by which you became human, you who by nature are God, without change or confusion, remaining the same, and that you have made me a god, a mortal by my nature, a god by your grace, by the power of your Spirit, bringing together as god a unity of opposites.

Hymns of Divine Love

Whenever someone sees God revealed, he sees light. He is amazed at what he sees – but at the same time he does not know straight away who has appeared. He does not even dare ask. How could he? He cannot even life up his eyes and gaze upon that majesty. Instead, overcome by fear and trembling, he looks down at his own feet.

On the Mystical Life

Gregory Palamas (c.1296–1359)

Since one can participate in God and since the super-essential essence of God is absolutely above participation, there exists something between the essence (which cannot be participated in) and those who participate, to make it possible for them to participate in God… He makes himself present to be all things by his manifestations and by his creative and providential energies. In one word, we must seek a God in whom we can participate in one way or another, so that by participating each of us, in the manner proper to each and by the analogy of participation, may receive being, life and deification.

Triads

He is being and not being… He is everywhere and nowhere; He has many names and cannot be named; He is both in perpetual movement and immovable; He is absolutely everything and nothing of that which is.

Apology

The king of all is everywhere, and his kingdom is everywhere. This means that the coming of the kingdom cannot mean that it is transferred from this place here to that place there, but that it is revealed in the power of the divine Spirit. This is why [Christ] said 'coming with power'. And this power does not come upon everyone, but upon 'those who have stood with the Lord', that is, those who are firmly grounded in the faith, such as Peter, James and John, who were first brought by the Word to this high mountain, in order to symbolize those who are thus able to rise above their humble natures. For this reason, Scripture shows us God descending from this supreme dwelling place and raising us up from our humble condition on a mountain, so that the one who is infinite may be surely but within limits encompassed by created nature.

Homilia 34

Anselm of Canterbury (c.1033–1109)

This [definition of God] is indeed so true that it cannot be thought of as not being true. For it is quite possible to think of something whose non-existence cannot be thought of. This must be greater than something whose non-existence can be thought of. So if this thing (than which no greater thing can be thought) can be thought of as not existing, then, that very thing than which a greater thing cannot be thought is not that than which a greater cannot be thought. This is a contradiction. So it is true that there exists something than which nothing greater can be thought, that it cannot be thought of as not existing. And you are this thing, O Lord our God! So truly therefore do

you exist, O Lord my God, that you cannot be thought of as not existing, and with good reason, for if a human mind could think of anything greater than you, the creature would rise above the creator and judge you; which is obviously absurd. And in truth, whatever else there be beside you may be thought of as not existing. So you alone, most truly of all, and therefore most of all, have existence: because whatever else exists, does not exist as truly as you, and therefore exists to a lesser degree.

Proslogion

Peter Abelard (1079–1141)

Indeed, how cruel and wicked it seems that anyone should demand the blood of an innocent person as the price for anything, or that it should in any way please him that an innocent man should be slain – still less that God should consider the death of his Son so agreeable that by it he should be reconciled to the whole world! These and like queries appear to us to pose a considerable problem concerning our redemption or justification through the death of our Lord Jesus Christ.

Exposition of Romans (3:19–26)

Now it seems to us that we have been justified by the blood of Christ and reconciled to God in this way: through this unique act of grace manifested to us – in that his Son has taken upon himself our nature and persevered therein in teaching us by word and example even unto death – he has more fully bound us to himself by love. The result is that our hearts should be enkindled by such a gift of divine grace, and true love should not now shrink from enduring anything for him.

Exposition of Romans (3:19–26)

Love is increased by the faith which we have concerning Christ because, on account of the belief that God in Christ has united our human nature to himself, and by suffering in that same nature has demonstrated to us that supreme love which Christ himself speaks... 'Greater love has no one than this' (John 15:13). We are thus joined through his grace to him and our neighbour by an unbreakable bond of love... therefore, our redemption through the suffering of Christ is that deeper love within us which not only frees us from slavery to sin, but also secures for us the true liberty of the children of God, in order that we might do all things out of love rather than out of fear – love for him who has shown us such grace that no greater can be found.

Exposition of Romans

Thomas Aquinas (1225–74)

It is commonly said that God is almighty. Yet it seems difficult to understand the reason for this, on account of the doubt about what is meant when it is said that 'God can do "everything"'... If it is said that God is omnipotent because he can do everything possible to his power, the understanding of omnipotence is circular, doing nothing more than saying God is omnipotent because he can do everything that he can do... To sin is to fall short of a perfect action. Hence to be able to sin is to be able to be deficient in relation to an action, which cannot be reconciled with omnipotence. It is because God is omnipotent that he cannot sin.

Compendium of Theology

A proper satisfaction comes about when someone offers to the person offended something which gives him a delight greater than his hatred of the offence. Now Christ by suffering as a result of love and obedience offered to God something greater than what might be extracted in compensation for the whole offence of humanity; firstly, because of the greatness of the love, as a result of

which he suffered; secondly, because of the worth of the life which he laid down for a satisfaction, which was the life of God and of a human being; thirdly, because of the comprehensiveness of his passion and the greatness of the sorrow which he took upon himself.

Summa Theologiae

Names applied to God and to other beings are not used either entirely univocally or entirely equivocally... They are used according to analogy... For, from the fact that we compare other things with God as their first origin, we attribute to God such names as signify perfections in other things. This clearly brings out the truth that, as regards the giving of the names, such names are used primarily of creatures, inasmuch as the intellect that gives the names ascends from creatures to God. But as regards the thing signified by the name, they are used primarily of God, from whom the perfections descend to other beings.

Compendium of Theology

Some have held that after the consecration the substance of the bread and the wine remains in this sacrament. But this position cannot be sustained. First of all it would destroy the reality of this sacrament, which demands that the very body of Christ exist in it. Now, his body is not there before the consecration. But a thing cannot be where it was not before, except by being brought in locally or by something already there being changed into it... Now it is clear that the body of Christ does not begin to exist in this sacrament by being brought in locally. First, because it would thereby cease to be in heaven, since anything that is locally moved begins to be somewhere only by leaving where it was... For these reasons it remains that there is no other way in which the body of Christ can begin to be in this sacrament except through the substance of bread being changed into it. Now, what is changed into something else is no longer there after the change. The reality of Christ's body in this sacrament demands, then, that the substance of bread be no longer there after the consecration.

Summa Theologiae

It is obvious to our senses that, after the consecration, all the accidents of the bread and wine remain. Divine providence very wisely arranged for this. First of all, men have not the custom of eating human flesh and drinking human blood; indeed the thought revolts them. And so the flesh and blood of Christ are given to us to be taken under the appearances of things in common human use – namely bread and wine. Secondly, lest this sacrament should be an object of contempt for unbelievers, if we were to eat our Lord under his human appearances. Thirdly, in taking the body and blood of our Lord in their invisible presence, we increase the merit of our faith [by believing against the evidence of our senses].

Summa Theologiae

Now according to this mode of his being under the sacrament, Christ is not moved locally in any strict sense, but only after a fashion. Christ is not in this sacrament as if he were in a place, as we have already said: and what is not in a place is not moved locally, but is only said to be moved when that in which it is is moved.

Summa Theologiae

Bonaventure (1221–74)

Whoever wishes to ascend to God must first avoid sin, which deforms our nature, then exercise his natural powers mentioned above: by praying, to receive restoring grace; by a good life, to receive purifying justice; by meditating, to receive illuminating knowledge; and by contemplating, to receive perfecting wisdom. Just as no one comes to wisdom except through grace, justice and knowledge, so no one comes to contemplation except by penetrating meditation, a holy life and devout prayer.

Journey of the Soul into God

Nothing can be understood unless God himself by his eternal truth immediately enlightens him who understands... God is to be called our teacher because our intellect attains to him as to the light of our minds and the principle by which we know every truth.

Disputed Questions Concerning Christ's Knowledge

In the Old Law, there were ointments of a kind, but they were figurative and did not heal. The disease was lethal, but the anointings were superficial... Genuinely healing ointments must bring both spiritual anointing and a life-giving power; it was only Christ our Lord who did this, since... through his death, the sacraments have the power to bring life.

Sententiae in IV Libris Distinctae, vol 2

John Scotus Erigena (c.810–77)

And what, O Lord, is that coming of yours but an ascent through the infinite steps of your contemplation? – for you always come to the intellects of those who seek and find you. You are sought by them always, and are found always, and are not found always. You are found indeed in your appearances, in which in many ways... you encounter the minds of those who understand you in the way in which you allow yourself to be understood – not what you are, but what you are not, and that you are. But you are not found in your superessence, by which you surpass and excel all intellect.

Division of Nature

John Wyclif (c.1330–84)

As far as the work of a prophet goes, it is clear from the example of John the Baptist and Christ that every prophet ought to speak the truth to the edification of the people until the day he dies.

Sermones I

Lack of faith is the cause of all unnecessary anxiety.

Sermones I

It is God's way to make his Words pregnant with the fruitfulness of many meanings.

Sermones IV

Endless peace in the world is not to be compared with the smallest peace of God, for it is uncertain, and dependent on the changing wishes of sinners.

Sermones IV

Scripture is a secure refuge to anyone who reads it with respect, because of its impenetrable depths.

On the truth of Holy Scripture I

If someone lives in grace, everything he does is directed by the Holy Spirit

On the truth of Holy Scripture I

Martin Luther (1483–1546)

Even if an angel were to come down from heaven and appear in front of me, it would not make me believe any more. I have the bond and seal of my Saviour, Jesus Christ. I have his Word, Spirit, and sacrament. It is on these that I depend, and I need no new revelations.

Table Talk

Faith does not merely mean that the soul realizes that the divine world is full of all grace, free and holy; it also unites the soul with Christ, as a bride is united with her bridegroom. From such a marriage, as St Paul says (Ephesians 5:31-2), it follows that Christ and the soul become one body, so that they hold all things in common, whether for better or worse. This means that what Christ possesses belongs to the believing soul; and what the soul possesses belongs to Christ. Thus Christ possesses all good things and holiness; these now belong to the soul. The soul possesses lots of vices and sin; these now belong to Christ.

The Freedom of a Christian

I hated that phrase, 'the righteousness of God,' which I had been taught to understand as the righteousness by which God is righteous, and punishes unrighteous sinners. Although I lived a blameless life as a monk, I felt that I was a sinner with an uneasy conscience before God. I also could not believe that I had pleased him with my works. Far from loving that righteous God who punished sinners, I actually hated him… I was in desperation to know what Paul meant in this passage [Romans 1:17]. At last, as I meditated day and night on the relation of the words 'the righteousness of God is revealed in it, as it is written, the righteous person shall live by faith,' I began to understand that 'righteousness of God' as that by which the righteous person lives by the gift of God (faith); and this sentence, 'the righteousness of God is revealed,' to refer to a passive righteousness, by which the merciful God justifies us by faith, as it is written, 'the righteous person lives by faith'. This immediately made me feel as though I had been born again, and as though I had entered through open gates into paradise itself. From that moment, I saw the whole face of Scripture in a new light… And now, where I had once hated the phrase, 'the righteousness of God', I began to love and extol it as the sweetest of phrases, so that this passage in Paul became the very gate of paradise to men.

Preface to the Latin Works

To receive this sacrament in bread and wine, then, is nothing else than to receive a sure sign of this fellowship and union with Christ and all the saints. It is as if citizens were given a sign, a document, or some other token, to assure them that they are indeed citizens of the city, and members of that particular community... In this sacrament, therefore, we are given a sure sign from God that we are united with Christ and the saints, and have all things in common with them, and that Christ's suffering and life are our own.

The Blessed Sacrament of the Holy and True Body of Christ

Where there is the Word of the God who makes promises, there must necessarily be the faith of the person who accepts those promises. It is clear that the beginning of our salvation is a faith which clings to the Word of a promising God who, without any effort on our part, in free and unmerited mercy goes before us and offers us a word of promise.

The Babylonian Captivity of the Church

Huldreich Zwingli (1484–1531)

I believe that in the holy eucharist (that is, the supper of thanksgiving) the true body of Christ is present by the contemplation of faith. In other words, those who thank the Lord for the kindness conferred on us in his Son acknowledge that he assumed true flesh and in it truly suffered and truly washed away our sins by his own blood. Thus everything done by Christ becomes present to them by the contemplation of faith. But that the body of Christ, that is his natural body in essence and reality, is either present in the Supper or eaten with our mouth and teeth, as is asserted by the papists and by some who long for the fleshpots of Egypt [Lutherans], we not only deny but firmly maintain to be an error opposed to God's word... The natural body of Christ is not eaten with our mouth as he himself showed when he said to the Jews who were disputing about the corporeal eating of his flesh, 'The flesh counts for nothing' [John 6:63]... The words 'This is my body' should be received not literally, but figuratively, just as the words 'This is the passover' [Exodus 12:11].

Confession of Faith

Faith exists in our hearts through the Spirit of God, and we are sensible of it. In fact, that there is an inward change of heart is not an obscure matter, but we do not perceive it by means of the senses... Although faith is hope and trust in things quite remote from sense, nevertheless it does not rest upon our decision or election. The things upon which we set our hopes themselves cause us to put all our hopes upon them; for if we were made believers by our own election or determination, all men could become believers by their own strength, even the impious... In short, faith does not compel sense to confess that it perceives what it does not perceive, but it draws us to the invisible and fixes our hopes on that.

On True and False Religion

John Calvin (1509–64)

Now we shall have a right definition of faith if we say that it is a steady and a certain knowledge of the divine benevolence towards us, which is founded upon the truth of the gracious promise of God in Christ, and is both revealed to our minds and sealed in our hearts by the Holy Spirit.

Institutes of the Christian Religion

There is within the human mind, and that by natural instinct, a sense of divinity. This we take to be beyond controversy. So that no one might take refuge in the pretext of ignorance, God frequently renews and sometimes increases this awareness, so that all people, recognizing that there is a God and that he is their creator, are condemned by their own testimony because they have failed to worship him and to give their lives to his service... There are innumerable witnesses in heaven and on earth that declare the wonders of his wisdom.

Institutes of the Christian Religion

The covenant of life is not preached equally to all, and among those to whom it is preached, does not always meet with the same reception. This diversity displays the unsearchable depth of the divine judgment, and is without doubt subordinate to God's purpose of eternal election.

Institutes of the Christian Religion

Wherever we see the Word of God purely preached and listened to, and the sacraments administered according to Christ's institution, it is in no way to be doubted that a church of God exists. For his promise cannot fail: 'Wherever two or three are gathered in my name, there I am in the midst of them' (Matthew 18:20) ... If the ministry has the Word and honours it, if it has the administration of the sacraments, it deserves without doubt to be held and considered a church.

Institutes of the Christian Religion

Westminster Confession (extracts)

The catholic or universal church, which is invisible, consists of the whole number of the elect that have been, are, or shall be gathered into one, under Christ the head thereof... The visible church, which is also catholic or universal under the gospel (not confined to one nation as before under the law), consists of all those throughout the world that profess the true religion, together with their children... Unto this catholic visible church, Christ hath given the ministry, oracles, and ordinances of God, for the gathering and perfecting of the saints in this life, to the end of the world; and doth by his own presence and Spirit, according to his promise, make them effectual thereunto... particular churches, which are members [of this catholic church] are more or less pure, according as the doctrine of the gospel is taught and embraced, ordinances administered, and public worship performed more or less purely in them. The purest churches under heaven are subject both to mixture and error; and some have so degenerated as to become apparently no churches of Christ. Nevertheless, there shall always be a church on earth, to worship God according to his will.

Westminster Confession

John Wesley (1703–91)

First let us agree what religion is. I take religion to be, not the bare saying of many prayers, morning and evening, in public or private; not anything superadded now and then to a careless or worldly life; but a constant ruling habit of the soul, a renewal of our minds in the image of God, a recovery of the divine likeness, a self-increasing conformity of heart and life to the pattern of our most holy Redeemer.

Letter to Richard Morgan.

I believe the infinite and eternal Spirit of God, equal with the Father and the Son, to be not only perfectly holy in himself but the immediate cause of all holiness in us; enlightening our understandings, rectifying our wills and affections, renewing our natures, uniting our persons to Christ, assuring us of the adoption of sons, leading us in our actions; purifying and sanctifying our souls and bodies, to a full and eternal enjoyment of God.

Works

Christian faith is then, not only an assent to the whole gospel of Christ, but also a full reliance on the blood of Christ; a trust in the merits of his life, death, and resurrection; a recumbency upon him as our atonement and our life, as given for us, and living in us; and, in consequence hereof, a closing with him, and cleaving to him, as our 'wisdom, righteousness, sanctification, and redemption', or, in one word, our salvation.

Sermon 1

Jonathan Edwards (1703–58)

The whole of God's internal good or glory, is in these three things, viz. his infinite knowledge, his infinite virtue or holiness, and his infinite joy and happiness.

Indeed, there are a great many attributes in God, according to our way of conceiving or talking of them: but all may be reduced to these; or to the degree, circumstances and relations of these… And therefore the external glory of God consists in the communication of these.

Works of Jonathan Edwards

We must *believe* in the Lord Jesus Christ, and accept of him as offered in the gospel for a Saviour. But, as we cannot do this of ourselves, Christ has purchased this, also, for all the elect.

He has purchased, that they shall have faith given them; whereby they shall be [actively] united in Christ, and have a [pleadable] title to his benefits.

'Wisdom Displayed in Salvation', Works of Jonathan Edwards

We have faith given us, principally that we might believe and live by it in daily applications of Christ. You may believe immediately (by God's help), but getting assurance of it may be the work of a great part of your life.

Quoted in The Religion of Abraham Lincoln

The enjoyment of God is the only happiness with which our souls can be satisfied. To go to heaven, fully to enjoy God, is infinitely better than the most pleasant accommodation here. Fathers and mothers, husbands, wives, or children, or the company of earthly friends, are but shadows, but God is the substance. These are but scattered beams, but God is the sun. These are but streams, but God is the ocean (2.244).

Quoted in Jonathan Edwards: A New Biography

Schleiermacher (1768–1834)

Any possibility of God being in any way *given* is entirely excluded, because anything that is outwardly given must be given as an object exposed to our counter-influence, however slight this may be. The transference of the idea of God to any perceptible object, unless one is all the time conscious that it is a piece of purely arbitrary symbolism, is always a corruption.

The Christian Faith

An essential element of our exposition in this Part has been the doctrine of the union of the Divine Essence with human nature, both in the personality of Christ and in the common Spirit of the Church; therewith the whole view of Christianity set forth in our Church teaching stands and falls. For unless the being of God in Christ is assumed, the idea of redemption could not be thus concentrated in His Person. And unless there were such a union also in the common Spirit of the Church, the Church could not thus be the Bearer and Perpetuator of the redemption through Christ. Now these exactly are the essential elements in the doctrine of the Trinity, which, it is clear, only established itself in defence of the position that in Christ there was present nothing less than the Divine Essence, which also indwells the Christian Church as its common Spirit, and that we take these expressions in no reduced or sheerly artificial sense, and know nothing of any special higher essences, subordinate deities (as it were) present in Christ and the Holy Spirit. The doctrine of the Trinity has no origin but this: and at first it had no other aim than to equate as definitely as possible the Divine Essence considered as thus united to human nature with the Divine Essence itself... In virtue of this connection, we rightly regard the doctrine of the Trinity, in so far as it is a deposit of these elements, as the coping-stone of Christian doctrine (*als den Schlussstein der christlichen Lehre*), and thus equating with each other of the divine in each of these two unions, as also of both with the Divine Essence in itself, as what is essential in the doctrine of the Trinity.

The Christian Faith

John Henry Newman (1801–90)

Natural religion is based upon the sense of sin; it recognises the disease, but it cannot find, it does but look out for the remedy. That remedy, both for guilt and moral impotence, is found in the central doctrine of Revelation, the Mediation of Christ.

The Grammar of Assent

Supposing it, then, to be the will of the creator to interfere in human affairs, and to make provision for retaining in the world a knowledge of Himself, so definite and distinct as to be proof against the energy of human scepticism, in such a case – I am far from saying that there was no other way – but there is nothing to surprise the mind if He should think fit to introduce a power into the world invested with the prerogative of infallibility in religious matters. Such a provision would be a direct, immediate, active and prompt means of withstanding the difficulty... And thus I am brought to speak of the Church's infallibility as a provision adapted by the mercy of the creator to preserve religion in the world, and to restrain the freedom of thoughts, which of course in itself is one of the greatest of our natural gifts, and to rescue it from its own suicidal excesses.

Apologia

Karl Barth (1886–1968)

Credo ecclesiam ['I believe in the church'] means that I believe that here, at this place, in this assembly, the work of the Holy Spirit takes place. By that is not intended a deification of the creature; the church is not the object of faith, we do not believe *in* the church; but we do believe that in this congregation the work of the Holy Spirit becomes an event.

Dogmatics in Outline

When Holy Scripture speaks of God, it does not permit us to let our attention or thoughts wander at random... When Holy Scripture speaks of God, it concentrates our attention and thoughts upon one single point and what is to be known at that point... If we ask further concerning the one point upon which, according to Scripture, our attention and thoughts should and must be concentrated, then from first to last the Bible directs us to the name of Jesus Christ.

Church Dogmatics

What took place is that the Son of God fulfilled the righteous judgement on us human beings by himself taking our place as a human being, and in our place undergoing the judgment under which we had passed... Why did God become a human being? So that God as a human being might do and accomplish and achieve and complete all this for us wrongdoers, in order that in this way there might be brought about by him our reconciliation with him, and our conversion to him.

Church Dogmatics

God is not an abstract category by which even the Christian understanding of the word has to be measured, but he who is called God [in the Bible] is the one God, the single God, the sole God.

The Christian Understanding of Revelation

It is impossible to listen at one and the same time to the two statements that Jesus of Nazareth is the Son of God and that the Son of God is Jesus of Nazareth. One hears either the one or one hears nothing. When one is heard, the other can be heard only indirectly, in faith.

Church Dogmatics

The very heart of the atonement is the overcoming of sin: sin in its character as the rebellion of man against God and in its character as the ground of man's hopeless destiny in death.

Church Dogmatics

Dietrich Bonhoeffer (1906–45)

If grace is God's answer, the grit of Christian life, then we cannot for a moment dispense with following Christ. But if grace is the data for my Christian life, it means that I set out to live the Christian life in the world with all my sins justified beforehand. I can go and sin as much as I like, and rely on this grace to forgive me, for after all the world is justified in principle by grace. I can therefore cling to my bourgeois secular existence, and remain as I was before, but with the added assurance that the grace of God will cover me.

The Cost of Discipleship

As they contemplated the miracle of the Incarnation, the early Fathers passionately contended that while it was true to say that God took human nature upon him, it was wrong to say that he chose a perfect individual man and united himself to him. God was made man. This means that he took upon him our entire human nature with all of its infirmity, sinfulness and corruption, the whole of apostate humanity.

The Cost of Discipleship

Of this man we say, 'This is God for us.' This does not mean that we know, say, at an earlier stage quite apart from Jesus Christ, what and who God is, and then apply it to Christ. We have a direct statement of identity; whatever we can say here is prompted by a look at him, or, better is compelled by this man.

Christology

God lets himself be pushed out of the world on to the cross. He is weak and powerless in the world, and that is precisely the way, the only way, in which he is with us and helps us... The Bible directs us to God's powerlessness and suffering; only the suffering God can help.

Letters and Papers from Prison

Here is the decisive difference between Christianity and all religions. Man's religiosity makes him look in his distress to the power of God in the world. God is the *deus ex machina*. The Bible directs man to God's powerlessness and suffering; only the suffering God can help.

Letters and Papers from Prison

Reinhold Niebuhr (1892–1971)

Without the public and historical revelation the private experience of God would remain poorly defined and subject to caprice. Without the private revelation of God, the public and historical would not gain credence.

The Nature and Destiny of Man

If I believe that the Christian understanding of man could help solve some of the crucial issues [economic injustice, fascist politics, and the impotence of liberalism in the faith of both] and could conserve the best achievements of liberalism better than traditional liberalism can conserve them, I do not for that reason wish merely to hitch Christian faith to this or that political task. Christianity faces ultimate issues of life which transcend all political vicissitudes and achievements. But the answer which Christian faith gives to man's ultimate perplexities and the hope which it makes possible in the very abyss of his despair, also throw light upon the immediate historical issues which he faces. Christianity is not a flight into eternity from the tasks and decisions of history. It is rather the power and wisdom of God which makes decisions in history possible and which points to proximate goals in history which are usually obscured either by optimistic illusions or by the despair which followed upon the dissipation of these illusions.

'Ten Years that Shook My World', The Christian Century

Nothing that is worth doing can be achieved in our lifetime; therefore we must be saved by hope. Nothing which is true or beautiful or good makes complete sense in any immediate context of history; therefore we must be saved by faith. Nothing we do, however virtuous, can be accomplished alone; therefore we are saved by love. No virtuous act is quite as virtuous from the standpoint of our friend or foes as it is from our standpoint. Therefore we must be saved by the final form of love which is forgiveness.

The Irony of American History

Paul Tillich (1886–1965)

A theological system is supposed to satisfy two basic needs: the statement of the truth of the Christian message and the interpretation of this truth for every new generation. Theology moves back and forth between two poles, the eternal truth of its foundation and the temporal situation in which the eternal truth must be received.

Systematic Theology

The name of this infinite and inexhaustible depth and ground of all being is God. That depth is what the word God means. And if that word has not much meaning for you, translate it, and speak of the depths of your life, of the source of your being, of your ultimate concern, of what you take seriously without any reservation. Perhaps, in order to do so, you must forget everything traditional that you have learned about God. Perhaps even that word itself. For if you know that God means depth, you know much about him. You cannot then call yourself an atheist or unbeliever.

Sermon on The Depth of Existence

The being of God is being-itself. The being of God cannot be understood as the existence of a being alongside others or above others. If God is *a* being, he is subject to the categories of finitude, especially to space and substance. Even if he is called the 'highest being' in the sense of the 'most perfect' and the 'most powerful' being, this situation is not changed. When applied to God, superlatives become diminutives.

Systematic Theology I

Jürgen Moltmann (1926–present)

We can therefore say that the historical church *will* be the one, holy, catholic church through the apostolic witness of Christ, and in carrying out that witness; whereas the church glorified in the kingdom of God is the one, holy, catholic church, through the fulfilment of its apostolate. Historically the church has its being in carrying out the apostolate. In eternity the church has its being in fulfilment of the apostolate, that is, in the seeing face to face.

The Church in the Power of the Spirit

Just as the coming kingdom is universal, so the gospel brings the liberation of men to universal expression. It seeks to liberate the soul and the body, individuals and social conditions, human systems and the systems of nature from the closedness of reserve, from self-righteousness and from godless and inhuman pressures.

The Church in the Power of the Spirit

Christ's surrender of himself to a Godforsaken death reveals the secret of the cross and with it the secret of God himself. It is the open secret of the Trinity.

The Church in the Power of the Spirit

Anyone who believes in the God who created being out of nothing, also believes in the God who gives life to the dead. This means that he hopes for the new creation of heaven and earth. His faith makes him prepared to withstand annihilation, even when there is nothing left to hope for, humanly speaking. His hope in God commits him to faithfulness to the earth.

God in Creation

The eschatological is not one element of Christianity, but it is the medium of Christian faith as such, the key in which everything in it is set, the glow that suffuses everything here in the dawn of an expected new day. For Christian faith lives from the raising of the crucified Christ, and strains after the promises of the universal future of Christ. Eschatology is the passionate suffering and passionate longing kindled by the Messiah. Hence eschatology cannot really be only a part of Christian doctrine. Rather, the eschatological outlook is characteristic of all Christian proclamation, of every Christian existence and of the whole Church.

Theology of Hope: on the Ground and the Implications of a Christian Eschatology

Wolfhart Pannenberg (1928–present)

The aspect of fatherly care in particular is taken over in what the Old Testament has to say about God's fatherly care for Israel. The sexual definition of the father's role plays no part... To bring sexual differentiation into the understanding of God would mean polytheism; it was thus ruled out for the God of Israel... The fact that God's care for Israel can also be expressed in terms of a mother's love shows clearly enough how little there is any sense of sexual distinction in the understanding of God as Father.

Systematic Theology

History is the most comprehensive horizon of Christian theology. All theological questions and answers have meaning only within the framework of the history which God has with humanity, and through humanity with the whole creation, directed towards a future which is hidden to the world, but which has already been revealed in Jesus Christ.

Basic Questions in Theology

Only at the end of all events can God be revealed in his divinity, that is, as the one who works all things, who has power over everything. Only because in Jesus' resurrection the end of all things, which for us has not yet happened, has already occurred can it be said of Jesus that the ultimate already is present in him, and so also that God himself, his glory, has made its appearance in Jesus in a way that cannot be surpassed. Only because the end of the world is already present in Jesus' resurrection is God himself revealed in him.

Jesus – God and Man

Glossary

Adoption
Christians are 'adopted' as sons and daughters in the family of GOD.

Advent (literally 'coming')
Refers to JESUS' first coming in his INCARNATION, and to his SECOND COMING, at the end of the age.

Agnostic
One who believes that spiritual questions cannot be settled one way or the other because of the limitations of human knowledge.

Alienation (literally 'estrangement')
Used by Karl Marx to describe how repetitive work estranges people from their creativity. Christians also sometimes use it of humanity's separation from the life of GOD.

Allegory
Speech or writing where the literal meaning takes second place to the symbolic meaning. Some BIBLE interpretation, especially in the early church, saw more allegory than is really there.

Almighty
GOD'S ability to do anything which is not against his character and laws.

Amen
The word Christians commonly use at the close of each PRAYER. It means 'let it be so'.

Analogy
The method of description which compares like with like. In religious matters, we often express ourselves through 'the language of analogy' as when we say 'God is Father', meaning that GOD'S relationship to humanity has some likeness to your own parenting.

Angel (literally 'messenger')
Spiritual being who serves GOD. According to the BIBLE, angels' chief role is worship, but they also undertake tasks that bring them into contact with human life.

Anglican
Member of the Church of England, or of a member-church of the 'Anglican Communion', the worldwide fellowship of churches in special relationship with the Church of England.

Anglo-Catholic
Member of the ANGLICAN Communion whose beliefs and practices are in some ways close to those of ROMAN CATHOLICS. Modern Anglo-Catholics are successors of the TRACTARIANS.

Apocrypha
See DEUTEROCANONICAL WRITINGS.

Apologetics (from the Latin *apologia*, a legal speech for the defence)
The study of how to justify Christianity in the face of ideas or cultures that oppose it. The Apologists were second-century defenders of the faith against both Judaism and polytheism.

Apostle (literally 'one who is sent')
One of the twelve men appointed by JESUS to 'be with him and be sent out to preach'. After Jesus' ASCENSION, as eyewitnesses of the RESURRECTION, the apostles (less Judas Iscariot) spread the GOSPEL and founded the church. (Paul was made an apostle through meeting the risen CHRIST.)

Apostolic Fathers
Christian writers and leaders in the time directly after the APOSTLES.

Arianism

The belief that the SON OF GOD is neither eternal nor divine; it thus undermines the belief in the TRINITY. Arius was condemned at the Council of Nicea (325), but Arianism continued for some time after that.

Arminian

One who holds that people are free to choose for and against FAITH in JESUS CHRIST, and that Christians can fall away from such faith. These beliefs, which derive from sixteenth-century Dutchman Jacobus Arminius, stand in opposition to some emphases within Calvinism.

Ascension

JESUS' return to his Father's GLORY and his exaltation as King. It took place in his DISCIPLES' presence forty days after his RESURRECTION and ten days before the giving of the SPIRIT at Pentecost.

Asceticism (literally 'training')

Self-denial and self-discipline, sometimes used by Christians to avoid being mastered by the world. Often a feature of monasticism.

Assumption (sometimes called 'Bodily Assumption')

The belief, not found in the New TESTAMENT but held by ROMAN CATHOLICS, that the VIRGIN MARY was taken up body and SOUL into HEAVEN at the end of her life.

Atheist

One who believes there is no god. This is not a very common belief, since many people without faith in GOD are in fact AGNOSTICS.

Atonement (literally 'at-one-ment')

The bringing of people back into a relationship with GOD. In the Old TESTAMENT this was achieved through animal sacrifices, but the death of JESUS made full and final atonement for everyone who believes in him.

Authority

That which can rightfully command our total acceptance and obedience. For Christians, authority lies in GOD through JESUS CHRIST. One great issue at the REFORMATION was whether God's authority comes to us through the church (as Catholics believe) or through the BIBLE (the Reformers' teaching). More recently, reason and spiritual intuition have become alternative authorities.

Baptism

The washing or immersion of a person in water in the name of the TRINITY, as a sign of all GOD promises to people who are IN CHRIST, such as FORGIVENESS, NEW BIRTH, membership of the CHURCH. Baptism is firmly linked in the New TESTAMENT to FAITH and REPENTANCE (see also SACRAMENT).

Baptism in the Holy Spirit

Where John the Baptist baptized in water, to signify repentance and forgiveness. JESUS' BAPTISM is in 'water and Spirit' to signify the greater gift of NEW BIRTH. There is a disagreement today as to whether this term refers simply to Christian baptism as such or also to a stage of becoming alive to the HOLY SPIRIT subsequent to CONVERSION as some Pentecostals and CHARISMATICS teach.

Baptist

Member of the worldwide fellowship of churches which teach that only people old enough to make a personal step of REPENTANCE and FAITH should receive BAPTISM. These churches are basically Congregational in church order.

Bible, The (sometime also called 'the Scriptures')

A collection of books written over a period of many centuries, which are recognized by the church as having GOD'S AUTHORITY. It is accepted, particularly by PROTESTANTS, that the Bible contains everything we need to know for SALVATION, and that beliefs not to be found in the Bible should not be made articles of FAITH.

Biblical Criticism
The scholarly study of the BIBLE, especially its historical background, language and literary styles.

Bishop (literally 'overseer')
In the New TESTAMENT, this means the same as presbyter, but by the second century bishops began to be in sole charge of CONGREGATIONS or of Christians in a town or area. In Catholic belief, bishops have a vital role in ensuring the continuity of CHURCH and FAITH.

Blessing
The giving of spiritual benefits, especially through the GOSPEL; sometimes refers to the forms of words used. Some Christians also use this word instead of CONSECRATION.

Bodily Assumption
See ASSUMPTION.

Body of Christ
The most characteristic picture of the CHURCH used by the APOSTLE Paul. The picture conveys that each member of the church has a role and that Christians depend on each other. Some also take it to suggest that through the church CHRIST is present in the world.

Calling (also known as 'election')
An invitation or summons GOD issues to people, initially to follow him but then also to perform specific tasks in the world or the CHURCH. God's calling is an expression of his GRACE. Not everyone who receives God's call obeys it.

Calvinist
One who draws his beliefs particularly from John Calvin's *Institutes of the Christian Religion.* The term has come to be used particularly of those who stress GOD'S sovereignty, and hold that God's PREDESTINATION is more important to a person's SALVATION than human FREE WILL. Calvinists are thus opposed to Arminianism.

Canon, The
The list of books regarded as rightly belonging in the BIBLE because they possess GOD'S AUTHORITY. This list was finalized by the CHURCH in the fourth century. Before that time there was some uncertainty as to whether a few books in the final list should be excluded or a few others included.

Canon Law
Laws made by some churches, such as the ROMAN CATHOLIC church or the Church of England, covering many matters of FAITH, discipline and morality.

Catechism
Body of basic teaching used to instruct new believers in the Christian FAITH, often in preparation for BAPTISM and/or CONFIRMATION.

Cause
Person, force or event as a result of which other events take place. Christians speak of GOD as the First Cause, through whom everything else came into being. They also accept secondary causes, bringing results which, while not outside God's PROVIDENCE, are not directly caused by him.

Charismatic
One who particularly stresses the importance of the HOLY SPIRIT in Christian life, worship and WITNESS. The GIFTS OF THE SPIRIT (*charismata*) also receive great emphasis. Charismatics have much in common

with Pentecostals, but also some differences. Some are separatists, but may remain firmly rooted in the main DENOMINATIONS.

Christ

The Greek word for MESSIAH, so that 'Jesus Christ' means 'Jesus the Messiah'.

Christ, In

A phrase frequently used by the APOSTLE Paul. Those 'in Christ' are identified with JESUS in his death and RESURRECTION, through which they have received FORGIVENESS and NEW BIRTH. BAPTISM is the sign of coming in CHRIST.

Christening

Sometimes used in the BAPTISM of infants, particularly by those who do not believe infant baptism is true baptism. It refers to the giving of a name to the one baptised.

Church

The worldwide community of all those who follow JESUS CHRIST. It includes the church militant' – all Christians now living – and the 'church triumphant' – all Christians who have died. Membership of the church is a vital part of what it means to be a Christian. Some distinguish the 'visible church' – a structured organization – and the 'invisible church' – those within the visible church who are truly regenerated. The word is also sometimes used of a CONGREGATION, of a DENOMINATION or of a building in which Christians gather.

Church Fathers (sometimes called Early Fathers)

Writers and thinkers in the first few Christian centuries who played a part in the formation of Christian belief.

Church Order

Matters to do with the government, structuring, ministry and discipline of CONGREGATIONS and DENOMINATIONS.

Circumcision

The removal of the foreskin as a sign of membership in the covenant people of Israel. This was done to Israelite males on the eighth day after birth and to non-Israelites on CONVERSION to Judaism. There was dispute in New TESTAMENT times as to whether GENTILE converts to Christianity should be circumcised.

Common Grace

See GRACE.

Communion of Saints

The fellowship of all Christians which extends beyond death.

Confession, The

The acknowledging of SIN, either individually or corporately. Fundamentally, we admit sin and ask forgiveness from GOD. But the New TESTAMENT also encourages Christians to confess to each other in some circumstances. Catholics believe sin should be confessed to a PRIEST, who is authorized to absolve the penitent or exact PENANCE. The word is also used for a statement of FAITH.

Confirmation

The service (Catholics would say SACRAMENT) in which people already baptized are received into full membership of their CHURCH and are admitted to HOLY COMMUNION. It is a feature of churches which have BISHOPS. Those confirmed repeat their baptismal vows and receive the LAYING ON OF HANDS from the bishop. In Catholic belief, confirmation is a sign of receiving the HOLY SPIRIT. Others see BAPTISM as a sign of this, and associate confirmation with strengthening in the Holy Spirit.

Congregation

Local community of Christians who come together regularly for worship and cooperate in Christian service and WITNESS.

Consecration

The setting apart of people or things for GOD's use. The word most normally refers to a believer devoting himself or herself to a holy life, but it is also used of setting apart bread and wine for use in the Eucharist or water for BAPTISM.

Conversion

Turning to Christianity from some other FAITH or world-view or from none. It involves REPENTANCE and faith, but in all other respects each person's conversion is unique to him or her; no fixed sequence of events is required. (See also NEW BIRTH.)

Council

A gathering of BISHOPS or representatives of the whole CHURCH, to take decisions on matters of belief or practice. Important councils have been: – the Ecumenical (or General) Councils, held between the fourth and the ninth centuries, whose decisions have held great AUTHORITY in the worldwide church ever since. They are particularly highly valued by the ORTHODOX CHURCHES; – the First and Second Vatican councils (1870 and 1962–65) of all the cardinals and bishops of the ROMAN CATHOLIC church.

Counter-Reformation (or 'Catholic Reformation')

A movement for reform and expansion in the ROMAN CATHOLIC church of the sixteenth and seventeenth centuries, partly in response to the REFORMATION. Among its key features were the Council of Trent (1545–63) and the beginnings of the Jesuit movement.

Covenant

A solemn agreement made by GOD with his people with the aim of securing a lasting relationship between them. The 'old covenant' (or TESTAMENT) included the giving of God's LAW and eventually failed through the people's inability to keep it. The prophesied 'new covenant', made through the death of JESUS, overcomes this drawback by ensuring FORGIVENESS and NEW BIRTH.

Creation

GOD's action in bringing into being the universe and everything in it. Humanity is the crown of creation. Belief in God as creator brings the conviction that the universe and life in it are ultimately purposeful. The question how God created has been widely debated since Darwin proposed the theory of evolution.

Creed

Formal statements of belief made in the early Christian centuries. The central creeds (especially the Nicene and Apostles' creeds) are accepted by all Christians and are used regularly in baptismal and other liturgies.

Cross

The wooden gallows on which JESUS was nailed to die (crucified). Sometimes used as a shorthand for the death of Jesus. The cross has become the central emblem of Christianity.

Deacon (literally 'servant')

In the New TESTAMENT, appointed initially to help in practical matters, but soon developed wider ministries. Since then 'deacon' has become a specific office in the CHURCH though interpreted differently in different TRADITIONS.

Deist

One who believes in GOD, but not that God has revealed himself to mankind directly. A deist believes in a this-worldly religion providing the basis for an upright life. This seventeenth-century philosophy was the basis for the eighteenth-century ENLIGHTENMENT.

Demon

Evil spirit working for the DEVIL against GOD and goodness. JESUS saw demons invading people's personalities, and frequently he cast them out. Belief in demons is common in primitive cultures but has only recently been re-emphasized in the West.

Denomination

Organized grouping of CONGREGATIONS with similar beliefs, CHURCH ORDER and/or LITURGY. These grouping are commonly international, and it is through them that Christians relate to other denominations, to civic structures and to governments.

Deuterocanonical writings

Books whose qualifications to be included in the CANON of the Scripture are disputed. Catholics include these writings as part of the BIBLE, but PROTESTANTS consider them to be of lesser AUTHORITY and leave them out or bind them separately. (Sometimes called Apocrypha.)

Devil, The (also called 'Satan')

A personalized power of EVIL, leader of spiritual forces opposed to GOD. His AUTHORITY is strictly subordinate to God's as Christian belief does not allow dualism. It is widely believed that the Devil is a fallen ANGEL, not created evil by God. The death of JESUS and his RESURRECTION have ensured Satan's eventual defeat.

Disciple

One who follows JESUS in order to learn from him and to grow to spiritual maturity. GOD'S plan is not just that people should become adherents of Christianity but that they should go on to be full disciples.

Dispensation

A distinct period during the history of SALVATION. Some Christians speak of the 'dispensation of the Law' (from Moses to CHRIST) or the 'dispensation of grace' (from Christ's first coming to his second). Dispensationalists (often to be found among the Christian brethren) believe that in each period God acts towards people in a way typical of that dispensation.

Divinity

The being of GOD. Christians believe that JESUS CHRIST shares God's divinity.

Docetist (from a Greek word meaning 'to seem')

One who believed that the SON OF GOD only seemed to live and die in the flesh. This early HERESY would have fatally undermined Christianity as FAITH in the INCARNATION.

Doctrine

A belief carefully formulated. 'Christian doctrine' can be used for the whole body of belief.

Dogma

Close to DOCTRINE, but can carry overtones of a fixed and inflexible system of belief. Dogmatics is the study of Christian doctrine, often in a way which centres on its philosophical implications.

Dualism

The belief that there are equal and opposite forces of good and EVIL at work in the universe. This is an old HERESY which it is all too easy to fall into when speaking of the DEVIL and the presence of evil. It was taught in an extreme form by the Manichaeans who spread widely from the third century.

Early Church

The CHURCH in the first few centuries, after the days of the primitive church.

Early Fathers

See CHURCH FATHERS.

Eastern Church

The churches at the eastern end of the Mediterranean, originally based on

Constantinople (Byzantium), which sought to be independent of Rome. These churches are largely Greek-speaking. This division became absolute after the Great Schism and the ORTHODOX CHURCHES are the heirs to the eastern TRADITION.

Ecclesiastical
To do with the CHURCH (the Greek word for church is *ecclesia*, 'assembly').

Ecumenical
To do with the unity of all Christians. The ecumenical movement looks to draw all Christians into one fellowship, as a witness to a divided world of GOD'S RECONCILIATION.

Election
See CALLING.

Enlightenment, The
An eighteenth-century movement believing that mankind should be guided by reason and not by external AUTHORITY, DOGMA or REVELATION. This movement has had great influence on the development of modern thought.

Episcopacy
Form of church government which treats BISHOPS as an integral part of the system.

Epistle
The old term for the letters, mainly written by APOSTLES, included in the New TESTAMENT.

Eschatology
The study of the 'last things', what will happen at the end of the age, and in particular at the SECOND COMING of CHRIST.

Essene
Member of a strict Jewish community based at Qumran on the Dead Sea. Their characteristic beliefs were kept secret, but some are now known from the Dead Sea Scrolls. They were in the third main division of Judaism in Jesus' time, along with the PHARISEES and SADDUCEES.

Ethics
The study of morality and moral choices. Christian ethics seek to relate the teaching of the BIBLE, and the long tradition of interpretation of the Bible's moral teaching, to contemporary thinking and decision-making.

Eucharist
See HOLY COMMUNION.

Evangelical
One in whose Christian FAITH great importance is given to the teachings of the BIBLE as the basis for belief and to personal CONVERSION as a necessity for true Christianity. Evangelicalism is in continuity with the REFORMATION but traces more direct lines of descent to the REVIVALS of the eighteenth and nineteenth centuries. Many evangelicals are in independent CONGREGATIONS but many are also within the main DENOMINATIONS.

Evangelism ('evangel' means the gospel)
Telling other people of the GOSPEL of SALVATION through JESUS, with the aim that they might repent, believe and find new life in him. The means used to spread the gospel are many and various; all need to be relevant to the particular culture of the people being approached. Evangelism is not the whole of Christian mission but many believe mission to be inadequate without it.

Evil
Harm which comes to human beings, turning us away from GOD and from goodness. Often divided into: – moral evil, harm which comes through other people's actions or our own, as in war, oppression, avoidable accident; – natural

evil, which comes through events in the natural order such as disease or natural disaster. The origins of evil are a MYSTERY, though there are hints that it connected with humanity's FALL.

Exodus, The
The escape of the Israelites under Moses from slavery in Egypt, resulting eventually in their establishment in their own land. The Old TESTAMENT and Judaism look back to it as GOD's greatest deliverance, when Israel became a nation. New Testament teaching about SALVATION sometimes makes use of exodus imagery.

Expiation
Making an offering or taking action that atones for SIN. Some believe this is the right word to describe the death of JESUS, but others feel it is too objective a term and prefer the more personal PROPITIATION.

Faith
Personal belief and trust in a person or an idea, such that loss will be inevitable if the object of faith proves untrustworthy. Christian faith in JESUS CHRIST is therefore more than an intellectual assent to beliefs: it is personal commitment to Jesus. Faith is regularly linked in the New TESTAMENT to REPENTANCE.

Fall, The
Humanity's choice to be independent of GOD and his will, a choice which we are all involved in and which has resulted in the deflection of humanity from the path God intended, the distortion of the image of God in mankind and the spoiling of CREATION itself. There is disagreement as to whether the fall was an actual historical event or expresses a truth about humanity's character and relationship to God.

Fatherhood of God
The quality in GOD which relates to humanity in a parental way, caring and guiding. It was JESUS' characteristic way of referring to God. Christians commonly speak of the first person of the TRINITY as 'God the Father'.

Fathers
See CHURCH FATHERS and APOSTOLIC FATHERS.

Fellowship
Doing things and having things in common with the Christian community. The emphasis is on shared participation rather than simply common membership or meeting together. Its New TESTAMENT usage makes clear that we are not intended to lead isolated Christian lives, but to find encouragement and support among other Christians.

Filled with the Spirit
Having our personalities and wills so open to the HOLY SPIRIT that we put no obstacles in the way of his enriching our lives and using us in GOD's service. The APOSTLE Paul teaches us that it is to be a continual rather than a once-for-all filling.

First Cause
See CAUSE.

Forgiveness
One of the great BLESSINGS made available through the death of JESUS is that people can know themselves to be forgiven by GOD, free of the guilt which would otherwise hold them apart from him. Just as forgiveness is a central feature of the relationship between God and humanity, so it is to characterize relationships between people: we are to forgive as we have been forgiven.

Free will
The quality in humanity which is able to make choices, not totally governed by outside factors. Christians disagree on how to relate our free-will decision

whether or not to follow JESUS to our understanding of PREDESTINATION.

Fruit of the Spirit
Quality in a Christian's life which results from the work of the HOLY SPIRIT in SANCTIFICATION. First place among them is given to LOVE, joy and peace.

Gentile
Term used by Jews of one who is not a Jew.

Gifts of the Spirit
Abilities given to believers by the HOLY SPIRIT, to be used for the good of the whole Christian body. The emphasis is on the gifts coming from GOD directly rather than just natural abilities. Also, the SPIRIT gives a variety of gifts so that each person has a distinct part to play.

Glory
A quality of the eternal GOD in his majesty, which he promises to share with believers hereafter. God's glory was seen in terms men and women can understand in the character of JESUS.

God
Christians believe, not vaguely in a god, but specifically in GOD whom JESUS called Father, the BIBLE's teaching about God is that he is HOLY, perfect and TRANSCENDENT, but also that in his GRACE and goodness he is close to us in our everyday lives, and relates to us in a personal way. He is creator of the universe. He sent Jesus, the SON OF GOD, to fulfil his eternal plan for humanity's SALVATION.

Gospel (written with a capital G)
One of the four accounts of the life, death and RESURRECTION of JESUS found in the New TESTAMENT. A Gospel is more than just a biography; it interprets the meaning of Jesus in a way that calls forth a response of FAITH.

Gospel (written with a small g)
The good news of what GOD has done through JESUS, and especially his death and RESURRECTION. He has made available to us FORGIVENESS and NEW BIRTH in the HOLY SPIRIT. It is through hearing the gospel that people can come to receive Jesus and find his new life.

Grace
Grace is always given, never earned. It is a relationship word not a 'force'. It is often divided into: special grace – FORGIVENESS and other BLESSINGS which come specifically through the death of Jesus; common grace – goodness in life and society which comes from GOD's creating and sustaining the world.

Heaven
The presence of GOD, where believers will find the final fulfilment of the LOVE, joy and peace they have begun to experience on earth. As well as representing the presence of God and his goodness, heaven also stands for the absence of SIN and all the disharmony that has resulted from the FALL.

Hell
The word translates two New TESTAMENT concepts: Hades, the place of the departed, an idea close to the Old Testament Sheol, and Gehenna, a place of torment. The concept of hell in the latter sense holds before us the fact that to reject JESUS CHRIST brings eternal JUDGMENT. There is disagreement as to whether hell actually goes on forever or is an experience of instantaneous destruction.

Hellenism
The predominantly Greek culture that began with Alexander the Great and continued for centuries alongside Roman culture. It was thus a very influential aspect of the cultural background to the New TESTAMENT.

Heresy

This originally meant simply a party or a school of thought, but Christians came to use it of a teaching that split off from and contradicted orthodox Christianity. Today it is confined to teaching that subverts a central Christian belief, such as the TRINITY, the divinity of CHRIST or the ATONEMENT, and thus results in something not truly Christian.

Hermeneutics

The study of how to interpret the BIBLE, in such a way as to be true to its original meaning and also relevant to today's questions.

Holy

A quality initially of GOD, denoting his separation from anything which is not wholly pure. The BIBLE also applies to objects, religious officials and so on who are set apart for use in GOD'S service. But ordinary believers are also called to be holy, to live lives that reflect the character of God as seen in JESUS. (See also SANCTIFICATION.)

Holy Communion

The service in which the CONGREGATION take a piece of bread and a sip of wine as a token that they owe their spiritual life to the death of JESUS. It was instituted by Jesus at the Last Supper, when he took bread and wine saying 'This is my body', 'This is my blood'. The service is also known as the Eucharist (meaning 'thanksgiving'), the mass (the ROMAN CATHOLIC term) and the Lord's Supper. (See also REAL PRESENCE, SACRAMENT.)

Holy Spirit

The personal presence of GOD, active in the CHURCH and in the world. He is the third person of the TRINITY, not to be thought of as a force or influence but fully personal. In the Old TESTAMENT, the SPIRIT was given to particular individuals for special tasks. But at Pentecost JESUS CHRIST gave the Holy Spirit to every believer and Jesus has been present with his people by the Holy Spirit ever since.

Hope

A Christian virtue only equalled in importance by FAITH and LOVE. It means the conviction that our life and our relationship with Jesus do not end at our physical death, and that therefore the spiritual dimension of believer's lives cannot be destroyed by any temporal forces. Hope is thus able to sustain Christians even in great adversity.

Humanist

One who sets great store by the capacity of human nature, by the aesthetic and moral sense, and by education. Today most humanists believe in humanism rather than in god, but there has been a long tradition of Christian humanism which started at the time of the RENAISSANCE.

Icon

An image, usually of JESUS or the VIRGIN MARY, used in worship in orthodox churches. They are not mere religious decorations but are seen as windows into a spiritual world.

Idol

Something physical or natural that people take for GOD and worship. Many tribal cultures have idols but there are a number of features of modern life which have become objects of worship, such as money, the state, science.

Immanence

The quality in GOD which causes him to be involved in the life of humanity and the world, and not stay remote from it. The chief evidence for God's immanence is the INCARNATION of the SON OF GOD. Christians try to hold belief in God's immanence in balance with belief in his transcendence.

Incarnation (literally 'taking flesh')

The action of GOD in becoming a wholly human person in JESUS of Nazareth, subject to place, time and all other human attributes. What made Jesus' humanity unique was his freedom from SIN. In his full humanity can be seen everything about the character of God which can be conveyed in human terms.

Indulgence

In Catholic belief, remission of the debt owed to GOD for SIN after the guilt has been forgiven. This is thought possible due to the 'treasury of merit' believed to have been built up by JESUS, the VIRGIN MARY and the SAINTS. It was the sale of indulgences for money which provoked Martin Luther to issue the theses which launched the REFORMATION.

Inerrant

The quality of being without any mistakes of fact or interpretation which some Christians attribute to the BIBLE. The word is used to defend the Bible's AUTHORITY in the face of those who are thought to take too low a view of its INSPIRATION.

Infallible

A term very close in meaning to INERRANT when used of the BIBLE. It is also applied by ROMAN CATHOLICS to the pope when he is pronouncing on a matter of DOCTRINE.

Inspiration (literally 'in breathing')

The means by which the BIBLE, a collection of books written by human writers became also the word of GOD. The HOLY SPIRIT is believed so to have inspired the writers that their books carry the meaning God intended, but without lessening the individuality of the writers.

Intercession

The aspect of PRAYER in which believers make specific petitions to GOD on behalf of themselves, other people or groups. The word also applies in the New TESTAMENT to an activity of JESUS since his ASCENSION; that he intercedes with GOD on behalf of humanity as humanity's REPRESENTATIVE.

Interpretation

The attempt to understand the BIBLE in a way true to its original meaning and apply it to present-day concerns. (See also HERMENEUTICS.)

Jesus (literally 'one who saves')

The man born in Bethlehem and brought up in Nazareth who became an itinerant teacher and healer, was crucified and rose again. His followers came to believe he was the MESSIAH (CHRIST) and the SON OF GOD.

Judgment

The activity of GOD in calling people to account for what they have made of their lives. Believers and unbelievers alike will face judgment, but there will be no condemnation for those 'in Christ'. JESUS claimed that God had given to him the AUTHORITY to judge, and this assures us that judgment will be fair and perceptive. It will take place at Jesus' SECOND COMING (see also HELL).

Justification

GOD'S reckoning of a person to be righteous before him, in standing rather than in the quality of life, though the second naturally flows from the first. It is an image from the law courts meaning 'acquittal'. The means of justification have been thought to be: – justification by FAITH, in that all that we need to be made right with God has been achieved in the death of JESUS, and believers simply receive it by faith (this was a key REFORMATION belief); – justification by works, according to which we are made though with God through our own righteous acts. This is widely seen as unbiblical today though many attempt a fusion of the two ideas.

Just War
The idea that war can sometimes be morally justified, but only as a last resort, and under strictly defined conditions. This teaching was put forward in medieval times, but attempts have been made to apply it through to the modern period, though some hold it is not relevant to nuclear warfare.

Kenosis (literally 'he emptied himself')
A theory about the INCARNATION which holds that, in becoming JESUS of Nazareth, the SON OF GOD put aside all distinctively divine attributes and revealed GOD simply and solely through his humanity.

Kingdom of God (or kingdom of heaven)
The rule and AUTHORITY of GOD and every person and community in whom that rule is accepted. The Jews had hoped for the kingdom of David to be re-established but JESUS brought a kingdom with a different kind of power, the quality of which was largely unrecognized. The kingdom of God is entered through adopting Jesus' way of living in the power of the spirit; its chief concerns are with the poor and oppressed. Though hidden now, the kingdom of God will finally overturn all earthly power at the SECOND COMING of Jesus.

Laity
The whole people (Greek, *laos*) of GOD, whether clergy or not. It has often been used for the people of God excluding the clergy with the result that a contrast has arisen between active ordained Christians and passive ones. This has harmed the mission of the CHURCH.

Lamb of God
A title for JESUS used by John the Baptist and by the writer of REVELATION, which highlights his SACRIFICE for our sins and the victory he won in his death.

Law, The
A set of God-given commandments, centred on the Ten Commandments but often thought of as including the first five books of the BIBLE. The Law is God's fatherly instruction to his people, outlining the pattern of behaviour through which they can best love him and their neighbours. We can never find SALVATION by keeping the Law, because we all fail to keep it fully. So the attempt to establish our righteousness by legal means is doomed and leads away from the GOSPEL of JESUS.

Laying on of hands
The identification of a person before GOD as the object of special PRAYER by placing hands on him or her. This was done in the BIBLE for healing, for ORDINATION and for receiving the HOLY SPIRIT. It is also used today by a BISHOP in CONFIRMATION.

Legalism
The approach to religion which sees its centre in keeping rules and regulations. While keeping God's law is important, the legalistic approach is deadening and undermines FAITH in the GOSPEL.

Liberal Theology
A type of theology which asserts the freedom to question alleged authorities and to avoid intellectual constraints. It is thus often critical of orthodox Christianity. It has flourished from the eighteenth century, though more dominant in some periods than others.

Liberation Theology
A movement which has arisen in Latin America in the last fifteen years, which looks to apply Christian beliefs in

concrete action (praxis), especially in the face of situations of oppression and political injustice.

Liturgy

A set form of worship, usually published in a book. Liturgy is sometimes followed word for word, and sometimes provides a framework within which there is some freedom of expression. It is characteristic of Catholic, Orthodox and ANGLICAN worship but not of the NONCONFORMIST (or 'free') CHURCHES, though this distinction is not absolute.

Lord, The

A title for GOD in the Old TESTAMENT, generally written 'the LORD' used because God's name, Yahweh, was too HOLY to be spoken. It was used in the New Testament of JESUS CHRIST and has become a key term in Christian worship of him.

Lord's Supper

See HOLY COMMUNION.

Love

The chief and most characteristic Christian virtue, so distinctive that the New TESTAMENT coined a new word for it, 'agape'. Christian love is more that an emotion: it is an active caring for other people whether they do anything or not to provoke it. It is a central quality of GOD and is seen at its most essential in JESUS.

Marcionite

One who followed in the teaching of Marcion in the second century, in particular that the GOD of the Old TESTAMENT is not the Father of JESUS CHRIST.

Martyr

One who dies for his FAITH, refusing to turn from it despite persecution. Christians are often martyred when the state takes to itself god-like powers. The word also means witness.

Mary

See VIRGIN MARY.

Mass

See HOLY COMMUNION.

Mediator

A title given to JESUS CHRIST, describing his function in bringing together GOD and humanity. He is uniquely qualified to do this because he is both human and divine.

Medieval

Pertaining to the time of the Middle Ages. In Christian thought this period was characterized by an appeal to natural theology and an attempt to harmonise BIBLE teaching with the philosophy of Aristotle.

Messiah (literally 'anointed one')

The one whose coming was prophesied in the Old TESTAMENT, who would set his people free and bring in the new age. Christians believe this Messiah is JESUS though he seldom openly claimed as much, as the Jews of his day expected a different kind of fulfilment. (See also CHRIST.)

Metaphysics

The study of what is fundamental to being. It has often taken the form of studying what is beyond scientific proof.

Millennium, The

A thousand-year period prophesied in the book of REVELATION when the righteous will rule on earth. This has been interpreted in three basic ways: – amillennialists hold that the thousand year period is symbolic and that JESUS' SECOND COMING will bring, not a reign on earth, but the eternal age: – postmillennialists believe that Jesus will come again after the millennium, which will be a period of spiritual prosperity; – premillennialists maintain that Jesus' return will happen before the millennium and that he will reign with his people on earth.

Ministry (literally 'service')

The whole range of service all members of the CHURCH offer to one another and to society as a whole. It is made up of many and varied particular ministries, according to the diversity of the GIFTS OF THE SPIRIT. That ministry for which ORDINATION is appropriate forms an important part of the whole of the church's ministry, but everyone is involved. The model for all Christian service is the ministry of JESUS.

Miracle

A mighty work, beyond the normal functioning of human beings which evokes wonder and in which we hear GOD speaking of his personal involvement with and care for people.

Mission (from a root word meaning 'sent')

The whole range of what JESUS has sent the CHURCH into the world to do: to bring the love of GOD to people in all their need. Jesus said 'As my Father has sent me so I send you,' which means that the church must fulfil all that Jesus did for people. This included EVANGELISM as central, but also service and care of the needy, together with what is now called 'humanization'; the helping of people to overcome political and other circumstances which reduce their humanity.

Monotheist

One who believes there is only only GOD. This belief is totally basic to Christianity, Judaism and Islam. Christian belief in the TRINITY in no way lessens Christian monotheism.

Mystery

Something that we can know but never fully understand, particularly the mystery of GOD himself. All religion contains mystery, which can present a problem to the tidier type of mind. But the fact that we cannot understand everything need not prevent us understanding as much as we can.

Myth

A story through which people seek to encapsulate a religious idea. Some myths are powerful means of conveying spiritual truths. There is disagreement about whether there are any myths in the BIBLE. In particular, is the story of the Garden of Eden a factual account or a myth?

Natural theology

Knowledge of GOD reached through reason alone, without resort to REVELATION. It is often thought of as complementary to revealed religion. This method was a feature of medieval theology, especially that of Thomas Aquinas, and has remained influential particularly in Catholic circles.

New birth (also called regeneration)

JESUS said 'Unless a person is born again he cannot see the kingdom of God.' Where CONVERSION describes a person's response to GOD, new birth describes God's work in a person through the HOLY SPIRIT, to give him a fresh start and a life in a new dimension. A Christian is not simply forgiven and called to try again in his own strength; he receives a new life in his relationship with God.

New creation

The realm opened up through the death of JESUS, his RESURRECTION and the giving of the HOLY SPIRIT. It contains possibilities otherwise closed to us through the FALL, particularly relationship with GOD and the whole spiritual life. Central to the new CREATION are the new community of the church and a restored HOPE of eternal life.

Nonconformist (in some places called 'free churchmen')

One who does not accept the established CHURCH of his nation and joins instead a DENOMINATION or CONGREGATION that is free of ties with the state.

Omnipotent

See ALMIGHTY.

Omnipresent

Present everywhere, describing the fact that GOD is not localized and can be known simultaneously by people all over the world.

Omniscient

Knowing everything, describing the fact that there are no limits to GOD'S knowledge.

Ontological

To do with the essential nature of things. Thus, the 'Ontological argument' for the existence of GOD maintains that, in the nature of beings, a being must exist who is greater than anything else or there would not be a supreme being.

Ordination

A commissioning of people into a particular ministry within the whole ministry of the church, normally involving teaching, pastoral care, ministry of the SACRAMENTS and leadership. It is performed by LAYING ON OF HANDS by leaders of a DENOMINATION, with PRAYER for the enabling of the HOLY SPIRIT. Many, particularly Catholics, believe that orders are indelible; once ordained, always ordained.

Original Sin

The predisposition towards SIN which is part of all humanity, believed to stem from humanity's FALL. This belief does not take away from individual responsibility, but it does highlight the inbuilt factors within environment and heredity which push us towards disobedience, and it corresponds to observable facts about universal human nature. (See also the FALL.)

Orthodox churches

One of the three great Christian traditions in continuity with the Eastern church and made more distinct from the time of the Great Schism. Orthodoxy includes Greek Orthodox, Russian Orthodox, Armenian, Coptic (Egyptian) and Ethiopian Orthodox churches. Its central characteristics are a prizing of TRADITION, a beautiful LITURGY and a deep continuity with the DOCTRINE of the ECUMENICAL councils.

Pacifist

One who believes that war is never justified and so refuses to bear arms. The majority of Christians in the EARLY CHURCH were pacifists, as were some Anabaptists who were persecuted by the state for it. A continuing pacifist TRADITION has run through the history of Christianity, and is probably stronger today than ever before.

Pagan

One who is thought to be unenlightened as to true religion. It is often used of adherents of primitive religions but is sometimes now extended to those who have no FAITH.

Panentheist

One who holds that everything exists in GOD, a view which is rather different from pantheism. It is an understanding popular in twentieth-century theology, with its accent on God as immanent and especially in PROCESS THEOLOGY.

Pantheist

One who holds that everything is divine, so that many pantheists worship nature. A tendency of pantheism is to be morally neutral, since everything is an aspect of the divine being. The idea is close to monism.

Parable

A story which conveys spiritual truth. It is a characteristic of JESUS' teaching method. He often used parables to bring home the unexpectedness of the KINGDOM OF GOD and the urgency of responding to himself.

Paraclete (literally 'one who is called alongside')

A term used in John's GOSPEL for the HOLY SPIRIT. It has been variously translated but in the context of John's teaching it seems to mean 'the one who is to us what Jesus was to the disciples'.

Paradise

A term used infrequently in the BIBLE meaning 'the blessed state hereafter'.

Passion

The Passion of JESUS is his suffering as his death approached, including his temptation in Gethsemane, his humiliation by Roman soldiers and his suffering on the CROSS.

Passover

God's action in preparation for the EXODUS of Israel from Egypt, when he 'passed over' the Israelite families while afflicting the Egyptians. The term is also used of the great Jewish festival which recalls this incident, and in particular the Passover meal in Jewish homes. It is thought that, at the Last Supper, Jesus used Passover symbolism in instituting the HOLY COMMUNION.

Penance

In Catholic and Orthodox belief, the performance of an assigned duty in restitution for SIN. It is held to be a SACRAMENT, and absolution of guilt may be made dependent on it.

Person

A technical term used in defining belief in the TRINITY, to describe the Father, Son and HOLY SPIRIT severally.

Pharisee

Member of a sect of Judaism, strict in observance of the LAW. Unlike the SADDUCEES, they taught the importance of the whole Law, not only the worship in the TEMPLE.

Pietist

Member of a movement in the seventeenth and eighteenth centuries that sought to bring back devotion and HOLY living into a Protestantism which had become rigid and theoretical. Without ever becoming a structured DENOMINATION, the Pietists contributed much to the development of Protestantism.

Pluralism

The existence of many religions side by side in the same community – a frequent occurrence in the modern world. It is sometimes used of the view that all religions are equally valid.

Polytheist

One who believes in more than one god. Polytheism was the normal religion of the Near Eastern, Greek and Roman cultures which predominated at the time of the beginnings of Christianity.

Prayer

The believer's conscious practice of relationship with GOD, sometimes taking the form of worship, sometimes meditation, sometimes INTERCESSION. Words are often used, though some people pray in thought only. All prayer is a two-way relationship. It is the central activity of the Christian life.

Predestination

GOD's deciding of a person's destiny in advance. Christians have always found it hard to reconcile this with human FREE WILL, and our responsibility to choose REPENTANCE and FAITH.

Priest

One who represents GOD to people and

people to God. The term is also used of one who offers SACRIFICES. The Old TESTAMENT priests were a central part of Israel's faith, but since the death of JESUS has opened the way for every believer to come to God, many hold that we no longer need a special priestly caste. On this understanding, every believer is a priest. But Catholics see a continuing role for special priests, as those who offer God's GRACE to the people at the sacrifice of the mass.

Process Theology

A modern form of theology teaching that GOD is involved in the whole process of evolution, holding good and EVIL together on the way to a resolution of the suffering in the world.

Prophet

One who prophesies, declares the WORD OF GOD as it bears on particular national, communal or personal circumstances. Prophecy also contains elements of prediction, though they are not its centre. Prophets were very important in Old TESTAMENT religion, bringing GOD'S REVELATION. They reappear in the New Testament, but stand in different relationship to the completed revelation.

Propitiation

The making of an offering that brings a person back into relationship with another who has been offended. Some believe this is the right word to describe the achievement of the death of JESUS in reconciling humanity with GOD, though others prefer the more objective EXPIATION.

Proselyte

A non-Jew who is brought to FAITH in Judaism and allowed to worship in the synagogue. The proselytes were often impressed by the early preaching of the Christian GOSPEL, which began in the synagogues.

Protestant

Member of one of the three great Christian traditions, besides Catholics and the Orthodox. It is a general title given to the successors of those who separated from the Church of Rome at the REFORMATION. Its particular features have been an emphasis on the AUTHORITY of the BIBLE above that of the church, and the rejection of any priestly caste. The latter has sometimes made Protestantism highly individualistic. Protestantism has also shown a tendency to subdivide into many different DENOMINATIONS.

Providence

The care GOD takes of all existing things. His acts of SALVATION, as in the death of JESUS, are part of his providence, but so is his care for us in COMMON GRACE. God is able to care for everything because of his universal sovereignty.

Purgatory

In Catholic belief, this is where the spirit goes after death, to be 'purged' and prepared for HEAVEN.

Rabbi

Jewish teacher who, in JESUS' time, would gather round him a group of DISCIPLES. Jesus was often called 'Rabbi' though his methods were often highly distinctive.

Ransom

Payment offered to secure someone's release. It is therefore sometimes used to describe what was achieved by the death of JESUS, being close in meaning to REDEMPTION.

Rationalist

One who believes that everything can be judged by unaided reason and that reason is superior to REVELATION (if any has been made). Rationalism was an important school of philosophy in the seventeenth and eighteenth centuries and its influence is still felt.

Real Presence

JESUS' presence as Christians take the bread and wine at HOLY COMMUNION. There are different views as to whether his is present in a miraculous, bodily way (TRANSUBSTANTIATION), or in a spiritual way.

Reconciliation

The bringing of two estranged parties back into relationship. It is one of the central images for what was achieved in the death of JESUS, bringing GOD and humanity into harmony and taking away the barrier due to SIN. Once reconciled to God, Christians are equipped to bring reconciliation across the divisions in the world.

Redemption

The buying of someone back from slavery to secure their freedom. It is a concept used frequently in the BIBLE, in the Old TESTAMENT to describe what GOD did for Israel at the EXODUS and in the New Testament as an image carrying the meaning of the death of JESUS.

Reformation, The

The great sixteenth-century movement to reform the Church of Rome which resulted, against the wishes of many of its leaders, in the division of the Catholic church. The key beliefs of the reformers were JUSTIFICATION by FAITH and the priesthood of all believers. (See PRIEST.) The division caused by the reformation has remained deep ever since though there are some signs that bridges are being built across it today.

Reincarnation

The belief that we live a series of succeeding lives, sometimes at different levels of being. This is not a Christian belief. It is important in Hinduism.

Renaissance, The (literally 'rebirth')

A group of movements in the fourteenth, fifteenth and sixteenth centuries, which marked the transition from the medieval period. It was marked by a great interest in the works of classical times and in classical forms of art. Another important feature was its deep humanism. The bearing of the renaissance on the REFORMATION is much debated.

Renewal

A return to a deeper Christian FAITH and life on the part of a person or a community. Renewal is generally preceded by PRAYER and a sense of something wrong, and results in increased SANCTIFICATION. The term is also used in a way close to REVIVAL or awakening.

Repentance (literally 'change of mind')

A complete turning around, from any way other than JESUS' way, to following Jesus. Repentance may be accompanied by feelings of remorse, but the key is the actual change of heat and life. Without repentance there is no real CONVERSION. It is often linked in the New TESTAMENT to FAITH.

Representative

A term used to describe the position JESUS held in his death. Being fully human and yet without SIN, he became the representative person, who died for us, representing the whole of humanity in its guilt for sin.

Resurrection

The action of GOD in raising JESUS to life from the grave. As the risen LORD, Jesus is eternally living and can still be known today. His resurrection also confirmed that he is the unique SON OF GOD. In his victory over death, Jesus has given confidence that death is not the end of all life.

Resurrection of the body

The belief that at the SECOND COMING of JESUS Christians will be raised from death to life with GOD, not in their physical bodies but in their essential selves.

Revelation

GOD'S action in making known to humanity his character, will and his ways. This revelation has been made in history, through specific acts of revelation, supremely in the life, death and RESURRECTION of JESUS. The record and interpretation of these historical acts is in the BIBLE, which Christians believe God has so inspired as to ensure that his revelation is fully accessible to us. (See also the WORD OF GOD.)

Revival

A turning of many in a community back to GOD, through an unusually powerful working of the HOLY SPIRIT. There have been many revivals in recent centuries, including several in different parts of the world in this generation.

Ritual

A symbolic action, usually in the context of worship, that points to a spiritual truth.

Roman Catholic

A member of the Church of Rome, acknowledging allegiance to the pope. The Roman Catholic church is the largest Christian DENOMINATION. For many centuries, especially since the REFORMATION, it was deeply conservative but since the Second Vatican Council (see COUNCIL) it has begun to be more open to RENEWAL.

Sabbath

The day in the week when people are called to rest from labour and reflect on GOD, as God rested on the 'seventh day of creation'. This practice ensures a rhythm of activity and recreation in life. Jews observe Saturday as the Sabbath (as do Seventh-Day Adventists). Christians keep Sunday in a similar though less rigorous way.

Sacrament

Augustine called this 'an outward and visible sign of inward and spiritual grace'. It is a sign, or dramatization, giving an effect more powerful than words. The two SACRAMENTS of the GOSPEL, ordained by JESUS, are BAPTISM and HOLY COMMUNION. Catholics also count other ceremonies as sacraments: CONFIRMATION, marriage, ORDINATION, PENANCE and extreme unction.

Sacrifice

In the Old TESTAMENT, animal sacrifice proved the means by which SIN might be atoned for and relationship with GOD preserved. The sacrifice of JESUS in his death was a full and final means of ATONEMENT. From that time there has been no need of further sacrifices, though Catholics see a representation of Jesus' sacrifice in the mass.

Sadducee

Member of a Jewish sect, powerful at the time of JESUS, who set great store by regular worship in the TEMPLE.

Saint (literally 'holy person')

In New TESTAMENT usage, anyone who is 'in Christ' so that the word is interchangeable with Christian. But Catholics reserve it for people of special holiness who are 'canonized' – authorized to be called saints. In Catholic belief, the saints can be called on to intercede with GOD for us.

Salvation

The rescuing of someone from danger. In the BIBLE it means bringing someone from captivity (to SIN) into fullness and freedom of GOD. Salvation has a past reference: a believer has been saved through the death of JESUS once-for-all; a present application: we can know God's freedom today through the power of the HOLY SPIRIT; and a future hope: believers will be rescued from all the effects of the FALL at Jesus' SECOND COMING.

Sanctification (literally 'being made holy')

The progressive conforming of a believer's life and character to that of JESUS, through the inward work of the HOLY SPIRIT. Where JUSTIFICATION is what begins a person's Christian life, sanctification is intended to mark its continuance. It will never be complete until the end.

Satan

See the DEVIL.

Saviour

One who brings SALVATION. The name JESUS means 'Saviour'.

Schism

A separation between two groups of Christians. The most important have been the Great Schism (between Western and Eastern churches) and the REFORMATION. But there have been many others before and since.

Scholasticism

An approach to theology in medieval times, of those who worked outside the monasteries, often in universities. The approach was detached and objective, using logic, debate and speculation.

Scribe

A Jewish teacher of the LAW. They often opposed JESUS' teaching.

Scripture

See the BIBLE.

Second Adam

A title sometimes given to JESUS, indicating that he stands at the beginning of a new CREATION, just as Adam stood at the beginning of the old, fallen creation.

Second coming

The belief that JESUS CHRIST will come again, publicly as Lord of all, to end the present age and introduce the eternal age. It will be the Day of Judgment but also the day when SALVATION is fully realized. Jesus frequently spoke of this but warned that we can never known in advance when it will be.

Secondary cause

See CAUSE.

Septuagint

A translation of the Hebrew Old TESTAMENT into Greek.

Servant of the Lord

A character who appears in four poems in the prophecy of Isaiah. In the New TESTAMENT, this concept of a person who would suffer for many is applied to JESUS.

Sin

Carries a range of meanings, including breaking GOD'S LAW and falling short of God's intention for human life. Sin includes both specific wrong actions and a condition, a fatal flaw in everything human beings do, even their best endeavours. It is because of our sinfuless, for which we deserve God's judgment, that we stand in need of the SALVATION that JESUS has made available. (See the FALL, ORIGINAL SIN.)

Son of God

A title given to JESUS CHRIST, designating him as one who is pre-existent and shares the being of GOD. It is as the Son of God that Christ is spoken of as the second person in the TRINITY.

Son of Man

The title JESUS most frequently used of himself. It seems to refer to a prophecy in Daniel about a divine figure who would break in from heaven. This one was widely expected in Jesus' time. The term highlights both Jesus' divinity and his humanity.

Soul

In the BIBLE, this term is used for the

whole self or person, body and mind. It does not mean some separate entity which separates from the rest at death. Christian immortality is an aspect of the whole person.

Speaking in tongues (sometimes called 'glossolalia')
Using languages unknown to the speaker, usually in praise of GOD, though sometimes carrying a message to others. When this GIFT OF THE SPIRIT is sued publicly, there should always be someone who can interpret the meaning. When used privately, its great value seems to be that it can give expression to emotions that are beyond words.

Special grace
See GRACE.

Spirit
That aspect of a person which can recognize the God-ward dimension and is open to relationship with GOD. It is therefore the most important part of us and the APOSTLE Paul often contrasts it to flesh. (See also HOLY SPIRIT.)

Stewardship
The relationship in which people stand both to GOD's creation and to their own abilities and possessions. We do not own these things; they remain God's, but we have the responsibility of using and managing them to the best of our ability as stewards.

Sustainer
GOD as one who holds the CREATION in continued being, providing and maintaining all the conditions necessary for life to carry on. This is an important belief, which contradicts the view that God started the universe off and has left it to its own devices.

Syncretism
The combining of different FAITHS in such a way to blur their distinctiveness.

This is fatal to Christianity, which maintains the centrality of JESUS CHRIST.

Temple
The building in Jerusalem which was set apart as the centre of Israel's worship and SACRIFICES. First built by Solomon but destroyed when Jerusalem fell to the Babylonians, it was replaced after the Jews returned from exile. In JESUS' time Herod's temple had been completed, but soon after this too was destroyed by the Romans and no Temple has since been built.

Temptation
The pull towards SIN which all humanity, including Jesus, experiences in different ways. To be tempted is not in itself sinful, just human. Sin only comes when a temptation is welcomed and yielded to.

Testament (literally 'covenant')
The two testaments together form the BIBLE. The Old Testament covers the period of the creation and the first COVENANT, made first with Abraham, renewed with Moses and struggled with throughout the history of Israel. The New Testament deals with the new covenant, made by JESUS. It describes his life, death and RESURRECTION, and also covers the life and growth of the CHURCH in the time of the APOSTLES.

Theism
Belief in GOD. Christianity starts with theism and builds from there, giving specific content to theism through God's REVELATION and particularly through the character and teaching of JESUS.

Theodicy
A JUSTIFICATION of the ways of GOD, particularly in the face of suffering and other things that make it hard to believe that he is both omnipotent and all-loving.

Theology

The study of GOD. Christian theology is not based on speculation about him, but sets itself the task of understanding and interpreting the REVELATION he has made of himself.

Tractarian

One of a group of members of the Church of England in the nineteenth century who tried to take that church back beyond the REFORMATION to its Catholic heritage. (See ANGLO-CATHOLIC.)

Tradition

What is passed on of the FAITH from generation to generation. Tradition gives Christianity its continuity but its AUTHORITY is always secondary to the BIBLE.

Transcendent

Extending beyond human and earthly limitations and concerns. God is transcendent and always stretches beyond our understanding. But he is also immanent so that his 'otherness' does not make him remote.

Transfiguration

The occasion when Jesus appeared to Peter, James and John in his full GLORY.

Transubstantiation

In Catholic belief, the view that the bread and wine in the mass miraculously become the actual body and blood of CHRIST.

Trinity

The threefoldness of GOD, as Father, Son and HOLY SPIRIT. Within the unity of God, the three persons are distinct and function in distinctive ways. This key Christian belief is required by the New TESTAMENT evidence that JESUS was the INCARNATION of the eternal God and that the HOLY SPIRIT is divine and personal.

Unitarian

One who believes that only the Father is GOD, and that JESUS and the HOLY SPIRIT are not divine. This is not a Christian belief.

Universalist

One who believes that all humanity will eventually receive SALVATION even if many have no FAITH in JESUS. This view is based on the New TESTAMENT teaching that all things will be summed up in Jesus CHRIST, but many believe this does not include those who have rejected him.

Virgin Birth

The belief that Mary conceived and gave birth to JESUS while still a virgin, through the miraculous intervention of the HOLY SPIRIT.

Virgin Mary

The mother of JESUS. A lady worthy of great honour. In Catholic belief, she has been elevated to high position and is called upon to intercede with GOD for believers. (See also ASSUMPTION.)

Vocation

See CALLING.

Western church

The CHURCH in the western half of the Mediterranean, based on Rome, Latin speaking. It developed its own form of life under the papacy and its successors are those in the Catholic TRADITION, and the churches of the REFORMATION.

Witness

The act of declaring all a believer knows about JESUS CHRIST and the GOSPEL. Although only some Christians have the ministry of EVANGELISM, all are called to bear witness when opportunity arises.

Word of God (with a capital 'w')

A title given to JESUS which points to him as the REVELATION of GOD, the communication of God to mankind. The idea has an extensive background both in Jewish and Greek thought. Its Greek form is *logos*.

Word of God (with a small 'w')

The REVELATION of GOD to be found in the BIBLE. Some Christians hold that the Bible is the WORD OF GOD; others that it contains the word of God. (See also INSPIRATION and REVELATION.)

Work of Christ

Everything CHRIST has achieved for humanity, especially in his death and RESURRECTION.

Worship

Bringing praise, thanksgiving and adoration to God as the central part of our service to him. Worship can be individual, but its focus is corporate, when a Christian community comes together. Music, PRAYER, preaching, the reading of the BIBLE and sharing in HOLY COMMUNION are key aspects of Christian worship. (See also LITURGY.)

Yahweh (rendered Jehovah in some Bibles)

The Hebrew name for GOD, thought too holy to be spoken in Old TESTAMENT times. (See the LORD.)

Zealot

Member of a Jewish sect in JESUS' time, which tried to overthrow the occupying Romans by force.

Index

**Bold entries indicate
main section on topic**

Picture Acknowledgments

Picture research by Zooid Pictures Limited

2/3 Alinari Archives/Corbis UK Ltd; 4 Armenian Cathedral and Museum, Julfa, Isfahan, Iran/Giraudon/Bridgeman Art Library; 9 Araldo de Luca/Corbis UK Ltd; 10 Alamy; 13 Dave Bartruff/Corbis UK Ltd; 14 © Stapleton Collection/Corbis UK Ltd; 15 Erich Lessing/AKG – Images; 16 Bridgeman Art Library; 18 Bettman/Corbis UK Ltd; 19 John Chillingworth/Hulton/Getty Images; 21 British Library; 22 Anton Meres/Reuters/Corbis UK Ltd; 23 Rhoda Hardie; 26 Archivo Iconografico, S.A./Corbis UK Ltd; 28 Nicholas Rous; 31 David Alexander; 32/33 Digital Vision; 37 Private Collection, Johnny Van Haeften Ltd., London/Bridgeman Art Library; 40 Susanna Burton; 44/45 Clay Perry/Corbis UK Ltd; 46 Anders Ryman/Corbis UK Ltd; 48 Otto Rogge/Corbis UK Ltd; 49 Susanna Burton; 51 Corbis UK Ltd; 52/53 Louie Psihoyos/Corbis UK Ltd; 55 Bettman/Corbis UK Ltd; 57 Gianni Dagli Orti/Corbis UK Ltd; 59 Tony Cantale Graphics; 61 Alamy; 64 Ashmolean Museum, University of Oxford, UK/Bridgeman Art Library; 64/65 Jon Arnold; 67 Bettman/Corbis UK Ltd; 68 Charles O'Rear/Corbis UK Ltd; 69 David Alexander; 70 Kevin Schafer/Corbis UK Ltd; 71 © Stapleton Collection/Corbis UK Ltd; 74 Jon Arnold; 75 Felix Simmons 76 Louie Psihoyos/Corbis UK Ltd; 77 Mark E. Gibson/Corbis UK Ltd; 83 Geoff Nobes; 86 Bettman/Corbis UK Ltd; 90 Armenian Cathedral and Museum, Julfa, Isfahan, Iran/Giraudon/ Bridgeman Art Library; 92/93 Archivo Iconografico, S.A./Corbis UK Ltd; 96 Alamy; 98 AKG – Images; 99, 102/103 Archivo Iconografico, S.A./Corbis UK Ltd; 104 AKG – Images; 108, 109 National Gallery Collection; By kind permission of the Trustees of the National Gallery, London/Corbis UK Ltd; 110 Dean Conger/Corbis UK Ltd; 112 © Stapleton Collection/Corbis UK Ltd; 113 Werner Forman/Corbis UK Ltd; 114 © Stapleton Collection/Corbis UK Ltd; 115 David Alexander; 119 David Townsend/Lion Hudson; 122 Sonia Halliday; 126/127 David Alexander; 129 David Alexander; 133 Kadriorg Palace, Art Museum of Estonia, Tallinn, Estonia/Bridgeman Art Library; 135 Alexander Burkatovski/Corbis UK Ltd; 138 Hermitage, St. Petersburg, Russia/Bridgeman Art Library; 141 Sonia Halliday; 147 Musee d'Unterlinden, Colmar, France, Lauros/Giraudon/Bridgeman Art Library; 148 Jon Arnold; 150/151 Sant'Angelo in Formis, Capua, Italy/ Bridgeman Art Library; 153 Jon Arnold; 155 Musee d'Unterlinden, Colmar, France/Bridgeman Art Library; 157 David Townsend/Lion Hudson; 163 © The Trustees of the Chester Beatty Library, Dublin/Bridgeman Art Library; 167 ImageState/Alamy; 171 Erich Lessing/AKG – Images; 172 NASA; 174/175 Ann Hawthorne/Corbis UK Ltd; 178 Patrick Durand/SYGMA/ Corbis UK Ltd; 180 Archivo Iconografico, S.A./Corbis UK Ltd; 183 Musee Conde, Chantilly, France/ Giraudon/Bridgeman Art Library; 188 Archivo Iconografico, S.A./Corbis UK Ltd; 191 David Lees/Corbis UK Ltd; 196/197 National Gallery Collection; By kind permission of the Trustees of the National Gallery, London/Corbis UK Ltd; 201 Bridgeman Art Library; 204 Stefano Bianchetti/Corbis UK Ltd; 209 British Library; 214 Francis G. Mayer/Corbis UK Ltd; 217 Archivo Iconografico, S.A./Corbis UK Ltd; 218/219 Gyori Antoine/Sygma/Corbis UK Ltd; 220 Alamy; 223 David Alexander; 224 Photofusion Picture Library/Alamy; 233 Archivo Iconografico, S.A./Corbis UK Ltd; 237 Alamy; 243 Jerry Bergman/Rex Features; 244 Alamy; 249 Alamy; 250/251 David Leeson/Dallas Morning News/SYGMA/Corbis UK Ltd; 253 Chris Hellier/Corbis UK Ltd; 254 Bettman/Corbis UK Ltd; 263 Bettman/ Corbis UK Ltd; 264 Vallon Fabrice/ KIPA/Corbis UK Ltd; 267 Arte & Immagini srl/Corbis UK Ltd; 270 Archivo Iconografico S.A./Corbis UK Ltd; 273 BBC TV 1998/Ronald Grant Archive; 274/275 Hulton-Deutsch Collection/Corbis UK Ltd; 278 Erich Lessing/AKG – Images; 283 Sandro Vannini/Corbis UK Ltd; 284 Bridgeman Art Library; 286/287 Francis G. Mayer/Corbis UK Ltd; 291 Palazzo Medici-Riccardi, Florence, Italy/ Bridgeman Art Library; 292 Reuters/ Corbis UK Ltd; 295 Corbis UK Ltd; 298/299 Digital Vision

Lion Hudson

Commissioning Editor: *Morag Reeve*
Project Editor: *Catherine Giddings*
Book Designer: *Nicholas Rous*
Jacket Designer: *Jonathan Roberts*
Picture Researcher: *Juliet Mozley*
Production Manager: *Kylie Ord*